12/92

D1006111

ONLY MAN

IS VILE

ONLY MAN IS VILE

The Tragedy of

Sri Lanka

WILLIAM McGOWAN

Farrar, Straus and Giroux

New York

Copyright © 1992 by William McGowan
All rights reserved
Published simultaneously in Canada by HarperCollinsCanadaLtd
Printed in the United States of America
Designed by Cynthia Krupat
First edition, 1992

Library of Congress Cataloging-in-Publication Data
McGowan, William.
Only man is vile : the tragedy of Sri Lanka / William McGowan. —
1st ed.
Includes index.
1. Sri Lanka—Politics and government—1978– 2. Sri Lanka—
Description and travel—1981– 3. Sri Lanka—Ethnic relations.
I. Title.
DS489.8.M4 1991   954.9303—dc20   91-20655 CIP

Map of Sri Lanka reproduced from
The New International World Atlas,
© 1991 by Rand McNally R.L. 91-S-211.
Used by permission

For my parents and family

—and for Mr. Crab

Acknowledgments

I'd like first to thank my agent, Lizzie Grossman, and my editor at Farrar, Straus and Giroux, Jonathan Galassi, for launching my boat, as well as Rick Moody, also of FSG, for helping me bring it to shore. Let me also thank my parents, whose understanding and financial support proved crucial in helping me complete the project, as well as Sandy and Peg Martin of Middlebury and Dave and Libby Seaman for their hospitality during a housing crisis.

Thanks, too, to the numerous people in Sri Lanka who provided assistance during my research—John Rettie of the BBC, the late John Guyer of the Asia Foundation, and the many diplomats and development officials who very generously gave of their time and shared information. Thanks as well to Jinx Pettus, Peace Corps volunteer, for her affection and insight.

My greatest gratitude, however, has to go to the many Sri Lankans of all ethnicities who took me into their confidence and allowed me to forge an understanding of their lives and of their society without which this book could not have been written. They are too numerous to name, and, considering the repression that continues in their country, some of them are probably best left unidentified. I hope they know who they are. In addition to teaching me about their much-troubled country, they extended an important lesson in how to live with grace under extraordinary pressure. For all of them, both living and dead, a salute—and a prayer.

Contents

THREE

FOUR

Preface

FOR MOST OF my time in Sri Lanka, I lived in a shabby old guesthouse down by the tracks in Bambalapitiya, one of a string of suburbs that stretched along the coast from Colombo. Early in the mornings, the houseboy, Goonatileke, would go out into the courtyard and rake up the frangipani flowers that the rain or the ocean breezes had blown down the night before. Heavy with morning inertia, I'd lie in bed and listen to him scrape his rake across the smooth dirt below. Later, he'd come upstairs and start sweeping out the rooms, one by empty one. The war had driven off most of the tourists, and, for most of the time, I was the only guest. After doing his raking and sweeping chores, however, Goonatileke would always let something distract him, and the morning's breezes would blow the piles of flowers and dust apart, undoing his efforts and ensuring him work for the next day.

I began to see something of a parallel between Goonatileke's circumstances and my own in trying to understand the situation I was writing about. Whenever I felt I had made sense out of Sri Lanka, some other force would emerge to scatter my carefully constructed logic. That this happened was not because of the fast-breaking nature of events or the complexity of the situation. It was just a fact of life in Sri Lanka. Every day, I had to revise my take from the day before. As a result, during most of my stay there, I rarely felt I had anything but the most tentative, uncertain grasp of the war and what it was about.

It is in the nature of awareness to doubt what you've thought previously. But there was something about Sri Lanka that made it doubly difficult for me to declare anything unequivocally. It took a long time to sense how profoundly different that culture was from my own—to see that it was scored in a different key—and even longer to gain some idea of the grammar of Sri Lankan thoughts and lives. Although the culture there had been profoundly affected, some would say bastardized, by the West, it was nevertheless deeply indigenous and deeply Oriental, resistant to casual penetration. Even those living in Sri Lanka for many years felt its fundamental impenetrability; the longer you lived there, the more you realized you'd never really know it. *An Historical Relation of Ceylon*, the account of a seventeenth-century shipwrecked English sailor held captive by the Sinhalese king of Kandy, is probably still the most incisive look at the Sinhalese mind, but it is written with such a sense of estrangement that Daniel Defoe is said to have used it as the major psychological source for the character of Robinson Crusoe. For me, the process of understanding the psyche and culture of Sri Lanka was like living in a house for years before discovering one day that there were wings, floors, entrances, and exits you'd never suspected existed. Every few months I'd uncover a new dimension that I hadn't understood earlier.

To complicate matters, Sri Lankans have a general cultural resistance to discussing the Big Picture. Rarely did I find anyone who could cross the lines of ethnicity or caste to comment on the country as a whole. So much of what was happening was covert or invisible, unless you made yourself familiar with the cultural idiosyncrasies at work. Essential issues were rarely mentioned in the papers or addressed explicitly in conversation because of the way Sri Lankans communicate—in an idiom of indirection. It was often maddening. Things said one way in conversation had the potential to mean something radically different. Even sentiments expressed in the most impeccable English had meanings I couldn't divine. Nothing was ever unambiguous. The cultural predisposition to avoiding negativity complicated my efforts, too. Sri Lanka was shot through with a psychology of avoidance and denial, linked, in part, to the crucial process of saving face. As a result, people were discouraged from discussing what might make them look bad in the eyes of a Westerner.

The time I spent in Sri Lanka coincided with the Indo–Sri Lankan Peace Accord, which was widely seen as a chance, perhaps the last, to correct the country's tragic course. But hope, or, more correctly, false hope, sprang eternal, shored up by the impulses of denial and avoidance, and in the end the Accord became simply another source of disappointment in Sri Lanka's post-colonial history. Political violence made avoidance more than just an Eastern idiosyncrasy: for many it became the key to survival. Over time I absorbed much of that ethic of avoidance. I became a "contact Asian," putting a great deal of energy into resisting the implications of what I had seen.

I did have moments of acute realization, however, most of them striking at about three in the morning, when the cheap arrack I drank had settled on my growling ulcer and the overnight train that ran along the coast roared past my guesthouse. As I lay there counting the number of cars, I would tick off the problems facing the country, each car symbolizing a factor in the war's tragic, mounting equation: militant monks condoning violence in the name of protecting Buddhism; opportunistic politicians of every ethnic stripe; death squads; cyanide suicides; caste hatred; unstoppable insurgencies; unstoppable economic deterioration; reckless blood-and-soil ideologies. The sum of these factors had the same quality of inexorable momentum as the hurtling, blaring train. It was then that I realized just how sadly irreversible the situation had become. By the time I got back to sleep, Goonatileke would have his piles all swept together, and the grim realizations of the night before would have subsided into a beautiful tropical morning. But soon after, I'd be eating breakfast, and the wind from the sea would start to scatter Goonatileke's piles, and whatever point I had put on things the night before would dull again, pitted by the sea air and the equatorial landscape. Ironically, it was Goonatileke who seemed to have the clearest picture of his native land. Day after day as I'd scan the morning headlines, he'd lean over my shoulder pretending to read. "Ah, Sri Lanka," he'd say forlornly. "Very very fighting. Very very bomb."

During all the time I spent thinking about and writing this book, I resisted the full implications of what I had seen and come to feel. I left Sri Lanka burned out, physically and emotionally, and I wanted to give myself some time to settle down before writing, to let the poison ease in me. Even though I had learned much over the two years I was there, I still had nagging doubts that I had missed some-thing, some avenue of hope. As bleak as the news reports were that reached me, there was always an accompanying sense that the Sri Lankans might, in the end, pull the rabbit out of the hat, might rescue the country from its various sources of dissolution—ethnic, religious, spiritual, social, economic, and political. The more things were deteriorating, the more peace seemed to be at hand. It was a country, after all, that Arab traders had once named Serendip, for its aura of accidental good fortune.

Although I no longer wake up to the overnight Colombo train, I do still nurse an ulcer in the early morning, and it was during these hours that I tinkered with this book, often with the same sense of toxicity that I had in Sri Lanka. If serendipity were to strike the island now, I'm afraid the dose would have to be massive.

Vijaya, son of King Sihabahu, has come
to Lanka, together with seven hundred
followers. In Lanka, O Lord of Gods,
shall my religion be established and flourish.
Therefore, carefully protect him with
his followers and Lanka.

LORD BUDDHA
The Mahavamsa, or the Great
Chronicle of Ceylon
SIXTH CENTURY A.D.

What though the spicy breezes
Blow soft o'er Ceylon's isle
Though every prospect pleases
And only man is vile.

BISHOP REGINALD HEBER
From Greenland's Icy Mountains
1811

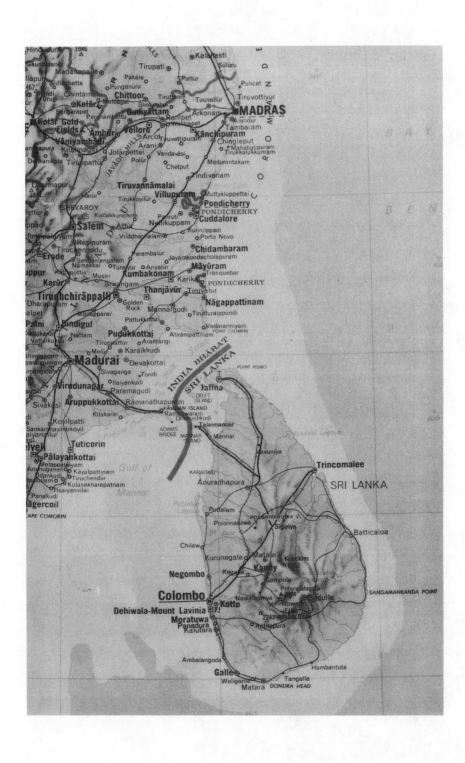

O N E

1 · Return to Serendip

"HOW CAN YOU describe the beauty? How can you imagine them hurting anything, anything at all?" The man seated to the left of me on the Air Lanka flight from London to Colombo was awed into incomprehension as he watched the long tapered hands of our stewardess flit over the snaps of her demonstration life jacket. He had been in the British Army during World War II and had been stationed in Ceylon. For the last five years, he had postponed his post-retirement trip back to the former colony because of the Situation. Now that India was sponsoring a peace accord which had halted, at least temporarily, the sectarian violence between the majority Sinhalese Buddhists and the minority Tamil separatists, he was going back with his wife to tour the places he had missed during the war years.

The Tamil woman on my right spoke with a different tone of incomprehension. "Mommy," she told me her five-year-old had asked her during the 1983 race riots that tore apart Colombo and killed as many as 3,000 Tamils, "why are they putting that tire around that man's neck if he's crying?"

She and her family had emigrated to the West, where her husband's medical practice was lucrative, and were returning now to present a new child to the grandparents. In 1983, however, they had barely been able to escape the mobs that rampaged through the streets with pickaxes and gasoline necklaces. It was the very moment when Sri Lanka, a country that had been smoldering in ethnic tension, finally erupted, formalizing the polarization that already lurked underneath.

Our steward, Trevor, was the embodiment of Sri Lankan hospitality, scurrying and scraping around the cabin. He wore a thread-bare dinner jacket and a drooping bow tie, and a distraught expression was evident beneath his perpetual bright smile. He resembled a bandleader whose musicians refused to play anymore. He was deracinated, like many in Colombo—neither Eastern nor Western. Our stewardess, Salome, on the other hand, was pure Sinhalese. She was from Kandy, I guessed, the cultural citadel of Sinhalese Buddhism. It was surprising to find a Kandyan in the position of air hostess, as their generally high caste status usually discouraged them from serving others. She was no charm-school graduate. I got on her bad side almost immediately when, after the in-flight announcements, I asked her whether the translations had been in Sinhalese or Tamil. A look of sharp disdain overcame her teeth-gritted smile as she hissed, "Sinhalese." After that, any interaction I had with her was tense and uncomfortable.

At one point, before a fueling stop in Bahrain, I woke with a headache and went toward the mess looking for some aspirin. Salome was hunched over her rice and curry, eating with her hands in the traditional manner, her long tapered fingers now greasy and yellow with food. I stood there for a moment before she saw me, when, with a look that could kill, she ripped the curtain across the doorway.

Welcome back to Sri Lanka.

I had originally gone to Sri Lanka the year before, in the fall of 1986, to run an American college semester-abroad program. I was a magazine journalist seeking a break from deadlines, as well as a little adventure. When the term was over, I stayed on for a while to work as a free-lance and acquaint myself with one of the world's nastier and more intractable ethnic conflicts, waged between the majority Sinhalese Buddhists and the minority, mostly but not exclusively Hindu Tamils. I felt that returning in the fall of 1987 was bound to be intriguing. Fighting between the Sinhalese-dominated government and the militant Tamil separatists struggling for an independent homeland had been calmed by a peace agreement brokered by India, which itself had a strategic interest in the island nation by dint of its proximity—just twenty-two miles across the Palk Strait. The peace accord held some promise of ending the fighting, but if it failed the results could be disastrous.

The nearly five years of ethnic strife had already left the country and its people, whatever their ethnicity, in very bad shape. Of the war's 8,000 victims, most were noncombatants killed in the hundreds of massacres that formed the bulk of the violence. More than 100,000 Tamil refugees had fled to southern India; another 100,000 were in camps in the Tamil areas of Sri Lanka, along with smaller numbers of displaced Sinhalese who were scattered around the country. Conditions in the camps were bad: the inmates were subject to official indifference, caste exploitation, and thuggery. There were 5,000 Tamil men in detention, thousands of widows, orphans, and amputees; there was destitution; there were outbreaks of malaria, encephalitis, and other diseases that the war's social chaos had allowed to return after their near-eradication.

While the casualty figures were not nearly as high as in such places as Mozambique and the Sudan, the violence in Sri Lanka had a devastating impact on the social and psychological fabric of the country. It suffered from chronic underdevelopment to begin with, and the war wiped away the already small accomplishments of daily life. In a society where sons and husbands were a source of both identity and livelihood, the loss of men gravely affected family security. In a society where female modesty was so important, the rape of women had an even more devastating impact than it would have had in the West, forcing many victims to commit suicide. And in a society where white-collar status was so overemphasized, the disruption of the educational process had a very profound impact on students in both Sinhalese and Tamil communities, increasing the already formidable emotional burden of war, especially among the poor and middle-class unable to flee like their wealthier compatriots.

At first, like many, I found it hard to accept that such awful political and ethnic violence could happen in a country so staggeringly beautiful and so outwardly suffused with Buddhist piety and passivity. Wasn't this the fabled isle of Serendip? The claim that the island was the site of the original Garden of Eden was one not entirely rooted in mere chauvinism; the island's aesthetics—its mist-draped vistas, its languid refulgence—seemed by themselves capable of overwhelming violent impulses. The agreeability and equanimity of the people, too, made the idea of political violence incongruous; I was often struck by how gentle and generous Sri Lankans as a whole could be and how remarkably tranquil the surface texture of life was. Even the combatants in the war—Tamil or Sinhalese, soldier or militant—would, like as not, shoo a mosquito away rather than smack it, in keeping with *ahimsa*, the South Asian doctrine of nonviolence.

It didn't take long, however, to sense that Sri Lanka, the Resplendent Isle as it was known in ancient Buddhist scriptures, had an underside. The surface texture of life, so full of ease and grace, rested atop great harshness and unpredictability—snakes with incurable venom, rogue elephants that rampaged through rice paddies, floods that erupted from nowhere, waves that rose and smashed whole hamlets to splinters. And what passed for equanimity was often an illusion beneath which raged emotions deeply repressed by Buddhist prohibitions.

If the political violence in Sri Lanka seemed incongruous in the face of its mesmerizing beauty and outwardly tranquil temperament, it also seemed ironic in face of the country's bright prospects in the era after independence in 1948. The British had left Ceylon with the most sophisticated political elite in all of Asia, with secular traditions and seemingly strong democratic institutions shaped in the image of Westminster democracy. There was an extensive infrastructure of roads and communications, a system of civil administration that worked efficiently, and great reserves in the treasury. The Ceylonese seemed to be doing well with what was left behind, at least at first. Education levels increased, and social welfare programs gave the country one of the best quality-of-life indexes in the developing world. Enthusiastic Western observers saw Ceylon becoming the Switzerland of the East. Though ethnic tensions simmered, relations were thrashed over in the gentlemanly spirit of parliamentary debate, and governments were regularly turned out by ballot in what was seen as a shining example of Third World democracy.

In less than two generations' time, however, the country became torn apart by its own internal divisions. The Ceylonese seemed to have absorbed only the most negative side of their relationship with the British. As Stanley Tambiah of Harvard points out, instead of maintaining itself as a model of Third World prosperity and secular pluralism, the country became a paradigm of the troubled former colony. What was heralded as the Switzerland of the East had become another Lebanon; instead of reviving its ancient reputation as a crossroads of trade and learning, Sri Lanka was becoming a backwater, increasingly insular and isolated.

And beyond what the country had squandered of its colonial inheritance, there was the legacy of its own Buddhist spiritual tradition that it had betrayed. According to a myth cherished deeply by the Sinhalese, the dying Lord Buddha had turned to one of his minions, pointed across the waters of the Bay of Bengal, and said, "In Lanka, O Lord of Gods, shall my religion be established and flourish." As a result, the Sinhalese believe that they are the chosen people of Buddhism, given a mission to preserve and protect the religion in its most pristine form, and that the island of Lanka is the repository of Buddha's teachings. But despite considerable government patronage and ostentatious displays of public devotion like the monumental Buddha statues scattered all over the country, Sri Lanka hardly became the island of the dharma celebrating the ideals of nonviolence and compassion. Instead, it had become a country of routine massacres, rampant human rights abuses, and moral obduracy where the implacable hatreds of race, class, and culture had created a nightmare world of viciousness, opportunism, and envy.

As compelling as it was to use Sri Lanka's fall from grace to understand the problems of many former Third World colonies, I was just as drawn to the situation there by what it said to the West. Obviously, Sri Lanka's predicament underscored its inability to

build a multiethnic, multicultural society based on equity and respect for principles of secular pluralism. This was something that
states in the West might take note of, I thought, as these societies
became more ethnically diverse and less certain about their essential
cultural identities.

Ironically, though, Sri Lanka failed to build a stable multiethnic, multicultural society because it embraced many of the very
concepts and ideas that multiculturalists in the West have advocated.
These included preferential policies for ethnic groups deemed historically oppressed; reform of the school curriculum to redeem
outdated cultural hegemony and promote ethnic self-awareness;
economic policies that stressed ethnic entitlement instead of merit,
efficiency, or economic expansion; linguistic nationalism indulged
at the expense of a common tongue; and other ideas shaped by a
romantic infatuation with the idea of distinct cultural identities
based on invidious scholarship and demagoguery. Sri Lanka, with
its own discrete historical and cultural context, was a remote war-
torn country in the underdeveloped world that many of my own
contemporaries couldn't find on a map. But its experience cast shadows toward the more stable and affluent Western countries which
those countries ignored at the risk of their own political and cultural
fragmentation.

For most of the first phase of the war that took place between
1983 and 1987, fighting had been restricted to the Tamil areas in
the northern and eastern parts of the country. During my first stay,
I rarely traveled out of the Sinhalese areas of the south, and thus
the war, for the most part, felt distant. By that time, the conflict was
deadlocked, with Tamil militants controlling most of their traditional homelands—which they hoped would one day become Tamil
Eelam, an independent nation—and the predominantly Sinhalese
army of the Sri Lankan government immobilized in their forts and
camps. Negotiations for peace had stalled as well.

But in the few months I was away, the situation had sprung
wide open. The new phase of the war began when Tamil rebels
ambushed several bus- and truckloads of off-duty military personnel
as they returned from a Buddhist New Year's celebration in April

1987. Around that time Tamil rebels also massacred nearly three dozen Buddhist monks and stepped up terrorist bombings in the capital, Colombo. They detonated one explosion at rush hour in the central bus station of the crowded Pettah market. The blast killed 113 people.

These attacks put extraordinary pressure on the President, octogenarian Junius R. Jayawardene, to mount a final offensive against the Tamil rebels in their bastion of Jaffna, a city in the north. For years, Jayawardene had been trying to settle the conflict through negotiation, but Buddhist extremists were making it impossible for him to resist using force, mounting demonstrations, making fiery speeches denouncing his inaction, and threatening a coup. "We have listened long enough," cried Jayawardene's own Prime Minister. "It is time to wipe this cancer out of our midst."

Jayawardene, aware of how many civilians would die in a major military strike against Jaffna and how quickly the international community would be prompted to condemn him (threatening the flow of foreign aid), moved tepidly at first, stepping up attacks on Tamil positions and conducting light aerial bombing missions against Jaffna. Soon, though, as Sinhalese fury deepened, he had no choice but to launch an all-out attack on the Jaffna peninsula by land, air, and sea. The Sri Lankan forces were able to seize considerable territory from the rebels, but Operation Liberation caused such major civilian casualties that Indian Prime Minister Rajiv Gandhi, at the behest of the 55 million Tamils in his own state of Tamil Nadu, intervened in the crisis, first by air-dropping food and supplies to the Tamils in Jaffna. Such violations of Sri Lankan sovereignty put the two countries at the brink of war. But Gandhi convinced Jayawardene to "invite" his troops into the country as peacekeepers under the terms of what became known as the Indo–Sri Lankan Peace Accord.

The Accord, and the agreement letters that went along with it, were designed to satisfy most Tamil demands, short of a separate state, in a way that the Sinhalese could accept. In return for the surrender of Tamil rebel weapons and cessation of hostilities on both sides, there would be a merger of the contested northern and eastern provinces—the area claimed as Eelam—which would be granted wide powers of autonomy to be guaranteed by India. Tamil and English, the former "link language" of colonial days, were to join Sinhalese as national languages, settling one of the conflict's thornier issues. Sri Lanka also agreed to make concessions to India in specific matters of foreign affairs, essentially consenting to Indian hegemony over the region, which had been challenged by the increasingly close ties that had developed between Colombo and India's regional rivals Pakistan and China, as well as the United States, Israel, and other Western powers. In line with this, the port of Trincomalee, one of the world's foremost deepwater ports and the object of some superpower interest, was to become a free port, the Indian Ocean equivalent of Danzig.

The intent of the Accord was multifarious. With the prospect of an outright Indian invasion, it gave President Jayawardene a way to save face internationally, and it also guaranteed his continued rule. For India, it provided control of a situation that had steadily threatened security interests on its southern flank for years and had become a domestic liability. Although India had originally backed the rebels to check Colombo's increasingly Western drift, they had become a little too independent, particularly the Liberation Tigers of Tamil Eelam, known as the LTTE, or the Tigers. And, apart from the self-interest of the various signatories, the Accord did provide breathing space, a break in the cycle of violence. Only in a ceasefire could there be a resolution of the conflict's more complicated issues.

From this angle, the Accord heralded a great breakthrough: journalists and statesmen from around the world sung its praises, and the international press portrayed the architect of the Accord, the Indian High Commissioner to Sri Lanka, J. N. Dixit, as a great genius. American officials praised the Accord's great courage and U.S. congressman Stephen Solarz even proposed that Gandhi and Jayawardene be nominated for the Nobel Prize, a suggestion that overlooked just how much both men had done to fan the flames of the fighting in the first place.

The Accord did bring peace for a few weeks. Desperate for

calm, many Sri Lankans of both communities danced in the streets and traveled to places unvisited for years. Although most had doubts about the Accord, few were immune from euphoria.

However high hopes were that the Accord would hold, there were troubling signs that it wasn't destined to last. Essentially an agreement between two governments, the Accord did not adequately account for the objections of either the Sinhalese masses, who were enraged by it, or the Tigers, who said it did not answer their aspirations. The Accord triggered mass nationalist hysteria among the Sinhalese, sweeping huge crowds into the streets. "This is it," one rabid young monk remarked at a demonstration beneath a sacred bo tree. "We must be prepared to sacrifice our lives." When Rajiv Gandhi helicoptered into Colombo to sign the Accord, he flew into a city ringed by marching mobs and smoldering fires. The Sinhalese had always expected the Indians to invade, but it was quite astonishing for them to learn that Jayawardene had actually invited them in on his own. Much of the mobs' destruction was aimed at government property—whole fleets of buses, as well as the central telephone exchange. From Colombo, rioting spread throughout the country, hitting hardest the Buddhist heartland along the southern coast. Through a nationwide curfew and mass detentions, Jayawardene barely averted anarchy.

There was no better symbol of the Sinhalese backlash than an incident that occurred at the Accord signing ceremony. As Gandhi was about to leave, he passed a guard of honor, one of whom tried to hit him over the head with the butt end of his rifle, a blow that would have surely killed him if Gandhi had not ducked. The blow landed on his shoulder instead. President Jayawardene, aghast, claimed that the man had merely fainted and had hit the Prime Minister by accident, a charge that Dan Rather, rerunning the tape on the evening news, found quite funny. The guard was arrested, put on trial, and convicted, but the incident cast a pall over the Indian bid for peace.

The Accord gave a new lease on life to a shadowy, ultranationalist Sinhalese extremist group called the Janata Vimukti Peramuna, the People's Liberation Front, or JVP, who capitalized on the resentment against the government in their drive to recruit new members. Having been banned from politics for some time, first for an aborted 1971 uprising and later after being blamed for the anti-Tamil riots that tore the country apart in 1983, the JVP returned in a much less overtly Marxist form and draped itself in the mantle of Sinhalese Buddhist nationalism, which many saw as a cover for a dangerous Khmer Rouge-esque underside. It was still being led, however, by its founder, an enigmatic Sinhala ideologue named Rohanna Wijeweera, who blended Maoist absolutism and Sinhala racism into a potent and appealing vision for revolution. No one knew how many cadres the JVP had, but it was feared that they had infiltrated the lower rungs of the government security forces, which had expanded their numbers in a headlong rush to fight the Tamils and had not conducted proper background checks. It was also feared that the JVP had set up an international fund-raising apparatus to buy arms, and were working busily in London among wealthy Sinhalese expatriates, a mirror image of the support network long established by the Tamils.

Fears of JVP infiltration were supported when, on the opening day of Parliament, an assassin threw grenades inside a chamber of officials, killing two government ministers and wounding the President. Clearly an inside job, the JVP's message to members of Parliament was unambiguous: pass the legislation needed to ratify the Accord constitutionally and you do so at your own peril.

Meanwhile, in the north, there were equally troubling signs that the Accord would not hold. Although he had given his consent to the Accord, the leading Tamil rebel commander, Vellupai Prabakeran of the LTTE, had done so only under pressure, after being flown to Delhi, held under house arrest, threatened with harm, and not even allowed to see a written copy of the agreement. Once he was allowed back into the country, his support for the Accord was tepid; he told an emotional gathering of Tamil rebel supporters in Jaffna that he agreed because "we had no choice." The only lasting solution, he said, was a separate Tamil state, which the Tigers would continue to struggle for "by other means," the details of which he left unspoken.

By then, the first detachment of Indian troops had been airlifted into the north and east as part of the peacekeeping force. But the arms surrender required by the Accord was an exercise in going through the motions. While the Indian High Commissioner claimed that 80 percent of the Tigers' weapons had been handed over, the Tigers were only turning over things they didn't need and had scattered large caches of weapons in Jaffna's lagoons for an inevitable renewal of hostilities.

I was still in the United States at the time, and relying on the media for most of my news of Sri Lanka. But no matter how loudly it was trumpeted, as soon as the Accord was announced I had the suspicion that it wasn't going to work out, at least not smoothly. Part of it was the Sri Lankan propensity for empty assent, the habit of nodding emphatically with no intention whatsoever of following through. Another source of pessimism lay in the Sri Lankans' cultural resistance to the kind of contractual obligations an agreement like the Accord represented, especially when made between parties of unequal social status and of different ethnicities. And with so many scores to settle for the prior five years, it would be hard to see either community laying aside their distrust. In the face of how deep and automatic vengeance was in that society, some thought it would take at least a generation for the anger to subside. "There are thousands of torture victims, rape victims, people without limbs," a Catholic priest running the Tamil Information Center in London told me when I paid him a visit on a layover. "There has been a change of ethos—an acceptance of violence in the people. At business levels, there might be links, but at other levels, the Tamils and the Sinhalese will never trust each other again. There will be a permanent lingering syndrome of distrust."

Now, flying over the Arabian Sea and down the western coast of the Indian mainland, I was filled with anxiety. There was the simple danger of traveling inside Sri Lanka. This time, to research my book, I would be going a lot into forward areas where things were unpredictable. The fighting in a war zone would be dangerous enough, but cultural factors unique to Sri Lankans would make it dicier still. Often, for example, when you'd ask Sri Lankans for directions, they'd just send you anywhere, worried to admit that they didn't know what you asked. What if someone sent me over a land mine or into a guerrilla ambush by mistake? The country also had the world's highest unpremeditated-murder rate, something that the strain of war certainly wouldn't help. I remembered how tempers, repressed by Buddhist notions of restraint, could flare suddenly. Though my foreignness gave me a certain exemption, I still didn't feel like testing the point. .

As we flew down the Indian coast, dawn quickly grew into morning. The view over southern India was of gentle switchback rivers etched into soft green and brown plains, and of mountains whose sides were carved and grooved. The land seemed old, in a way that suggested the crackling of a distinctly human, as opposed to a geological, antiquity. As we approached Sri Lanka, I thought of the legends of Buddha projecting himself astrally across the twenty-two-mile Palk Strait below, on his mission of consecrating the holy isle of Lanka. The clouds around the plane, however, reminded me of antiaircraft flak and mortar rounds.

The jet, that masterpiece of twentieth-century technology, filled with Sri Lankans returning from remittance work in the Middle East, had taken on aspects of a South Asian village. People were sleeping on the floor curled up on mats, others were lined up at the toilets in back as if at the village well. I wondered if some of the Tamil Hindus there were performing ritual ablutions inside or simply readying themselves for the long wait many of them would have to endure at the hands of Sinhalese customs agents once we landed.

The visibility fell to practically zero as we crossed over land into Sri Lanka. The plane seemed to hang in the sky, without weight, without momentum. Through meager sight lines the land below was raw. The mists that rose from the jungle made the scene look creational, as if it were just cooling off—even the paddy land and the rows of coconut plantations spoke of an order that man had been allowed to impose only on sufferance. Occasionally we could make out the red tile roofs of old Portuguese Catholic churches, and the newer roofs of seaside tourist hotels. Not far away hills had been gouged out for clay, and large scattered swatches of jungle had been charred for planting crops.

My dread grew more pronounced as the jungle became more articulated below us. The jungle seemed inert and dead in a harsh, malignant way. The amount of time in the air had left me feeling dislocated; time no longer seemed like a measurable quantity. Our descent had the same quality of inertia as the jungle beneath. But the jungle soon became more animated. It had a raw and visceral look to it now, the pulpiness of freshly wounded flesh. It was as if some gigantic malevolent machine or beast had rampaged through it, bruising and smashing along its way. Touching down, the jet broke the stillness with a roar, a roar that seemed to come out of the jungle itself.

"Hello, my dear!"

Evidently, I wasn't going to get the third degree at the airport, although I had taken the precaution of listing my occupation as educator, not journalist, on the arrival card. Trying to get a reading on what was happening on the ground, I feigned nervousness, asking the customs guard if there had been any fighting lately. "Fighting? What fighting?" answered the guard, a tall, thin Sinhalese with a broom-handle mustache. He wiggled his head agreeably. "Now there's no fighting. Only tourists coming. Season starting soon. Only tourists coming now. No problem."

After receiving several preposterously high bids on a taxi trip into Colombo twenty miles away, I settled with a pair of men in their thirties, dressed in crisp white shirts and slightly bedraggled bell-bottoms, their slightly conked, carefully combed hair tucked behind their ears. As usual, I couldn't tell if the driver and his sidekick were Sinhalese or Tamil, although most drivers now were Sinhalese, since Tamils were hassled too much by the police at checkpoints and roadblocks. After my exchange with Salome the stewardess, I thought it best to be less direct than to ask outright. "So how are things in Ceylon?" I asked. Tamils who objected to the name change in 1972 still tended to use the old colonial name, while the Sinhalese bristled. "You mean Sri Lanka, sir?" the driver returned matter-of-factly, without further elaboration.

The traffic on the road seemed exceptionally chaotic, in direct contrast to the inertia of the jungle as it had looked from the sky. It was muggy and extremely hot even at eight in the morning, but already people were moving purposefully. I was able to focus only on isolated snapshots: the emaciated cow wandering across the road, a bullock cart being pulled by an ox with jouncing flanks, the little girls in white school uniforms walking across a sodden field. We passed a man on a bicycle wearing only a loincloth; behind him a huge fish was strapped across a wooden box. Women with long, beautiful black hair and bright-colored saris glided along the road-side. In the other direction, a truck top-heavy with mats made from palm leaves was careening toward us, the men on top wearing rags around their heads.

"Is it the rainy season?" I asked the driver, trying to start some conversation. Last year, it had been a cabbie who had left me with one of my most enduring impressions of the ethnic situation. "You know the way the Nazis treated the Jews," he, a Sinhalese, had told me. "Well, that's the way we have to deal with the Tamils. They can't stay here."

I couldn't tell whether the driver was peeved at me for my use of the term Ceylon or whether his inability to grasp my question stemmed from poor English and the habit many Sri Lankans had of pretending to understand it. It was common for people to start shaking their heads from side to side and say, "Yes, yes," before you even finished a question. After several false starts, the simple question about that year's monsoon was understood. "Not really rainy season yet, sir," the man answered. "Last year was very dry." He paused for a few minutes as we passed by an accident on the side of the road. It was a head-on collision. People had clustered around to gawk, but no one seemed to be doing anything to help the victims, who were slumped onto the shoulder. When the driver resumed, his voice had taken on a nervous, slightly emotional edge. "Actually, sir, you know everything here is going wrong. First it was rainy season, and then there was no rain. Now the rainy season is over, but it starts to rain. It's raining when it should be sunny. No tourists when it should be tourist season. It is all screwed up. People are still fighting. The Tamils and Sinhalese are still fighting and no

tourists are coming. All the planes are off. Still, even with a settlement, they are not coming. The Tamils, sir, are crazy. It is such a
small country. A small land. We are fourteen million here." He was
underestimating by three million. "Seventy-five percent Buddhist.
Only ten percent are Hindu Tamils, sir. They want half the land for
their own government, sir, and really this is difficult to do. It is a
small island. You can't give half away. Where can the Sinhalese live
then?" His voice had assumed a rasping pitch. "So that is why we
fight." he continued. "The Sinhalese have nowhere else to go, sir.
We shouldn't have to go anyway. It is our country. We will stay. The
Tamils have India, where they can go if they want to. India is a very
big country. Sri Lanka is so small. What are you thinking about
these problems, sir?"

I had learned well enough from my first trip not to be too
straightforward either; candor was not a highly valued trait. I told
him that as an outsider I was confused. He let the subject drop.
"Confusion. Yes, confusion," he muttered.

The morning promised a sweltering day, but for now colors
were still sharp and brilliant, and people who would be paralyzed
by the heat moved with a quick, easy sway. At roadside stands,
vendors were selling huge globular coconuts the size and color of
small basketballs. A tiny thatched hut had an array of souvenirs
outside it and was framed by a set of gigantic curving elephant
tusks crossed by swords. Thick green mold grew on the walls of the
concrete houses by the side of the road, presumably on the side
where the monsoon would approach. There was a lot of construction
going on almost everywhere, but it was hard to tell which things
were being built and which things were falling apart. Everything
seemed to slope.

The grand, if unsettling, overview I had from the air approaching the airport had been replaced with a feeling of claustro-
phobia. Already the "crowded surrealism" that Pablo Neruda, who
had been a diplomat in Ceylon in the late twenties, had described
was closing in on me. Everything seemed like a tropical miniature,
lacking the sweep and sprawl that I had associated with Asia in prior
travels. Though joined to India by a series of sandy reefs known as

Adam's Bridge, Sri Lanka felt more like a totally separate continent—lush and friendly where India was stark and harsh, lithe and svelte where India was big and muscular.

Most of all, however, Sri Lanka seemed deracinated, its Asian identity diluted by things such as welcome signs from the Rotary Club of Wattala and the Colombo Jaycees. Statues of saints stood before hulking Iberian-style Portuguese churches, and right in the middle of the grimiest tin-roofed slums were signs for color film and air-conditioning services.

For all its vivid strangeness and sensuality, Colombo's environs were like an overcrowded tropical suburb. The first impression I had had of the place the year before was that it was the Long Island of Asia. On his first trip to Sri Lanka in the late sixties, Thomas Merton had said that driving into Colombo by night had been like riding through Flushing, Queens. "There is very little here that seems Oriental," he wrote in his journal, a disappointment shared by me and even more so by the students in the semester-abroad program who were with me. It had been the billboard for Rambo that caused the most distress. One student who had preconceptions of the primal spirituality of Asia later told me that he really did expect saffron-clad holy men in meditational rapture beneath the swaying palms. The dirt, the Western consumerism, the shapelessness, and the suburban sprawl had crushed his fantasies.

As we got closer to the city, the slums thickened. Many of the dwellings were hardly more than wooden packing crates with sheets of tin for roofing, held down by stones so that the wind, or the gigantic Sri Lankan crows, wouldn't carry them away. Outside, younger women wrapped in sarongs squatted next to spigots, pummeling suds into dirty laundry while their naked children scampered into the road. Old men and women, shriveled and stooped to right angles, shuffled along aimlessly through the playing children. By now, exhaust fumes had coated the road with a thick, foul dew. We were trailing behind a particularly overloaded truck filled with coconuts and what seemed to be a kind of jute-like material. The truck was listing badly to the right and belching great clouds of carbon monoxide as it backfired, which made me both nauseous and jumpy. Just as we veered to pass, a bus hurtled out of the black clouds. We ducked back into line behind the truck with barely an inch to spare. No matter how insane the driving could be in Sri Lanka, it usually worked. One came to accept a level of chaos and clamor that one would never dream possible in the West. Nonetheless, this had been a close call. "Jesus Christ," I winced, clutching the back of the driver's seat.

"Ah, I see you are a Christian," the driver said with crazed enthusiasm. It struck me as funny. In a country torn by culture and religion, why wouldn't the choice of profanity be a giveaway? "Catholic or Protestant?" he asked with finely tuned sectarian awareness.

"In Sri Lanka, is everyone some religion?" I asked.

"Yes, yes, of course, sir," the driver answered, his sidekick coming out of his stupor to shake his head vigorously in agreement.

"It is not possible to have no religion?" I asked facetiously.

"It is not a good way to be, sir. Not a good way to be. Here everyone goes somewhere. To the monks. The Hindu priests. The Catholic priests. The mosque. It is all very important."

The response roused the secularist in me. "Yes. It is a very religious place," I replied. "But if it is so religious, why are there so many problems between the religions?"

The one looked at the other, and both shook their heads, smiling awkwardly.

2 · Arrival

ALTHOUGH I had broken up the trip with the layover in London, I was completely discombobulated by the time I got into Colombo. I couldn't tell whether it was Saturday or Sunday until we got into the city and I saw the sea of school kids and government clerks—all in brilliant white uniforms—making an early break for the customary half-day Saturday. Whatever day it was, it was indisputably laundry day. Row after row of dull public housing projects and pitiful slums were festooned with the uniforms and long colorful bolts of sari cloth hanging out to dry. Even the tonier wards that we passed through—Colombo Five, Colombo Seven, Colombo Three—were similarly draped, though the government clerk's outfits were replaced by Western-style shirts and the sari cloth looked more expensive.

When I reached the hotel my houselady, Mary, and her lover, Nimal, refused to make me breakfast, whether because of resentment tied to the Situation or simply because they were too lazy to do it, which, from my stay the year before, I knew to be quite possible, I couldn't tell. I was the only guest in the place, which could make one expect better service, but it seemed to them that the absence of tourists generally was something to be blamed on the foreigners who did come. We were also expected to make up for lost revenue by paying more, not less, for the service we did receive, despite the elementary laws of supply and demand. As a result, Mary refused to make an arrangement that would discount the nightly rate for the length of time I planned to stay. No matter how I tried to explain it, she felt I was swindling her. I decided to pay the full rate.

If the proprietors lacked hospitality, the hotel itself was worse. In the six months since my last stay there, the Ottery had deteriorated noticeably. With so few guests, Mary had little cash flow to keep up with the rain, the humidity, the termites, the rust, and other agents of decay that constantly ate away at everything on the island. I peered into the kitchen once and vowed never to do it again.

Nevertheless, I liked staying at the Ottery. It was favored by a regular clientele of younger expatriates who came in from their development-related jobs in the bush and kept me abreast of things happening close to the ground. It also had great character. At one time, it must have been an elegant place. There was a piano in the lounge downstairs, now warped and barely playable, and a huge billiards table. The felt was still intact, though crudely stitched from many rips over the years. I had been stuck at the Ottery during a curfew the year before and played game after game of billiards. We put Band-Aids on the cues to simulate tips. It was a grand time amidst a funny, rummy lot. A Vietnam veteran named Tony—in Sri Lanka doing some kind of business for friends in the Rotterdam underworld—had kept us entertained with tales of his life as a fugitive throughout Europe and Asia.

I don't think Mary really liked any of us at all. She was a Tamil who had inherited the place from her husband, a Sinhalese, and was very worried about its reputation. We were hardly raucous, but the constant fear of being "blackguarded"—the practice of gratuitous, almost reflexive character assassination pervasive with Sri Lankans but particularly acute among the face-conscious Sinhalese—made her uncomfortable when the house was spirited and full. But whatever the demeanor of the proprietor, the Ottery made me feel closer to the culture and its myriad idiosyncrasies.

As I tried to unwind over a cup of Mary's metallic tea, I read the morning's papers. In addition to several different papers in Sinhala and Tamil, there were three English-language papers—the

Sun, the *Island*, and the government-controlled *Daily News*. The English papers were written for a very small yet influential English-educated elite that dominated government, business, and intellectual circles, despite giving more than thirty years of lip service to the Sinhala-speaking native. Because of this, they often reflected a class bias.

There were other problems, as well, with trying to figure out what was happening through these English papers. The English press gave a false sense of accessibility to the local mind. The copy might be written in English, but the grammar of Sri Lankan thought was often in an entirely different idiom. Reflecting the cultural aversion to the Big Picture, articles would often lack focus or the crucial paragraph that situated its information in context. The papers also skirted anything too troubling. It was all right if you were an insider intimate with the ebb and flow of developments and knew what the otherwise unimportant buzzwords meant, but until then, it was hard to puzzle out what was really happening.

That day, however, it wasn't hard to see that things weren't going well. A major Tiger rebel leader had starved himself to death in Jaffna to protest Indian duplicity in the northern and eastern provinces, which were to be made autonomous. The Tamils believed that they had been promised domination of an interim Provincial Council until elections were held. As a result, tension was mounting in the region.

There was also an article about fighting between rival factions of Tamil militants, some of whom supported the Accord and others, like the Tigers, who did so only with their arms twisted behind their backs. The militants fought with each other as much as they did against the government, and internecine grudges from the war's earlier phase were now being settled.

The paper contained many tributes commemorating the anniversary of the birth of Solomon West Ridgeway Dias Bandaranaike, the former Prime Minister of Sri Lanka, who was revered by the Sinhalese as a patriot. By fanning the flames of Buddhist nationalism, he rode into power in the fifties, during the first major deterioration of relations between the major ethnic groups. Article after article, piece after piece sung his praises.

Impatient to get a sense of things at hand, I embarked on my first walk around town. It was too soon to do any good, however. Colombo wasn't speaking to me, at least not on the subject of the war. The state of affairs was diffuse and submerged, its edge, if there was one, buried deep down. The Situation was everywhere, fouling the air like the local exhaust fumes which coated Sri Lankan palm leaves. In spite of its invisibility, though, it was virulent, but it wasn't the sort of virulence that could be conveniently labeled.

Signs of rioting and looting from the summer were hard to miss, but a wholesale revolt against the government had not yet materialized. A crackdown, employing mass detentions, and a quick redeployment of government troops—from the north to the south—had done the trick, although how long such measures could contain Sinhalese fury was open to question.

I had gotten to know Colombo fairly well the year before. Its surface easygoingness usually masked a subterranean capacity for violence. The memory of the riots of 1983, which killed thousands of Tamils and spurred what was then a small separatist struggle into a full-blown insurgency, clung to the back of the national mind.

In 1986, obvious signs of the war in Colombo were few and far between. There had been bombs detonated in the post office, in the telecommunications building, and in one of the five-star hotels. But the only real signs of the conflict had been the nightly ambulances from the military airport outside of town ferrying back the day's casualties. Then, struggle was something remote, at least to a culture so laden with denial that "out of sight" wasn't just "out of mind," it was nonexistent.

Colombo lived in perpetual dread that the Tigers would launch a new wave of bombings in the city. (The conventional wisdom held that the Tigers would relish a backlash, which would drive into their fold those Tamils not yet totally alienated from the government.) Bracing for that eventuality, Colombo reacted with the appearance of vigilance: handbags were searched on the way into government buildings and hotels, and checkpoints ringed the city. But such precautionary measures were always an exercise in formalism. Bribes were effective at checkpoints, and the tropical climate made attention spans short. Security was tight for a few weeks and then the city grew porous again, vulnerable to attack.

Things had changed. The places I was comfortable at the year before made me nervous now. Was I more at risk? Could I trust the men making the kissing noises—not a sign of lewdness but a way of getting attention—who were beckoning me to come over and have a conversation? Were the students or the young people on the streets asking for my address really interested in being pen pals or would they soon be writing for sponsorship in trying to emigrate to the United States? Was it safe to eat in my favorite restaurant in Colombo, the Tamil-owned Greenlands Hotel, or would grenades sail through the windows? Jet lag had finally caught up with me. Befuddled, confused, and overwhelmed by the foreignness of sight and smell, I limped back to the Ottery and its cool red cement floors to listen to the sea breezes stir in the palm trees before sleeping the sleep of the dead.

"*Kiri, Kiri,*" the man delivering the milk called from the street outside, tinkling the glass bottles together while waiting for Goonatileke to open the gate and let him in. "*Malu, malu,*" hawked the fishmonger in his weird glottal cry as he traveled from house to house. Across his back was a springy "pongi" stick with heavy platters of bloody fish dangling from each end.

Waking up the next day, I decided I would ignore the Situation for a while and indulge, instead, in the sensuality of the island. Just outside my window, I could hear Goonatileke raking the courtyard. At a well somewhere in the backyard, there was the dunking and splashing of people bathing; it was as mechanical as the raking, reminiscent of the Dutch colonial passion for order, regularity, and cleanliness. Through the rusty bars of my window, I could see a crow high up in a coconut palm. Across the street, the roofline of the buildings was Moorish. Atop the smooth whitewashed walls, the jagged edges of broken glass protected against invaders.

On the street, children swarmed in white ducks and jumpers, while a coolie, naked but for a sarong and a rag atop his head, pushed a wagon laden with round green coconuts. In the most stylish of cars—Rolls-Royces, Morris Minors, even a Stutz Bearcat—the

Sri Lankans of that well-to-do neighborhood dropped off their children for school, sometimes pausing to buy crabs or lobster from the barefoot hawkers on the corners.

I tried to get an early start, before the sun paralyzed the will. Even sticking to the shadows, though, I was soon drenched in sweat. Then the rain began, a lazy Asian rain, slowing everything, isolating Colombo's pulsing colors and unfamiliar shapes.

The central artery leading into town, the Galle Road, was a war zone all by itself. The traffic was murderous, but the pedestrians and the draft animals sauntering along it didn't seem to notice. In such traffic, merely stepping across the road seemed a strenuous karmic exercise.

Straining to revive the little Sinhala I knew from the year before, I faltered when I tried to engage people along the way, not so much from lapse of memory as from an inability to get my mouth and tongue around its rapid cadences and long, serpentlike sounds. Passing by open-air elementary schools, I heard the singing of schoolchildren as they recited their lessons. It reminded me of poet Michael Ondaajte's description of the Sinhalese style of singing: "Like a scorpion being pushed through a glass tube, like someone trod on a peacock, like someone pulling barbed wire through a stone courtyard, like a frog singing at Carnegie Hall."

There was no way to differentiate any one sound in the cacophony of the Pettah, Colombo's crowded central market and bus stand. According to Paul Bowles, who lived for a time in Sri Lanka, it was customary to say the word "Pettah" with a little disgust in the voice—perhaps because of the preponderance in an earlier time of "black" Tamils and Moors occupying its stalls. At this time of the day, it was clamorous, and the fish lying in the gutter, some the size of fully grown men, had taken on an awful aroma, despite the ample portions of kerosene poured on them to drive away the flies. Occasionally the odor of spice dampened the putrefaction, but most of the time I was nauseated. A small toothless man with striped gums stood on the corner and sold betel nut wrapped inside a bright green leaf. (A dollop of lime paste on the sides of the nut numbed the mouth while chewing.) Around him stood a number of market workers, chewing. The men had caked the ground around them with brilliant red betel juice.

I had a conversation with a little Sinhalese man fixing shoes beneath an umbrella. As I stopped to watch him work, the man smiled broadly and wiggled his head, saying hello, which prompted me to do the same. He wiggled more. I did the same. After a while several of his children appeared beside him, curious at the *suddha*, the white foreigner, who was so fluent in the national head wiggle. In no time there were ten of them lined up before me, with wide smiles and bobbing heads, not a word uttered between us.

At points as I walked through Colombo that afternoon, I felt that I was dreaming. Culture shock? Jet lag? As I walked through the back streets of Colombo's Slave Island, named for the auctions the Dutch conducted there, face after face reminded me of someone I knew in America. The features were almost exactly alike. Only the polished mahogany and teak of Sri Lankan skin tones and the gauntness caused by poverty seemed different. The impression intensified as dusk settled over the seaside promenade, known as the Galle Face Green—a broad treeless strip of grass and dust favored by Colomboans for their own sunset walks. "I know of no nation in the world," wrote Robert Knox, the seventeenth-century shipwrecked English sailor, "who do exactly resemble the Sinhalese as the people of Europe." Although the Sinhalese claim of Aryan lineage was difficult to prove anthropologically, the racialist folk belief seemed to have some basis that night at least.

By night, viewing it from the taxi I had hired, Colombo was gray and obscure. Trishaws that had buzzed through the traffic were now huddled in clumps under the dim light of streetlamps. Profuse insect life swarmed around these lights. In the Muslim quarter, off Slave Island, men squatted in the doorways of eateries, their sarongs tucked up between their legs. Mangy dogs reclaimed places from which they had been shooed away all day. Occasionally my taxi passed a knot of bare-chested day laborers standing idly around a fire. Outside the shuttered stalls in the market, homeless people were preparing cardboard mats. Beside them, piles of bananas were being guarded from the night, the curl of the fruit resembling the curl of the Sinhala graffiti on roadside walls. Later, the city was pounded by a furious rainstorm, to be measured more appropriately in decibels than inches.

One day at the end of the week I paid a visit to my friend John Rettie, a Colombo-based correspondent for the BBC. The son of a tea planter, he had been born in colonial Ceylon, though he left at the age of three months when his parents divorced and his mother returned to England. Rettie manned the BBC post ably, which meant that his reports upset the government with great regularity. He had been especially accurate describing the human rights abuses that were going on all through 1986 and 1987, and, as a result, he was frequently denounced on the floor of Parliament.

Because Rettie was the only full-time foreign correspondent in Colombo, he had a far-flung network of sources and contacts with whom he was in touch daily. Rettie was especially popular with the "old boys" of Colombo, owing to their Anglophilic fondness for a vestige of a time and a social scene now gone by. His nerve center was on the second floor of the Galle Face Hotel, an old Raj-era building crumbling slowly from neglect and mismanagement at the hands of an eccentric Tamil Christian millionaire.

Rettie was on the phone when I arrived, so I busied myself wandering about the garden outside. The garden of the Galle Face fronted onto the ocean, facing west, and from its broad veranda, surrounded by its wicker furniture, silver tea sets, and immaculately dressed waiters, one could almost see the old colonials snapping their fingers and scowling.

Rettie, who was on the threshold of retirement and had come back to Sri Lanka as one of his last assignments, was in "fit nick," as the Anglophilic old boys would have said. But he had "lost his color" in the time since I'd last seen him, which in local parlance meant that he, a white man, had acquired a tan, of dubious cachet in that supposedly Aryan society where fairer skin meant higher status. As we sat talking about the Situation, he reminded me a little bit of a merchant in the bazaar, dispensing information instead of tea or bolts of linen.

I was distracted from time to time by the beauty of the ocean shimmering beneath the window. I was also a bit amused by the sight of the giant chessboard in the garden just below—something right out of *Alice in Wonderland*. It was not a regulation board, however, but one with an extra row of dark and light squares running all around it. This seemed appropriate. With the Indian intervention and intramural violence between Sinhalese over the Accord, the Situation was ever more Byzantine. Rettie needed a scorecard that was bigger than regulation size.

He had been on leave when the Accord was signed in the summer, but was initially confident it could be pulled off. As the weeks went by, however, the fault lines in the agreement were becoming more apparent. First, the Accord was seen in entirely different ways by the two primary signatories, Delhi and Colombo. For India, the agreement was a way of inducing necessary social change in order to ensure Tamil rights. For Sri Lanka, the objective was simply to ameliorate terrorism. In addition, the Accord had glossed over some of the conflict's most central grievances, leaving decisions about land settlement and policies covering language issues, education, and employment to be worked out at a later date.

That week, the snags in the Accord, all connected at some level to the more substantive issues, were threatening to scuttle the whole peacemaking effort. One of these involved a disagreement over who would have pride of place in the interim government that would rule the Tamil areas in the north and east. While the Indians and Sri Lankans wanted the seats on this council equally divided between the various Tamil rebel groups and the Muslims living there, the Tigers were demanding a majority of seats. Another snag threatening the agreement involved disagreements over the resettlement of refugees who had been displaced by the war. While the Sri Lankan government insisted that the Sinhalese who were returning to the north and east had lived there before, the Tigers were claiming that they were new colonists sent there to dilute Tamil control. Government soldiers were also said to be blocking Tamil refugees from returning to their homes.

A final point of contention concerned Tamil men in detention. The Accord said they would be released, but almost two months after the agreement several thousand still languished in Sinhalese camps throughout the south, many of them high-ranking Tigers. To add to the confusion, factional fighting had broken out among the various Tamil militant groups, some of it, it was said, secretly backed by Indian intelligence.

Rettie was also getting disturbing reports from the south that week. The government's summer crackdown hadn't been as effective as it would have liked. Every day, there was news that the shadowy Sinhala nationalist group, the JVP, was assassinating government officials and elected representatives who backed the Accord, a campaign that would make it impossible for the government to follow through on the settlement. In order for the Accord to be legally binding, it had to be ratified by Parliament, but doing so looked unlikely if the JVP was effective in carrying out its death threats. One influential MP had been shot already, and Rettie was getting reports that JVP units were starting to attack government offices and security installations in the deep south. A full-blown rebellion might be in the offing, one that could overwhelm the forces that had been dispatched from the north.

"Why don't you go and have a little look-see?" Rettie suggested with a smile, arranging for me to meet up with another British reporter, Derek Brown of the *Guardian*.

It was refreshing to get out of Colombo, with its blinding carbon monoxide haze and pitiless noise. As the train lunged down the coast, I was captivated by the musty vapors of the jungle, the salty tang of the sea, and the secretive quiet of the lagoons, where I spotted a minotaur dragon from time to time slicing through the water like a prehistoric beast. Fishermen slept on the decks of their boats bobbing gently nearby. But a clearer picture of what was happening in the south was hard to get. We were traveling through towns along the coast that made up the Bible Belt of Sinhalese Buddhism, places where the JVP was said to have been assassinating and assaulting three or four government functionaries and ruling-party officials a night. Yet it was impossible to get anyone to talk about what was going on, and those who would talk did so only in the most indirect and oblique manner, in bits and pieces.

The frustration we had in getting civilians and officials to talk about the Situation left me and Derek with the increasing sense that we had fallen into some kind of purgatory. The region was on the threshold of explosion, but no one would admit anything. It was as if an elephant was rampaging but people refused to acknowledge it.

Part of this pretense was the traditional culture of avoidance. Because they lived in a society with a strong emphasis on maintaining face and equanimity, the Sinhalese approached our questions with polite and smiling dismissals, with repeated assurances that there was "no problem, no problem." These words took on the aspect of a mantra after a few days.

Government officials were also deeply reluctant to let such information get out. Concerned that reports conveying the success of JVP efforts might undermine the Accord, the government was making sure to minimize the extent to which the JVP was able to challenge its power. This meant that we got many "no problems" from senior police officials and local civil administrators, too, and lame assertions that what was being portrayed as regional unrest was actually the work of random thugs and opportunists.

At times, these denials were almost comic. Although the town of Galle, at one of the most southern points of the island, had been aflame during the rioting the month prior to our trip, the senior police commander there said it had been spared any violence whatsoever. We must have been confusing his district with the adjacent one, he explained. His was absolutely trouble-free.

Such unflappable denial was also the style of a young politician from the ruling United National Party (UNP) whom we met in another small coastal town. His father, the local member of Parliament, had been assassinated just a few weeks before, making the son the new MP. But it was not the JVP who did him in, the son maintained. It was a band of brigands in the jungle who had attacked his father's fancy car. "He was merely driving on the wrong road at the wrong time," the son explained, playing nervously with the white string around his wrist that Buddhists wore for good luck. Reports about the situation in the south getting out of control were entirely fallacious. The situation was actually improving, and in a few weeks' time it would be settled.

Having only just arrived in the country after a significant time away, I was a little clumsy in the way I formulated my questions, which didn't help. I was happy, then, to have Derek along, since he had spent so much more time in South Asia. Unlike many reporters who grew impatient and testy with the swamps of official denial and fundamentally different cultural conceptions of truth, Derek pursued his questions like a gamesman and grew more amused as the lies became more implausible.

We were able to pick up a few tidbits here and there, most of them suggesting that the situation was about to get nasty again quite soon, and on a much wider scale than we were now seeing. According to some officials, weapons were making their way into the hands of JVP rebels, some from Tamil rebels in the north who had accepted the Accord and wanted to make some money from their guns, others from smugglers along the unpatrolled southern coast. Over 40 percent of the people in the south were behind the JVP, reflecting bitter resentment over the Accord. "The south is like a soda bottle," one local headman in a small jungle village maintained. "All shaken up and ready to explode."

One of the more ominous indications of instability and in- creased JVP activity had to do with the extent to which the govern- ment's security forces had been infiltrated by the JVP, or those Sinhalese sympathetic to the JVP cause. Many with JVP sympathies had gotten into the security forces and had received extensive train- ing in the use of weapons. Many had since deserted, taking with them their guns and their expertise, which would make the JVP much stronger than had been estimated originally. "They have been deeply infiltrated," said Don Windsor, a crusty old Anglophile with portraits of the queen in his house and a Morris Minor outside. He had leaned over conspiratorially, so that his servants wouldn't hear. "The government pretends to be calm, but they are deeply, deeply worried."

However formidable their powers of denial and avoidance, of- ficials had a hard time maintaining the appearance of equanimity as we ventured inland from the coast. In almost every one of the small agricultural settlements that we drove through, there had been some JVP activity that week—an attack on a government installation, an assassination, or a kidnapping. The area was also awash in graffiti—a combination of messages written by the rebels and those written by government counterinsurgency forces in response. "Fight the monkeys. Fight against the Indians for the survival of the country," read one JVP graffito. "You will deliver our youth unto death once again," read a government inscription, directed at the JVP leader, Rohanna Wijeweera, whose last attempt at revolt in 1971 had resulted in the deaths of nearly 10,000 Sinhala youth. As we slowed to read the graffiti, I noticed that swarms of yellow butterflies were tracing arcs in the air above bulbous Sinhalese script. The island's lithe, delicate beauty and its violent hatreds, as always, were not two steps away from each other.

The afternoon we were to head back toward Colombo, we had gotten word that there had been an attack on a police station along the route we were to take. I was a little nervous about going out to investigate the incident; just before I had gone to bed the previous night, I finally caught up with that day's paper and saw a tiny item about the number of Sinhalese "home guards"—a kind of civilian militia—who had not handed in their weapons. Almost 8,000 had still to comply with a government order to do so, the paper said. So there were at least 8,000 guns in the hands of the most patriotic Sinhalese in the country, many of whom lived in the area we were driving through. Derek Brown, despite his Oliver Hardy–like corpulence, was gung ho, however, so off we went into the scrub jungle of the interior, with the central highlands looming in the distance.

As we proceeded inland, the vegetation grew more sparse. Coconut palms gave way to fields planted with sugarcane. The land became arid, too; the only water in the area came from ancient, man-made lakes called tanks that were used for irrigation.

The land was profoundly inert. We headed to the area's biggest town, which turned out to be a single row of dirty tea boutiques, a few shops, a post office, and some government buildings. A sign in front of a burned-out structure identified it as a government nursery school, which had presumably been destroyed in the summer upheaval.

We sat inside one of the grimiest tea stalls, sipping tea that was far too sweet, drawing little attention beside the giggles of a shy little girl who kept staring at my blue eyes. Then, after a little while, a man claiming to be the owner of the place sat down with us. He seemed to know what we were interested in. There had been two or three killings every night in the district, the man told us, his mouth ringed red from betel juice, and the victims had been supporters of the ruling party or those who were thought to be police informers. Most of them had been sent letters of warning first, he added, though he was vague about how he knew. The police had swarmed the main roads but were not going any farther now, because they were worried about ambushes. Last night's attack had taken place in a hamlet not far from where we sat. Three men had been shot.

Generally, the owner said, the extent of the unrest and violence in the area went unreported. There were many highway robberies, some in broad daylight, and JVP cadres had insinuated themselves so well in small underdeveloped villages that they were impossible to detect. Just then, however, an army jeep drove by, followed by two buses filled with commandos. Our friend immediately moved to the back of the shop. He didn't want to be seen talking to us.

We spoke, instead, to a young army lieutenant who was the officer in command of the detachment, which numbered about four dozen commandos. The lieutenant admitted they were on their way to raid a JVP camp. But later, speaking to Derek he changed his story, maintaining that they were merely on a training mission. "Oh, what a ratbag," Derek said when we compared our contradictory notes. The officer also told us that what we had heard about the attack on the police station was wrong and that everything in that district was fine. It was in the next district that there had been some activity the night before. "So there's an elephant right in front of us and then no elephant at all," Derek sighed. "Oh, what a ratbag."

We decided to go with what the man in the tea stall had told us. But finding the hamlet wasn't easy. The peasants we stopped for directions and information feigned ignorance. The fact that there had been local violence complicated the task of getting clear directions.

We drove aimlessly for several miles, stopping along the road. Two men wiggled their heads to signal they had heard of an incident, but it had taken place the week before and was in a village whose name we did not recognize. We entertained the possibility that the tea-shop man could have fabricated the report of the killings, for our attention, or to fan a rumor he wanted carried back to Colombo.

We passed by an old checkpoint that dated from the JVP insurgency of 1971. At that time, explained our driver, it was the police who had infiltrated the JVP, forcing them to mount their insurrection prematurely. This time, the JVP seemed to have moles inside the police, he explained, which would account for the number of police informers who had been successfully targeted and the number of ranking officers who had been kidnapped, intimidated, or killed.

The land again changed character as we drove; it was full of giant anthills that gave it a lunar aura, and red clay roads. It was eerily empty—road and scrub, scrub and road. Certainly not a place you'd want to be at night, when, as we were to find out, the JVP could roam unhindered.

We reached a town called Midieniya, and went directly to the police station, a mud-walled, two-room structure, where we spoke to the assistant superintendent of police for the district. Like his colleagues on the coast, the police superintendent tried to put a good face on what was happening in his subdistrict. He was sorry we had come so far, he said, smiling weakly, but there was, in fact, "no problem" last night, or any other night, for that matter. Maybe we were thinking of something that happened during the summer's troubles, he said. But recently? No. We must be mistaken.

The superintendent's denials, though, were contradicted by several things. He was wearing civilian clothes—so he wouldn't be such an obvious target; he had a Chinese automatic pistol unholstered on his desk, ready to be used; and only a few yards from where we sat, his staff car sat with a line of fresh bullet holes all along its right side. He might already have served as target practice.

Nevertheless, the officer insisted that there was "no problem." Yes, okay, there had been an incident several days before, but it was a grudge shooting between two Buddhist laymen over a contested temple election. Could that be the seed of the rumor that had brought us all the way out here? Yes, of course. That must be it, for all the talk about the JVP was only that—so much talk.

It was obvious that something had taken place, but to admit it would cause the officer a loss of face. Responding to these cultural subtleties, Derek gave me the high sign and we thanked the superintendent for his time, explaining that we had to hurry on to Colombo if we were to return before dark. "Not to worry," Derek explained. While we were having our conversation on the porch, the driver had been conducting his own interview with the officer's driver over in a corner of the courtyard outside.

Four men had been shot the night before in a JVP ambush, the man had told him. All had been police informants, some of them petty big shots in the local UNP political hierarchy. None were killed, but all were hospitalized, in critical condition. Derek smiled ironically as we drove home through thick walls of scrub jungle. "You don't keep a loaded gun out on your desk all day long and not expect trouble. 'Problem? What problem?' 'Elephant? What elephant?' Oh, what a ratbag it is indeed."

3 · Trinco Burning

OUR TINY SIX-SEATER gained altitude quickly. Within seconds we had a spectacular view of the island. On one side, thin, wraithlike clouds corkscrewed over tea estates. On the other, the broad muscular ridges of the island's central highlands waded in a sea of cumulonimbus. The most prominent landmark was the crisp triangular shape of Adam's Peak, also known as Sri Pada, a mountain of more than 7,000 feet, where Lord Buddha was supposed to have left his footprint as he ascended into nirvana.

Beneath us, rice paddies cut long tapered fingers into the jungle, and the country's longest river, the slow brown Mahaweli, snaked its way across the island to the northeast port city of Trincomalee, or Trinco. In the middle of the island, we crossed an invisible line that separated the abundantly fertile wet zone of the south from the dry zone in the north and east. There were few paddies here, but furrowed fields of chilis and onions stretched out in large rectilinear blocks, irrigated by the water of ancient tanks.

As we approached Trincomalee, we arced widely at a high altitude to avoid sniper fire from below. From the air there was hardly a sign of the wear and neglect that Trincomalee had suffered during five years of fighting or during the rioting and burning that had broken out again that week. But as we got closer, we saw that whole neighborhoods had been blackened or gutted by fire.

When Derek Brown and I got back to Colombo after a few frustrating days in the south, the sense of tension in the country had come to a head, and Trinco was already in flames. The Indian High Commissioner and the Tiger leader Prabakeran had worked out what seemed to be the final snag in the Accord—a debate over who would have pride of place in the composition of the interim Provincial Council that would preside over the new autonomous Tamil province. Prabakeran had been given everything he had asked for, much to the dismay of the Sri Lankan government and its Buddhist hard-liners. Then, for no apparent reason, the Tigers had reportedly burned thousands of Sinhalese out of their homes in Trinco. The Indian Peacekeeping Force failed to protect them. As a result, whatever momentum the Accord may have gained had come to an end.

There were wild discrepancies among the various versions of the events. The Indians claimed the violence was not as bad as reports suggested, and was chiefly the fault of the Sri Lankan military, who were undermining the Accord with covert operations. For their part, the Sri Lankan government was making an effort to present itself as a victim of India's cynical indifference to the Sinhalese plight.

The first reports were of smaller incidents: a few homes burned here and there, several people killed by the peacekeepers in the course of quelling a few small riots, mostly in mixed-ethnic neighborhoods. Then the violence escalated. Entire villages were attacked by various armed groups. Sri Lankan soldiers were reportedly seen in civilian clothes shooting at Indian patrols. Groups of Tamil militants were roaming freely through the district, in some cases in full view of the Indian forces. And Indian patrols had fired on Sinhalese settlements, killing several people in the process. In addition, four police constables taken into Indian custody had been assaulted, and a prominent local Buddhist monk had been killed in a confrontation with Indian troops, news of which was spreading through the south.

The climate of hysteria and rumor had been fanned by Sinhala extremists in the government, and the fear was that the commandos and soldiers of the Sri Lankan forces, who had been confined to their barracks in the north and east under the terms of the Accord, would break out and avenge the killings of Sinhalese civilians with retaliations against unprotected Tamils. This would, in turn, trigger open warfare between the Indian peacekeepers and the Sri Lankan forces and plunge the country into an awful conflict between two armies that would make the low-intensity guerrilla activity of the last five years look mild.

We flew over Trincomalee's harbor, which the British admiral Horatio Nelson had called "the finest harbor in the world." To naval historians, it had been the taking of Trincomalee harbor, not the taking of the Khyber Pass, that had allowed the British to control the Indian subcontinent. Centuries later, the British Seventh Fleet was anchored there throughout World War II, protected from attack by rocky promontories and the seven scallop-shaped bays that creased Trincomalee's coastline. For the Indians, ensuring the neutrality of Trinco had been a primary reason for involving themselves in Sri Lanka's domestic conflict in the first place. A deal struck here between the Sri Lankan government and a Singapore-based American company to renovate an oil-tank installation had been seen locally as a ploy by the American CIA to secure alternatives to U.S. bases in the Philippines. Trinco would be an ideal base for nuclear subs, which could, it was said, dive low enough there to avoid radar and sonar detection.

In the visions for Eelam, the Tamil homeland, Jaffna, the traditional cultural center of the Tamils in the arid north of the island, would probably become the political capital, but Trinco would become its economic hub. What the Tamils saw was a kind of South Asian Hong Kong, where the blessings of a strategic location for shipping and the natural commercial instincts of the Tamils would be a prosperous match. The Indian-authorized peace accord might have crimped dreams of a separate Tamil state, but it did see a vital role for Trinco in the economic life of the new autonomous province; development funds were scheduled to pour into the region.

Trinco was also important because, with an equal proportion of Sinhalese, Muslims, and Tamils living there, it was a microcosm of the island's internal ethnic and political dynamics. Maintaining peace in Trinco was one of the most important elements of the

Accord, a necessary step in resolving difficulties among the three groups. The Sinhalese had to be convinced that they could live in Trinco safely. Muslims had to be convinced that the Tamils now dominant in the north and east wouldn't turn around and exploit *them* as a minority. For their part, the Tamils had to be assured that the Sinhalese-dominated government in the south would follow through on the promises of autonomy and goodwill stipulated in the Accord. But in the face of the recent tumultuousness, none of this looked likely. "Today," read one of the editorials that I read on the plane, "Trincomalee epitomizes the tinderbox that Sri Lanka has become. Any event, be it assassination attempts or routine disputes, now has the potential to blow up the fragile accord."

The violence was hard to figure. Why would the Tigers, who had been given so large a role in the post-Accord order, explode into such a frenzy of violence? Critics claimed such action showed that the Tigers were incapable of accepting political solutions and that they were afraid of democracy. The destruction of Sinhalese homes and businesses in Trinco was a systematic effort to drive the Sinhalese out of the area for good—"gerrymandering by genocide," as the editorialists described it.

Such denunciation did not allow, however, for the covert operations mounted both by the Indians and by the Sri Lankan government, which, in violating the terms of the Accord and threatening the Tigers, may well have provoked them to violence. Having grown increasingly weary of its inability to control the Tigers as firmly as it wanted to, India, particularly the faction of intelligence officials within the Research and Analysis Wing, its CIA, had been encouraging rival factions of Tamil rebels with covert aid. To the Tigers, this suggested that India was planning to liquidate them, despite the assurances embodied in recent agreements.

Tiger suspicions were also fanned by continued government attempts to pack the eastern province with Sinhalese colonists. The peace agreement had specified that Colombo would cease these West Bank-style settlement programs in areas that the Tamils claimed as their "traditional homelands," and Tamils suspected that the Sinhalese refugees being returned were really new colonists.

Meanwhile, a Sri Lankan naval patrol in waters off the island's northeast coast intercepted a Tiger trawler allegedly filled with materials for making land mines. Seventeen Tiger cadres were arrested, including two lieutenants who were wanted for some of the conflict's most savage terrorist attacks. Factions within the Colombo government demanded that all seventeen be transported from temporary detention in Jaffna to Colombo for trial, where it was almost a certainty they would be tortured or killed. For several days, there was a tense standoff between Indian diplomats, whose credibility with the Tamils depended on the detainees remaining in the north, and a faction of Sinhalese hard-liners out to sabotage the Accord. His position already weak, President Jayawardene capitulated to the hard-liners, but as the Tigers were being readied for transfer to Colombo, they each bit down on the cyanide caps Tiger cadres regularly carried in order to avoid divulging secrets. Twelve died, including the two lieutenants.

The suicides destroyed whatever little credibility the Indians had had with the Tigers. Rajiv Gandhi had assured Prabakeran that his men would be safe if they laid down their arms; according to some reports, he had even given Prabakeran a bulletproof vest as a personal reassurance of his commitment to the Tigers' safety. But on the heels of India's support for rival militant groups and continued Sinhalese aggression, Gandhi's assurances that he would protect Prabakeran's men—and his clear inability to do so—were meaningless. Soon, Trinco was burning.

Given the situation, we were lucky to have gotten the small charter flight. The island's only charter company had claimed that the weather was too uncertain. The real problem was that they were having a hard time finding a pilot willing to go. We were especially keen on getting there for the funeral of the slain Buddhist monk, but wondered whether the government would permit foreign journalists at such a sensitive event. The government spokesman, however, said we'd have "no problem." "With your charm," he chided Derek Brown, who had organized the excursion, and who had displeased the government with his candid reporting, "you should be able to get a seat right on the pyre."

We missed the funeral, but an afternoon on the tarmac at the airstrip outside of town was worth the wait, yielding hints that the Indians had let the situation spin out of their control. Fear of Tiger snipers had led the Indian officers to peel off their rank and regimental insignia. We waited on the tarmac for two hours before the Indians and the Sri Lankans could make a joint decision to let us pass into town. It was only one of many signs of the poisoned chemistry between the two ostensible partners in peace.

Later, when we finally got a chopper—with machine gunners ready to rake the area below if we were fired upon—we saw how badly chewed up the town was. Many of the buildings below were either presently in flames or charred from earlier fires. Our pilot, circling around the devastated town like a vulture looking for carrion, screamed about the way the Indians had left Sinhalese residents unprotected. Just the night before, between forty and fifty houses had been gutted. "They did nothing to stop them," the pilot insisted over the roar of the blades. He dove at a steep angle to pass over the monk's funeral at a temple below. "The Indians have let these animals run free. In fact, they helped them. Their sympathies are with the Tigers."

When we landed at the Sri Lankan military's Joint Operations Command, inside the sprawling navy complex on the outskirts of town, a contingent of dignitaries from the south were coming out of a briefing with the ranking commander and his staff. "What we are seeing is the systematic destruction of the Sinhalese in a place which has not been touched before," said one of the most prominent Buddhist laymen in the country, the director of a Gandhian social services organization called Sarvodaya. The fact that such a grim pronouncement was coming from a man revered for his nonpartisanship did not bode well for stability.

We had to wait another hour before we were cleared to tour the town in a jeep provided by the Sri Lankan Army, driven by an official escort, an ebullient Muslim named Colonel Mustafa. Derek Brown nicknamed him Colonel Happy because of his enthusiasm. Colonel Happy was determined that we see what dire things were really happening in town, that we "see the facts for ourselves," as he emphatically stated it, and to show his determination, he drove like a man possessed through the tense, ramshackle downtown streets. Trinco looked macabre, its alleyways pitted, scarred, and strewn with rubble and makeshift roadblocks. With a curfew from the night before in force until noon, the streets were absolutely empty, except for Indian sentries crouching with machine guns on the rooftops above us.

At noon, the curfew ended, and the roads were instantly filled with Sinhalese families who had fled their settlements. Trucks, vans, cars, and bicycles were piled high with seat cushions, glasses, chairs, cups, rugs, and other fugitive odds and ends. An elderly Sinhalese confronted Colonel Happy immediately. "Seven days they are not helping us. The Indian Army is even firing at us when we are running away. From this side we are shot at by the Tigers, from that side by the Indians. We are in the middle. You promised peace. You promised security, and look at us now. We have no homes. No lives. We do not even have a cup of tea."

An Indian officer pushed the elderly man away. The colonel cursed this Indian as he had others, but got back into the jeep to drive us to a refugee camp where medical care was being dispensed to lines of small skinny children. "What can be done?" the colonel said woefully. One of the doctors at the camp said that she had heard that the Indian soldiers were supplying kerosene to young Tamil boys to burn down Sinhalese houses, a claim echoed by some of the other Sinhalese refugees.

Later, we stopped at a rather desolate-looking crossroads, where a small crowd of Sinhalese were gathered. A row of shops and several vehicles had been firebombed. As we stood in the sun and tried to determine what had happened, the crowd grew bigger in size and nastier. The colonel was worried we might ignite a riot and draw Indian fire. Some of the people claimed to have seen Indian soldiers loot the stores after bands of Tamil boys drove away nearby residents.

A woman in late middle age beckoned to me to follow her down a small lane. She took me through the charred, empty shell of her house, pointing to where the Tamils had beheaded a statue of the Buddha and had ripped the rubbery croton plants out of the walkway in the front. "We had so many Tamil friends," the woman explained, her eyes ringed with dark circles. "We had no idea they had this intention. At the moment of the attack, the vehicles of the IPKF (Indian Peacekeeping Force) were right here. Six people were in the house at that time. We have no place to live now."

"J.R. has made a great mistake in this peace accord," moaned her husband. Like many Buddhists, he wore a white string around his wrist for good luck. He was sorting through the few of their possessions that were salvageable. "We have no faith in the government anymore." Nearby, a flock of large, screechy crows flapped their wings nervously, mirroring the agitation of the crowd that had meanwhile encircled Colonel Happy.

"It's all over," said Derek, who had traveled down several other lanes and had joined up with me to compare notes. "There doesn't seem to be anything sporadic about this at all. An organization has simply decided to systematically wipe out this entire area."

At the Indian military command center inside the Trincomalee city hall, the captain made a feeble attempt to apologize for the commanding officer's absence. It was the old runaround, brought to an almost surreal level of implausibility by the bureaucratic idiosyncrasies of the Indian psyche. "The competent man who would be able to give you an assessment of the situation is not here," the captain said, with the superior visible inside the office. "He is at the moment fifteen miles away. You should have made arrangements."

After that, we stopped over at the Sri Lankan Joint Operations Command again, where they were only too happy to give us a briefing, in an effort to discredit the Indians. We were first treated to a chronology of the preceding week's escalation of violence. As we were briefed, the Reuters reporter wrote her notes in a thick diarylike book filled with many similar chronologies from the earlier phase of the fighting.

"It has been impossible for us to assess the extent of the deaths and property damage," said a strapping colonel named Liyanage—whose demeanor personified the warrior spirit of the Sinhalese lion on the Sri Lankan flag. "But it is clear that it is the work of the Tigers, backed by the Tamil community and given the tacit permission of the Indians." In fact, the Tigers were roaming freely now, not even trying to hide their guns. Forty to fifty houses were burned just the night before. Whole villages had been emptied throughout the district, a sure sign that Tamil rebels were trying to force out the Sinhalese in anticipation of the upcoming referendum. Would Sri Lankan forces stay in their barracks, we asked, or would they retaliate against Tamil civilians in response? "What we see makes our people frustrated," the colonel replied. "But we are civilized people."

It was time to get back to the airstrip for the flight back to Colombo. I was prepared to stay a few days longer but had decided against it after seeing how dangerous Trinco really was. As we stood by the plane waiting to board, I reconsidered and decided to stay. I asked Colonel Happy, who was making his gregarious goodbyes, what he thought. "Well," he said, laughing. "If you don't take too much sun the rest of the time you're here and don't get a deep tan, you should be okay."

Colonel Happy's encouragement did not account for logistics, however. While he roared off on the next chopper, I had to wait behind for another one. An hour stretched into two, and when a helicopter finally arrived the pilot was on orders to wait until there were at least two passengers for the trip into town. As a result, I wasted the whole afternoon watching Sri Lankan Air Force training missions skid and hop across the tarmac in their World War II–era single-prop Marchettis.

I was rescued by two chopper pilots who took me up to the officers' mess, an old British club situated on a knoll overlooking manicured green gardens and shrubbery. The second pilot, who, like his colleague, wore Porsche aviator glasses, spoke in the crisp, fluting voice of the upper classes. He had been in Jaffna the day that the seventeen Tiger cadres had bit down on their cyanide. His account was laced with generous amounts of professional respect and intimacy, like the stories of big-game hunters paying compliments to the endurance of their prey.

The pilots asked what other conflicts I had covered. They seemed disappointed when I told them that this was my first. They both had a gracious, Old World manner, but it was hard to tell what ranks they held because of the lack of insignia on their flight suits.

Both had spent the bulk of the war flying missions against the Tigers in Jaffna; if they were downed it was probably better for them to keep their real identities hidden.

I was interested in learning as much as I could about their training. There were persistent reports that American mercenaries, perhaps part of a CIA-directed covert assistance program, had helped train Sri Lankan security forces. There had been an American, one of the pilots admitted, a Vietnam vet, who had in fact flown in several operations, contradicting the U.S. ambassador's heated assertions that any talk of American mercenary involvement was "utter crap." Later, in the air over Trinco, on the way back to the naval base for the night, the pilot realized that he might have been a little too loose-lipped. "You have written that man's name down?" he asked. It would have been easy for him to have me thrown out of the chopper if he thought his loose lips would have caused him trouble later on.

Once we flew over the town I relaxed, though about the same time the night before, several choppers had been hit.

Below, about a dozen houses had been set ablaze, the flames eating steadily away at the roofs. Dark, smoldering plumes of smoke dispersed into the evening sky. Dog packs skulked along deserted streets, and the last refugee stragglers could be seen limping into the camps that had been set up in town to protect fleeing Sinhalese.

It was just after the seven o'clock curfew when we landed at the Joint Operations Command. The ride that Colonel Happy had promised me to the refugee camp where I wanted to spend the night was nowhere to be found. It was probably better, since the militants were watching all movements closely and I didn't want to appear associated with the military. In the next few days, I wanted to make contact with the guerrillas. I set out for the refugee camp on foot.

According to local superstition, dusk was the time of the *gra-hayas*, supernatural spirits of malignant inclination. As crows and fruit bats swarmed through the nighttime streets, a conversation that Derek and I had about kidnapping came back to me. The militants just might want to make international headlines, he'd said, and grabbing a journalist might be a quick way to do it.

Not a hundred yards from the naval base, an entire neighborhood was festooned with Tiger flags. Soon after, I was surprised to pass by a set of Indian Army tanks. The lights of a truck held me in their beams. Guns were trained on me. Someone at the base might have radioed ahead to inform them I was on my way. I braced for surly treatment, but a soldier simply leaned over and reminded me that it was after curfew. All around him, the Indian troops practiced their English with me. "Hello, good evening." "Hello, good evening."

The streets were littered with broken glass and charred debris. I could hear voices coming from behind the tin fences and cadjan walls which enclosed the houses still standing. The voices were hushed. I had only about four hundred yards to go to get to the camp, which was across a flat open space where Indian tanks had arranged themselves around a small stone fort. About halfway across, I was surprised by a brilliant flash of light. Inside another fort, on a rocky promontory nearby, searchlights had suddenly illuminated a giant white plaster Buddha, three or four stories high, which now stood sentinel over the town.

I followed a truckload of late-arriving refugees to the makeshift camp. It was filled to overflowing. The government, wary of the political impact of bringing refugees south, had dragged its feet in sending trucks to the region to relocate them. Every nook and cranny of the school buildings which served as the camp were filled with families who had fled their homes. Most were scattered on the floors, chatting nervously as the light flickered from power surges. The vast majority of refugees were Sinhalese, of course, but I did meet a small Tamil boy named Johnson, who was playing with his Sinhalese friend, David, in the room where I was supposed to sleep. Many Tamils in Trinco had long relationships with their Sinhalese neighbors. But those relationships meant little now. Even if the militants were not killing Sinhalese wholesale, it was clear that they were being driven away and would be killed if they resisted. And any Tamil citizen who objected to the militants would be shot, no questions asked.

I had a meal with the director of the camp, a Sinhalese Buddhist named Pieris. He was running the facility single-handedly now—his co-director had fled earlier in the day after hearing that two young

Tamil employees, once fired from the school, were readying their long-planned revenge. Because he had not made any enemies, Pieris was left with only political uncertainties to worry about, in addition to feeding and caring for several hundred people in a space taxed beyond all its usual resources.

"They wanted to destroy the Sinhalese and their property," Pieris said dejectedly. "The aim was not to kill them. If they wanted to do that they'd have been able to kill thousands." Pieris had worked for nearly ten years in Trincomalee, dividing his energies equally between Tamils and Sinhalese. Whatever he had accomplished had been wrecked. We were watching the refugees, most of them poor and barely literate, clustered around the television set. The evening news was severely underplaying the extent of the damage done to Sinhalese interests in Trinco. They watched the broadcast three times—once in Sinhala, next in English, and then finally in Tamil—but because TV news was controlled by the government, it gave little sense of what was happening.

I was the object of a great deal of attention in the camp, particularly from the younger children. It was likely they had never seen a Westerner before. I tried to have some fun with the kids, and put my flashlight up to my chin, distorting my features into what I thought would make a funny face. But the kids, already having seen enough monstrousness for the day, ran to their mothers, who scowled at me. I made another faux pas when I tried to give a bar of soap to a teenage girl I had caught looking through my bag. She took the soap, removing the wrapper and putting it up to her nose to sample its bouquet. Then she handed it back. "Lux soap?" she hissed. "I don't like Lux." So much for charity, in the face of teenage consumer awareness.

I had a hard time sleeping. I listened to the people in the dark around me, the couples trying to reassure each other, the old people mumbling to themselves. Oddly, the languages were no barrier; the tone of worry and bewilderment came through most clearly. Outside the window, Indian tanks had backed their rear ends right into the camp to guard against a possible raid. If there was an attack, there'd be little chance of getting out uninjured.

The next morning Pieris warned me not to go too far into town.

I was leaving with a batch of refugees who were heading back to check on their homes and businesses. Evidently the night had been fairly calm, by the standards of the last week, and the Indian commanders had therefore lifted the curfew at six that morning. The Indians still insisted that they had the area under control, but a Chinese man told me panic was still widespread. The owner of the ravaged Hotel Blue Note, a small guesthouse across the road, agreed. "The Tigers are all over," he told me. "They are everywhere in Trinco." A Muslim I met, however, told me there had been no trouble at all, gingerly stepping over a tangle of wires in the middle of the street. "No trouble?" I asked incredulously. "No problem in my area anyway," he said over his shoulder.

The first neighborhood I walked through, a Sinhalese area, had taken a horrible beating. Most of the streets were littered with debris. It was as if debris, not ideology, was the driving force of wars. I was momentarily stopped and questioned by an Indian police inspector. The inspector told me he couldn't comment on the situation, and resumed the patrol, with his pistol drawn.

Later, I strayed into a Tamil neighborhood. It was untouched by violence. I was pretty sure that the boys who had invited me inside a small concrete house for tea were Tiger sympathizers, if not militants themselves. "You've got it all wrong," one of the Tamil boys insisted, a row of heads nodding behind him. "It is the Sinhalese who burn the Tamils out."

"The Indian Army was very good; gentlemen, even," declared the boy next to him. "It was the Ceylon Army, the Sinhalese, who were the dangerous ones. Firing at innocent Tamils. Drawing their blood, burning down their houses for the last five years. This week? It was all overrated. And anyway, after five years, what goes around comes around, no?"

"These boys have lost their mothers, fathers, sisters, and brothers," said an older man, perhaps an uncle, who had slid into the room. "The Sinhalese have brutally raped, assaulted, and killed, in front of their very eyes. What would you do if they held you in a detention camp for four years on suspicion?"

Another youth joined in. "Yesterday they brought ministers, but only after there were Sinhalese victims. Did they ever visit when it was our people? And that curfew? You'll notice they made the announcement in Sinhala and English, but not in Tamil. They don't care for us in the least."

"This is the way of life as it is lived in Trinco now, as it is in all of Ceylon," growled the first boy again, seeming to like the sound of his own voice. "Do to them or die. Do or die."

There was hardly any sympathy for the Sinhalese victims from the children I interviewed, even those Tamil kids who sought the protective confinement of Sinhalese refugee camps. "They are burning their own homes," said one little girl, with the aid of a translator. "They burn them, blame the Tamils, and then start a fight."

Even the clergy, who might have been immune from partisanship, seemed to gloat. "Most of those people leaving their homes are not refugees at all," said a young Tamil Roman Catholic priest. "The government is merely emptying the town of them as an act to show the outside world." In any case, he explained, there was a history here I had to understand. If the Indian Peacekeeping Force had not come, the Sri Lankan forces would have eliminated all the Tamils in Trinco by now. "The Sinhalese want to stamp out the Tamils, the individuality of our language and our culture," the priest insisted. "That is why this fighting has come again."

"Every action has a reaction," added an elderly Tamil man. "Earlier, it was the Tamils who were burned. Now it has taken a complete turn. Now the Sinhalese are suffering for their past sins. This is a payback for 1983 and all those years when they attacked us, going back to 1956. Will it ever stop? I do not think it will. But at least with the Indians here now, we have some peace. If they were to leave, however, it would mean death to all Tamils. They will kill every one of us. If the Indian Army leaves, we will have to jump into the sea."

Things were different in Trinco when I had visited it the year before. While control of the rest of the eastern province was split between the rebels and the government, Trinco itself had remained in Sinhalese hands, mostly due to the presence of the Sri Lankan naval and air force bases around the harbor. Few of the younger

Tamil men would dare venture out of their homes, for fear of being detained for interrogation—or worse.

I had planned on my first visit to stay at a small guesthouse run by an expatriate Chinese—one of the few prewar hotels still open—but his retarded son, traumatized by the violence, wailed incessantly. I decided to stay at a rest house nearer to the naval base. At night, soldiers and sailors off duty would come in and drink arrack into the night. Even then, everyone in town was drunk and jumpy, especially the owner of the rest house, a tall Muslim man who was leery of foreigners.

When I stopped by the rest house this year on my way back to the Joint Operations Command, I found that this year's chaos had sobered the owner up, and instead of looking for someone to intimidate he was looking for a sympathetic ear. He showed me how close he had come to being hit by stray bullets—presumably from the Tigers, but perhaps, too, from the Indians—the day before while playing in a card game in the back. The bullets had traveled through three sets of windows, over the card table, and into the wall he was leaning his head against. "Business? What business?" He scowled. "My whole staff is leaving now. Even my cousins—their mother came from Kandy the other day to drag them back by the ears." His sourness contrasted with the upbeat kitsch of his decor, which included wall-sized posters of Brooke Shields, Jodie Foster, and Lassie. Surprisingly, the owner wouldn't let me pay for a soda water when I offered to. He made a big production out of his bunker generosity. As soon as I was outside, however, on my way to the Joint Operations Command, the manager of the rest house was right on my heels. "Sir. A small problem with the bill," he apologized, wiggling his head amiably.

Colonel Happy personified the mood at the Joint Operations Command later that morning: a mixture of despair and exhilaration. Attacks had occurred in the last twenty-four hours all over the north and the east, a quantum leap from the low-level violence of the previous week. Reportedly, thirty to forty Sinhala civilians had been massacred on a train at Batticaloa, the second-largest town in the east. There were also reports that about thirty miles up the coast from Trinco, a small Sinhala fishing village had been all but wiped out. Tamil militants swooped down and shot more than twenty inhabitants, most of them children.

"Looks like war again, no?" the colonel said to me with the same screwball enthusiasm he had projected the day before. "Well, at least you know where you are, huh? It's back to normal now, huh, on the war footing again, and we'll be on it for a good long time. You can shake hands after a cricket match or boxing, but after this fighting, it will be a long, long time."

Colonel Happy procured a telephone line for me, so I could talk with Derek Brown in Colombo. Both he and John Rettie, the BBC man, had asked me to file any reports I heard while I remained in Trinco, on-the-spot information of vital importance as they sifted through the propaganda coming at them from all sides. I was hoping that Colonel Happy could get me on a chopper for the fishing village where the massacre took place so I could confirm that story. He disappeared for a while, checking with a logistics officer about the availability of the chopper. Then he returned, slapping me hard on the back. "We're in business," he said, though we would have to wait for the area to be secured to make sure there were no "terrorists" lying in wait. Sri Lankan forces were going to evacuate the survivors by boat.

But soon after this announcement, a radioman burst into the Situation Room to tell the colonel, in rapid Sinhala, that a truckload of Sri Lankan soldiers out on a provisions run had been blown up by a land mine. "Fuck," said the colonel. "They must not want our men in that area." The incident meant that I would have to wait quite a while for a chopper to the massacred village, but the colonel promised that he'd get me there and be my escort.

In the meantime, I just sat around the Situation Room, out of the pounding sun, in the company of the two old war-horses, Colonel Happy and his counterpart, Colonel Sam De Silva. Both had been retired but had come back to active duty when the riots of 1983 turned a relatively small-scale Tamil revolt into a full-blown civil war. Both had been educated in English-style schools in old Ceylon.

Colonel Happy was a Muslim, Colonel Sam a Buddhist, I think, but both were of the generation that put fidelity to a secular, united Ceylon ahead of ethnic passions. The war had been good for military careers, however, Colonel Happy explained. Most of his "batch mates"—those who had graduated with him from the service academy—had made it to major general, and coming back from retirement had meant, for him, a lot more pension money.

Colonel Sam had worked for the British Navy during World War II and had made a number of friends among the British officers he had served with. While I was waiting for the chopper, he produced a letter that one of his old British "chums" had written to Margaret Thatcher, explaining that the Tamil separatist cause on Sri Lanka was but a thinly veiled adjunct of the international Communist conspiracy whose "evil" agents had infiltrated the BBC—witness the sympathetic reports on the Tamil struggle that were being aired in England.

While Colonel Sam was showing me the letter, Colonel Happy engaged himself intently in a tête-à-tête with a Sinhalese Catholic priest. The colonel nodded his head deferentially a few times before returning to Colonel Sam's desk. "A silly man, that priest. A very silly man," said Colonel Happy. "Imagine. He wants blood for the people in the hospital. The only people left in the hospital are Tamils! Let them go to their own families for blood. Mobilize their own for their own. It's always the same story. Cheer their boys, but go to the government for help."

Just then, word came in of a chopper transporting the wounded men from the earlier land-mine incident. One of the soldiers had died instantly; four others needed immediate emergency care, which would be provided by a team of surgeons from the French humanitarian organization Doctors Without Frontiers. When the helicopter landed, the casualties were unloaded in a blur of stretchers. Colonel Liyanage, the second-in-command, watched with evident disgust. "There is no peace accord anymore, but the Indians will never leave," he said, practically within earshot of a high-ranking Indian admiral. "They will be here a thousand years. All this bloody stuff is happening and yet our movements are restricted by those bloody bastards." Later, he said, "Actually, that wasn't too bad. We have seen land-mine victims in pieces. We have had to round them up and throw them into sacks."

Refugees were continuing to stream into the naval base; their vehicles were stacked with chairs, cabinets, carved wooden doors, and any other prized possession they could strap down for the ride. A man wearing a hat that read, "Official Hawaiian Bikini Inspector," came up to Liyanage just then. He said that the Tamils had hacked his father to pieces and burned his body on the spot. All the while Indian soldiers stood by, doing nothing. Liyanage launched into a tirade. He had heard other reports of Indians looting the abandoned homes of Sinhalese refugees, of truckloads of Sinhalese property being brought into Indian Army camps.

I was skeptical. "Why doesn't India acknowledge any of these things? Their denials have been consistent right on down the line."

"Acknowledge!" he exploded at me. "What is there to acknowledge? They are directly involved!"

Meanwhile, Colonel Happy returned. "We're in business." He slapped me hard on the back once again. The chopper was ready to leave. The colonel wore a walkie-talkie on his belt. His sidearm was carried by his orderly, a young corporal, who stayed two paces behind us as we walked out to the landing pad. I wasn't exactly sure why he wasn't carrying it himself. Perhaps an unarmed man was less likely to be shot at by a sniper, or perhaps he did it out of some technical compliance with the rules of the now near-irrelevant peace accord. "That pistol is not meant to be taken seriously," the colonel explained, considering the firepower the Tigers had. "What can you do with a pistol anyway?"

The information that we had gotten earlier about the massacre had been mistaken, Happy explained rather matter-of-factly over a huge meal of rice, curried vegetables, and fish heads, for which we had stopped at a small Sri Lankan naval outpost up the coast. "They have not been shot. They have been hacked and cut." After the meal, Happy belched loudly and washed his hands from a jug of water on the table. "Now we are ready for any eventuality."

The village that had been massacred was a settlement of Sin-

halese fishermen who had been moved there as part of the government's colonization program. It had been attacked once before and
abandoned, and then resettled on the highest government orders.
Most of the survivors were being evacuated. The dead had been
buried, the colonel said, which would complicate my verification of
the numbers killed and the circumstances involved. On top of that
it was already late in the day and the rest of our trip to the village—the last leg by boat—would have to go smoothly for us to get
back by dark.

We motored up the coast in a dorylike vessel manned by a dozen
armed sailors, more than the small boat would normally carry. The
coast grew even wilder. It was a tropical version of the coast of
northern Maine. We passed two large fishing boats, each carrying
about forty villagers toward the relative safety of the naval bunker.
A few miles behind them was another boat, this one carrying about
twenty.

When we arrived at the village, the last of the villagers were
wading into the water to load their meager possessions—pots, a few
sticks of furniture, bicycles—onto the remaining vessels. When we
landed on the beach, the sailors had their guns cocked and ready to
fire. The mood was eerie: most of the small cadjan houses had been
burned to the ground, leaving only a few charred and twisted poles
and several roofless concrete houses that had not yet been finished.
Behind the clearing where the village once stood was a cliff covered
with jungle, fine cover for an ambush. Once we got out of range of
the surf, not a sound disturbed the area.

I was able to break away from Colonel Happy long enough to
ask several of the remaining villagers how many were killed the
night before, establishing that nineteen had died. Contrary to the
colonel's latest update, only one man had actually been hacked to
death. Twelve of the victims had been children under the age of ten,
one of them an only son. His father told me, tearfully, that he was
now left with only daughters—a curse in Sri Lankan culture.

To make sure that the world believed that the poor Sinhalese
of that village had really been butchered, the colonel volunteered to
dig up the graves. A face-off ensued. Although I protested that it

really wasn't necessary for him to do so, the colonel urged some of his sailors into action. Part of me, however, did want to make sure the story wasn't falsified, as often was the case. Before they had dug down very far, however, the horror of the scene I was sure to see made me walk away. They stopped digging.

Colonel Happy ran up behind me, to fill me in on little details about the village, as though the preceding incident had never taken place. All of the people in the village, he explained, were Sinhalese Catholics from an area outside of Colombo called Negombo, where Tamils and Sinhalese had intermarried for generations. The Tigers had been after Sinhalese Buddhists, he told me, but the irony was that they killed people with their own blood in them, and Catholics to boot. "All the poor Marys and Josephs," lamented the colonel.

The colonel enlisted the help of a teenage girl, an eyewitness. It had been about nine o'clock the night before, she told us, when about fifteen terrorists walked quietly into the settlement and demanded that the villagers open up their doors. From where she had been watching, she saw them drag the father of one family out of his dwelling. The man was down on his knees begging for his life, touching the feet of the militant with his forehead, one of the most powerful forms of pleading in that culture. It didn't work. The Tiger stepped back from the man and pumped his rifle right into the man's head. He then set the house ablaze, the screams of the children mingling with the roar of the flames as the girl ran out of her home and into the jungle for safety.

We walked solemnly among the other ruins. In one, there was blood splotched across a hearthstone; in another, the clay floor had been dyed a grim shade of crimson. As we walked farther from the beach and closer to the edge of the clearing, the colonel suddenly scolded our armed escorts for keeping their backs to the jungle. "They could still be in there watching us," the colonel whispered firmly, explaining that one of the LTTE's regional offices was only a half mile away. One of our naval escorts pointed up into the trees abruptly, causing me to look for cover, but all he had seen was a Tiger banner strung between two trees. It was a bright orange-red with a bloodcurdling image of a roaring, fanged Tiger framed between two AK-47 rifles. One of the sailors climbed the tree to retrieve it, and the colonel gave it to me to keep as a souvenir. He warned me not to let any of the other officers see it, though, since they might not understand why I wanted to keep such a thing. "This is the Situation," the colonel said with a deep sigh. "The Tigers don't want our people here. The government does. These poor people are stuck in the middle."

Back at the beach, it became clear that the colonel's men had nearly permitted our boat to drift out to sea. They had been keeping a close watch on the jungle. "If that boat was lost, there'd be a court-martial," Colonel Happy warned. "Our people are not very good with these things. That is why the Tamils are so effective. Give them a rule book and they will digest it."

As the remaining survivors boarded their overburdened craft, Colonel Happy grimly summarized the occasion while pointing at the rusted carcass of an old Morris Minor left stranded in the sand: "A silent reminder that all the good things the British brought here are all but completely gone."

Down the coast where we were to get the chopper, a storm was brewing, causing the palms to bristle with an almost erotic intensity. I hoped we'd put into the base before the rains began. We were way overloaded and taking on water, which the crew bailed out desultorily. Coconuts lurched back and forth in the boat. At times, because of the combination of bad currents and sloppy navigation, we were moving in large sweeping circles. Colonel Happy sat athwart the gunwales, his hat cocked at a dopey angle, his shirt half untucked and his pistol, which he was now carrying, threatening to unholster itself. The crew looked equally disheveled. The afternoon had drained everyone. The protection we were supposed to be giving the refugees had been spotty at best. At one point, we passed what we thought was a corpse floating in the water, perhaps a villager who had run into the sea to avoid the slaughter. If it was a human being, there didn't seem much point in stopping for it. "It's a dog," the colonel declared, and everyone shook their heads in agreement. "Yes, it is a dog. I am sure of it."

* * *

In the refugee camp that night, the power of the Indian radio transmitters—erected to communicate between Trinco and military bases in southern India—interfered with local television reception. What did come across, however, was as grisly as that afternoon's journey to the massacred village. More than 127 Sinhalese civilians had been killed that day by the Tamil Tigers. The news reported that forty alone had been killed after fleeing from a train that had been set ablaze. Unlike past nights, there was little restraint in the reporting, and the broadcasts emphasized India's shock and revulsion. India, it was said, would take direct and decisive action to keep the peace.

Clustered cheek by jowl around the television, the ever-swelling numbers of Sinhalese refugees watched in silence—beaten, sullen, and anxious. Even if India did deliver on its promise to mount a counterattack against the Tigers, Indian slogans meant little to people whose homes and businesses had been systematically destroyed. "*Dukkha, bomo dukkha*," a little Sinhalese boy sighed in the flickering blue light of the television news. Suffering. Much suffering.

Though urgency had made its way into official Indian statements, local commanders in Trinco were still making an effort to minimize that week's debacle. "People are overreacting," said the Indian colonel who agreed to see me the next day. We chatted inside the headquarters of the Indian Peacekeeping Force in downtown Trinco. What impressed me most was how he said such things with a straight face. "There is no real reason these people should be leaving anyway," he continued. "Hundreds of houses destroyed? Nonsense! And anyway, don't blame the Indians. It is the fault of the communities here that the Accord hasn't worked. And how many more would have been displaced if the Indians hadn't come?"

Then, as we were speaking, a call came in over a special radio line. The colonel blanched. "I have just been informed that you will have to talk to our officer who specializes in relations with the press. He is now in Madras and only when he returns can we give you any information. In the meantime, I am asking you as a gentleman to disregard my comments. Can I have your word that you will?"

"We are all living dramas here now," cried Colonel Sam in his arch, Victorian style as I entered the Joint Operations Command center in the naval dockyard later that morning. Already another Sri Lankan Army vehicle had been blown up by a rebel land mine outside of Trinco. Colonel Liyanage shook visibly as he told me about it. "You should see the bodies," he said, his voice choked with a mixture of rage and sorrow. "You should see the bodies and then you'll be able to see what we are up against."

Then he took me to the mortuary. It was too dark inside the cool, clammy room to see until a few minutes had passed, and even when my eyes did adjust to the light, there was a moment before I could recognize what was before me. The smell, however, was unmistakable, and it wasn't long before I ran outside to vomit. Back inside, I surveyed the carnage. The blast had left two of the victims reasonably intact, but the other two were hideously dismembered. One was just a pile of body parts, the merest suggestion of a human being. They had arranged the parts in ascending order: a foot, a calf bone, a midriff with intestines coiling into what might have been a chest cavity. There were two arms yoked together with a length of brown skin, half a face, and a scalp with pieces of a service hat embedded in it. The next set of remains was somehow even more disturbing: the head had been blown completely off, exposing the stem of the brain.

Leaning over the bodies, a doctor in a stained Western-style suit labored, his eyes gluey from too much arrack. I was glad I had a camera with me so I didn't have to look at the gore straight on, but even with the buffer of the lens, I felt another wave of nausea. "We were a contented nation at one time," I heard the doctor say as I wiped the tears from my eyes. "A contented people, until these terrorists came."

There had been land-mine attacks that morning all over the north, and I was getting a little worried about how I was going to get out of Trinco safely. There were no planes that I could hop on for a ride back to Colombo and little fuel left for nonessential helicopter flights. I was quite reluctant to ride in a military convoy, the only option available that day, as the Tigers had demonstrated unusual precision in finding and blowing up Sri Lankan military vehicles, a precision that may have come from sympathetic Indian soldiers.

After lunch with Colonel Sam (a difficult experience after the mortuary visit), I tried to find a safe ride out of Trinco in Fort Frederick, a military installation overlooking the town. Several thousand refugees were packed onto the grounds awaiting government evacuation. It seemed safe to assume that the militants wouldn't attack refugee convoys, but Colombo had not yet sent vehicles to carry people out, fearing the political consequences of evacuation.

The fort was bedlam incarnate. Leaving behind a shrill loudspeaker announcement for missing family members, I went for a walk up the hill behind the fort's barracks in search of a Hindu temple located there. Though few Tamil Hindus visited the shrine, the structure itself went untouched, as did the old bearded Brahman man who kept the ritual flame burning inside it. "All are good people, sir," the man told me, oblivious to the fires that were, at that moment, sending up thick plumes of smoke in settlements to the north and west of town.

Later that night, the sky over that part of town glowed red. More fires had been set that day than any before it. Whatever the Sinhalese left behind when they fled was burned that night. The Tamils wanted to make sure that if the Sinhalese did return they'd be coming back to nothing. You could almost hear cries of jubilation and glee issuing forth from the flames. Behind the despondent row of spectators, the illumination of the camp's Buddha statue cast a weak pallid light by comparison, silent and remote. Heavy rains knocked the power out and the Buddha's light flickered several times before going out completely. "Maybe the rains will put out the fires," Pieris, the camp director, joked forlornly behind me.

When I woke the next morning, I decided to cancel the meeting I had arranged with the leaders of the Three Stars militant groups, a consortium of three Tamil rebel groups allied with the Indians against the Tigers. Some of their cadres had stopped me on the street the day before. My heart was in my mouth most of the time. They seemed like pretty hardened sorts, capable of anything, and I was surprised to learn that they were only in their late teens and early twenties. All of them claimed to have spent at least half a dozen years in "the movement." After their interrogation—at one of their safe houses—I asked a few questions about the situation in Trinco, which prompted interminable ideological discourses in reply. They were emphatic about taking me to one of their commanders, who had taken refuge in an Indian Army camp outside of town, but I wasn't eager to be seen by the Tigers in their company, and managed to make an appointment to go out the next day.

Instead, I thought I'd try to make contact with the Tigers. I walked through the ravaged Sinhalese section of town toward the neighborhood where they were headquartered. I was apprehensive about meeting them, too. They had formally renounced the Accord after the recent cyanide suicides, and with it any notion of a cease-fire. At that very moment, in fact, four Sinhalese technicians from the Sri Lankan Broadcasting Corporation had been taken hostage by the Tigers. Had I known that I would not have gone near the place.

Huskinson's Road, named for the last British government agent in the district, was the Tigers' address. I had expected to have some trouble finding it and was surprised when I came upon a tidy bunga-low with a huge red Tiger banner flying outside it. This flag was about twelve feet by twelve feet and was visible throughout the entire neighborhood.

The house, however, was empty. A small boy in shorts met me at the gate and walked me inside the courtyard, explaining that all the cadres had left that morning "to go back to the jungle," leaving behind a shrine, made out of palm leaves fashioned into stick figures, to their fallen comrades who had taken cyanide a few days before.

The situation was accelerating. Prabakeran had publicly flouted the authority of the state. President Jayawardene had put a million-rupee price on his head. And the Indians, pushed into a political corner by the grisly events in Trinco that week, were readying to strike at the Tigers and bring them finally to heel, a move that would further jeopardize the peace accord. From this angle, the Tiger banner billowed and strained like a bloody sail.

4 · Operation Wind

THE PLIGHT OF Trinco's Sinhalese refugee population had been a godsend to Sinhala Buddhist chauvinists, who had predicted such a catastrophe as soon as the peace accord was announced. While I was in Trinco, stories abounded concerning the Tigers' mutilation of Sinhalese villagers. Sinhala extremists in the government made a point of housing refugees at temples around the city whose monks had particularly harsh reputations for militancy, thereby wrapping the refugee issue in the saffron mantle of the clergy's special authority and power. Some Sinhala politicians even warned that they might instigate violence against Tamil civilians living in the south. As a result, when I returned from Trincomalee, Colombo was a city poised on the edge of a terrible convulsion.

There was great pressure on President Jayawardene to let the armed forces, which the newspapers were calling "prisoners of peace," out of their barracks. To prevent this, and to maintain the legitimacy of its role as the guarantor of the peace agreement, India had to stand up to the Tigers. A few days later, therefore, Indian troops launched an offensive on Jaffna, the rebel bastion of the north. The offensive, which they called Operation Pawan, the Hindi word for "wind," was expected to last no more than two days.

There was considerable irony in India's action against the Tigers, to whom they had once given arms, training, and direction.

India had also long warned Colombo that a military strike against Jaffna would never work and would entail heavy civilian casualties. But there was a certain inevitability to the clash. The Indians may have supported the Tigers in their struggle for Eelam, but it was not to establish the separatist homeland so much as to destabilize the Sri Lankan government. In fact, the Tigers were Delhi's pawn in an international chess game, and once India could control the situation directly, under the auspices of the Accord, the Tigers were expendable. Whatever outward support India showed the Tamils, Eelam was a threat to the integrity of India as a nation. The last thing Delhi wanted was an independent Tamil state in the north of Sri Lanka, which would surely fan separatist fires among the fifty-five million Tamils on Indian soil.

A showdown was inevitable from the Tigers' perspective as well. Although the Tiger leader Vellupai Prabakeran had publicly supported the Indian role as a guarantor of the peace agreement, he had never really renounced the goal of Eelam. Once India put its foot down and made it clear that it did not want a separate state but, rather, autonomy within a unified Sri Lankan state, the Tigers began to view the Indians as a force to be circumvented. While the Tigers continued to surrender some of their arms as called for by the Accord, they were busy hiding old weapons and smuggling in new ones.

"Heading off in search of truth and accuracy?" I called jokingly across the lobby of the Meridien Hotel to Peter Hillmore of the London *Observer*.

"Well, yes, sort of," he replied with understated British sarcasm. "I was heading over to the Indian High Commission for a briefing, if that's what you mean."

Like the other foreign correspondents who had swarmed into Colombo in the few days that I was away, Hillmore was trying to maintain his genial spirits while placating anxious editors and scooping his rivals. The story that had brought the journalists into town was a compelling one, as siege stories always are: a few thousand guerrillas, mainly teenagers, were taking on the forces of the

Indian Army—the world's fourth largest—as it tried to overrun Jaffna. The stakes were high: the Indian drive had the potential to end the five-year civil war or to make it even more unresolvable, turning India's peacekeeping gambit into exactly what many of its critics had predicted: its Vietnam.

There was great copy to be written about the Tiger insurgency: their devotion to Prabakeran, considered a genius in guerrilla warfare; their puritanical sense of discipline—they spurned alcohol and sex; their cyanide caps; and their unswerving commitment to a separatist homeland in the northern third of the island. Most observers thought the Tigers would never surrender to the Indians, who would easily break their backs in a blitzkrieg on Jaffna. They would commit mass suicide in a final act of defiance and martyrdom, and this, in turn, would inflame the next generation. The normally staid *Economist*, for example, likened the Tigers to Japanese soldiers at the end of the World War II, "fanatically brave, appallingly cruel and committed unto death."

Smelling blood, then, members of the international press corps usually based in Delhi invaded Colombo in full force. Hardened reporters, called "firemen," who made their living traipsing from one global flash point to the next, had been rushed in as well. Overnight, Colombo was transformed into a media circus, with hotel lobbies full of men in safari suits and combat vests trading business cards and bonhomie. Although he was one of the last to arrive, the man from *Time* magazine had the story all figured out: "It'll be a Jonestown, boys, a Masada. They're a bunch of horny teenagers with cyanide caps and a death wish. We might even have a cover story."

Journalistic glory would have to wait, however. No one could get anywhere near Jaffna. We were all stranded in Colombo, our only link to the fighting being the inane daily briefings at the Indian High Commission.

Worried about any unflattering international attention, India preferred that the press corps learn about the fighting in Jaffna from a safe distance. Several hundred thousand residents of the area had already fled, but there were more than 500,000 remaining who might be trapped in the cross fire. India was making sure that the world knew as little about their fate as possible. Delhi refused to provide a press plane—the usual policy under the circumstances—claiming conditions were too dangerous, and talk of press pools came to nothing. In case anyone was tempted to sneak into Jaffna without proper permission, the Indians reminded us that they were patrolling access routes heavily with helicopters. What's more, by killing four Sri Lankan journalists, the Tigers left us all uncertain about the reception we'd get even if we did reach Jaffna.

A few people tried to get in on their own but were unsuccessful. One photographer from Agence France-Presse almost had his car stolen by bandits posing as militants, and John Swain, Peter Hillmore's rival from the London *Sunday Times*, had been turned around at an Indian checkpoint just on the lip of the action. Swain had made his reputation in Cambodia, where he'd been captured by the Khmer Rouge. When Swain returned to Colombo frustrated, the prospects for travel north dimmed considerably. Not that all the correspondents were raring to go. Heading off independently would anger Indian officials, and could prompt them to withdraw the press credentials essential to those based in Delhi. Trips overland to Jaffna would also mean days without the necessary telecommunications to "feed the news dragon," as one reporter called his copy-hungry editor.

The Indian briefings, dubbed the Five O'Clock Follies in tribute to the fantasy-ridden official U.S. briefings during the Vietnam War, at least gave us a few scraps with which to cobble a story together every day. This also suited the rather bureaucratically minded reporters on the scene, whose august institutions favored official pronouncements of embassies more than vivid on-the-scene reports. Most of them didn't seem to mind being grounded in Colombo. They were waiting for the Indians to stop stringing us along and follow through on their promise to chauffeur us all to Jaffna for an official tour. The Jaffna dateline would mask the fact that it was a relatively safe government-sanctioned sightseeing trip. Everyone would be content to sniff around, grab some color and some quotes, and head back to Colombo the same day, in time for deadlines, dinner, and, if the old bones could take it, maybe even a little disco.

Characters like Hillmore certainly kept the scene entertaining. A former gossip writer for the *Observer*, Hillmore had just returned to "fireman" duty and was champing at the bit. At one time he had been a public-school boxing champion, but a brain abscess had paralyzed his left side and gave him a distinctive limp. He couldn't write well with his left hand and he took few notes, but Hillmore had a withering eye for detail and an awesome memory, which made him a formidable journalist.

The morning I saw him in the Meridien, Hillmore was hiding behind a potted plant to avoid having to share a cab with Bruce Palling, another London newsman. Hillmore was socially connected in London and had little patience for the Australian Palling's persistent imitation of an upper-class Englishman. Palling didn't drop names, Hillmore exclaimed, he hurled them, especially those with hyphens. "You've heard of social climbers?" Hillmore asked. "Well, Palling is a social mountaineer. I'm surprised he doesn't carry a copy of *Burke's Peerage* around with him to tell him if people he meets are the right sort to know."

"Start the cartoon," one of the reporters said derisively in the briefing room of the Indian High Commission. Derek Brown of the *Guardian* had nicknamed the space the Blue Lavatory because of the revolting hue of its tiles. The Indian spokeswoman was a balloonish yet foxy woman in a sari who reminded me of the voluptuous Hindu love goddesses on ancient bronzes. The hundred or so reporters clustered before her were an impressive lot, but they treated her rather gently, hoping to get information on the side. Mrs. Puri was a bit of a pawn herself, informed of operational details only to the extent that the policymakers in Delhi wanted her to be. In another testament to the Machiavellianism of Delhi, Mrs. Puri was six months pregnant, a condition that mitigated the professional bile of even the most profane in attendance.

At the front of the room sat the correspondent from the *Times* of London. Nicknamed "the Brigadier" for his silver hair and lordly bearing, he had heard a vital bit of information that day wandering around Colombo: where to get "massages." A famed Vietnam-era reporter for the Washington *Post* had been dispatched from Rome to cover for their regular man, who was down with Delhi Belly. There was also a BBC "fireman" who had been sent in to provide color reports, but who, in the venerable tradition of British journalism, seemed to turn ashen whenever he was too long from the bar.

Hillmore was happy to see Swain sitting there among the others, Swain with his scuffed loafers and Oxbridge bad-boy manner. Hillmore turned to wave to a competitor from one of the British tabloids. "He's in his element," Hillmore explained in his trademark conspiratorial whisper. "With a story like this, it's always more important to send in somebody more skilled at inventing the facts than in ferreting them out. There's an old saying on Fleet Street: 'Make it early. Make it short. And if you have to, make it up.' "

The prize for fiction, however, went to the Indian spokeswoman, Mrs. Puri. Anything that contradicted the official version of events was labeled "disinformation," "blatant lies," or "a canard"—the last pronounced with a provocative sneer. The Indians, according to Mrs. Puri, were noble peacekeepers fighting a band of ruthless terrorists. Part of the dynamic behind Mrs. Puri's misinformation was the simple nature of propaganda, but some of it was cultural, too, reflecting a Hindu worldview that Nehru had once described as a "divorce from life itself, a credulity, a woolliness of mind where facts were concerned," which rendered reality wholly subjective and mutable, a product of wishful thinking and self-delusion.

In an earlier phase of the war she had been one of the best sources in town. When the Indian High Commission was trying to hector the Sri Lankan government before the Accord, Mrs. Puri became the conduit for information on human rights abuses and atrocities committed against the Tamils. She had put together an extensive, grass-roots network of Tamil civilians in the affected areas of the north and east who supplied her with the most reliable eyewitness information anyone could get, which she then funneled to journalists in Colombo. But now that India was inflicting the harm, Mrs. Puri had neutralized the effectiveness of that network. As a result, the Indian version of events skewed Western news coverage in even the most rigorous publications.

Within a week's time, it became clear that the original Indian plan for a two-day blitzkrieg had gone awry, though in general we still had no idea what was going on. There was still very little solid information about the fighting and no way to verify conflicting claims. The Indians alleged that they were close to taking the entire city, while other reports suggested that there were entire sectors they hadn't even stepped into yet. The Indians claimed they had attacked only military targets, but others spoke of wide swaths of destruction from indiscriminate shelling. The Indians said their tanks fired only at LTTE bunkers, but there were reports of people so badly crushed by tanks that they literally had to be scraped from the roads with shovels. The questions of air support and large "area" weapons like mortars and artillery were important to determine, as they spoke clearly of Indian's commitment to minimizing civilian death and hardship. No offensive air support had been used, in theory, but the man from the *Daily Mail*, a London tabloid, came up with a transcript of a radio intercept between Sri Lankan helicopter pilots and Indian spotters on the ground in which it appeared that Tamil civilians were rocketed and bombed from the air and that areas designated for refugees had been shot at as well. Earlier in the week, Mrs. Puri had denied such reports, but did eventually confirm that a few untoward incidents had in fact taken place. "Well, you know, this is not a game of hide-and-seek," she allowed. "This is a shooting war."

It was also unclear just how many Indians had been killed in the fighting, a figure that might have had great power to affect popular support for the Indian action domestically. Some reports held that India had sustained far greater losses than it was admitting, and that bodies were being shipped home clandestinely to avoid public outrage. Reporters were also unsure about the basic details of the Tigers' struggle. What was their numerical strength? How were they supplied? The Indians had painted a picture of blood-crazed fanatics holding out on crackers and soda pop, ready to fight to the last man. Would the cadre split from the leadership under the conditions of an amnesty the rank and file were being offered? And what about Prabakeran, the mythic Tamil guerrilla leader—would he try to negotiate a peace, be captured or martyred? Would his death mean the end of the movement, or spur yet another generation toward sacrifice for Eelam?

There were indications that civilian casualties in Jaffna had been high. Jaffna Hospital reported it had performed 166 operations in one day, when the usual figure was about three. Most of the people needing operations were over forty, suggesting noncombatants were being hit at quite a high rate. The few refugees trickling into Colombo spoke of hunger verging on starvation and people shot on sight as they tried to make their way to designated camps. The Tigers were apparently holding whole villages hostage, using them as human shields to blast their way past the Indians.

Reports of looting and rape by Indian soldiers were also steady, the latter of which our friend Mrs. Puri labeled "sexist rubbage, a vicious canard," despite medical verification. Reprisals against civilians were also rumored as well. In one particularly gruesome report, after the Tigers had ambushed a crack unit of Indian para-commandos, Indian soldiers stormed a nearby village and massacred between forty and sixty civilians, killing some by running over them in armored personnel carriers.

Every evening after the Five O'Clock Follies our ad hoc professional organization, Press Hacks Under Custody in Colombo, or PHUCC, met in the lobby of the Meridien for a burst of pre-deadline plagiarism, with notes, quotes, and spelling instructions swapped with gusto. As the dinner hour neared one night, Hillmore asked, "Is anybody hungry, or should we just send out for some receipts?"—alluding to the acknowledged liberties that many correspondents took with their expense vouchers. There was also talk of the young girls that the hotel management had flown in from Bangkok. "Yes, I've heard that before," sniffed Hillmore. "She was thirteen but had the body of a twelve-year-old, right?"

The auspicious, late arrival of *Time* photographer Dieter Ludwig guaranteed more diversion. Known as Field Marshal Ludwig for his Prussian severity and martial obsessions, he had spent twenty years crisis-hopping across Asia. His apprenticeship took place in Vietnam under Horst Faas, the photographer famous for declaring, "Vot I like is boom-boom."

Ludwig boycotted the briefings at the High Commission, claiming that they were an insult to his intelligence, but the briefings also conflicted with his nightly gambling. The consummate armchair analyst, he could spin wild theories about what was going on behind the lines, all based on the two weeks he had spent with the Tigers right after the Accord was signed the previous summer.

Like many other journalists in Colombo, Ludwig was fixated on the idea of the Tigers' last stand, a scenario fueled by reports that Prabakeran had barricaded himself into the Nallur Kandaswamy Temple—an ancient Sri Lankan Tamil Hindu shrine just outside of Jaffna—and was using the thousands of civilians taking refuge there as a human shield. The situation was parallel to the Golden Temple attack in the Punjab, which had occurred several years before. The theory was that Prabakeran would force the Indians to attack him there, that he had ordered the "necklacing" of five Indian soldiers held prisoner in the temple precincts as provocation. The Indians seemed to be readying for just such a move, announcing their view that a temple lost sanctity when wanton acts of barbarism were committed inside it.

Breakfasting late one afternoon in the hotel coffee shop, Dieter spoke gravely about the Tigers. "They are ready to go down in flames," he said solemnly. "To fight to the last man. They want to inflict the maximum 'fuck you' on the Indians. You have to see that they are completely governed by death fantasies. The leadership is probably right now calling in all their best fighters to Nallur Temple for the last stand. Now they must die, because if they surrender, they are dead forever as a movement. But if they go down together"—he broke off for a moment and made a twisted face as if he had bitten into a cyanide cap—"they will live forever in myth. If they live, they die, but if they die, they live, and another generation will rally to the cause." His speech had left him winded, and Dieter chuckled to himself as he caught his breath. "Then again," he said in self-deprecation, "I do like to explore the extremes."

We moved from the sublime to the ridiculous that afternoon, with a briefing from the British military attaché. It was presumed that he had more of an idea of what was going on in Jaffna than

most of the other Western diplomats we were all quoting authorita-
tively. He had been up to Jaffna a few times and had come away
impressed by the Tigers as a guerrilla force, particularly with the
way they had fortified the city in a labyrinthine network of tunnels
and secret passageways. "How long can the Indians continue to take
such heavy casualties?" one reporter asked. "I dunno," the attaché
replied, without even a hint of irony. "But this is the Orient, you
know. Life doesn't really have any value here. They have millions
of them, don't they?" A Filipino reporter working for Reuters was
flabbergasted.

Later that day, the Five O'Clock Follies again required a sus-
pension of disbelief. Most of the journalists who were still attending
the sessions had given up on Mrs. Puri's squalid disinformation.
Driven to distraction by the Indian stonewalling, Hillmore and
Derek Brown were holding their own news conference in the back.

"We are doing our best to minimize coverage," Hillmore wrote
in a note that was passed around the room. "Occasionally, however,
copy has gotten through."

"After ten days of fierce invention and plagiarism, essential
supplies are running low" read the handout from Derek Brown.
"There are only a few adjectives left, and our heavy amount of simile
and metaphor are virtually exhausted. The situation is dire: we are
reduced to the aimless tossing of homemade clichés."

By Sunday, everyone was bouncing off the walls. Rain had
imprisoned PHUCC in the hotel lobby. Stories from the London
papers had arrived via fax, allowing the British guys to read what
their competitors had turned out. When he saw someone holding a
copy of his latest story, Hillmore, who had stretched things a bit to
make it sound like he had gotten close to the action, abruptly ambled
off. "I think I'll go defend the swimming pool," he said sheepishly
over his shoulder. "But it's raining, Hillmore," someone reminded
him. "Well, then, I guess I'll go defend the bar."

A letter of professional protest that had been submitted to the
Indians resulted in nothing but the cancellation of the Five O'Clock
Follies. In a defiant mood, we batted around a variety of strategies
for forcing the Indians to let us into Jaffna. Death fasts, threats of

mass suicide through the consumption of hotel coffee, and a convoy to the front with reporters perched valiantly on top of taxicabs were some of the more desperate suggestions.

"I can hear enemy fire," cried Derek Brown, imitating a radio reporter in the thick of battle.

"That's my typewriter," replied Hillmore, puncturing the idyll.

"I can see smoke furling lazily through the palm trees," Brown continued.

"Sorry. That's my cigarette."

Later that day, though, came news that finally prodded us out of Colombo. The ashen-faced BBC "fireman" had been taken to Jaffna by the Tigers and, with the battle raging about him, was going to do an on-the-scene report. He was about to scoop us all. The last I had seen of him, he was leaning into a weekend, asking directions to the southern beaches. He went on the wagon, literally, to get into Jaffna: the Tigers had lashed him to a tractor.

The next morning, Hillmore and I, along with a photographer, left for the front.

"Move! Move!" our Tiger guerrilla guide screamed at us as we ran along the empty road. "Down! Down!" he screamed again as three shells landed nearby, followed by the sound of dirt sifting through the rubbery jungle leaves. I hunkered down to avoid flying shrapnel, then sprang up again, like a madman, with the guide barking orders from behind. At that point, I was no more worried about Hillmore—who couldn't run very well—than I was about the sunglasses that popped out of my pocket and were crushed as we began our scrambling, frantic retreat.

What looked as if it might end in tragedy had begun lightheartedly enough; for three days we had merely flitted around the edges of the fighting. In the car driving up, Hillmore was like a kid going to his first fox hunt. "What fun!" he exclaimed. "An adventure!" I did have misgivings about going off with him because of his limp, but Hillmore's keen sense of journalistic ingratiation compensated for his disability. And his British wit made him a fine traveling companion. "We'll have to tell the Tigers that we've come to witness their brave stand against the murderous Indians," he said as we set off. "Then we'll have to tell the Indians that we've come to witness their victory against the bloodthirsty terrorists. Then we have to hope that they're not eavesdropping on each other."

Our driver was a Muslim, but he was stopping at every roadside shrine we passed—Muslim, Christian, Buddhist, or Hindu—just to be on the safe side. So we thought, until we realized that he was nipping from a bottle of arrack at every stop as well. Partway up, we took down the press sign we had taped to our windshield, worried that the word might be misconstrued as "police" in certain well-armed circles. Still it was hard to think about danger, given the tropical beauty of the landscape. Every ten miles or so, we'd pass through swarms of yellow butterflies, as they spun lazily along the road.

Hillmore was at his best, dishing tidbits from his days as a gossip writer—the one, for example, about the famous American model who had left her signature in an old English manor house by dipping herself in ink and sitting on the open pages of the guestbook.

Getting into Jaffna and getting out again would be no mean feat. The funeral banners stretched across the road as we drove through the tiny villages began to take on a greater significance. We'd have to circumvent Indian checkpoints somehow, and then boat across the lagoon to the Jaffna peninsula. And then there was the small matter of avoiding rebel land mines until we could make contact with a guerrilla escort. The image of the soldiers killed by the mines the previous week, the leaky burlap body bags, was something I just couldn't get out of my mind. Hillmore, on the other hand, complained that he'd not had the chance to use his favorite line about a bombing victim: "Friends ran to his side, while others ran to his legs."

As we drove, the traffic evaporated. We had crossed an invisible line. I tried to concentrate on what we were trying to learn: the casualty rate for both combatants and noncombatants; the tactics and weaponry involved in the fighting; the treatment of prisoners; the condition of refugees; and, perhaps most important, the popular sentiment about the Tigers. We were heading into a major military offensive by what had originally been a peacekeeping force in a town that had only a month before garlanded this same force with flowers.

We stopped for the night at a rest house about three-quarters of the way to Jaffna. We had been told we might pick up an escort there who could smuggle us into the action. Run down by years of conflict, the rest house had a desperate air. The proprietor, who said he was a guerrilla sympathizer, blew gusts of whiskey into my face: "You must tell the world what is happening to our people. You must!"

We arranged for a guide to meet us the following morning at the crack of dawn. There were reports that the Indians had captured the ferry slip where we hoped to cross into Jaffna, and we felt very nervous about proceeding. I was beginning to lose patience with the photographer that the *Observer* had assigned to accompany Hillmore, a strapping Englishman named John Reardon. He had only been in the country once before, for two weeks, but he carried himself as if he were an authority on the conflict. Like many war photographers, he had a romantic view of war and sympathies for Third World liberation movements, although his feelings for Third World peoples were a little less generous.

I was having second thoughts about going into Jaffna, though the honor of being the first American print man into the battle was seductive. Suddenly, however, as we were arguing over the next morning's plans, we heard familiar voices. "So where the hell is the fax machine?" someone called, as a group from the hotel strolled in. They assumed that we had already been up to Jaffna and back. "Indescribable," Hillmore said, summarizing the scene when asked. "I'm having a hard time putting my experience into words." There was no room at the inn, however, and the only place in town where they could sleep was the mortuary across the street.

Next morning, the cook wouldn't make us breakfast because it was the Hindu holiday of Deepavali, the festival of lights, which celebrates the vanquishing of evil by one of the gods. Hillmore tried to pay him off with a fistful of rupee notes. "This should straighten out his calendar," he said. The guide was late, but at least he had shown up. Despite the delay we got off earlier than the others, who must have risen feeling pretty uncomfortable from their night in the mortuary. The road swarmed with Indian soldiers on a sweep of the area, and they eyed us suspiciously as they searched our vehicle and interrogated our guide. The soldiers believed the story we had concocted—that we were only heading two miles up to visit an Anglican minister Hillmore knew. We wove our way along the narrow tracks threaded between rice paddies and small hamlets. There were no signs that the Indians had any foothold at all in the interior; as in Vietnam, the army controlled the roads, and the guerrillas controlled everything else.

A few hours later, we raced toward the ferry slip at Pooneryn. Boats were still making the crossing. Along the way, we had stopped to talk to a busload of refugees who had just escaped from the city. Some children showed us bullet casings from helicopter strafing. Hillmore, squinting into the sky, looked equal parts blithe and anxious. "This is when you start feeling a little guilty," he said. "You've come all the way up here—a grown man—just for a little pop-pop over your head."

It was astonishing that ten days into the offensive the ferry slip for crossing the Jaffna lagoon was not under full Indian control. The "ring of steel" with which the Indians said they had surrounded the city was actually much flimsier. Refugees, profiteers, and Tiger resupply missions were crossing back and forth as we climbed into a boat.

A band of teenaged rebel sympathizers met us on the other side and swept us into a van. It was a bone-jarring dash to the Tiger command center on the city periphery. Across the low scrub and brackish lagoons of the Jaffna landscape, we could see pillars of smoke rising from the city, several miles away. We crossed an expanse of salt marshes before plunging into the narrow winding alleyways of town. At one point we hit a bump so hard that I thought we had struck a land mine.

After the trip, the lazy atmosphere of the Tiger camp seemed incongruous. The guerrillas, clad in sarongs and rubber slippers, hardly appeared to be ruthless terrorists bent on annihilation. The town seemed equally casual. It would inevitably fall to the Indians, and there was a twenty-four-hour curfew in force, but people strolled nonchalantly. The sounds of helicopters and shelling in the distance were no more threatening than locusts on a town green in Iowa.

It was this surreal continuity of war that I found most intriguing, and most Asian. Despite the fighting, people hung out their laundry, merchants continued to sell their wares, fishermen bobbed in the lagoon, and peasants planted rice in the fields behind their homes.

The Tiger command center was a small house that had been converted into a communications center. It reminded me of a suburban homestead where the parents had gone away for a vacation and the kids had taken over. The house was also doubling as a rest and recuperation center, and Tiger cadres were sprawled on mats inside, some sleeping, others reading adventure novels.

Instead of taking us right into the fighting as we had asked, the Tigers insisted that we have lunch, and escorted us to a small nearby café. We asked if the Tigers would leave Jaffna and take refuge in the bush. One of the cadre smiled a little eerily and said, "It is not easy to get out of Jaffna these days, no?" We asked another, a rather zealous-looking sort, if any of the Tigers had been taken prisoner. "None," he said, holding up his cyanide cap.

The persistent surrealism of the north was more in evidence as the rebels carted us closer to the battle zone. Our van was full now, since the other reporters had arrived on our heels. Though the area bore signs of fierce fighting, with its shattered houses and rubble-strewn streets, the scene appeared more like a large-scale version of capture-the-flag than the defeat of a rebel bastion. In the eye of the storm it was calm, if creepy. As we got closer to the fighting, however, we had to make ever more frequent stops under cover to wait out passing helicopters. When the ground started rumbling with the concussive force of approaching artillery and mortar fire, we turned back. We spent the rest of the day in a safe house.

The original plan for taking Jaffna had called for a four-pronged attack on the center of the city, after which those four columns would link up with an advance guard already stationed in the Jaffna fort downtown. But Clausewitz's ideas on "friction"—the countless minor factors that distinguish real war from war on paper—had played a much bigger role than anticipated. As a result, all four of the Indian columns were stalled by Tiger resistance. The force garrisoned in the fort, meanwhile, was so heavily pinned down that it took more than a week for them to break out. What had been originally seen as a two-day siege ultimately became a three-week bloodbath.

Primarily, Operation Wind was an intelligence debacle. Dismissing the Tigers as low-caste youth whose cyanide caps were a joke, the Indians made little effort to deepen their understanding of the Tigers' military organization or to familiarize themselves with the topography of Jaffna. Indian commanders did not learn, for instance, that the Tigers had the capacity to intercept their radio transmissions, which enabled the Tigers to ambush them, and their maps of the area were inadequate, causing patrols to get lost in Jaffna's streets.

India had also made fundamental logistical errors, despite the meticulous planning that went on in Delhi. Most of the units it had to rush into Jaffna were understaffed, underequipped, underbriefed, and tired after long transits across India. There had been inadequate airlift planning: at one point, the army had to commandeer civilian airliners to ferry in troops. Heavy weapons were left behind in the initial stages, leaving an insufficient ratio of armor and artillery to infantrymen, and plans for resupply did not foresee a protracted conflict.

Tactical mistakes were costly, too. In their rush to vanquish Jaffna, Indian units blitzed the Tigers instead of moving patiently with the men in the rear covering for the men advancing. LTTE snipers perched in trapezes hung in trees were exceptionally effective at cutting down officers, which hurt Indian morale and discipline. A common Tiger trick was to yield the first line of defense, which encouraged the Indians to advance, in order to attack from the rear through a tangle of local byways and back alleys. The Tigers also made use of civilian shields, forcing noncombatants to walk in front of their patrols toward the Indians before being ordered to drop to the ground so the Tigers could fire.

Another factor stalling Indian progress was the Tigers' facility with land mines. Jaffna had been heavily mined before the peace accord; along the roads we traveled were the scars of blasted culverts and destroyed bridges. Many of the mines used against the Indians were already in place from an earlier phase of the war, and all the Tigers had to do when hostilities resumed was reconnect the wires that controlled them. Many LTTE land mines were nonmetallic, and therefore difficult to detect; sometimes a mine was nothing more than an explosive coconut shell. The standard LTTE mine, however, was a 55-gallon barrel packed with enough TNT to rip the belly from the underside of a tank. Some of the mines were even bigger, approaching one kiloton in explosive force. Tiger land mines were made even deadlier when the LTTE developed the capacity to detonate them by radio. Consequently, Indian armored columns moved carefully along their approaches, and the Tigers used the time to fortify their own positions or arrange tactical retreats.

After waiting out the nearby artillery attack, we were shuttled to another safe house several miles away. There we set up our short-wave radios to listen for developments from Delhi and Colombo. We were disappointed to learn, however, that the BBC man had made it in and out ahead of us. He had already filed an impressive eyewitness report.

Later, several "community leaders," clearly LTTE sympathizers, treated us to a barrage of revolutionary rhetoric as we waited for word on where we would spend the night. War, it seemed, was often as it had been described: hours of tedium with moments of intense panic and fear.

"Oh, look," Hillmore said, interrupting one of the sympathizers to point at three young Tamil women walking toward the house. "Maybe they're going to have a disco."

The three were part of the women's wing of the Tiger movement—a subject that intrigued most of the reporters. The group peppered them with inane questions. How did they wear their hair in battle? What hobbies did they have? Had the movement offered them equal opportunity? They answered obligingly at first. Their irritation became obvious, though, when the photographers closed in on them, asking them to pull their cyanide caps out of their frocks for the camera. "The pictures are useless without the capsules and the black ribbons in the hair," complained Reardon, Hillmore's photographer. "Do you think you can pull the caps out again for me?" he asked impatiently. The performance was pretty degrading.

Next, a teenaged boy was brought in—an eyewitness to gang rapes committed by Indian soldiers. The question of rape had been the most difficult of all the atrocity and brutality reports to confirm. Rape was potentially more devastating than execution in traditionally conservative Tamil Hindu society. A rape victim lost almost all marriageability and would be a burden on her family for the rest of her life. Consequently, it was hard to get victims to admit to the crime.

The boy, swathed in bandages, began a breathless litany of details. He had been stopped on a road near the center of town and taken, blindfolded, to a bus station a few miles away, joining a small group of Tamil teenagers suspected of links to the guerrillas. Then Gurkha soldiers stripped three girls of their clothing and attempted to rape them. Some of the Tamil boys tried to intervene; three were shot point-blank. The bodies were dragged to the other side of the bus station, where they were piled on top of six naked corpses, covered with rubber tires and kerosene, and burned. The boy and the others in his group were bound and beaten, saved from death by the arrival of Tamil-speaking Indian soldiers who called the Gurkhas off.

We had great doubts about the boy's story. The Tigers were as adept as the Indians at coloring the impression they wanted to give, so we tried to sniff out any possible disinformation. The boy was straightforward and consistent in his story, however, and answered all the many questions we threw at him as quickly as he could.

The houses where we stayed for the night were festooned with portraits of fallen Tiger martyrs, but it was hard to tell whether the families living there genuinely supported them. It was clear the next morning, however, as we tried to pick our way through the suburbs to the center of the city, that the population was certainly stirred up. The Tigers—known in Jaffna as "the boys"—were readying themselves to take on far superior forces in sectors of the city that had not yet fallen. Even if the population as a whole was ambivalent about the Tigers and the legitimacy of the militant struggle, they clearly had the loyalty of every teenager in the city.

Young boys relayed orders from street corner to street corner, as cadres at crossroads prepared their grenade launchers and assault rifles. Civilians, in the meantime, huddled nervously in doorways. With Tiger help, we corkscrewed through lanes and back alleys dense with foliage. Every move that the Tigers made along our course was exact, each move anticipating the next. Their machine was precise in a way that the Sinhalese generally were not.

We spent yet another morning in a safe house, waiting to interview the Tiger leadership. We were told that the house where we had slept the night before had been shelled just after we had left. That sector of Jaffna had passed into Indian hands. We were now in the northernmost point of the peninsula, where the rebel leader Prabakeran had grown up. The safe house once belonged to a captain in the Sri Lankan merchant marine, and there was a beautiful crystal chandelier still intact in the living room. All else had been ransacked. On the floor were scattered photos of weddings and graduation ceremonies past—during "those days," as all Sri Lankans mournfully referred to an earlier, happier era. We had thought that the Tiger leadership would make it a point to brief us personally, but the military commanders were either stuck in the fighting downtown or didn't want to give away their whereabouts. We did get to talk to the political director of the Tiger movement, a slippery Tamil intellectual named Anton Balasingham, who had taught at several universities in the West. He was known for his Marxist ideology, which was uncharacteristic of the Tigers as a whole.

Balasingham, however, turned out to be a good second-best. He outlined the strategy the Tigers would follow from now on. Jaffna would fall, no doubt, but the Tigers would not bite into their capsules en masse. They would return to the jungle. There would be some suicide missions to protect the retreat, but the Tigers would bide their time in the bush and resume the struggle later. Jaffna would be a Pyrrhic victory for the Indians, who would find themselves in the quagmire that critics had foreseen from the beginning.

We were getting a bit tired of waiting out the action. It was almost beyond doubt that there were massive civilian casualties, rapes, looting, and indiscriminate shelling into civilian areas, but we needed better, irrefutable proof to offset the weight of the official denials.

Just then, a Tiger cadre ran into the house with a radio report that Jaffna Hospital had been stormed by Indian troops—a major violation of the Geneva Accord. Both patients and staff were said to have been slaughtered, but we needed corroboration before we could report the story. Ironically, Jaffna Hospital was visited by many Indian Tamils who crossed the narrow Palk Strait seeking medical treatment. We were given the name of a doctor who had witnessed atrocities and then fled.

As easy as it was to be stirred by the energy of a city under siege, it was equally hard not to be affected by the tragedy we saw. The hospital we went to was up to its rafters in war victims, mostly civilians shot at or shelled at random by the Indians. The wards were open to the air, but they still stank from grimy bed linens and unclean wounds. Flies clustered in the eyes of the wounded who were too weak to brush them away. One sobbing woman with a tube draining a wound in her back told a story echoed by a hundred others. Too frightened to go to a refugee camp, she had remained at home with her family until Indian troops, searching for guerrillas, had broken down her door and sprayed the house with bullets. Her husband and children were killed, and she was left for dead as well. The Indians, overlooking the fact that many civilians couldn't or wouldn't leave their homes, assumed that if they were still in the area they were guerrillas or supporters.

In a corner of one of the wards, a group of Tiger cadres kept watch over a comrade. We noticed that he didn't have his cyanide cap around his neck anymore. "We hold on to it while he's in pain, just so he doesn't get tempted to swallow it when the pain becomes too bad," one of the attending Tigers explained. "When he gets better, then we give it back. But while he's sick, we hold on to it."

"Your safety is our priority," read the leaflets the Indians dropped on Jaffna at the beginning of Operation Wind. They counseled civilians to seek safety in three designated refugee camps. This is where we searched next for the doctor who had seen the hospital attack. But the way the Indians handled the refugee problem was a clear breach of the Geneva Convention—noncombatants were not to be moved unless it was imperative to do so, and then only when the refugees' safety, hygiene, and nutrition were ensured. The Indians had misunderstood the psychology of the Jaffna Tamils, and the result was a great loss of civilian life. In the end, there was simply not enough room in the three areas to accommodate the several hundred thousand refugees who sought space as the shells began raining down on Jaffna. Many of the refugees had been roaming desperately for two weeks, though the trip would have ordinarily taken only a few hours had they not had to dodge Indian fire. All told, there had been at least 1,400 civilians killed, an assistant government agent in a refugee camp told us later that evening.

The roads leading into the camp were choked with jalopies, bicycles, oxcarts—every possible type of conveyance. In the bedlam, only blaring horns could rise above the overpowering din of crying infants. Families searched desperately for relatives. The faces of the refugees were ghostly, hopeless.

I began to feel a little guilty. Had the international press corps spent less time pinned down in the lobbies of Colombo in the early days of the offensive, international pressure might have been brought to bear on the Indians. Rajiv Gandhi had been in Washington, D.C., the week before, and a few tough stories might have forced a change of tactics, perhaps a moratorium on offensive air attacks and indiscriminate shelling, which had recently intensified.

The refugees felt completely trapped, unable to leave the Jaffna peninsula. "Give us security! Give us security!" they cried as they surrounded our group.

"Now it has come to the point where we can't even give the new refugees a cup of tea," sighed one of the self-appointed refugee coordinators, a retired civil servant. "If it rains we cannot give people shelter. They can only get wet. We are surrounded by the Indian Army. If we want to go, we can't. They have blocked us here and there. We do not know what will happen to these lives. Rajiv Gandhi says he has controlled everything. But it is not so. The man who came to give us peace is now killing us."

In the end we never found the doctor we were looking for.

Since the refugee camp was soon to be cut off by an advancing Indian column, we zipped across one of the principal axes of attack just a few minutes before the Indians arrived. "It's getting interesting now," Hillmore said abstractedly as we waited to cross an open stretch of road. "It's getting to be an interesting story." Meanwhile, in the back seat, someone was reciting an old nursery rhyme, with a twist. "Star light. Star bright," he said, looking into the darkening sky with apprehension. "Hope it's not a helicopter."

We had dinner in the gloomy Tiger café, which now had an air of a World War I bunker about it. Our numbers had been swollen by the arrival of several French journalists, who were entertaining everybody with imitations of the heavy ordnance they had weathered in Beirut. There was also a photographer airlifted in the night before by *Newsweek*, who was a raging caricature of a jaded war junkie. "It's an easy story," he snapped flippantly. "Tomorrow morning I'll get refugees, I'll get bang-bang, and then I'll be gone."

At the other end of the table, Hillmore was keeping everybody laughing with declarations of love for the Tigresses, cracks about his editor, and facetious toasts to the wretchedness and suffering that were fueling our story. We became worried, however, when a rumor circulated that the Indians knew we had defied their ban and were searching for us. If we left first thing in the morning, we might be able to get out all right, but if we went on an operation with the Tigers, there was great likelihood that the Indians would intercept us, with uncertain results.

The beer I was drinking was helping to unleash the fear I had suppressed. I had been quite affected by a videotape at the Tiger command center that the other guys had skipped. It was a tape of civilian casualties, with very little left to the imagination, body parts and brains liberally presented in full color, close up. One of the advantages of buddying up with Hillmore was that in the end I figured he wouldn't go too far into the action; his limp was my excuse. But Hillmore threw me a curveball. "Going to the war to-morrow?" he blithely asked.

I guess the barrage we were in the middle of was light, but every round knotted my stomach anew. Fear surged through me. When we retreated far enough, falling against the skeleton of a half-built house, it took me about a half hour to catch my breath. Everyone had made it, except Hillmore, lost somewhere in a forward position.

We waited in the house with some Tigers for about an hour as shells began to drop along another line of fire. The guerrillas were hardly fazed. "The Indians aren't very brave," one cadre explained, as he kept watch with his M-16 and grenade launcher nearby. "They tend to clump together, making them easy to hit. They're very bad fighters, but their mortar fire is too much for us."

The Tigers seemed to have the measure of the Indians' artillery tactics, knowing where the shells would fall and how much time they had before they really needed to worry. What was terrifying for me was as predictable as a minuet for them. They even broke for midmorning tea—a villager brought out a tray of it, along with an unexploded mortar shell. I hoped that Hillmore might somehow be on the van that was to evacuate us. Having gone in with him originally, I felt a little responsible now that he was missing. I tried to busy myself by taking some notes, but concentration was impossible. I was having a hard time thinking straight, fixing details to their implications.

Just as we were about to give up on him, Hillmore arrived on the back of a motor scooter, his bulk incongruous next to the skinny frame of his guerrilla chauffeur. Behind them was a patrol of Tigers, strolling lazily in the sun after having detonated another mine. "Only way to see the country really," Hillmore said triumphantly, as we welcomed him back into the fold of the living. The rebels brought us coconuts that had been knocked down in the attack. "Funny little war," he mumbled cavalierly. Hillmore had been close enough to the Indians to have heard the snortings of an armored personnel carrier and, unlike the rest of us, had actually seen Indian soldiers—well, one Indian soldier anyway, sprawled dead in a field. Nonetheless, Hillmore was not taking any undue chances. "My God! Are you mad?" he exclaimed when one of the boys offered him a drink of water from a nearby well. "You can die drinking that stuff!"

During our desperate retreat, Hillmore was lolling in a rice paddy with one of the Tigers, having a smoke and chatting about London, where the guerrilla had studied. "It's all a bit like being a tourist, isn't it?" he said quite happily. "You can almost set your watch by it. Six o'clock coffee. Seven o'clock refugees. Two o'clock back to Colombo. I'll go tell the Indians that we have had enough for the day, thank you very much. Game over."

As we walked to the van, though, Hillmore's limp was much more pronounced. "I was after some pop-pop," he said with his typical Oxbridge understatement. "But what I didn't expect was such heavy boom-boom." He looked down at the dirt he was picking out of his ears. "Bloody awful, shelling."

The game, as Hillmore had called it, was far from over, however, as the business of getting out of Jaffna was still at hand.

We decided against taking the boat the Tigers offered us, opting instead to go back the way we came in. It would be risky. We still weren't sure what kind of reception we'd get from the Indians, and the Tigers scared us with talk of being shot right on the spot. They were abandoning Jaffna as well; the town that boasted the first command and communications post was soon to be rocketed from the air. The Tigers, though, wouldn't tell us how they were getting out.

Most of us were pretty sure we'd at least be intercepted and detained by the Indians, and prepared for that eventuality by stuffing notes and rolls of film in bodily orifices, hoping that the Hindu caste taboos on excreta might get us through body searches. Hillmore even went into a tailor's shop and had two white surrender flags sewn for us, which we waved as we crossed the arid salty no-man's-land into a nervous detachment of Indian soldiers on the other side of the ferry slip.

Happily, the major in charge of the Indians was a gentlemanly sort and chatted with us instead of shooting us. They had already detained several Tiger suspects before us, and these cadres were now lying facedown off to the side of the road. They were, at the very least, going to be beaten and perhaps tortured for information;

most likely they would be shot after we had moved on. We were instructed not to look to the left or the right as we walked along a causeway, escorted by Indian infantrymen, their fingers polishing their triggers as we marched in step with them. "Gentlemen, and I do appeal to you as a gentleman myself," the major said politely as we began another harrowing leg of our trip back to Colombo. "I ask you as gentlemen not to look from side to side and not to take any photographs of those suspects over to your left. If you do, gentlemen, I have to warn you that it will be my duty, gentlemen, to shoot you dead."

5 · Colombo I

CAIRO WAS insufficiently Oriental, wrote Mark Twain in his collection of travel essays called *Following the Equator*. It was a tempered Orient, one where the West intruded too deeply on his desire for the exotic and mysterious. "That feeling was not present in Ceylon," he wrote. "Ceylon was oriental in the last measure of completeness—utterly oriental and utterly tropical and indeed to one's unreasoning spiritual sense the two belong together. All the requisites were present: the costumes were right, the black and brown exposure unconscious of immodesty were right, the juggler was there, with his basket of snakes and mongoose, properly out in the country were the deadlier snakes. And there was a swoon in the air which one associates with the tropics, and that smother of heat, heavy with odors of unknown flowers and that sudden invasion of purple gloom fissured with lightning, then the tumult of crashing thunder and the downpours, and presently all sunny and smiling again. All these things were there, the conditions were complete, nothing lacking."

The American college program that first sent me to Sri Lanka as its director in 1986 accented cultural immersion and required that the students live in homes with various Sri Lankan families. What we got, however, at least in the first round of homestays, were families that mirrored the homestay coordinator's rather insular vision of Sri Lankan society—Christians from the Westernized elite, some Tamil, some Sinhalese, all intent on showing off how much like us they were. The expectations couldn't have been more at odds. We were there for an indigenous experience, to learn about life in a completely different culture.

As a result, almost as soon as we arrived for our stay—it was required of me, as director, to participate as well—we were on a nonstop tour of Colombo's Western elite. We were taken to shopping malls and ice-cream parlors, we were encouraged to watch *Dynasty*, and we were asked about which models we admired back home. One of the students, who played guitar in a rock-and-roll band, was placed with a family who sang old Carpenter tunes and Christian hymns. This part of the program lasted for a week. It was a week of parties, tennis outings, and lunch at the YMCA with the Lions Club. The families' irrepressible imitativeness was as bad as the deracination. While the Westernized upper class claimed to be "more English than the English themselves," this was essentially a secondhand cultural identity that did not quite fit. Even though Western influences and values were widespread, they were superficial, and left those in the Westernized cultural orbit with few powers of originality, even if the capacity for mimicry was formidable. As a result, the Westernized elite seemed like a parody of an antique Anglophilia, spouting "righto," "cheerio" and other Victorian clichés, as well as a social outlook dating from another era.

The weeklong tour we took next with the families proved even more unendurable. One of the reasons we were traveling with the native Sri Lankans was so that we might get to know the culture in detail. In the south, however—the heartland of Sinhala Buddhist culture—it was impossible to get any answers from our guides about religious matters. They seemed to know less than we did. It was more than the disdain of the cosmopolitan for rural unsophistication. It was as if, for them, Buddhism was slightly barbaric. Why would we want to stop at the largest Buddha statue on the island when a Dutch church built in 1640 was in the next town over? Why would we want to know the myth of the Sinhalese princess who was put out to sea and rescued by the gods? Likewise, our hosts avoided talk about the ethnic conflict, as one might try to avoid painful questions about family alcoholism or incest. When pressed, they grew offended. They were part of a secular world, and the bloody battle that was consuming the rest of their fair country was something they tried to conceal.

The homestay experience left all of us in the group feeling frustrated and completely confused. At first, I, too, had thought the whole exercise a waste of time and had recommended that the Colombo homestay be struck from the next itinerary unless a different batch of families could be found. But later, as I began to understand what a significant role the problem of cultural identity played in the country's troubled political life, I came to rethink the experience.

By the time that I returned to Sri Lanka in the fall of 1987 I had begun to see that the Colombo elite as a whole, like the homestay families that had stepped around questions about the ethnic conflict, was skilled at avoidance. They avoided, for example, the question of their own relevance in a world rapidly drifting from the secular moorings of the past. At times, the persistent denial of political and social realities could seem surreal, as if the entire community was living the old Ceylonese adage that "a well-told lie is worth a thousand facts." It was startling to me, upon returning to Colombo, to see how easily the Jaffna offensive had been swallowed up by the "no problem" mentality. "Situation is getting cool now, man, tourists are coming. Everything's back to normal," said a playboy on the beach out at Mount Lavinia, where I'd gone to try to shake off the persistent buzz of mortar shells in my ears.

It was often hard to feel the conflict in Colombo itself, however grisly some of the bombings could be there. Among the many divisions and subdivisions that fractured national life in Sri Lanka, none was quite as profound as the rift between the urban and the rural. Although much of the Colombo elite had economic ties to land owned and leased in rural villages, there was little social contact, as the elite became more concentrated in metropolitan comfort over the years. Caste, too, put barriers between the capital and the provinces, as much psychological as physical, diminishing the humanity of those outside the boundaries of a particular caste group.

But what most affected the way Colombo looked out upon the Situation was a simple and powerful streak of denial. In the older, Anglicized generation, denial largely took the form of self-conscious nostalgia for the golden age of the English-speaking elite—"those days," before an upsurge of Buddhist majoritarianism swept them from political power shortly after independence. "Those days" had been times of secular amity, when members of prominent families from all the communities got along in Anglophilic good cheer. Tamils and Sinhalese, along with mixed-race Eurasians known as Burghers, attended the same schools, belonged to the same clubs, and had little truck with communal politics. For them, ethnic consciousness was bad form; they considered themselves Ceylonese. In many cases of generations of intermarriage, ethnicity was notional at best. "Emil Daniels summed up the situation for most of them," writes Michael Ondaajte in *Running in the Family*, his account of the flapper era excess of his parents' generation, "when asked by one of the British governors what his nationality was. 'God alone knows, your excellency'."

Those days had been a time when, as a prominent Burgher architect told me, "you could be stupid as a way of life." It was a world of jubilant delinquency and madcap indulgence, a world of pranks and harmless philandering, of beauty queens and magic-carpet rides from party to party. "Love affairs rainbowed over marriages and lasted for years," Michael Ondaajte was told by nostalgic relatives, "so it often seemed that marriage was the greater infidelity." Men worked in order to gamble; it was the only thing that could distract them from drink and romance. To be sure, those days had been a time of learning and erudition, too, a time of civility and tolerance when men of ideas, no matter how ideologically opposed, were from the same elite and could therefore ground their political differences in the green turf of a cricket pitch or the cool night of a beachside dance.

Mostly, the effort to revive the world of those days seemed forced and ineffectual, a sad echo of what had once been natural and vibrant. Finding myself in such scenes, I often thought of the rusted-out Morris Minor on the beach up near Trinco, forlorn and haunting. But there were times when the old Ceylon would leap to life as before. While I was in Sri Lanka there was a marriage between two of the more prominent and affluent Muslim families on the island. With more than 1,700 guests, it was the largest wedding that had taken place in quite some time. The groom had gone to Oxford, and had put up a dozen of his classmates for a week at one of the priciest hotels in Colombo. A throng of male guests were invited to the bachelor party a few days before at the Hill Club in Newara Eliya, an old British hill station in the tea-planting highlands that had been preserved like a Disneyland exhibit. It was a black-tie affair, but after tubs of Pimm's, gin, and scotch, the party got raucous, and the guests tore down an old oak door. Instead of being distressed, though, the management was practically beaming at the reminder of better times, of the antic decadence that Old Ceylon was famous for.

Another reminder of those days was schoolboy cricket, particularly the annual match between the two most elite Colombo prep schools, Royal and St. Thomas colleges. The match drew thousands of spectators, especially the "old boys" who had gone on to become captains of industry and leading politicians. Cricket was "a virtual religion," explained a news columnist, "which contained in miniature the Victorian code. One had to play the game. The umpire's rule was law. It was a code of voluntary self-denial . . . a code which perfectly buttressed the existing social and political structures. . . . Here is the political and power elite assembled under one roof for three days to propitiate the ancestral gods and thank them for favors done."

Hysterical hedonism was another form of the Colombo elite's psychology of denial. It was played out in tinselly nightclubs, casinos, and coming-out parties. If the older generation was lost in nostalgia for yesterday, the younger crowd was consumed by the psychology of "no tomorrow." Colombo was awash in new money swept in by the economic liberalizations of President Jayawardene's open economy. Kickbacks from arms sales and funds skimmed from foreign-aid development were two prevalent money schemes. As a result, Colombo took on a rakish, *Miami Vice* style, becoming a carnival of the well scented and the sleazy. The discos were packed with the children of the parvenu class. Balls and fashion shows were undeterred by the tension, and the five-star hotel casinos issued curfew passes for patrons so they could get through nighttime check-points. "One cannot help wondering how long the carnival can go on," wrote a news columnist, marveling at the ardor of the elite as it pursued the palliative high life and glamorous distraction.

Most of my excursions into the Colombo night were in the company of Tilak, a half-Sinhalese, half-Tamil Westernized Sri Lankan, who was one of the more interesting characters on the scene. Cocktail parties made him anxious, Tilak explained one night, not long after I had returned from Jaffna, when we had all been invited over to his friend A.J.'s for drinks. He was getting older in Sri Lanka and had no future.

Tilak had dark, shaggy hair, a beard that covered most of his face, and he stood about six feet tall. He had been raised in England, but it wasn't really home. Home wasn't really home either. And so Tilak was the archetypal "man adrift," trapped between two warring political factions, as if his state of cultural alienation was his very cultural identity.

The decor of Tilak's bachelor pad spoke eloquently of the way East had melded with West on the island. On one wall was an Andy Warhol print, reproduced by a deaf-mute on the island who did everything freehand and had taken the natural cultural talent for mimicry a step further. On another wall hung a collage of old post-cards of the lost Ceylon of the 1920s, sepia images of toddy tappers, bare-chested Tamil maidens, and Kandyan dancers in ritual finery.

As we sat waiting for Tilak to get dressed, the sounds of the Pentecostal mission across the street came in through the open windows—the faithful speaking in tongues. It was a strange cacoph-ony punctuated by shrieks, clapping, and stomping feet. Sometimes I could make out a word in Sinhala, Tamil, or English. "Bloody fools," Tilak moaned, in his usual mellifluous voice. "Bloody, bloody fools. It's the one thing about living here I just can't stand. And, of course, they're always starting up at the wrong times, when you come in at 2 a.m. and want to go to sleep, or when you're sleeping in the morning after an exceptionally hard night." Sometimes when he came home drunk, he'd go over and wake them. "I'm the bloody devil to that crowd. They're probably praying for me or about me right now."

For people of mixed blood, like Tilak, the question of identity was a daily challenge, however much class privilege softened the sting. Just the day before, he had skidded on his motorcycle on the way to the airport. Before saying anything to him, before even asking if he was all right, the policeman who stopped to attend to him asked Tilak's nationality. "Imagine, here I am, covered with blood, and they want to know whether I'm bloody Tamil or Sinhalese. And if I couldn't speak English and I only spoke Tamil, they would have probably thrown me in bloody jail without even bringing me to the hospital. Tells you what this whole country is bloody well about, let me tell you."

Tilak asked me to accompany his friend Christo to the Oberoi Hotel, where we were to pick up ice for the party's refreshments. Christo, whose family was Christian and had accumulated a fortune as morticians, made his living wholesaling Sri Lankan labor to contractors in the Middle East, Kuwait and Bahrain for the most part. Christo lacked Tilak's easy confidence, perhaps because of his heavily accented English, and asked me to go into the hotel to pick up the ice. If the arrangement didn't work, he would not risk being shamed in front of me by the staff. It would be easier for me to command attention and get the job done because of my white skin. As expected, Tilak's reassurances about the ice were unfounded. I had to wait nearly an hour while the steward checked with the bellman, who checked with the food-and-beverage man, who checked with the bartender, who checked with the night manager, before the ice bag was delivered. And then we had to wait for a coolie to carry it out because only coolies did things with their hands. Christo had parked where the chauffeurs normally parked, so when the doorman leaned into the microphone to summon him, he paged "Driver Christo" in a summary manner, which I knew must have sent shivers of anger and humiliation down Christo's spine. "He is my friend Christo, not my driver," I told the doorman, who immediately changed his tone. "Would *Mister* Christo please come to the front?" he said.

The guests had arrived by the time we returned. We were swamped by arrack drinkers waiting for something to cool their drinks. A.J., the hostess, was complaining about her job at the Sri Lankan Broadcasting Corporation, where she was a television producer. In her late twenties, A.J. was neither girl nor matron, a difficult position in Sri Lankan society, where her Westernized upbringing already made her a cultural misfit to begin with. She was complaining about the broadcasting service's requirement that all employees speak Sinhala proficiently, a condition she had not yet met. "It's like they are treating me as if I were a foreigner," she bitched.

"But we're all foreigners here, local foreigners, black foreigners, *kalu suddha*, as they say," answered Tilak from the chaise longue where, drink in one hand, cigarette in the other, he was reveling in his marginality.

And life at the television station had not become any easier with the peace accord and the emotional backlash it had triggered. Sinhalese chauvinists were becoming more strident in their demands. Militant monks had been at the station several times to register displeasure over one thing or another. "Rogues in robes," A.J. called them. "I don't feel safe even looking at them," she said. The JVP had made the normally fraught situation even more tense, she added. Some correspondents were so afraid of the JVP that they refused to go out into the field. The politics of management were bad as well. Announcers had been sacked by ministers of state for reporting the slightest controversies. "It's a propaganda machine, that broadcasting system. Every one of the ministers has a finger in it. It's so sad, because there's neither creativity nor credibility anymore. The pay is bad, we're all exploited, and now they are killing our colleagues. No wonder no one wants to do anything there."

Outside, Tilak and a few of the others were making plans for the rest of the evening—the Blue Elephant at the Hilton for dancing, and the casino later still. The night would be a game, but essentially a pale imitation of what their fathers and mothers might have known. In a bygone era, as Michael Ondaatje wrote in *Running in the Family*, there were routine nights where young people crashed sports cars through moonlit frangipani and went swimming "with just the modesty of the night. . . . An arm touched a face, a foot touched a stomach while champagne corks bobbed in the surf. . . . They could have almost drowned or fallen in love and their lives would have been totally changed."

"Another night in bloody Colombo," Tilak sighed. "The whole bloody syndrome yet again, one more time."

Even with all the distractions of the Colombo high life, it was hard to avoid the developing pathology of the Situation, as the fear of Tamil terrorism became overshadowed by the political violence of Buddhist nationalists. A grim archaeology could be read in the walls that surrounded the nicer homes and family compounds. Year by year they climbed higher, the ends of last year's walls visible beneath the added foot or two, turning the nicer sections of Colombo into fortified canyons, complete with guard dogs and sentries.

Along with basic political terror came a surge in basic criminal terror. Not a day passed without a killing, a Chicago-style bank robbery, or a gem heist. "It's even more dangerous than gangland Chicago," an opposition party leader exclaimed. "You are looking over your shoulder all the time around here now."

Colombo was the objective correlative of the Sinhalese psyche—full of agreeability and menace. Although many of its residents were gentlemanly to the bone, the city had never really absorbed the dictates of British civility. There was no avoiding the memory of the riots of 1983 with its immolations, dismemberments, and murder in the streets. No matter how bright the sun, how blue the sky, how sweet the ocean breeze, how weightless the air, the memory adhered to the back of one's mind.

It began when Tamil Tiger guerrillas bombed a Sri Lankan army patrol in Jaffna and shot the survivors during the last week of July 1983—an act of revenge for the earlier killing of a Tiger leader. A lone survivor crawled to a nearby bus station, after which news spread quickly around the island.

Nearly 8,000 Sinhalese congregated at the burial ground where the victims were to be brought. A delay in bringing the bodies riled the crowd. Rioting broke out. What followed was five days of pillage and slaughter aimed at Tamils living throughout the south and their businesses and property. As many as 3,000 Tamils are said to have been killed, nearly 60 percent of the Tamils in Colombo were turned into refugees, and most of the Colombo Tamil business community, which had accounted for over half the city's commercial infrastructure, was ruined. Many Sinhalese burned down their own workplaces, targeting, in particular, Tamil-owned garment factories. Much of the wholesale food district of Colombo was destroyed. The stately Victorian railroad station in the center of the city had to be converted into a morgue to accommodate the corpses.

The violence spread from Colombo along the southern coast, into the highlands of the tea country, and into the eastern province. Trincomalee burned for nearly a month. In Colombo, the looting and arson at the beginning of the week grew into a frenzy of assassination on what became known as "Tiger Friday"—the day on which it was rumored that Tiger hit squads were readying to attack Colombo in revenge. Eyewitnesses to the carnage spoke of it in detached, almost operatic tones. "Forty years later," wrote a Jewish poet who had fled Nazi Germany and married a Ceylonese in Colombo. "Once more there is burning / the night sky bloodied, violent and abused." Along the skyline of Colombo, columns of smoke billowed and swirled, while on the street long bolts of expensive sari cloth looted from Tamil stores were set afire and bodies were burned around the clock. One Westerner who was driving up the coast road after a long weekend in the south was amazed at the things he saw being taken from Tamil homes to be burned—marriage licenses, family photo albums, deeds—irreplaceable things and objects of sentimental value. What the Westerner found most disturbing, however, was the look of glee on the faces of the mobs, as if in the midst of torching houses and factories, the Sinhalese were realizing their greatest desires.

Others told of mobs surfacing from the depths of arrack dens, to stomp old men and violate young women: petty thieves, bazaar

workers, and bus drivers venting long-suppressed hostility, resentment, and envy. Soldiers roamed the beaches, firing randomly. No
phones, no radio, no television. Curfew was imposed, but only after
several days, and was enforced spottily.

For some Tamils, the week was one long flight. Many were
killed right near the perimeter of refugee camps. Some Sinhalese
did in fact hide their Tamil neighbors, but the numbers may well be
exaggerated. Some Tamils were saved by acts of brave intercession
by Sinhalese who knew them and were able to convince the mobs
to back off. A lawyer interviewed afterward by the BBC spoke of
being cornered, stripped naked, and nearly immolated with a "necklace" when one of the petty thieves he was defending on a pro bono
basis stepped forward to rescue him with testimony of his generosity.
Other Tamils saved themselves by being able to pronounce certain
Sinhalese words that most Tamils can't without telltale incriminating sounds. Still others lived to savor the irony of being stopped
while driving by Sinhalese mobs who mistook their ethnicity, demanding that they be given petrol so they could "burn Tamils."

One of the more terrifying accounts of the riots is from the diary
of a Tamil man whom Shiva Naipaul quotes in a collection called
Unfinished Journey. Traveling on a bus when a mob laid siege to it,
the man watched as a small boy was hacked "to limbless death."
The bus driver was ordered to give up a Tamil. He pointed out
a woman who was desperately trying to erase the mark on her
forehead—called a *kum-kum*—as the thugs bore down on her. As
the witness melted into the crowd, the woman's belly was ripped
open with a broken bottle and she was immolated as people clapped
and danced. In another incident, two sisters, one eighteen, the other
eleven, were decapitated and raped, the latter "until there was nothing left to violate and no volunteers could come forward," after
which she was burned. While all this was going on, according to the
diarist, a line of Buddhist monks appeared, arms flailing, their voices
raised in a delirium of exhortation, summoning the Sinhalese to put
all Tamils to death.

Many witnesses spoke of soldiers and policemen who simply
watched as Tamils were beaten and slain, or of police and soldiers

openly siding with the mobs and taking part in the gruesome chores. In two separate incidents, Sinhalese prisoners got out of their cells in a jail outside of Colombo and murdered the Tamil political prisoners incarcerated there.

Whether the government actually instigated the riots remains unclear. According to eyewitness testimony, some mobs were led by people in possession of government voting registries, which allowed them to pinpoint Tamil property. Government vehicles may also have brought mobs into the suburbs, where the wealthier Tamils resided. As Shiva Naipaul noted in *Unfinished Journey*, the Sinhalese mobs needed some help in distinguishing Tamils from their own: "Their bloodlust was in effect regulated by the bureaucratic endeavors of the civil service. Before the axes could be wielded, before the petrol bombs could be thrown, before the pillaging could begin, a little paperwork had to be done."

After several years, the most plausible theory about the 1983 violence held that the government had planned some kind of strike against Tamils in Colombo, particularly against businessmen thought to have been funding the Tigers in the north. The operation was meant "to teach the Tamils a lesson" by sobering them to the realities of Sinhalese power and reminding them of their own subservient minority status. The funerals of the thirteen soldiers ambushed in Jaffna provided a pretext, and the initial attacks were pinpointed and methodical, led by political organizers who had been issued written instructions.

But what the government saw as a coercive twist of the arm was taken by some as a license to launch "a final solution." As a result, a brownshirt force of government thugs in the pay of certain militant parties were joined by lumpen Sinhalese on the street, triggering violence beyond calculation.

Almost as disturbing as the riots themselves was the Sinhalese reaction to them. During the carnage, the government was silent, and when the President finally did make a statement over the national broadcasting network, it wasn't an appeal for reconciliation or a reassurance to the Tamils cowering in hiding. Instead, President Jayawardene pledged to safeguard the rights of the Buddhist majority. There would be no concessions to terrorists bent on dividing the Sinhalese nation that had been indivisible for 2,500 years. Yes, the violence had been a setback to economic development, but he understood the Sinhalese reaction.

Rather than seeking out the real hidden hand behind the violence, the President sought scapegoats, banning the JVP, then a legal political party, and later proscribing the moderate Tamil United Liberation Front, a party advocating the peaceful division of the country by constitutional means.

Not a single Sinhalese politician visited Tamil refugee camps in Colombo. Instead, one of the cabinet ministers, Lalith Athulathmudali, who was later to become Minister of National Security, became anguished at the sight of Sinhalese lined up to buy bread in the aftermath of the violence. Other high-ranking officials justified the Sinhalese reaction as an appropriate response to the threat represented by Tamil separatism, which would spell the end of the Sinhalese as a race.

Four weeks after the riots subsided, the Minister of Tourism summed up the government's ideas on what kind of soul-searching was needed. "The sun is shining, the flowers are blooming, and the people are smiling again," he told reporters. But years later, many Sinhalese in Colombo still talk about the riots as if the perpetrators were an invading force. They blame the violence on slum pathology and the effects of angel dust that was fed to the poor by mob manipulators in league with "foreign hands." Meanwhile, many Sinhalese still talk of "killing them all," "making them all pack up and go," and the like. Admissions of collective Sinhalese guilt are frequently viewed as treasonous. As one of the more chauvinistic monks told me, "If we were really like that, the Tamils would no longer exist."

After 1983, life for Colombo Tamils was changed irrevocably. Many of those who fled into refugee camps never returned to their homes. Instead, they traveled to Tamil areas of the north and east, or abroad to India and Western Europe. Ironically, many of the Tamils victimized in Colombo were strong opponents of Tamil separatism and were loyal to the President's ruling United National Party. With the riots, though, a good number of those patriotic

Tamils who had resisted rebel propaganda began to wonder whether they could rely on the state for basic security.

However deep the trauma, the legacy of 1983 was hard to see in everyday relations between Tamils and Sinhalese, which were almost always superficially cordial. This was especially so among the upper-class groups that had once studied and socialized together. For them, from the cozy world of drawing rooms and clubs, the conflict engulfing the rest of the country was something happening "out there." Within these circles, it was considered impolite to delve too deeply into the root causes of the conflict. If anything, the Situation encouraged greater solicitude between groups and a self-conscious, exaggerated pride in such interethnic amity as the number of mixed marriages in "their" crowd. "Even with their extraordinary capacity for violence, I'd still rather have a Sinhalese than a Tamil for a best friend," exclaimed an older Tamil journalist at a mixed dinner party I attended. "A Sinhalese friend will drink from six to midnight with you, and pull out a knife and stab you after an argument. But then he'll take you to the best hospital on the island, meet with all your friends, pay the hospital bills, and take you to a five-star hotel for a week at his expense, out of remorse. A Tamil, on the other hand, will plan your death down to the exact detail."

Up until the riots of 1983, the Tamils in Colombo might have been able to indulge illusions of ethnic harmony. Generally opposed to separatism in the north, they felt perfectly safe in Colombo and continued to flourish in business and in the public sector, many of them occupying top positions as judges, police commanders, and select political appointees. But many Tamils left Colombo completely after the riots, selling off land and jewelry at fire-sale prices. And those who remained kept a very low profile, some of them even going so far as to change their names to something less obviously Tamil-sounding. Tamils also became less public about celebrating their rituals out of doors. After a time, I began to realize that while Sinhalese all had numbers posted on the walls surrounding their houses, Tamils generally didn't, the better to confound any mobs who might again use voter registration lists to attack them. And as the war ground on in the north and east, Tamils in Colombo were sure to lock their doors, windows, and security gates, lest a government loss in the field become an excuse for the Sinhalese to scapegoat them.

Though the Tamil militants looked upon the upper-class Tamils in Colombo as quislings who were only useful for their money, the Sinhalese saw them as a potential fifth column residing behind their lines. Most Sinhalese made no distinction between the Tamils still living in the south who were largely loyal to the government and the militants in the north who wanted to break away. "Yes, they all say they are loyal to the government, but scratch a Tamil, any Tamil, and beneath the skin there is an Eelamist," one Sinhala businessman explained acidly. "Three drinks and they're all toasting Prabakeran."

The urban Tamil population was disturbed, meanwhile, to find that many of their educated, liberal-minded Sinhala friends refused to condemn the riots. "Except for my most immediate friends, I got the feeling that few of the Sinhalese in my social circle were really and truly outraged," explained a woman I met, a Tamil whose prominent political family formed the very bosom of the establishment. "After that I went through a period of deep emotional alienation from my social set. We were all too oversaturated with what had taken place. There was a certain understanding. I just didn't go when I was invited. And even now, although things have normalized somewhat, I am still not comfortable in those circles. They think I am a Tigress. Okay, with my friends it is different. But among the same people I grew up with in my social set from the fifties and sixties, I feel like a fish out of water."

Until the peace accord of 1987, it looked as though the Tamils who had chosen to remain behind were doing better than those who had fled north and lived between the retaliations of Sinhala security forces and Tiger "revolutionary justice." Life among the Sinhalese, although tense, was bearable, and though the government failed to discipline Sinhala soldiers guilty of human rights abuses in the north, there were few instances where Tamils in the south were harassed in any organized fashion. But the Sinhalese backlash against the Accord suggested that whatever separate peace the Tamils might have enjoyed in Colombo since 1983, it was no longer tenable.

This was made clear to me the night we returned from Jaffna. We had commandeered a Tamil bus once we were released by the Indians at the ferry slip. After running a gauntlet of Sinhalese army checkpoints well after curfew, we thought we were home free once we neared the Colombo city line. But right near the airport, a detachment of soldiers manning a roadblock stopped the bus and made us all get out—ten correspondents, our diminutive Tamil journalist colleague Sentile, the bus driver and his conductor, as well as two Tamil boys we had picked up along the way. These boys, we discovered, did not have their national identity cards. Sentile tried to convince the captain that the boys were only villagers seeking a ride into the city, but the captain became suspicious. He pushed Sentile up against the side of the bus and threatened him. "Bloody fucking Tamil. You all think you're so smart!" Our presence, however, deterred any violence, but just barely.

Tamil insecurity wasn't mitigated by newspaper editorials that congratulated the Sinhalese for their restraint under "severe provocation," or by politicians like the opposition leader Anura Bandaranaike, son of the Sinhala demagogue S. W. R. D. Bandaranaike, who reminded the government that "when stepped on, the worm turns."

Day-to-day life deteriorated in the wake of the Accord. With the JVP targeting supporters of the Accord as "enemies of the people," many Sinhalese liberals became intimidated. Any Sinhalese who stood up to protest treatment of the Tamils had to contend with the possibility of JVP reprisals.

"You hear it still," a young British engineer told me. "You actually hear it more now than before. Casual references to killing all the Tamils, to sending them all packing. It hasn't gone away." As a result, Tamil emigration was surging again. "They are resigned to their situation," said a Burgher woman I met. "The optimism they had ten years ago is completely gone. Slowly, their community is being decimated. Their educated elite has all gone abroad. Some are still here trying to organize a dialogue to carry on, but others are all packed to go. Any Tamils remaining in Colombo have all put their children abroad and are living with one leg here and one leg there. They have accepted the providence of God."

Being an avowed atheist, my Tamil friend N. had not accepted the providence of God. Nor had he made any plans of his own to leave, although the tension of remaining in Colombo had driven him further and further into the bottle and into despair. "Sleep is my god," he said wearily, rubbing his eyes the afternoon I met him. He had told me to come promptly at five, but when I arrived I was told that he was asleep. His servant wouldn't wake him, and so I waited downstairs. The premises had a run-down, dissipated feeling. The only light was from a heavily shuttered window. Through its slats, I could see that a high wall, topped with glistening shards of glass, had recently been added on to one side of the house.

N. was the son of a knight of the crown, a Tamil who had been part of that Anglicized elite who had known no ethnic feeling, who had higher loyalties to empire, and later to an independent Ceylon. He had been schooled abroad, and had returned to a career, first in the diplomatic service, then in academia.

When he woke he began smoking incessantly, as practically all Sri Lankans did. "I must have a cigarette and a cup of coffee before I wake up, before I can talk," he said. He quickly chose a new libation, however. "Let us have a drink," he said with gusto, and then shouted to his servant. "Christopher," he cried toward the kitchen. "I surrender. Where have you hidden the bottle? And get us some ice so we can drink."

After the servant had left and we had our drinks, N. turned to me. "I have such a problem talking sensibly and normally to people like you. The bottles are here, but they don't really help. I am the last of my generation. Everyone else has left. But I don't know if I know anything any longer about this place either, because I don't know if I belong here anymore. One knows about a place from the feeling one has of belonging to it. And I only belong to this"—he raised his glass in the air, exposing a scaly wrist. "Nothing means anything to me anymore, because I have belonged and lost every-thing."

He had an eighty-five-year-old mother in the house next door. Each time he heard a gun discharged he had to take her out of the house and hide her somewhere safe. "But still I'm here, never knowing which wall they'll jump over." In 1983, he had sent the family off to a safe house, remaining behind with a Spanish friend while a mob terrorized the neighborhood outside. It reminded him of 1958, the year of the first ever large-scale Tamil-Sinhalese riot. "When you want another drink just get it yourself," he said. "I pour the first, then I walk around." He began to circle the room counterclockwise. "At one level I felt protected. My father's name is an institution in this country, and even the rabble respected that. At another level, I felt completely vulnerable, though I knew what to do if they came in. When the trouble had first started that week, my good Sinhalese neighbor, a good Sinhalese Buddhist, told me flat out, 'Get yourself a knife.' "

The problem, as he explained it, was the romanticization of the concept of identity. "Identity was never a question for thousand of years. But now, here, for some reason, it is different. We live in the past now, a past that has given us an idea of who we are that is entirely rooted in false notions of race, which are handed down from father to son but never existed in the past at all. Friends that I grew up with, fucked with, got drunk with, now see an essential difference between us just for the fact of their ethnic identity. And there's no obvious differences at all, no matter what they say. I point to pictures in the newspapers and ask them to tell me who is Sinhalese and who is Tamil and they simply can't tell the difference. This identity is a fiction, a fiction, I tell you, but a deadly one. You want to talk about culture?" he said, parodying the tone of recent debates about identity. "Wait a second and lemme get my gun.

"I have been lucky. Through all this trouble I have been able to remain aloof. I was not required to avenge anything or anybody. But if my mother or father or sister or brother had been killed in that riot, I would have had no choice but to avenge them. That is the way we live in Asia. It is the same in Teheran, as it is in Beijing, as it is in Colombo. We have no choice but to avenge. One has to. All of our societies are like that because there is no in-between position in our culture, no liberal positions that let us think about the future, about the wife and kids we'll be leaving behind, perhaps, to accomplish our vengeance. Instead, we are bound by blood to the past. You won't find one Asian civilization where vengeance is not the rule. You have to see we are so different from you. You have such a sense of the future, of making things better, while we are obligated to the past. My brother, the son of a bitch, has been living in America, and he comes back here now and then and starts spouting stuff like 'the human species is all one and we are all in it together.' True enough, my friend, but it is a mirage half the time, metaphysics and mysticism. Rubbish. If that's what you think humanity is all about, I tell him, then, as the great Sam Goldwyn said, 'Include me out.' "

"The Sinhalese have everything to pay for," N. declared as we walked through his neighborhood looking for a taxi to take us to lunch. Squinting into the sun, he pointed out the homes of friends who had already left, explaining how, in his own extended family, the two hundred relatives on his mother's side had now been whittled down to twenty by the great Tamil exodus. "They are scattered about the globe. Anyone who can is getting out. A half a million people have left in four years. An entire generation that should be getting ready to run the country has left. Yes, they have everything to pay for, the Sinhalese. They thought we would never fight, that they could take up the knife and kill and we'd simply take it. Well, we didn't."

We crossed a street. "Never look a mad dog in the eye," N. snapped, studiously avoiding the glare of several rough-looking Sinhalese youths clustered at the corner. "And when you get into the cab, be careful what you say," N. insisted as we finally hailed a trishaw. "These fellows do not speak English very well, but they recognize the words. These are the measures we have to take these days. Those days, when we could speak our minds freely, are all gone. But," N. said as we climbed into the cab, in a voice designed for our driver's consumption, "if the Tamils were the majority, the whole thing would be much worse. But don't quote me, please. If those bloody Tigers heard me, they'd tie me to a lamppost and shoot me through the balls."

6 · Colombo II

COMPARED WITH Jaffna's nerve-shattering chaos, Colombo was calm and soothing. But as the second week of November drew near and it became time for Parliament to ratify the peace accord, the city tensed. It was widely believed that opponents of the Accord would disrupt the voting with violent action. Such action, if successful, would amount to a profound crisis. Without parliamentary ratification, the Accord would have no legal basis and President Jayawardene would have to either order the Indians home, risking a major confrontation, or let them stay, which would create the impression of occupation.

Jayawardene faced opposition to the ratification of the Accord on a number of fronts, not the least of which was the Sri Lanka Freedom Party, which hewed to an ardent Sinhala Buddhist nationalist line and received support from the more militant Buddhist monks. Less obvious though no less formidable was the resistance from within Jayawardene's own government, including a faction of Sinhala patriots within his cabinet who were intent on sabotaging the agreement in order to salvage their nationalist credentials and political careers.

The most dangerous resistance, however, came from the JVP and its powerful alliance of younger monks and university students. For months, the JVP had issued death threats against members of Parliament and had backed up these threats with assassinations throughout the south. And as if that wasn't enough to worry about, there were also reports that the Tigers might launch attacks as well, as if to remind the Sinhalese that they were still in the picture.

In the face of such widespread opposition, Jayawardene was taking no chances. To ensure the support of MPs and government ministers, Jayawardene had threatened to release incriminating evidence of high-level government corruption. Against the threat of JVP terrorism, Jayawardene had moved all the MPs into five-star hotels throughout the city and put them under heavy guard. He had also ringed the city with tanks and armored personnel carriers, placed heavily armed paracommandos on virtually every street corner, and brought 2,000 civilian "home guards" from the militias of the countryside to Colombo to keep things under control. The city looked like it was in a heavy state of siege.

Backed up by the formidable powers of the security forces, the eighty-one-year-old Jayawardene gave the appearance of confident control. As a result, the likelihood of a vote against ratification was low, although Parliament's consent could well be taken as yet another insult to the sensibilities of the Sinhalese masses. The elaborate measures taken to prevent terrorist attacks in the city were not as effective, though. At rush hour on the Monday evening before the vote, a huge explosion was detonated, turning midtown Colombo into a charnel house.

I was visiting Dieter Ludwig, the *Time* photographer from Delhi, when I heard about the bomb. The blast was near a major road-and-train junction downtown. Ironically, I had just been complaining to Dieter that Colombo was getting a little dull. "Yes, yes," he said. "You want more of it, don't you? It is because your body never feels more alive, your consciousness is never as sharp, as when all that adrenaline is surging through your head. But you see, there is a price you pay for that, and that is this craving you are now feeling. What goes up must come down, no such thing as a free lunch, huh?" He laughed at these American idioms. "The problem is that you start craving that feeling so much you go and do it again. And again. And again."

We followed an ambulance through the streets, skirting a gathering crowd. Helicopters circled high overhead, with searchlights trained on the people below. Armored personnel carriers were parked on the side. The authorities were bracing for a riot. A ring of riot police stood with their rifles ready across their chests.

The epicenter of the explosion was eerily quiet. A hideous, overpowering smell hit me as we got close to the scene, the smell of charred flesh, gasoline, and undigested rice and curry from lunch. The car bomb had exploded in the middle of the street, substantially demolishing seven or eight vehicles and incinerating the people inside them. Some of these vehicles were buses, packed with passengers on their way home from work. A school was also located near the blast.

Through the helicopter searchlights, I could make out several corpses inside the vehicles—they were burned unrecognizably. When the light passed, I was grateful for the dark. Windows running down the entire length of the street had been blown out, paving the area with glass dust and shards that sparkled in flashbulbs and television lights.

"The incident is still under investigation," said a police officer standing in the middle of a circle of television cameras. "It was very powerful, very big," said another inspector officiously, wearing, I noticed, the familiar white Buddha string around his wrist for good luck. "I think maybe we should get the civilians out of the area." Shouts from the burgeoning crowd of onlookers grew louder, along with the sirens of ambulances and security vehicles racing through the streets, underscoring the eeriness of the scene.

We were careful to stick to the middle of the street. Whole doors, fenders, even the windshields of cars had been blown into nearby trees, some as far as fifty meters away. These fell to the ground when police poked the trees with long bamboo poles. In the middle of a spreading bo tree near the police station was what I thought was an arm or a child's leg.

The police inspectors told us we had to go, but Dieter continued to snap away, lingering on a bus whose seats had been burned down to the metal springs. A corpse inside was indistinguishable from the burned wires of the bus's charred electrical system.

Practically running in the dark, Dieter looked at his watch with dismay. "Already too late to get these photographs on the flight to London tonight," he hissed. "This is the trouble with these fellows, the JVP." He had no doubt it was them, though he was later proved wrong. "They have no sense of deadlines. Maybe they need a media adviser. Anyway, let's go back to the hotel, put the equipment away, and get something to eat. I haven't even had any breakfast yet."

An agreement like the peace accord was, viewed from the outside, the only way peace could come about, given the momentum of the conflict. But insecurities shaped by myth and by history, deep antipathy to the idea of Indian-sponsored Tamil autonomy, and broad dissatisfaction with the country's ruling elite created profound emotional resistance among the Sinhalese, making fierce opposition to the Accord inevitable.

According to a deeply cherished Sinhalese myth, just before he ascended into the state of nirvana, the Buddha had chosen the Sinhalese to be the protectors and preservers of his teaching. "In Lanka, O Lord of Gods, shall my religion be established and flourish," the ancient Sinhalese Buddhist chronicle the *Mahavamsa* quotes the Buddha as saying as he gazed across the waters and saw Vijaya, the progenitor of the Sinhalese race, making his way to the island in an open boat. "Therefore carefully protect him with his followers and Lanka."

According to other parts of the sacred mythology, the establishment of Buddhism in Sri Lanka had endowed the Sinhalese with abundant prosperity and had been integral to the creation of the great Sinhalese Golden Age, from the second to the thirteenth century. But that Golden Age, says the *Mahavamsa*, was destroyed when Tamil invaders from southern India attacked and dismembered the Sinhalese kingdom, sowing disorder that centuries later left the Sinhalese defenseless in the face of Western colonialism.

In the Sinhalese worldview, autonomy for the Tamils was equated with separatism and the creation of Eelam, the mythical Tamil homeland. Any breakup of the country would have been abhorrent; one of the corollaries of Sinhalese Buddhist mythology held that the island in its entirety must remain under Buddhist control, imputing mystical properties to the unitary character of the Sri Lankan state. But Eelam, many Sinhalese feared, would only serve as a springboard for modern-day Tamil invaders to sweep down on the Sinhalese once again, threatening their sacred mandate. Such atavistic fears were hardly allayed by the Tiger rebels, who self-consciously adopted the symbol of the ancient Chola invaders. "The Tamil people, they did it then, and they are doing it now," whispered a tour guide in broken English inside the ancient ruins of an image house in the sacred city of Polonnaruwa, ransacked by south Indian invaders in the thirteenth century. "Always a problem, India and Sri Lanka. Even then. Even now."

Given the degree of Westernization among the country's elite and the outward façade of Western-style democratic institutions, it was easy for outside observers to dismiss these myths and atavistic memories or to diminish their importance. But such mytho-history was still very much alive among the Sinhalese people, cementing a link between their fate as a nation and that of their religion. "Deep down, Buddhism is still the most important thing in people's lives here," explained a young Sinhalese academic recently returned from doctoral studies in America. "It is like Islam is to Arabs and Zionism is to Israelis: the most important thing. People will sacrifice their lives to protect it; it is seen as a noble and high duty to lay down one's life to save it. You are taught from the time you are a child to the time you are in university that foreigners are out to destroy Buddhism and that the most noble thing to do with your life is to protect it and the Sinhala language. Even the most educated people feel these things, however much they are taught to view things rationally."

Thus, the rhetoric of monks opposed to the Accord struck a deep, resonant chord among most Sinhalese. "History shows that whenever the Tamils were in power, they destroyed Buddhist places of worship and the Buddhists," thundered one influential Buddhist cleric. "If we are inactive, soon Buddhism and Buddhist culture will fade from our land. The anti-Buddhist forces are invading our temples, our villages, and even our homes. We should be cautious and resort to well-organized action to counter the situation."

Sinhalese paranoia and the general opposition to the Accord it triggered was also a function of demographics. While the Sinhalese were, with 74 percent of the island's 17 million people, a majority on the island, they were a minority when the 55 million Tamils on the Indian mainland were counted in, an imbalance that filled them with cultural and political insecurity and fueled what analysts have called their "majority with a minority complex." The more hysterical among them saw Tamils in the northern third of Sri Lanka uniting with the Tamils of Tamil Nadu, who would then use Sri Lanka as a rear base in their struggle to break away from the central government of India. More modest expansion scenarios predicted that once an autonomous Tamil province was inaugurated, it would not be hard for Tamil leaders to manufacture a grievance to press for full secession and, after seceding, to mount a putsch for territory in the Sinhalese south, most likely the central highlands, where the lucrative tea crop is grown.

The Sinhalese were also worried that conceding territory would open the door for the island's other disgruntled minority communities. If there was a recognition of traditional Tamil homelands, then the Muslims, at 8 percent of the population, might want a state of their own someday, too, as well as the 6 percent who were Indian Tamils—a community in the tea country separate from the Sri Lankan Tamils by history and caste.

There were objections to Tamil autonomy for economic reasons as well. For nearly ten years the government had been building a gargantuan and costly series of irrigation dams and hydroelectric power plants in the central and eastern parts of the country. The purpose of the project was to expand agricultural production and to provide space to resettle landless Sinhalese peasants from the severely overcrowded southern portions of the island. But nearly 60 percent of the lands were in the Tamil areas of the north and east, which threatened the project entirely or ceded much of it to the despised Eelamists. An autonomous Tamil state would also mean more competition for international development aid.

The bulk of Sinhalese opposition to the Accord, however, was rooted in a fear of its architect, India, and the perception that the agreement had cost Sri Lanka its sovereignty. According to this analysis, aid to the Tamil rebels had been part of a plot to destabilize the island and make Indian intervention unavoidable. It was widely believed that the Accord laid the basis for an outright annexation. Many thought there were secret agreements written into the Accord that would cede much control of Sri Lankan affairs to the Indians. There was also fear that if Jayawardene was to die, whatever promises India had made about Sri Lanka's independence would be broken, a legitimate worry in a culture where backsliding on agreements is not unusual. "India wants to control the entire Indian Ocean," exclaimed a Sinhalese attorney belonging to the opposition party. "And in that drive Ceylon is an expendable little pawn."

Sinhalese suspicions about India's presence were further exacerbated by the way Gandhi and his major military advisers spoke of their venture. To audiences in India, Gandhi boasted of having been powerful enough to hand "one-third of the land of Sri Lanka to one-eighth of its population." Elsewhere, Rajiv asserted that the merged north and east would enjoy as much autonomy as any state in the Indian Union. Indian generals were similarly indiscreet, insisting that they took orders from Rajiv Gandhi, not President Jayawardene.

The significance of every utterance and every transaction between the two countries was magnified and scrutinized: the fact that goats were brought into the country to feed the Indian soldiers without a proper quarantine, that the soldiers were marrying Tamil women or were siring illegitimate children, that customs inspections in the north had been suspended as well as rules of civilian aviation, that journalists were barred by Delhi now instead of by Colombo. It was not surprising, therefore, that the importation of Indian nurses, civil servants, and teachers to help rebuild Jaffna became another cause for suspicion.

Popular Sinhalese resistance to the Accord was also fueled by broad disaffection with the ruling party. This class had betrayed the country, it was charged, not only by relinquishing its sovereignty but by eroding democratic traditions and encouraging an economic program that was at odds with Buddhist cultural ideals and values. Although the Sinhalese backlash against the government was triggered by the signing of the Accord, the agreement only revealed undercurrents of political, social, and economic alienation that had been boiling beneath the surface for years. "The country has yet to see a party that stinks as much as the UNP," barked an opposition party member in Parliament. "The internal sores of the UNP are emanating a foul smell. . . . But one day the people will rise against the government to win back their rights. Nobody can suppress the people all the time. The sovereignty of the people cannot be destroyed."

To many, Jayawardene's role in the creation of the peace accord, which had been conceived of in secret and agreed to without popular endorsement, had only been the final step in what was seen as a long, steady slide toward dictatorial control and subversion of the democratic process. Western-style democracy, like Western culture, had really only sent down shallow roots. "We have a façade democracy," cried one newspaper reporter. "Nothing more than a bloody façade. No one will ever confront J.R. or challenge him. Not even his ministers will raise points against him in policy debates. There is no check on his appetite for power at all. Whatever he wants is done."

Jayawardene had come to power in the 1977 election for Prime Minister on a platform that called for a "*dharmistra* society," a program that embodied an old Buddhist notion of *sasana*, which combined ideals of social justice and moral righteousness with faithfulness to institutional Buddhism. But Jayawardene's devotion to Buddhist moral principles and democratic ideals was merely rhetorical. Claiming that only a strong central executive could carry the country over the threats represented by separatists and subversives, Jayawardene rewrote the constitution to make himself a Gaullist-style President. He also allowed parliamentary reforms that made it impossible for MPs to "cross over" and join the opposition party, and stripped the judiciary of its powers to strike down laws that had failed its judicial review. Then, citing a wholly fictional conspiracy against the government, he canceled the 1982 general elections and held a referendum instead, seeking popular approval for extending Parliament another six years. The measure squeaked by though surrounded by charges of egregious electoral fraud and voter intimidation.

Once Jayawardene had secured his "Long Parliament" in 1982, there was little to check his power. Having solicited letters of resignation from all of his party's MPs, he could fire anyone who criticized or opposed any of his actions. And with the power to pick new MPs to replace slots that had been vacated, he could reward party hacks with these seats. Because they were accountable to Jayawardene and not to a constituency that had voted them into office, these MPs grew divorced from the electorate and used their positions instead for personal gain.

Another manifestation of the increasingly authoritarian nature of the regime was the rise in political thuggery, a common staple of South Asian politics which Jayawardene's rule brought to a new level of perniciousness. UNP politicians made alliances with criminal kingpins or formed goon squads on their own from the ranks of the unemployed and discontented, paying them out of funds set aside for patronage. The police, too, became cat's-paws of local political bosses. Those who tried to resist found themselves transferred to hardship posts, denied promotions, or worse.

Political thuggery led to the suppression of legitimate political dissent. Striking workers, voters at polling stations, opposition political operatives, intellectuals, even justices of the Supreme Court were intimidated. The police rarely intervened. In some cases, they were even promoted for their actions. In return for "political service," local officials allowed these thugs license to run rackets like timber smuggling and illicit alcohol production, and to commit crimes against the local population with impunity. "Ten years ago, we were a country of open houses; all these security precautions were unheard of," a Tamil scholar who had recently returned from Cambridge University told me. "Walking down the street you could see people inside their homes, playing with their children and watching TV. Now you see razor wire and guard dogs."

As the government stepped up its response to "southern subversion," as JVP activity was called, each MP was allowed to hire 150 men as a private militia for their own individual protection, a step that dangerously increased the number of civilians with guns and the power to terrorize. "Earlier, these thugs operated clandestinely," explained my friend from Cambridge. "But now they have been legitimized, made to appear essential to the preservation of democracy, when in fact all they are really doing is shoring up the MP and guaranteeing that his henchmen get their kickbacks and patronage so they can stay in business. There were always hatchet men in the pay of the MPs—doers of dirty work and providers of prostitutes and protection. But now they have become a force all their own. How can you run a society where there are one hundred and fifty thugs trained to shoot who are allowed to settle scores, often private scores, in the name of the political process? And because the state needs them, action against them is impossible. They are a Frankenstein monster. These militias are really death squads, just like in El Salvador. Soon they will be knocking on people's doors and taking them away. What is happening here is the process of Latin Americanization. And in my opinion, it means the end of democracy. Our British parliamentary system is a thing of the past. How can you have elections in the midst of all this? Or keep the people from reacting with violence of their own kind?"

Along with an unpopular concentration of political power, there was an objectionable concentration of wealth. Riding into power on the discontent created by the failed socialism of its predecessor, the UNP shaped its economic vision around what it called the "open economy," which would make markets free, attract foreign investment, and turn Sri Lanka into another economic miracle like Singapore or Korea. As a result, special free trade zones flourished, where favorable tax incentives coupled with low labor costs encouraged foreign firms in the textile, shoe, and electronics industries. Tourism soared, too, taking in $100 million in 1982 before the war crimped that industry. Unemployment decreased from 30 to 15 percent, and per capita income rose to $300.

Beneath the surface prosperity, however, the open economy had done very little to ease the crushing burden of poverty. By the late eighties, almost 50 percent of all families lived on food stamps. Debt was most widespread among public-sector employees, but salaried employees in the private sector were pinched, too, as even those with reliable incomes and solid educations struggled to keep pace with the galloping cost of living. Tax cuts to the wealthy elite, which were absolutely necessary to stimulate business investment, deprived the state of revenue needed for social welfare programs, as did the removal of price subsidies for rice and other essentials.

Government policy also favored investment in the service and import sectors, ignoring industries that might have created better-paying jobs for a greater number of people. Instead of investing in the country's base of production, most of the country's business class jockeyed for lucrative import licenses, the better to satisfy the elite's craving for conspicuous consumption.

Disaffection rooted in the inequities of the open economy was compounded by the extent of the official corruption that had seeped into every pore of public and private life. Jobs in the public sector required the "chit" of an MP, and the notes were given only to those with proper caste and class connections or those who had paid appropriate bribes. In time, MPs also began to control investment and jobs in the private sector, too; soon having a job, any job, depended on being in with the ruling party and being from the right families within it, which often made opposition party supporters virtually unemployable.

Government officials also skimmed huge amounts of international development money into offshore bank accounts or lavish consumer lifestyles. Projects were approved less for what they would add to the country's development effort than for what they could do for the ministers. As a result, money that was desperately needed in rural areas stayed in Colombo, feeding economic disparity.

Equally egregious was the official corruption in health care and education, despite the high priority Jayawardene had given them in his vision of the *dharmistra* society. Although under the national health care system medical treatment was supposed to be free, doctors sold medicine on the black market, gouged patients in private

clinics, and forced many into usurious debt for the simplest of procedures. Equally callous were the depredations of teachers who refused to teach in regular classes so they could make money in private
tutorials—a form of exploitation that status-anxious parents submitted to, often mortgaging all they owned so their children could pass
university entrance exams.

Disaffection from the economic inequity spawned under Jayawardene's rule would have strained any Third World country's social
fabric, but the peculiarities of the Sinhalese psyche made it even
worse. An extremely status-anxious people, the Sinhalese are acutely
conscious of social standing. The good fortune enjoyed by others
often arouses tremendous, even irrational, feelings of envy—feelings
that the Sinhalese call *irishywa*. The wealth and enhanced status of
Colombo's elite enraged those who were not so fortunate, especially
the young who had expected their educations to earn them white-
collar employment and the prestige that went with it.

The open economy was identified with alien, Western values by
Sinhala Buddhist nationalists. One of the promises of the *dharmistra*
society had been that the government would cast itself in the mold
of ancient Buddhist kings who had provided for the general welfare
of the entire society. But the increasing misery of the poor and the
superheated consumerism of the very rich, epitomized by restaurants
featuring expensive sacrilegiously named soups like Buddha Jumps
over the Wall, betrayed that promise badly, encouraging the impression that the regime was culturally estranged from the people at
large.

During the ten years it had been in power, the UNP rationalized
the steady erosion of civil liberties and democratic institutions as a
necessary and temporary response to "Tamil terrorism." The Tamil
problem also provided a ready scapegoat to distract the Sinhalese
from their economic difficulties as well as the social tensions sim-
mering in their society, repeating a pattern seen in many other
nations where the ruling elite plays the race card to obscure essentially class-based inequities. But by the time of the peace accord, the
Sinhalese could no longer ignore the fact that fundamental things
were wrong. The institutions of Western-style democracy endured

but their substance had withered. General elections had not been held in over ten years and legitimate political protest was entirely banned. The free trade union movement was dead, student protest had been smothered, and those political leaders who criticized the ruling party feared retaliation from government-sanctioned goon squads. Economically, there was a tiny fraction of wealthy Sri Lankans on one side and the rest of society on the other, slipping deeper into poverty, unable to afford housing, education, and all-important dowries for marriage. It was abundantly clear that elections were absolutely necessary, that they were the only way to purge the government of corruption and to restore its popular legitimacy. But elections were unlikely, as the threat of JVP subversion, fed in large part by the absence of elections, became a handy excuse for the government to justify withholding elections even longer. Terrorism must be wiped out first, Jayawardene said; only then can democracy return.

Nationalist hysteria and the sense that the country's political system was beyond redemption had given a tremendous boost to the JVP. Riding a wave of despair and betrayal, the JVP gained a much broader base of popular support than it had before the agreement. While it was an underground party, many Sinhalese were put off by the party's Marxist-Leninist leanings and commitment to revolutionary violence. After the Accord, however, the JVP could present itself as a party of national salvation. The JVP was broadly xenophobic, toward both India and the West, and it also championed the economic rights of Sinhalese "sons of the soil" who had been ignored in the UNP carnival for the rich. It was the government's repression of dissent, however, particularly the heavy hand with which it put down protest over the Accord, that most propelled the JVP forward. "If people are not allowed proper channels to deal with the situation," warned one prominent monk at his temple on the outskirts of Colombo, "people will find alternatives."

As the JVP slowly emerged in the wake of the Accord, analysts in Colombo were divided about its primary color and character. Was it a vessel for Buddhist nationalism, was it a social revolt fueled by the regime's corruption, or was it a Marxist-Leninist organization?

Much as the populace embraced the JVP on patriotic grounds, most middle-class Sinhalese held the movement's violent tactics and ultimate goals at arm's length. For them, the JVP was a vehicle of convenience.

There was little ambivalence about the JVP, however, among Sinhalese university students and younger monks. They saw the JVP as deliverance from a system shot through with contempt for their identity and aspirations. The majority of university students and monks were from the deep Sinhalese south, the area of the country where political disaffection was the most profound. Unemployment in some parts of the south was topping 35 percent, malnutrition and debt were high, and the entire southern province had seen very little of the development funds that had been siphoned off or misspent in other areas of the country. The south was also one of the most populous areas in the country, and its population was overwhelmingly young.

I spent the bulk of the week after the rush-hour bombing roaming Colombo with Dieter Ludwig. We wanted to be in position if the JVP tried to follow through on its threats against members of Parliament. Most of the other foreign correspondents had left Colombo, but Dieter was growing more fascinated by the situation every day. "You could win a Pulitzer here in a very short time," he insisted. "It's like being in a kitchen with all the right ingredients. Rich versus poor. West versus East. City versus country. Caste. Religion. Regional power plays. Superpowers in the shadows. A very interesting place."

During the week of the vote in Parliament, President Jayawardene was at pains to present the illusion of a Sinhala consensus behind the Accord. Threats to destabilize his regime, he said, were insignificant. But with MPs unable even to make their own way to Parliament without fear of being killed, with tanks surrounding the city, and with security forces on every corner, such claims seemed ludicrous.

And even with their formidable powers of denial, the people of Colombo weren't having it. Half the city's work force had stayed home that week. It was a sizable victory for the JVP, though in actuality it had been the Tigers who detonated the bomb earlier in the week. In the far south, the government's authority had failed almost entirely: drivers for the state-run bus system had refused to work after JVP warnings, government workers were calling in sick in droves, and the police were hardly moving out of their stations.

"Just as I suspected," Dieter said, congratulating himself on his intuition. "One bomb yesterday and half the work force doesn't show. Another one tomorrow and the rest will stay home, too."

I wondered aloud where the next strike might take place.

"It would be very clever for them to set off a bomb in the exact same spot the very next day," he said. We were stuck in traffic right where the bomb had exploded the day before. He wasn't trying to joke.

In front of the police station, the remains of the car that had contained the bomb had been reassembled piece by piece, for forensic purposes. Only its four springs were recognizable. "Very, very clever. You know, any one of these buses could have a suitcase of explosives inside."

Swarms of flies hovered over spots where blood had pooled the night before. We went by the train station and then headed out to Parliament—several miles outside Colombo—following a convoy of tanks for a mile or so. All along the route, commandos and army personnel lined the streets. The police and the army had blocked off access to Parliament. A Sinhalese police inspector explained to us his theory of the Situation. "Tamils may have started all this rain, but the government certainly doesn't want it to stop. When it's raining you have an excuse not to leave the house, eh?"

Students and monks at a demonstration at Colombo University, a known hotbed of JVP activity, were not so subtle in their disparagement of the regime. "If this government continues to violate democracy, then violence is the only way we can overcome them," intoned one student agitator as he stood on a log in front of a group of a hundred and fifty or so. "The main thing is that the President did not think about the consequences of his actions when he invited in the Indians. He only thought about remaining in power. The root cause was that he did not allow the democratic process to work. They have interfered with the democratic process and that has led to this."

"We are in a totally desperate state," said another student, more diminutive but more forceful than the other. "The government is heavily armed, but the people have no vote and no arms with which to win it. If somebody gave us arms, we would surely fight against them."

One of the monks jumped up and began flapping his robes. "To save the Motherland we must do something. So we are readying to get arms and fight the government. Even though I am a monk I have to do it for the people. I won't have any hesitation. If there is a need, I will take up arms. If the government kills the followers of Buddhism, and tries to protect its social and political privileges with its own weapons, then we must do something to protect the people and our rights."

At another university, on the other side of the city, the students were even more emphatic. They had mounted a hunger strike as part of their protest. By the time we got there, several had already passed out from lack of food and from sunstroke. The atmosphere was now fairly low-keyed, with many of the students—all male—relaxing on the ground. Occasionally one or two would come over and present their case to us. Students had to fight government repression, one said. "We have lost our privileges and our rights. And because of that we have decided to arm ourselves. To take up weapons like the students did in South Korea. The repression is so strong that without weapons we cannot oppose it. We want sophisticated weapons. For security reasons, we can't say where we'll get them, but we will get them, you can be assured."

"Yes, we have to get weapons," a wild-eyed monk exclaimed. "We must take up arms to kill the traitor J.R. and all his stooges. We need to get rid of this government and get a patriotic one. First it is essential to safeguard the Motherland. Only after that comes Buddhism."

Would he consider immolating himself in protest? Dieter asked him. "Yes," the monk responded soberly. "Self-immolation would be an appropriate tactic. If the government puts down the people, if there are massacres of Buddhists, we will do that."

The JVP was very big, a waiter at the Chinese Dragon told me later that evening. Besides the students, the waiter class of Colombo was almost solidly behind them, too, most being frustrated students. Frequently, college-age Sri Lankans were unable to get into university because of the educational bottleneck. The JVP drew most heavily from this very population: the educated sons of poor Sinhala lower-caste families who were either jobless or underemployed—the same stratum that had filled the ranks of the Tiger militants in the north. "Yes, just like the Tigers," my waiter added enthusiastically.

If they had gotten more than 100,000 votes in 1982 when they were legal and Wijeweera ran for President, then their numbers must have swollen many times over by now, my waiter continued. From the rhetoric he used and from his political sharpness, I suspected he might himself be a cadre in the movement. "Everyone must work, no?" added one of his colleagues, who had just finished serving a table of double-chinned members of the Colombo privilegentsia. He launched into a tirade over the property that UNP ministers had bought all over the world, citing especially Minister of Lands Gamani Dissanayake, whose holdings in Australia, he alleged, made him one of the richest men in the world. "Little people are working, but the big people are sitting home living off our work. Everyone should work, no?"

The size of the JVP would remain a mystery for some time, but the question of its effectiveness was being answered all across the island as it stepped up attacks on military targets and acts of sabotage against the island infrastructure. Over and over it was demonstrating a capacity to paralyze the country and, even more important, to strike psychological terror into those who feared it. It had attacked both the government and the privately owned bus systems, and halted the delivery of government-owned newspapers, a highly symbolic strike against national authority. It had also blown up electrical pylons, interrupting the flow of electricity, which in turn paralyzed the water delivery system in some parts of the country. The JVP had toppled a telecommunications tower in Kandy, a well-guarded installation, and it had ripped up long sections of railroad track. Though the government was doing its best to minimize the significance of the sabotage by presenting each act as isolated, the coordination was obvious. The fact that a bomb went off in the middle of Colombo during an intensive security alert—whoever had set it off—increased no one's confidence in the government's antiterrorism capabilities.

The Colombo bombing kept most people home for the week. In the evening, trains that were practically empty clattered along the tracks. There was a Sunday desolation all the week long.

I had begun to feel claustrophobic in the city. There really wasn't any safer place and there really wasn't any safe way to get there if there was. The north and east were full of Indians trying to mop up the LTTE; the south and central areas of the country were full of JVP hit squads. Furthermore, the JVP had not yet established its policy toward Westerners or journalists. Would they be like the Khmer Rouge and kill any reporter who got near them or would they strike a more sophisticated media posture?

Although I had been in Colombo during earlier alerts, the bombing had driven the reality of urban terrorism home graphically; even after a washing, the smell of charred corpses still clung to the shirt I had on that evening, or so it seemed. I was jumpy around government buildings and avoided the post office and the telecommunications center. I also limited whatever business I had to conduct downtown. By the end of the week, I had a crick in my neck, from looking over my shoulder all the time. This habit was born out of experience: especially at night when knots of whispering men would form on street corners and unmarked vans of plainclothes security men prowled the empty streets.

On Thursday November 12, 1987, Parliament passed the Provincial Council Bill, ratifying the peace accord. But however loudly the government tried to present it as a milestone toward the country's recovery, most knew it augured chaos and polarization. An important threshold had been crossed, signaling both the loss of the government mandate to rule and the gaining momentum of antigovernment forces, with the people taking the passage of the Accord as another sign of the regime's estrangement.

That Saturday, I sat on the second-floor porch of a restaurant on the Galle Road watching the office workers and bureaucrats who had stayed all week in Colombo to avoid commuting after Monday's bombing. It was an elegant-looking place but smelly from nearby garbage fires and the humidity. "I am thinking it will end up in a war," said a waiter who was watching the melancholy procession along the road. "End up in a war?" I asked him. "What about the last four years?" "Ah, sir, that was just a medium war, no? Next will be a full war. A very, very bad one."

TWO

7 · Buddhism and the British

AS WE DROVE along the hairpin curves and plunging jungled hillsides outside of Kandy, I began to appreciate the way such inaccessible terrain had slowed the British when they tried to conquer the kingdom there. I also realized why, to this day, Kandy had remained somewhat distinct from the rest of the country, culturally and psychologically. For nearly three centuries after the Portuguese had established themselves as the first colonial power on the island, the Kandyans had maintained their independence. Even now, the Sinhalese considered Kandy the cultural capital of their society, the repository of all that was most pure and most authentic.

The historian I was going to visit was considered an expert on the social and cultural impact of British colonialism. Given the generous material benefits left behind by the British—well-developed industries such as tea, rubber, and coconuts, as well as schools, railroads, telephones, and Westminsterian democratic institutions—social and cultural wounds were often overlooked by many historical analysts. But understanding the damage inflicted by the British, the historian insisted, was essential to understanding the larger context of the ethnic problem. "You must never forget," he said, clad in the white shirt and sarong favored by Sinhalese cultural nationalists. "We were under foreign domination for five hundred years. As a people we lost so much. Our language. Our religion.

Even our ability to write our own history. It has been a long, long struggle to win it all back, a struggle that continues even as we speak."

The first two Western colonial powers in Ceylon, the Portuguese and the Dutch, left a legacy of violence, though they managed to do little lasting damage to the social or cultural fabric of traditional Sinhalese society. That was left to the British, who fought the Dutch for control over the island's coastal regions in the late 1790s and later subdued the entire island by taking the kingdom of Kandy in 1815.

At first, the British left the kingdom's cultural and social institutions alone in the larger pursuit of political domination. Having correctly understood that political legitimacy required the sanction of religion, the British assumed the former Sinhalese king's responsibilities toward the institutions of Buddhism, thereby winning over the Sinhalese with a minimum of bloodshed. "The religion of the Boodoo," read the historic fifth clause of the 1815 Kandyan Convention, the treaty that first articulated the British role in colonial Ceylon, "is declared inviolate, and its rites, ministers, and places of worship are to be maintained and protected."

Although many of the Kandyans, especially the Buddhist monks, were not convinced by the British commitment to Buddhism, their suspicions were allayed by the first British "resident" or colonial agent in Kandy, John D'Orly. Following through on the promises of the Kandyan Convention, D'Orly demonstrated an uncommon degree of cultural sensitivity by learning Sinhala and by personally participating in Buddhist rituals. "We have not come to this country to destroy the religion of the Boodoo and the gods that have prevailed from ancient times in this country," D'Orly told the monks, "but to protect and promote it."

Such sensitivity worked, or so it seemed. So much did the Kandyans trust D'Orly that they brought back to Kandy the sacred relic of the Buddha's tooth—believed to confer mystical powers of kingship—from the jungle where it had been hidden in advance of the British expeditionary force some years before. After that, D'Orly presided over the annual Kandy Perahera, a ten-day series of elephant processions in which the tooth relic was paraded around sacred Kandy Lake.

There were precedents in Sinhalese history for non-Buddhists being invested with such political and religious power. The last line of kings in Kandy had been part of the Nāyakkar dynasty, Hindus with Tamil blood who were given the royal mandate in Kandy when the Sinhalese did not have a successor of proper royal lineage. Although it was foreign, the Nāyakkar dynasty ruled according to the hallowed Sinhalese traditions, the first and foremost obligation of which was to maintain Buddhism. With that precedent in mind, the Sinhalese expected the British authorities to follow through on their pledge, which in their eyes meant not just the protection of the religion but the management of its internal affairs as well—maintaining clerical discipline, administering important religious rituals, and dispensing government patronage.

In time, however, differences began to surface between the Sinhalese and the British over what the Kandyan Convention really meant. To the Sinhalese, the agreement was an immutable, inviolable covenant. But for the British, D'Orly excepted, the Convention had been an expedient to consolidate their power. While D'Orly paid it deference, most British colonial officials looked upon Buddhism as outright heathenism—"a gloom of ignorance and superstition that had enveloped the region to be dissipated by religious knowledge," according to the colonial governor Herbert Brownrigg.

Differences between the British and the Sinhalese came to a head over the restoration of the monarchy. The British refusal to allow the Sinhalese to install a new king revealed the true nature of British political and military domination. In 1817, a former monk who claimed to be part of the last, deposed Kandyan monarchy, and therefore a successor to the throne, launched a rebellion centered in remote areas of the kingdom. Sensing an opportunity to throw off the British, the Kandyan chiefs recognized the pretender, even as they disputed the legitimacy of his claim. The Great Rebellion, as this revolt was called, spread throughout the kingdom. The British were nearly routed by the successful guerrilla tactics of the insurgents; disease had depleted much of the British regimental strength and the inaccessibility of the areas in which they were forced to fight made it hard to mount an effective counterinsurgency. Only the most brutal scorched-earth policy, the starvation of a substantial percentage of the peasantry, enabled the British to turn the situation in their favor.

It was not British military skill, however, but their luck in sapping the morale of the insurgents that led to the victory. The inability of the rebel leaders to overlook their rivalries long enough to mount sustained coordinated operations led to several important losses in jungle redoubts. The rebels also lost momentum when the pretender was captured and unmasked. What really drained the cause, however, was the recovery of the tooth relic. Early in the rebellion it had been spirited away by bhikkhus and hidden in a jungle sanctuary. But a British patrol stumbled upon it and took it back to the Temple of the Tooth in Kandy—a propaganda victory from which the rebels never recovered since British possession was taken as a sign they were fated to rule Ceylon.

Shortly afterward, there was a decisive shift in the policies of the Colonial Office toward Buddhism, a shift instigated under increasing pressure from British missionary forces. Before the revolt, missionaries in England had protested the fifth clause of the Kandyan Convention, but were not powerful enough to do anything about it, except to conduct a campaign of slander against John D'Orly. Around the time of the revolt of 1818, however, a new generation of civil servants in the British Colonial Office gained influence, a generation that was much more inclined to scorn alien cultures and traditions.

From the floor of the British Parliament, William Wilberforce, one of the foremost evangelical leaders of the day, argued that the continued force of Buddhism was thwarting conversion efforts. If Buddhism was "disestablished," the field would be wide open for proselytizing. Concerned about the resentment disestablishment would stir in the Sinhalese, British civil servants in Ceylon objected, but missionary policy won the day, with the help of allies in the Colonial Office. The colonial government of Ceylon gave up formal possession of the tooth relic and British officials were no longer allowed to participate in Buddhist rituals.

Behind these sentiments were mercantile interests who saw the fatalistic streak in Buddhism as an obstruction to the kind of commercially dynamic society they wanted. "The religion and manners of the orientals naturally support one another," wrote Lord Acton, in reference to the same problems he encountered in India. "Neither can be changed without the other."

More disparaging were the comments of the American clergyman Maturin M. Ballou: "As one regards these lazy betel-chewing irresponsible children of the tropics idling in the shade of palms it does not seem strange that they should lead a sensuous life, the chief occupations of which are sleeping and eating. All humanity here seems to be more or less torpid. There is no necessity to rouse man to action—effort is superfluous. The very bounty of nature makes the recipients dirty, lazy and heedless. They live from hand to mouth, exercising no forecast, aiming no provisions for the morrow. It is the paradise of birds, butterflies and flowers, but man seems out of place. He adds nothing to the beauty of his surroundings. He does nothing to improve such wealth of possibilities as Providence spreads broadcast only in equatorial regions."

In response to Ceylon's continuing fiscal crisis, two British lords, Colebrooke and Cameron, were sent to the East by the Colonial Office on a fact-finding mission. They spent two years making an exhaustive analysis of the country's political, economic, and social conditions. The result was a series of legislative measures called the Colebrooke Reforms, one of the most thoroughgoing examples of cultural imperialism in the modern world, which changed Ceylonese society irrevocably.

One of Colebrooke's most far-reaching changes was to abolish the old feudal system, called *rajakariya*, of compulsory service to the king. *Rajakariya*, it was said, blocked the fluidity of labor, and hence the creation of a capitalist society, by restricting the mobility of workers and by maintaining the institution of caste. Colebrooke and Cameron objected to the caste system because it violated the ideal of equality and also because it would inhibit the creation of an indigenous civil service based on principles of merit and efficiency.

The Colebrooke Reforms also aimed at overhauling the fatalistic Sinhalese "attitude to life." One way the reformers proposed to do this was by promoting English as the language of education and administration. Vernacular Sinhalese lent itself to a nonrationalist worldview, it was said, while English was progressive. Another avenue of reform involved a system of Western-style education, which would be put in the hands of missionaries and require conversion.

Disestablishment, and the social reforms it entailed, opened wounds that have still not healed. First, it deprived the Sinhalese of a king and of the moral force that goes with monarchy, which was critical in traditional Buddhist political culture with its emphasis on maintaining *sasana*.

Without a king playing an integral role in institutional Buddhism, the sangha, as the order of monks was known traditionally, fell prey to indiscipline, doctrinal schisms, sectarian squabbles based on caste, and corruption.

Further damage was inflicted by the British in their attempts to abolish the caste system, which was seen as a violation of another pledge made in the Kandyan Convention to retain the "respective ranks and dignities" of Sinhalese society, particularly those of the Kandyan aristocracy, whose cooperation was essential for the British to defeat the king. Although Buddhism was in essence a revolt against the caste excesses of Brahmanic Hinduism, caste was nevertheless all-important in traditional Sinhalese society, fueling an intense preoccupation with status and honorific deference, especially among the topmost caste, which included almost 50 percent of the people. In traditional society, for example, there were at least eight personal pronouns to denote position within the hierarchy; so obsessed with status were the Kandyans that wives of noblemen who had been executed by the king would often commit suicide rather than live among the outcastes as commanded. While efforts to outlaw caste did not finally succeed, the status that the British bestowed upon Christianized Ceylonese created deep and widespread resentment among the Sinhalese, hitting them exactly where they were most sensitive.

These feelings were especially sharp among the traditional Sinhalese elite—monks, schoolteachers, and Ayurvedic physicians who saw their position in society plummet as the new comprador class rose to the top, through schools barred to non-Christians, through the civil service, which favored English speakers, and through wealth created by concessions given to Christian families in tea, rubber, and the production of alcohol. That Christian Ceylonese would make money from the production and distribution of alcohol was particularly offensive to the more puritanical Buddhists, who not only looked askance upon drinking but were outraged that the government could sanction and encourage its production and raise revenues by taxing it.

The new class created by the British was comprised of Christian Tamils and Burghers as well, but most were Christianized Sinhalese. Together, they became perhaps the most willing colonial subjects in the history of imperialism, putting up little resistance to the plans the British had for remaking their society and imitating their master's customs, manner of dress, and moral values with impressive alacrity. An ancestor, a skilled botanist, "knew of at least fifty-five species of poisons easily available to his countrymen," writes Michael Ondaajte, "none of them used against the invaders."

The willingness of the Ceylonese to convert made missionaries rapturous. "There are good grounds for believing that Buddhism will at no very distant period disappear from this island," wrote James Alwis, a nineteenth-century Bishop of Colombo. "I anticipate that Buddhism, shorn of its splendor, unaided by authority and torn by internal dissension, will not long have power to retain even its present slight control over the action of its votaries and will fall into disuse even before Christianity is prepared to step into its place."

On the surface this looked quite possible. Since the colonial government gave Christian missionaries a monopoly on education, which in turn gave them complete control over almost all avenues of upward mobility, the missionaries had many converts. As a result, Buddhist clerics fretted about the future prospects of their religion. "After reigning for more than twenty centuries," noted one pessimistic pamphleteer, "the Buddha, the dharma and the sangha were about to be cast as rubbish to the void."

Buddhism was not in such dire circumstances, however. The

domination of the Christian elite was limited and did not extend very far outside the cosmopolitan confines of Colombo, leaving traditional village hierarchies essentially intact, if demoralized. Missionaries there were often having much more difficulty making anything more than superficial conversions. The realities of going into the bush were much different from what they had been led to expect by seminary instructors who told them that as soon as they opened their mouths "willing hearers would flock around" and receive the message "with breathless attention and joy." Conversion statistics were misleading, often masking the way that the Sinhalese would embrace Christianity for practical purposes without relinquishing Buddhism, which to their minds involved no contradiction or apostasy.

Christian missionaries often had a hard time competing with Buddhist monks, who had a tradition of opportunities for daily contact with the villagers. Many Sinhalese looked upon the missionaries as dupes or meal tickets and often demanded arrack as a bribe to sit and listen to them. "We often meet with little but contempt, opprobrium and laughter," noted one dejected proselytizer. Often, missionaries had better luck with the Tamils in the north. The frustrations that missionaries faced in reaching the Sinhalese were frequently a function of cultural misunderstandings. Most of them didn't read or speak Sinhala, or when they did it was with little patience for nuance or idiom. In preaching, for example, the missionaries used language and terms of address that were unsuitable to an audience of widely varying social status and refused to make accommodations when advised to do so by Sinhalese Christians.

A controversy of this kind developed over the translation of the Bible into a more accessible form of the vernacular than the high Sinhalese in which it was originally written. Missionaries wanted a simplification and put out a second edition that used only one form of the pronoun "you"—in flat opposition to Sinhalese usage. The Colombo Bible Society, a group of Sinhalese Christians, strenuously objected and even went so far as to point out to the missionaries that their use of "you" could be considered an actionable offense if low-caste people used it to address high-caste Sinhalese, much less the

Redeemer himself. The director of the Bible project sniffed dismissively, calling the controversy "a prejudice that we have surest grounds to conclude will be constantly weakened and diminished when opposed by the mighty power of simplicity and truth." The Sinhalese reaction, however, was harsh. The translation was full of "blasphemous expressions toward our Creator, Redeemer and Sanctifier," one dissenting faction wrote. Thereafter, many prominent Sinhalese Christians withdrew entirely from the Anglican Church.

Meanwhile, as Buddhism was degenerating in its traditional center in Kandy, it was gaining strength along the southern coast, where it was never dependent upon official patronage. Ecclesiastical discipline may have broken down and the status of monks may have declined, but the severed link between the state and the sangha had allowed the latter to assert itself. Monks, therefore, revived their role as protectors and preservers of Buddhist culture, defining it in opposition to a foreign Western culture. In the process, Buddhist revivalism became a vehicle for Sinhalese nationalism, with the monks playing a major religious as well as political role.

Once official patronage was no longer available, the monks had to rely on laymen for donations and support. Many of these newly influential laymen had attended Christian schools and were reacting to Christian evangelicism by renewing their interest in Buddhist roots.

Both the monks and the laity involved in the Buddhist revival were galvanized by the arrogance of the missionaries and their contempt for Buddhism. The frustration that missionaries encountered in the bush found expression in increasingly shrill denunciations of Buddhism in missionary pamphlets. In these publications, Ceylon was depicted as a "stronghold of Satan"; Buddhism was "a stupor of ignorance"; and monks were "indolent, apathetic and indifferent to all matters of religion" and their faces had the appearance of "great vacancy, amounting to imbecility."

Such comments at first confused the monks, who had largely looked upon the Christian missionaries as colleagues in promoting religious virtue with whom they tried to share their spiritual and literary knowledge in an essentially noncompetitive relationship. After complaints to colonial authorities elicited no satisfaction, they grew angry and mounted a pamphleteering campaign of their own. In answer to the Society for the Propagation of the Gospel, Buddhist laymen started the Society for the Propagation of Buddhism, marshaling a growing body of lay activists into a broad-based social, political, and spiritual cause.

One of the highlights of the early Buddhist revival was a series of debates between missionaries and monks in February 1865 that the British hoped would publicly embarrass the Buddhists. The first debate, before a huge throng of Sinhalese Buddhists in a small town on the southwest coast called Panadura, demonstrated how badly the missionaries had underestimated their opponents. To the dismay of the Christians, the Buddhists did exceptionally well in defending their cosmology, parrying gibes about the historicity of the Buddha with their own about the historicity of Christ and taking aim at the vulnerabilities of the Christian creation myth by invoking the current arguments about evolution. They came across as erudite, learned, and witty, while the Christians seemed stodgy and flat. Reports of the monks' performance circulated quickly about the island, hastening the tide of popular revivalism. Some missionaries began to cast doubt on popular assessments of Buddhism's inevitable decline. "It is not yet conquered, not near it," wrote the Bishop of Colombo in 1879. "In the fullest sense it is the religion of the mass of the Sinhalese. There is little doubt that Buddhism is far more vigorous in Ceylon than it was 150 years ago."

The Buddhist revival picked up even more steam with the arrival of Henry Steel Olcott, an American, in 1880. Olcott, a veteran of the Civil War and founder with the Russian-born Madame Blavatsky of the Theosophical Movement, which envisioned the mystical union of all world religions, had read about the Panadura debate and was stirred to visit Ceylon to see if he could "do something if only a little" to fight the Christian missionaries. Although his original intent in going to Ceylon was only to expand interest in Theosophy, he was hailed by the Buddhists as a "defender of the faith" and soon dragged into the thick of the battle.

Olcott arrived with the zeal of an Old Testament prophet. He received a rapturous welcome, with crowds shouting, "Sadhu! Sadhu!"—a holy Buddhist chant—as he walked down the steps of the jetty on a white cloth that had been spread before him for the occasion. Monks came in droves to bless Olcott and his retinue. Buddhist lay dignitaries arrived from all over to meet him, and lavish floral arrangements and foods were spread before him at receptions throughout the southern part of the island. That a Westerner of Olcott's eminence would praise Buddhism in front of self-satisfied Christian missionaries was an incredible boost to Buddhist self-esteem. "It was this," Olcott noted, "that filled their nerves and filled their affectionate hearts to bursting."

Olcott began a series of tours around Ceylon intended to rouse popular interest in Buddhism. He was so successful at it that the monks invested him with the power to conduct Buddhist baptisms. He described his group's grueling schedule: arriving at dawn, preaching all day, and then moving on to another town, sleeping as best they could en route. "And I saw the people at their best," Olcott noted in great satisfaction. "Full of smiles and love and hospitable impulse and have been welcomed with triumphal arches, and flying flags and wild Eastern music and processions and shouts of joy. Ah! Lovely Lanka. Gem of the Summer Sea. How doth thy sweet image rise before me as I write the story of my experience among thy dusky children, of my success in warming their hearts to revere their incomparable religion and its holiest Founder. Happy the karma that brought me to thy shores!"

In the service of securing Buddhism against the depredations of Christian missionaries, Olcott wrote a popular Buddhist catechism and designed a seven-colored Buddhist flag that is used to this day. He also helped establish Buddhist schools to compete with the ones run by the Christians. At the time of his death in 1907 there were 205 Buddhist grammar schools and three high schools, a significant accomplishment.

Olcott's most important contribution to the revival, however, was the influence he had in inspiring a young Sinhalese Buddhist nationalist, Dharmapala, who had served him as an interpreter and aide-de-camp. Before Dharmapala, Buddhist revivalism had not yet achieved political density of any kind and posed little threat to colonial power. While some revivalists wanted to oust the British, others merely wanted the colonial authorities to reassume the responsibilities they had agreed to in the Kandyan Convention. Dharmapala injected the politics of revivalism with a fierce militancy, rallied the Sinhalese for a fight against colonial bondage, and gave ideological shape to the concept of Sinhalese Buddhist identity. Part messiah and part Malcolm X, Dharmapala is considered a pivotal figure in the struggle for Sinhalese redemption. "Low though the fortunes of the dharma had sunk," a biography of Dharmapala remarks, "the great beam of national karma was beginning to right itself and gigantic forces were about to be set in motion which in the future would lift them to a position high, even as their present one was low."

According to the biography, Dharmapala's mother prayed before a statue of Buddha every morning and received subtle spiritual emanations which made her "a fit receptacle" for the "Great Being" who was to come. During the third term of her pregnancy, monks came to the house every day to chant and light incense. Then, "like a vivid flash of lightning from a black and stormy sky," Dharmapala was born, "as though to strike evil at its very heart."

Dharmapala came from a traditional high-caste family of wealthy entrepreneurs who had made a great deal of money making and selling furniture in Colombo. He was trained in Buddhism early on by his parents, even though he was sent to Christian schools. He learned the Bible by heart but was expelled from one school when he drew a picture of a monkey and labeled it "Christ." Dharmapala then went to the prestigious St. Thomas College, a secondary school just outside of Colombo, where he was caned for going home to spend the Sinhalese New Year with his family in violation of the warden's instructions. Riots that broke out in Colombo between Catholics and Buddhists led Dharmapala's father to remove him from school.

Dharmapala became a clerk in the Education Department in Colombo and passed tests for promotion into the elite Ceylon civil service. When he heard Olcott preach favorably about Buddhism, he was so stirred that he joined the Theosophical Society and put himself at the service of Olcott and Madame Blavatsky. Dharmapala learned Pali, the language of the ancient Buddhist scriptures, and traveled the countryside with Olcott, sleeping in the lower bunk of Olcott's two-tiered oxcart.

During this time, Dharmapala came to an understanding of how deeply Western culture had tainted Sinhalese society and culture. "He saw how the influence of the missionaries had eaten into the vitals of the people and was corroding all that was noblest in their national character," the biography explains. "He saw that the dharma was crumbling and used all his efforts to amplify and broadcast Olcott's vindications of Buddhism and the appeal for a revival."

In Dharmapala's demonology, both Christianity and the British were threats. Christians were "slaves of passion," he wrote, controlled by baser instincts. The British, similarly, were still living in a state of savagery, little different from the days before they were conquered by the Romans. "Although they are a powerful race today their hereditary tendencies of primitive barbarism still cling to them. Cruelty, drunkenness, slaughter of innocent animals, wifebeating, roasting the whole ox on feast days, promiscuous dancing of men and women regardless of the laws of decency are the vestiges of the primitive customs when they lived half naked and painted their bodies and wore skins to ward off the cold. . . . Practices which were an abomination to the ancient noble Sinhalese have today become tolerated under the influence of Semitic sociology: opium, arrack, alcohol, ganja and other poisons distributed in the villages without regard for the degenerating effect they have on men. . . . The sweet, tender, gentle Aryan children of an ancient historical race are sacrificed at the altar of the whiskey-drinking, beef-eating, belly-god of heathenism. How long, oh how long, will unrighteousness last in Ceylon?"

Dharmapala's remedy for Sinhalese moral degeneration was the rediscovery of Buddhism, which would not only redeem the society culturally but lead to political freedom as well. "In the dharma is embodied all that is useful for the salvation of all beings," wrote Dharmapala. "It has one taste—the taste of emancipation." He also insisted that the Sinhalese look for inspiration to their own "brilliant" history, which he called "the literature of the science of patriotism." What he was referring to, though, was neither history nor science, but a set of Sinhalese folk myths drawn from ancient epics like the *Mahavamsa*, composed in the sixth century by monks, which highlighted a militant role for Buddhism and a romantic view of the past. "Let the *Mahavamsa* be your guide," Dharmapala exhorted.

According to the *Mahavamsa*, the Buddha foresaw the demise of Buddhism in India, where it was born, and a bright future for it on the island at its southern tip among an Aryan people from northern India whom he would divinely steer there. First, however, the island had to be cleared of the supernatural demonic beings who lived there, the Yakkas, deemed unworthy of spiritual enlightenment by the Buddha on one of his earlier visits. Calling forth a chaos of wind, rain, and darkness, the Buddha expelled the Yakkas to an island he made materialize off the eastern coast.

Meanwhile, as this *dharmadipa*, or "island of the teaching," was being purified, the forebears of the Sinhalese race were making their way across the waters of the Bay of Bengal, led by Vijaya, a renegade prince. As a punishment for a life of extortion, pillage, and terror, Vijaya and his seven hundred followers were set adrift in unseaworthy boats. Certain doom was in store for them until the Buddha, now on his deathbed, saw Vijaya and his men and implored the gods to protect him, so that Buddhism could transplant itself from India and thrive on the Lankan isle. After that, an emissary of the Buddha flew over the men, sprinkled holy water over them, and tied white strings around their wrists for protection, enabling them to land safely. Eventually, with the help of imported "Aryan" maidens said to have blood ties to the family of the Buddha himself, Vijaya and his band established the Sinhalese race, which prospered as it readied the island for the coming of Buddhism. Several centuries later, the Buddhist emperor of south India, Asoka, sent an emissary to convert Mahinda, a Sinhalese prince, who in turn converted his father, Tissa, a powerful Sinhalese king.

A later installment of the *dharmadipa* myth took up the story a few centuries later when a powerful Tamil king, Elaru, had taken control of the Sinhalese throne and allowed Buddhist institutions to wither. A young Sinhalese prince, Duttugemunu, raised an army from a splinter Sinhalese kingdom in the south and marched north to "reconquer" the island. Taking up arms had not come easy for the good Buddhist prince and his followers. His father had forbidden it. But the demise of Buddhism threatened the Sinhalese, and the prince despaired. Why was he doubled up in bed? his mother asked him. "Over there beyond the river are the Tamils pressing in on me," replied the prince. "And on the other side is the speechless sea. So how can I lie with outstretched limbs?"

Disobeying his father's instructions (in keeping with his name, which translates as "Undutiful"), the prince eventually went north to vanquish the Tamils with an army of thousands, including a column of five hundred monks. In some accounts, the prince held a spear with a relic of the Buddha embedded in its tip. After a long siege against the capital city of Anuradhapura, in which thousands of Elaru's followers were killed, the battle was decided in heroic, single-handed combat between Duttugemunu and Elaru, each mounted on an elephant. Younger, stronger, and filled with the righteousness of the dharma, Duttugemunu vanquished the Tamil king, and Lanka was reunited as a single Sinhalese kingdom.

"Not for glory but for the religion do I wage this battle," Duttugemunu was said to have declared. Nevertheless, his conscience bothered him, until a group of Buddhist holy men absolved him of guilt. "By this deed there is no obstruction to thy way to heaven," they explained. Only one and a half men were really slain in the battle, as only one of Elaru's men had been a Buddhist—another was half converted at the time. "Unbelievers and men of evil life were the rest, not more to be esteemed than beasts. But as for thee, thou wilt bring glory to the religion of the Buddha in many ways. Therefore cast away care from thy heart, O Ruler of Men." All he had to do to atone was to implement a program of state patronage toward Buddhism. Duttugemunu therefore constructed holy shrines and underwrote a massive public works program in the name of Buddhism, inaugurating the great Sinhalese "Golden Age."

According to myth, the Golden Age was a time when Sinhala kings held dominion over the entirety of ancient Ceylon and were guided by Buddhist principles and ethics. "Our ancestors, like the ancient Greeks," Dharmapala explained, taking a decidedly romantic view of the past, "were free from pride and envy, crime and luxury. There were no capitalists and landowners, but everyone had his own chena field and the village forest and village pasture gave them the right to graze their cows and cut firewood. Buddhism gave them the religion of the middle path and the Sinhalese did not care for wealth but cared more for virtue and courage."

Anuradhapura, the first of the two great Sinhalese kingdoms, had "a dazzling magnificence," with nine-story houses—taller than any in the world at that time—and streets crowded day and night by throngs of pilgrims and traders. The atmosphere was saturated with the fragrance of sweet-smelling flowers and delicate perfumes. Shouts of "Sadhu! Sadhu!" filled the air. The king was filled with great charity, giving land for widows and bulls to carry cripples. He also built hospitals and dispensaries, luxuriant parks and an extensive network of tanks and irrigation canals. "All was done by the impelling force of the religion of the Buddha," Dharmapala remarked.

Dharmapala's revival of the memories of ancient Sinhalese greatness coincided with the restoration of the ruins of the ancient cities of Anuradhapura and Polonnaruwa, the second great Sinhalese capital, both of which had been rediscovered by British colonial officials in the nineteenth century after being swallowed up by the jungle. In the later 1800s the British began archaeological excavations, envisioning the political prestige to be had in restoring the ancient sites as centers of regional administration. The Sinhalese, however, took a different lesson from the project, finding in the two lost cities a symbol of their reawakened national grandeur.

The resuscitation of ancient Sinhalese myth may have encouraged Sinhalese national pride and raised consciousnesses for the struggle against British colonialism, but for the ethnically mixed society that Ceylon had become it was divisive, racist, and aggressive.

"This island belongs to the Buddha himself," read one of Dharmapala's favorite mythological passages. "Therefore the residence of wrong believers on the island will never be permanent, just as the residence of the Yakkas of the ancient past was not permanent. Even if a non-Buddhist should rule Ceylon by force for a while, it is a particular power of the Buddha that his [the non-Buddhist] line will never be established. As Lanka is suitable only for Buddhist kings, only their lines will be established." Such literal interpretations of the myth justified violence, even genocide, in the name of Buddhism.

Furthermore, Dharmapala's resurrected mythology presupposed a Sinhala national identity based on a common Sinhala language, a common Buddhist religion, and a common Aryan racial stock. In fact, such an identity was really the recent creation of a nationalistic imagination, devoid of anthropological and historical validity. Anthropological evidence suggests that the term "Sinhalese" was not a broad ethnic term but only described a tiny political and social elite that may not have spoken Sinhalese exclusively or even practiced Buddhism.

Dharmapala also claimed that a "unitary state" had existed since the consolidation of Lanka under the first Buddhist king, Tissa. In fact, there was rarely a single unifying government in control through most of early Lankan history. When there was, it was unlikely that it was exclusively Sinhala Buddhist in character. In the south, there was constant fragmentation due to rivalries among various Sinhala rulers, and for many centuries a Tamil kingdom controlled the north, separated from the south by a thick growth of jungle across the country's midriff.

Still another historical fallacy lay in the idea that the Tamils and Sinhalese were locked in a primordial battle for survival—genocidal contests between whole populations on each side. Reality was not so clear-cut, however. More evidence suggests that these wars were really struggles between two kings over issues of fealty and dynastic expansion. Linked to the idea of Tamils and Sinhalese locked in inexorable wars of racial extinction was the false claim that it was the invading Tamil armies of south India who were exclusively responsible for ruining the great Sinhalese Golden Age. Completely ignored was the darker, more fractious side of the Sinhalese national character. Although Tamil invasions played a role in bringing down these kingdoms, so did civil wars and bloody succession battles, often involving parricide and fratricide.

But the most dangerous fallacy perpetuated by Dharmapala was the so-called Aryan origins of the Sinhalese. Dharmapala claimed that the Sinhalese originated in northern Indian Aryan stock and had retained that racial purity over the centuries, which, combined with their sacred Buddhist mandate, made them an exceptional people of great historical importance. In fact, the Sinhalese did speak a language that was rooted in Sanskrit, which is classified by linguists as an Aryan tongue. But the Sinhalese assertion that they were an unsullied Aryan people withered before a wide body of archaeological and anthropological evidence. Historical patterns of migration had mixed the Sinhalese in with peoples of south India as well as aboriginal Lankans. Tamil-Sinhalese and Aryan-Dravidian distinctions were therefore impossible to draw.

Nevertheless, like their German counterparts, Sinhalese intellectuals used Aryan theory to define their own glorious national identity and to denigrate minorities. A magazine called *The Aryan* was started in 1906 and a book of "Aryan" Sinhalese names was a best-seller around that time, too. In the late thirties there was much cheering for Hitler's racial programs, especially his policies banning mixed marriages. As Sinhala nationalists called for a struggle to cleanse their society of elements that were *thuppai*—a derogatory term for something bastardized and impure—Nazi propaganda poured into the country and comparisons were drawn between the Thousand-Year Reich and the multimillennial reign of the Buddha outlined in ancient myth.

Assertions of Sinhalese singularity contradicted the strong cultural similarities between the Tamils and the Sinhalese that had existed for centuries. In physical appearance, kinship networks, caste organization, and diet, the two groups show a long history of intertwinement. Though the initial Sinhalese migrants to Lanka were probably Indo-European speakers from Aryan northern India, practically all later arrivals were Tamil-speaking south Indians who were absorbed into the Sinhala Buddhist polity and given status through the operation of the Sinhalese caste system, the very existence of which, in a Buddhist country, was a declaration of the deep penetration of Hinduism in Sinhala Buddhist culture.

The most obvious symbolic expression of the symbiosis that existed between the two groups was the Nāyakkar dynasty that reigned over the Kandyan kingdom from 1739 until the British seized power in 1815. Lacking a successor to the throne of appropriate royal lineage and high ritual status, Sinhalese chiefs in Kandy were forced to solicit a Tamil Hindu prince from south India. In fact, one of these Tamil-blooded kings of Kandy sponsored a mini-revival of Buddhism and Sinhala arts and literature.

There was also a great deal of interplay between the two religious traditions, especially in the great number of shared gods and spiritual concepts. Although these differed slightly, they could still be considered leaves from one tree. Unlike more exclusivistic religions like Christianity and Islam, Hinduism and Buddhism are syncretic, allowing the absorption of other practices within their own spiritual framework. In many Lankan temples the image used to depict the Buddha had elements common to the portrayal of the god Vishnu, the Hindu Preserver. Furthermore, some places of worship now considered exclusively Hindu or Buddhist were for long periods of time holy to both, where worshippers bathed together before going to different shrines that shared the same ritual ground.

Whatever its fallaciousness, Dharmapala's mytho-historical revisionism struck a deep chord in the minds of the Sinhalese Buddhists, providing a way for them to assert themselves against the Westernized Ceylonese elite. Although only 8 percent of the island's population was Christian, this minority had a monopoly on positions of influence in society and set the cultural tone in a decidedly Western key. With extensive holdings in land, industrial concessions bestowed on them by the British, and plum positions in the civil service and political establishment, they had disproportionate privileges and status that made Buddhists almost pathologically envious.

Its members also led a lifestyle that was unquestionably decadent by the puritanical standards of the revivalist Buddhists, featur-

ing gambling, promiscuity, and drinking. The egregious sycophancy
and comic imitativeness of the elite toward the British drew scorn,
too. Even worse was the superior attitude that these Westernized
Ceylonese displayed toward the Buddhists, the way they viewed local
customs in the same way the British did: as the residue of Oriental
barbarism. "They made us feel like mutts," one Sinhalese monk
said of the Christian Ceylonese, with barely suppressed anger.

Restoration of the traditional Buddhist order, then, would be
more than simple cultural rectification. It would also provide a vehicle for moral revulsion, class envy, and deep pools of humiliation
that had accumulated through centuries of alien rule, to be driven
less at the overlords than at the "black Englishmen" who had been
their compradors.

8 · 1956: Cultural Revolution

INDEPENDENCE in 1948 did little to relieve Sinhalese Buddhist political and social discontent. Although the British gave Ceylon its freedom, the Westernized elite that took power remained opposed to the kind of traditional society Buddhist nationalists envisioned. It wasn't until the national elections of 1956 that the slowly rising tide of Sinhalese nationalism made itself felt. When it did, the effect was sweeping—the old order was submerged forever, and with it the old elite and their vision of a secular Ceylon.

Ironically, the man who vanquished that old political elite rose up from their very ranks. The Oxford-educated scion of one of the country's Anglicized families, Solomon West Ridgeway Dias Bandaranaike never learned to write the language of the Sinhala Buddhist community he championed. As with many other elite families, the Bandaranaikes had graciously served the British in important positions as headmen, judges, civil servants, and political appointees. An ancestor, Don Stephan Bandaranaike, even received a medal from the British extolling his loyal service during the Kandyan Uprising of 1818. The Bandaranaikes took ocean liners to England, wore Western clothes, had British accents, read Tennyson, fussed over visiting British royalty, and took pride in their light-colored skin. By the mid-1800s, according to one family history, some of them had "sloped so distinctly to the West" that they lost the ability to converse in Sinhala.

S.W.R.D. Bandaranaike's father had been knighted by the British and had led the life of a country gentleman. He wasn't particularly interested in politics and was a great believer in class privilege. Lower-caste women on his estate, for example, were forced to go topless, as caste requirements ordained, and members of the laboring castes knew better than to look Bandaranaike Sr. in the eye if he passed them on horseback. He was a loyal and conservative member of the Anglican Church and he named his son after Sir James West Ridgeway, then the British governor.

On the face of things it would seem baffling that the junior Bandaranaike felt alienated from his class. He was born with all the appurtenances of wealth and privilege. After graduating from Colombo's St. Thomas College, Bandaranaike headed to Oxford, where he was profoundly disillusioned by British racism. Some scholars date Bandaranaike's cultural awakening to the day that he lost the Oxford Union election—a large contingent of voters came out because they didn't want to see a "black" man win.

Nonetheless, back in Ceylon, Bandaranaike resumed the Anglicized life, courting maidens along Lady Horton's Drive in Kandy and enjoying other Westernized pleasures like dog shows and horse races. But he also became interested in Ceylonese politics. Like other politically ambitious Sinhalese Christians of that pivotal time, Bandaranaike converted to Buddhism. At independence in 1948, he became part of the government that took power from the British. And in 1956 he ran for Prime Minister himself, and was swept into power on a wave of popular Sinhala Buddhist nationalism.

As the candidate representing revivalist efforts to restore Buddhism to its proper place and to redeem Sinhalese society from Western decadence, Bandaranaike was given a great boost by the coming of the Buddha Jayanthi in 1956. Jayanthi was the 2,500-year anniversary of the Buddha's enlightenment, the very epicenter of his 5,000-year teaching. At that point, Buddhists believed, the dharma would be spread throughout the world and would produce an unprecedented spiritual awakening. In Lanka, Jayanthi had even greater significance, marking the completion of 2,500 years of Buddhism, the life of the Sinhalese race, and the length of recorded history and continuous political institutions, a threefold event of great mystical power in the Sinhalese mind.

Jayanthi quickly became a rallying point for revivalist political energies. The government gave large sums of money to various Buddhist groups for Jayanthi celebrations, and these flattering attentions filled Buddhist leaders with a new sense of their own potential power and political importance.

Preparations for Jayanthi prompted the Sinhalese to make an unsparing examination of the inferior place that Buddhism had in Ceylonese society, a condition that was even more troubling to them now that the country had been given its independence. A Committee of Inquiry compiled a catalogue of complaints in a report entitled "The Betrayal of Buddhism," which Bandaranaike endorsed. "In this country now, although there is no visible foreign yoke in the form of a colonial government," the report insisted, "we are as subject as we were before we broke loose from the British bond a few years ago to the invisible yoke of evil, unenlightened teachings, practices, habits, customs, and views fostered by the British. Thus we are still in moral bondage to the West."

The report clearly assumed a connection between the health of Buddhism and the fate of the Sinhalese people. The dharma, "the quintessence of human thought," it explained in its introduction, was comparable to the air the people breathe or the blood that flowed in their veins. "With the abandonment of the dharma, the people of the country shall wither, fade away, or perish. Therefore those who are trying to make the people of this country accept false teachings, all the apostles of unenlightened teachings in this country, are undermining the foundation of the social structure of Buddhist Lanka."

After more than a century and a half of British efforts to destroy the Lankan legacy, the report enumerated British infractions against Buddhism as an institution. The British attempted to break down the old system of obligatory labor owed to temples, they stole 800,000 acres of temple land by registration fraud, and they used legal rules to block transfer of ownership and bequests of private lands to temples, according to the report. It also criticized the government for allowing Christian religions too much institutional influence in the country. As a result, the report declared, "Christianity sits enthroned, and Ceylon, bound hand and foot, has been delivered to the foot of the Cross."

The report also articulated widespread Buddhist complaints against government education policies, which were dominated by the Christian missionaries. Such policies had produced a "denationalized" people who were ashamed of their own history and culture, the report maintained. Other complaints involved the disparities in funding between Buddhist schools and those run by Christians and the overrepresentation of Christians in policymaking and teaching positions. Turning its critical eye on government social services, the report saw the same wrongs in hospitals and orphanages as it did in schools: undue attempts to use these services in the pursuit of conversions, and preferential treatment for Christians at the expense of Buddhists.

In addition to its far-ranging critique of contemporary Ceylonese society, "The Betrayal of Buddhism" set forth a program for reform. In so doing it affirmed the importance of governmental action for the protection of Buddhism, articulating a role for democratic government much akin to the religious responsibilities of the traditional Sinhalese king. The Committee of Inquiry called for the establishment of a Buddha Sasana Council, invested with all the old powers of the Sinhalese kings, which would be made up of both monks and laymen. It would be the government's responsibility to pay a certain yearly sum, reparations in effect, to the Sasana Council to compensate for the numerous administrative acts during the colonial period. With those funds, the Sasana Council would implement more specific reforms in schools, social services, the economy, and laws governing public morality.

In education, the report recommended that Buddhists be given equal opportunity to rectify imbalances favoring Christians and called for curriculum reform that would produce students with an intimate awareness of the national language, history, and culture instead of narrow skills useful to the colonial civil service.

In social services, the committee wanted to make it a punishable offense for an orphanage run by one religious sect to take an orphan of another religion into its care. It also wanted to terminate the contracts of religious workers in state-run hospitals. Conversion of a child without the parents' awareness and permission would also have become criminal.

Arguing a link between economic prosperity and a revivified Buddhism, recommendations for economic reform were bound up with reforms that would regenerate traditional morality and discourage the excesses of the Westernized elite. Buddhists, it was said, should promote a movement for plain living, discourage ostentation in cars and houses, and ban the consumption of liquor at governmental functions. These changes would do more than encourage traditional moral values, however. They would also free up resources for investment in the country's economic development and stop the outflow of precious hard currency that was being spent on foreign luxury items at the expense of local industries.

The committee closed its report with a disclaimer. It was not attempting to gain a favored position for Buddhists at the expense of other religious groups, however much they have suffered at their hands in former times. "We ask no favors nor expect none. But we do ask for and expect the right to a decent education for our children, the right to save our country from becoming an Eastern outpost of the Vatican, the right to be allowed to profess and practice our religion without let or hindrance, material or spiritual, secular or religious, in a free and democratic Ceylon."

During the time of the Buddha Jayanthi, many popular prophecies were revived which held that a universal king, a bodhisattva or Buddha-in-progress, would arrive and redeem the Sinhalese from degraded subservience. Such prophecies spurred a popular cult of the Diyasena, or Great Deliverer, with an undercurrent of millennial longing that Bandaranaike was able to exploit, largely through charismatic oratory. (He may never have mastered written Sinhala but his command of spoken Sinhala was magnificent.) Many of these speeches were delivered at the sacred cities of Anuradhapura and Polonnaruwa. "It was not right," he thundered to his audience during one speech, "that a servile race should inhabit the same locality which their ancestors inhabited in power and glory."

His political genius was to shed his Westernized identity and to depict his political motives in a vocabulary that embodied the chief impulses of Buddhist revivalism. In doing so, Bandaranaike self-consciously sacralized his populist appeals with references to the glorious Sinhala past. It was a responsibility of the secular ruler to oversee and regulate Buddhist affairs, he claimed, and to rule in accordance with the principles of the dharma, "lest disaster befall the country." Bandaranaike also depicted his political agenda as a modern-day "reconquest," although his militancy was directed less against foreign invaders themselves than against the damaging impact of colonialism. Since more than two-thirds of Ceylon was Buddhist, it was "inevitable" that Buddhism would become the "state religion," he remarked. Making Buddhism the state religion would usher in an era of "religio-democratic socialism" in which the Sinhalese would have a dominant position, politically, economically, and socially, consistent with their status as the majority community.

Bandaranaike's election manifesto embraced the "Betrayal of Buddhism" report, which earned him great support, especially among two key constituencies, Sinhalese Buddhist monks and the Sinhala-speaking intelligentsia. Traditionally, the monks had been seen as the moral guardians of the nation and had operated as both teachers and advisers to the king. They had also been leading figures in the educational and religious life of the Sinhalese village. Under the British, the monks had grown irrelevant, and after independence, their advice and perspective were still not solicited. Promising them a larger role in the restored Buddhist society he envisioned, Bandaranaike was able to unite them.

Concerns for status were also paramount in Bandaranaike's other core constituency, the vernacular-educated intelligentsia, which included teachers, Ayurvedic physicians practicing indigenous medicine, clerks in the lower rungs of the civil service, and others aspiring to coveted white-collar positions. An increase in the number of secondary schools in the south meant that there was a wider pool of Sinhalese who wanted jobs in the government sector.

But better and more numerous jobs went to Tamils, who received better training in English in the missionary schools in the north. If Buddhist interests took over the government, positions in the apparatus of government would open up for them, as Bandaranaike had guaranteed job quotas that reflected their numbers as a majority.

The issue that burnished Bandaranaike's appeal more than any other was his support for legislation that would make Sinhala the official language of government, which had been a major recommendation of the "Betrayal of Buddhism" report. Although only a tiny minority of the country spoke it eight years after independence, English was still the language of the courts and the police, of parliamentary debate and government administration, as well as banking and university instruction. This fed a deep sense of alienation among vernacular speakers.

Initially, the Sinhala-language movement was purely anti-Western, but later it began to develop anti-Tamil overtones as well. Originally, both Tamil and Sinhalese nationalists agreed that English should no longer be the official Ceylonese language, and embraced the movement for *swabasha*, a term meaning "mother tongue," which would have given equal status to Tamil and Sinhalese. Soon, however, "Sinhala Only" became the battle cry in the language issue, as the Sinhalese majority asserted its nationalist agenda and Bandaranaike leapt to exploit its power. "You know, my dear fellow," he told an interviewer, "I have never found anything to excite the people in quite the way this language issue does."

For monks, Sinhala Only provided an avenue for the reclamation of the lost status and influence they enjoyed in traditional society. It would also give a boost to the general level of religious practice in the country; in their minds the health of the language was inextricably bound up with the vitality of Buddhism itself. For teachers in the vernacular schools it meant the end of a two-tiered pay scale in which their counterparts in English-language schools were paid nearly twice as much and were accorded considerably higher status. For Ayurvedic physicans, Sinhala Only meant renewed respect for their indigenous medical tradition, long under assault by their Western-style colleagues. Many students who would face either jobless-ness or severe underemployment believed that once Sinhala was made the official language it would be they, the sons of the soil, and not their English-educated mates, who would be given plum spots in law, medicine, engineering, and in the ranks of government service as clerks. Sinhala was the language of the majority, Bandaranaike reminded the crowd. "The unemployment and economic problems of the country can be solved to a great extent by making Sinhala the state language."

Heading into the elections of 1956, the candidate of the United National Party, the incumbent President, Sir John Kotelaluwa, looked assured of victory. The UNP was the very embodiment of the political and social elite that British colonialism had left behind. Looking forward after independence, they had seen a bright future for themselves and their nation. In the short period since independence, Sir John had established himself on the international scene and was a source of great pride to the island. Among the UNP's accomplishments were social and economic advances. The number of children attending primary school and going on to secondary education was at an all-time high, there were steady increases in tea, rubber, and coconut production, and the country was steadily developing and expanding the infrastructure of transportation and power grids left behind by the British.

Beneath the surface, however, there was much political disaffection, especially among the Buddhists. Although elements of the liberal, Westernized elite had appealed to the Buddhist majority and promised to revive tradition after independence, those appeals were forgotten. Instead, the government adopted a policy of bemused neglect toward the Buddhist majority in general and toward the Buddhist establishment in particular.

Such neglect was underscored by the relative economic deterioration of the Sinhalese majority under the first eight years of UNP government, despite superficial appearances of economic prosperity. Housing programs established for the poor were more than outweighed by mansions built by the rich. Increases in rice production and surging exports were more than offset by population increases. And increasingly, the nation's schools were churning out graduates, particularly graduates educated in the vernacular Sinhala, who had little hope of finding adequate employment.

Economic disaffection was sharpened by the film of petty scandal, official corruption, and moral taint that hung over the UNP government. It was widely held that Sir John was a friend of big business. He was also seen as out of touch with Buddhist morality and the conventions of a puritanical Eastern society. Some monks even went so far as to read aloud from his memoirs in temples to prove that his uninhibited worldliness and immoderate deeds made him unfit for high public office, stressing his renowned sexual appetites and champagne tastes.

A famous political cartoon of the day depicted him as leading the forces of Mara, the god of evil, as he attacked the Buddha while he sought enlightenment beneath the bo tree. A dead calf in the foreground alluded to Sir John's shocking decision to carve a calf in public view at a barbecue. In the background was the figure of Uncle Sam holding dollar signs aloft, as well as a bevy of wanton-looking Westernized women. "The fight against the forces of evil—2,500 years ago and now," the cartoon caption read. "In this year of Buddha Jayanthi, rescue your country, your race and religion from the forces of evil."

Bandaranaike embodied an entirely different cultural orientation. Although his Sinhala identity was assumed in later life, he was attentive to its nuances. Although he was a democrat, his vision of democracy was shaped by his feeling for the collective consciousness of the Sinhalese as expressed in the ancient chronicles. And his high-caste status and family connections in the south helped him a great deal, too, especially among the vernacular elite.

The key to Bandaranaike's electoral success in 1956 was the organizational weight and support of the monks, who buried long-standing doctrinal and sectarian disputes to help get out the vote. Cruising villages in cars, walking in their yellow robes on lonely jungle roads, and going door to door, monks proclaimed that a vote for the UNP and Sir John was a vote for the shadowy conspiracy called Catholic Action, while a vote for Bandaranaike's party was a vote for Buddhist rights and the restoration of the proper order.

In the monks' millenarian vision, Bandaranaike's coalition was a cleansing force that would sweep away things alien and impure. Even if the peasants weren't ardent Buddhists, the villagers' sensitivity to Sinhala Buddhist national symbols elicited a strong response. "The end of the *sasana* will not be long if we remain in silence," according to a pamphlet circulating at the time. "We appeal to bhikkhus to visit every Buddhist home and direct them on the right path. You may have to confront many difficulties. Be ready to sacrifice your life to restore a Buddhist Ceylon."

The 1956 election was a crushing landslide victory for Bandaranaike, sweeping an entirely new breed of government officials into power. Except for Bandaranaike himself and one other minister, the entire government was new to public office. At the opening of Parliament later that year, the cultural shift was symbolized in the Sinhala language and music that was used in the opening ceremonies as well as the national dress—white sarong and banyan cloth—worn by all the officials. In the galleries above sat row upon row of robed monks. Afterward, at a reception, coconut milk and soft drinks were served.

Bandaranaike's victory had its positive aspects. It opened up the political system to greater grass-roots participation, and it gave a boost to popular Buddhism. Additionally, many secular intellectuals who had once disdained Buddhist culture were starting to explore its more esoteric strains.

But in the long run, the Buddhist resurgence of 1956 became a vehicle for the darker elements in the Sinhala psyche. "That year, 1956, had great intentions behind it," Reggie Michael, an elderly Tamil journalist from "those days," explained one afternoon as we drove by the Bandaranaike family home. "The problem was, as we all now know, the road to hell can be paved with incredibly good intentions."

The first casualty of 1956 was the concept of a multiracial, secular society. The result was a decline in relations with the Tamils. In the beginning, Sinhalese Buddhist nationalism was born as a reaction to Western colonialism. To the extent that there was anti-Tamil sentiment, it ran beneath the surface. Buddhist revivalists generally considered Hinduism a sister Eastern religion also suffering oppression from Western Christianity. After 1956, however, the course of Sinhalese Buddhist nationalism veered in a decidedly exclusive direction.

The trajectory of this broad shift in dynamics between the two communities was written in the politics of language. Though originally the fight against English as the "official" language of government was a bipartisan effort, the movement for *swabasha*, or "mother tongue," soon became dominated by those backing Sinhala Only. They claimed that the Sinhala language needed affirmative action to bolster it after centuries of the primacy of English. Sinhala Only advocates also worried that if Tamil was given parity, it might overtake Sinhala, since so many more people in the region spoke it, and the cultural orbit of south India was so wide.

Had the original intent of language reform remained the implementation of both vernaculars instead of just Sinhala, the process of communal fragmentation in Ceylon would have been far less sharp. Sinhala Only, however, was a huge threat to Tamil interests, mainly in the form of jobs from which they could be excluded through hiring quotas and requirements for proficiency in Sinhala. Tamils would also suffer by being forced to conduct business with any level of government—police, banks, courts—in a language that many did not speak. Almost as bad was the severe slight that Sinhala Only represented to the culture of Tamils, who felt that their language was superior. Many Tamils would have learned Sinhala, it was said, just as avidly as they had learned English had they not been forced to, which spurred resistance. At the time, wiser minds warned that maintaining both vernaculars as the official languages of the nation was essential to future peace and unity. Two languages would make for one unified nation, they advised. But one language would surely result in the division of the country into two separate nations. Such sage counsel, however, did not stop the passage of the Sinhala Only Bill in 1956. As a result, relations between the two communities grew poisoned.

The British imagined they were leaving behind a society that accepted European notions of nationalism and civilization. But while

British colonialism inculcated the upper classes with a sense of national identity, a Ceylonese national identity did not exist outside this small, culturally estranged elite.

One reason for this was that Ceylon had not fought for its independence; a common struggle might have forged closer bonds between the various ethnic groups. The British were also adept at exploiting the natural divisions in Ceylonese society to thwart independence movements. Furthermore, nationalism, at least in the Western sense, was a foreign notion. In fact, the closest word for "national feeling" in the Sinhalese language was one that literally meant "race consciousness." Recognizing this, the Donoughmore Commission, a group sent by the British in 1928 to look into the prospects of establishing democracy in Ceylon, had warned: "It is almost time to say that the conception of patriotism in Ceylon is as much racial as national, and that the best interests of the country are synonymous with the welfare of a particular section of its people."

Increasing hostility between Tamil and Sinhalese was a function of the economic legacy of colonialism as well. British tactics of divide and rule favored the minority Tamils over the majority Sinhalese in terms of government jobs. Tamils also enjoyed other advantages. Perhaps because of the more capacious, flexible nature of Hindu traditions, Tamils were able to become Christians without losing their cultural identity, which made it easier for them to absorb a Western work ethic in turn, leading to greater opportunities in government bureaucracies and the professions.

After independence, middle-class Sinhalese began to assert their ethnicity as a weapon in the public competition for privilege and position. By the time Bandaranaike had come to power, Buddhists believed a long-overdue rectification had arrived. "The thinking was this," a prominent Buddhist government official told me. "Let us not annihilate the Tamils, but let us reverse our positions with them in order to get our due."

The Sinhalese bid to reverse positions with the Tamils, however, came at considerable cost to the country as a whole, and to themselves. Bitter over the perceived advantages that the Tamils received under colonialism, the Sinhalese cut their nose to spite their own face by embracing measures that retarded economic growth and lowered standards, just as long as they brought the Tamils down a peg in the process. Perhaps the most destructive legacy of colonialism was the psychological one, which as the years progressed saw relations between the two groups increasingly governed by the politics of spite and the urge to level.

As the darker side of the revolution of 1956 became more apparent, Tamils grew alarmed and began a program of nonviolent protests aimed at ensuring their rights and opportunities. Even Bandaranaike was surprised by the momentum of his policies. According to historians, Buddhist nationalism was less a matter of conviction than a vehicle for his own ambition; he had never intended that policies designed to exalt the Sinhalese should penalize the Tamils unfairly. As James Manor, one of his biographers explains, Bandaranaike told Sinhalese crowds what they wanted to hear, and reserved the right to change course after they melted away. Once in office, he planned to restore harmony through quiet concessions that would soothe Tamil anxiety and disaffection. Consequently, Bandaranaike tried in a very statesmanlike way to make Tamil a language of government in the north and east and to grant Tamils a limited form of autonomy in relation to the central government.

But the Sinhalese masses, led by opportunistic Sinhala demagogues and militant Sinhalese monks, responded with howls of protest. "The time has come for the whole Sinhalese race, which has existed for 2,500 years jealously safeguarding its language and religion, to fight without giving any quarter to save its birthright," warned the future president J. R. Jayawardene.

Bandaranaike was unable to check the Sinhalese passions on which he had ridden into power. In 1958, the island was rocked by riots, in which several hundred Tamils were killed, the first in a series of anti-Tamil pogroms to come. In some cases, trains and cars were stopped by angry mobs, their passengers assaulted and burned alive. Bandaranaike claimed that tensions and turmoil were inevitable for a country going through a major cultural transition. It was days before he declared martial law, and afterward the Tamils were deeply shaken.

Bandaranaike personally fell victim to the very forces of Sinhalese Buddhist chauvinism he had unleashed. He owed a great debt to the monks who had supported him in the 1956 campaign, and had paid off that debt by rewarding them with positions of influence in his government. According to some accounts, these monks functioned as a kind of shadow cabinet or Star Chamber to ensure his orthodox Buddhist sentiment. One of the inner core was a monk named Buddharakkita. He was a kind of Sinhalese Richelieu or Rasputin who lived luxuriously, kept a mistress, dispensed personal patronage through a variety of contacts, and was treated with deference by the Prime Minister.

Bandaranaike had drawn criticism from Buddharakkita and his lieutenants for dragging his feet on the Sinhala Only Bill and for not responding aggressively to the Tamils when they took to the streets in protest. Bandaranaike's biggest mistake in Buddharakkita's eyes, however, was to deny the monk government permission to continue some profitable, largely illegal operations. On September 25, 1959, an assassin hired, it is said, by Buddharakkita arrived on the porch of the Prime Minister in the guise of a monk seeking an audience. While Bandaranaike stooped down to pay his ritual respects, the monk withdrew a pistol from the creases of his robe, took several steps back, and fired four shots into Bandaranaike, who died the next day.

"He thought he could run with the hares and hunt with the hounds," sighed Reggie Michael, who had been a young English-speaking Tamil journalist in the fifties, as we passed by Bandaranaike's family home. "He was wrong."

9 · Polarization

ALTHOUGH THE assassination of Bandaranaike prompted a back-lash against direct clerical involvement in Ceylonese politics, it in no way blunted the messianic energies of the cultural revolution of 1956. The following years saw the growth of a Sinhalese form of manifest destiny in which the majority used state power to restore the "just and proper order" that had been destroyed by colonialism. Justifying their claim to proprietary rights over the island with pas-sages in the ancient scripture, the Sinhalese institutionalized what scholars have called "the myth of the reconquest," vanquishing the Westernized elite and the overprivileged Tamils through legislation and government action in the same way that the hero Duttugemunu had defeated the armies of invading outlanders centuries before.

As a result, the government became a vehicle for Sinhala he-gemony, targeting the various sources of perceived historical oppres-sion. "The Tamil people must accept the fact," explained Bandaranaike's widow, who assumed power after his death and became the world's first female Prime Minister, "that the Sinhala majority will no longer permit themselves to be cheated of their rights."

One of the priorities of the government was to place control over the country's educational system in the hands of Buddhists. Although educational opportunities for Buddhists had expanded, both through their own schools and through free education in government-run facilities, the best schools were still run by Christian missionaries, who received state subsidies.

However, the drive to nationalize the schools gave rise to a backlash among Sinhalese Christians and Burghers who dominated the armed forces. This was only a temporary setback for Buddhists. After a revolt was quashed in 1962, the Sinhalese instituted policies that separated students into three language "streams"—English, Tamil, and Sinhala.

The policy of separate language streams in the schools was implemented in the name of protecting the cultural identity of all students. Yet it had the effect of discriminating against non-Sinhala speakers, particularly the Tamils, in barring them from learning that language, which had become the ticket for upward mobility. But more damaging than the discrimination against one group was the divisiveness that linguistic separatism in the schools sowed throughout Ceylonese society after 1956. Lacking a shared language, which English had been for their elders, albeit a minority of them, a generation came of age with little ability to converse with the other side, much less address the issues that divided them or build a common sense of national identity. Instead, there was social distance, which gave rise to mutual stereotyping and corrosive suspicion.

The Sinhalese also introduced major curriculum changes, laying a great emphasis on rewriting the country's history. At first, each ethnic group was allowed to teach its own version of history; the results were equally chauvinistic accounts. Later, the Tamils were able to study a history imbued with a sense of shared nationhood, while Sinhalese children were taught accounts from the *Mahavamsa*, a text that Buddhist fundamentalists took literally and which bolstered ethnic self-esteem.

Course work was laden with a strong sense of Sinhala domination. Culture and history were presented with absurd monocularity as well. Independence in 1948 was seen as independence for the Sinhalese people, not Sri Lanka, and what was presented as the Sinhala New Year ignored the fact that Tamils celebrated the same day. In addition, no Tamil-language version of the national anthem was ever composed, and the only folk heroes who were studied were Sinhala Buddhist ones. Great heroes were those who defended Lanka against invaders or restored its respect when stripped of it, somehow neglecting the many, many Tamil and Christian leaders who were in the forefront of the more secular-minded nationalist drive for freedom. "If a child's knowledge of Sri Lanka was confined to these readers," wrote a scholar who studied the curriculum during those years, "he would not even be aware that there were any people in Lanka who were not Buddhists."

Cultural chauvinism in education was matched by ethnic favoritism in economic policies, in the form of affirmative action programs for the majority in both the public and the private sector based on strict proportionalism. In the government service, which provided the single greatest source of jobs under the socialist governments elected in the sixties and seventies, rigid quotas were established for each ethnic group. Promotions were guided by ethnic favoritism as well, since they were based on mastery of Sinhala, by then the official language.

Economic preference for Sinhalese was also attained through the nationalization of much of the private sector. Invoking ancient scriptural precedents in which the Sinhalese king was expected to provide for the economic welfare of the people, the government created state corporations which were used as employment agencies for Sinhalese workers and managers to the exclusion of other groups and at the expense of overall productivity.

During the height of nationalization in the period 1970–77, in the second term of Mrs. Bandaranaike's rule, the numerous state trading corporations created in textiles, petroleum, pharmaceuticals, chemicals, fertilizers, building materials, tractors, and motion pictures were entirely dominated by the Sinhalese. Sinhalese were also given preference in the management of the tea estates, an enterprise which the Tamils had run very effectively up to that point. But government efforts to control and direct economic advantages for Sinhalese were more insidious than outright discrimination or affirmative action. To get an appointment in a newly nationalized industry, at almost any level, required the backing of a politician, usually an elected representative to Parliament belonging to the party in power. And as both the ruling and opposition parties in power in the post-1956 period were distinctly Sinhalese parties favoring their own party supporters, Tamils had very little patronage open to them. A new parliamentary system of proportional representation also cut the number of seats that Tamils could win.

The results of nationalization were clearly in favor of Sinhalese interests. By the mid-eighties, when they had 74 percent of the population, they had 85 percent of all public-sector jobs, 82 percent of all technical and professional positions, and 83 percent of all managerial and administrative appointments, a vast improvement over their pre-1956 condition.

Another expression of Sinhalese economic aggrandizement was the preference they granted themselves in land-settlement policy. At the heart of the Sinhalese longing for the lost Golden Age was the resettlement of lands in the central dry zone that had once comprised the ancient Sinhalese kingdoms. Centuries of invasions and the depredations of disease had long ago led to the dissolution of those kingdoms. One of the priorities of the Sinhalese-dominated governments after 1956 was to reopen these lands to colonization schemes. This was to be done through large-scale government irrigation projects that would make these areas habitable and arable again, followed by programs that would shift substantial numbers of Sinhalese into them from the overpopulated southern portion of the country.

Such government irrigation and colonization schemes were modest in the fifties and sixties, but in the seventies their scope widened significantly when the government launched the colossal Mahaweli Development Scheme. The project called for the Mahaweli River to be dammed at a dozen places along its course, and its waters used to irrigate rice farming through a series of reservoirs and other public works.

The Mahaweli touched chords deep in the Sinhalese psyche, reflecting an almost mystical connection between blood and soil. Redeeming those lands was part and parcel of the larger process of cultural and political redemption attempted in other parts of the society. Symbolically, the Mahaweli replicated the irrigation networks built so spectacularly by the Sinhalese kings of old and celebrated so grandly in the *Mahavamsa*. In some cases, the new irrigation works even incorporated the old structures, using the very same canals and tanks that had carried water to fertile paddies more than a thousand years before. "Agricultural resettlement paves the way for a return of our people to the very plains where their forefathers retreated," said a minister in dedicating one of the Mahaweli projects, "when the large-scale irrigation works so painstakingly built by our Sinhala kings were destroyed by invaders."

The assertion of Sinhalese entitlement, however, was not shared by the Tamils. For one, the lands being developed and colonized by Sinhalese had long been considered part of the Tamils' "traditional homelands." Like all historical claims, this was part truth and part revisionism; in fact, over the centuries the land had been populated with scattered settlements of both major ethnic groups. But the colonization efforts definitely represented a threat to Tamil control, politically and socially. Tamil-owned land in the area was also often appropriated by new Sinhalese settlers—in some cases where crops had already been sown by Tamils.

Preferential policies for admission into the universities and professional schools created the greatest controversy between the two communities. The policy of Sinhala Only had reduced places for Tamils in the civil and administrative services, and nationalization of industry had shut them out of state-owned corporations as well. But Tamils had still retained superiority in the professional services—law, medicine, engineering, academia, and accounting—because admissions policies in the universities had been protected from Sinhala chauvinism. By some estimates, Tamils accounted for up to 60 percent of the professionals in the country, which greatly exceeded their percentage of the population.

The issue of university admissions was always divisive. But by the mid-seventies, when the issue came to a head, competition for university places had grown intense. There were six qualified secondary school graduates for every one place in the university, and the ratios in professional schools were even worse. Furthermore, even those who got degrees had trouble finding jobs, creating vast pools of unemployed and underemployed young people in both communities.

The difficulties that the Sinhalese had in getting into universities on merit alone made them very receptive to conspiracy theories about the Tamils. Graders of Tamil-language exams, it was said, were handicapping the tests of Tamil students to boost admissions. "How many poor, deserving Sinhala medium students failed to gain admission to the university after years and years of study before the flickering lights of bottle lamps in their poor homes?" asked one Sinhala chauvinist. "How many such innocent intelligent and able Sinhala medium students who failed to gain admission to the university would have cried out their hearts in despair at their failure? How many students would have torn out their hair, sobbed on their pillows in the silence of the night . . . ?"

Such conspiracy theories were used to justify Sinhalese calls for a quota system that reflected the ethnic composition of the population at that time. Thus 72 percent of the university places were to be held for Sinhalese, 11 percent for Jaffna Tamils, 9 percent for Indian Tamils, 6 percent for the Muslims, and 2 percent for other minorities, mostly meaning Burghers, who had begun to flee the island in droves, fearing exactly this kind of Sinhala majoritarianism. "The prospect of 60 percent of the professionals being Tamil while 70 percent of the population is Sinhalese was self-evidently horrible," said the same outspoken Sinhalese chauvinist, "unless the experts who determine the admissions policy at the university have become mentally retarded, innocent and imbecilic infants."

As a result of the controversy, beginning in 1972 Sinhalese taking university admissions exams were given a handicap in their favor, in a racially preferential program called "the standardization of marks." The numbers of Sinhalese gaining entry to top universities increased, but their access was bought at the expense of Tamils who had scored higher.

Meanwhile, there were also changes in the basic nature of the

Ceylonese state which had profound political consequences for Tamils. Although the country's original constitution at independence had promised a secular democratic state, the constitution was changed in 1972 to reflect the increasingly Buddhist character of the state. The 1972 constitution changed the name of the country to Sri Lanka, its name during the time of its ancient glory. Sinhala was reaffirmed as the sole official language, rectifying a slight liberalization which had taken place during the late sixties. The 1972 constitution also eroded assumptions about the secular character of the state. "The Republic of Sri Lanka," read one provision, "shall give to Buddhism the foremost place and accordingly, it shall be the duty of the State to protect and foster Buddhism . . ."

The new constitution also made a distinction between "persons" and "citizens." No "person" could be deprived of life, liberty, and security, but only "citizens" were accorded freedom of thought, conscience, religion, speech, publication, movement, choice of residence, and the right to promote their own culture. In addition, no "citizen" could be discriminated against on grounds of race, religion, caste, or sex, or arrested, held in custody, or detained except in accordance with the law.

While another constitution in 1978 guaranteed wider rights for those deemed noncitizens, and accorded a wider role for the Tamil language in government administration and the courts, these constitutional changes clearly reflected Sinhalese domination in almost every facet of public life. "For the non-Sinhalese, even if they do not have Sri Lanka as their homeland, their races have other countries of their own," wrote the Sinhala arch-chauvinist Cyril Matthew in the foreword to his *Diabolical Conspiracy*, a screed on university admissions. "Hence their races will never get annihilated. But the Sinhalese have one and only one country, and that is Sri Lanka. Sri Lanka is the only country in which Sinhalese live. If the Sinhalese get annihilated in Sri Lanka as a race, they are lost forever."

Unlike the Sinhalese, Tamils had looked forward to independence as a chance to build a secular, culturally neutral nation on the foundations of freedom, equal rights, and social justice. But as

Sinhalese Buddhists grew more powerful after 1956, Tamils became more concerned for their rights in the fledgling democracy of Ceylon. They were particularly distressed by the role that militant monks had won in shaping government policies and by the way that the *Mahavamsa*, with its implicit assumption of Sinhalese proprietary rights, had been absorbed into the country's politics. The effects of the various measures taken to give preference to Sinhalese and discriminate against Tamils were devastating for the minority. In 1948, before Sinhala Only, the civil service was made up of 30 percent Tamils; in 1983 the figure was 6 percent. Between 1956 and 1970, out of the 200,000 people recruited for the newly created state corporations, nearly 99 percent were Sinhalese. Government policies also deprived Tamil areas of an industrial infrastructure—the roads, bridges, harbors, rail lines, and factories other than what was built there under British rule. They also withheld from Tamil farmers credit and other subsidies that were lavished on their Sinhalese counterparts in the south. As a result, per capita income for Tamils declined. The increasingly violent nature of politics was also a factor in Tamil economic estrangement: as the targets of Sinhalese "pogroms," Tamils had to limit their economic activity to areas in the north and east where they had traditionally been dominant.

It was the university admissions controversy and the policy of "standardizing" marks on entrance exams that did the most to disenfranchise Tamils, though. Besides the huge insult that standardization implied, with its presumption of institutionalized Tamil cheating, standardization was a stinging blow to the Tamils, wiping out their last resort economically: university educations and the professions they opened up. In 1970, Tamils accounted for 40 percent of all engineering and medical students, but by 1975, when the effects of affirmative action in favor of Sinhalese could be seen, their ranks had dwindled to 17 and 14 percent, respectively.

The sense of wrong was particularly sharp in the ranks of the educated lower middle class that had long looked to university education as the sole means of upward mobility. Unlike the upper-caste Tamils or agrarian Sinhalese who had land to fall back on, these middle and lower middle classes had no other economic lifeline but the civil service and the professional positions which required university education. For these Tamils, a central artery of life had been cut, along with the social mobility and economic security that it entailed.

The result was a generation of disaffected youth. It was these men and women who gave shape to a desire for separatism that had been building in the corners of Tamil society since the cultural revolution of 1956.

Originally, Tamil leaders had met the increasing militancy of Sinhalese Buddhist nationalism with great concern. Some had argued for the creation of a separate Tamil-language state within a federal union of Ceylon as early as 1956. But most Tamil politicians had only gone as far as to demand more constitutional protections for Tamils and greater autonomy in their areas. As relations deteriorated and it became clear that a fundamental aim of Sinhalese policy was to marginalize Tamils through institutional discrimination, more Tamils began to lose faith in the power of protest and began to think in terms of a federalist arrangement which would recognize the unitary nature of the nation of Ceylon but would at the same time grant Tamils needed control and autonomy in areas of land settlement, economic development, and language policy. But in the face of continued Sinhalese efforts to deprive Tamils of their economic and political rights, even federalism was eventually seen as an inadequate response. Radicals began calling for an independent Tamil nation that would spurn the central government entirely. "I think that every year, the development of events in the south leads us to the irresistible conclusion that the hopes of union are fading further and further," said one prominent Tamil leader in 1964. "If the leaders of the Sinhala people persist in this attitude, I say that when you are advocating federalism, we will rather choose to have a division of the country."

It took a while for such a profoundly radical shift to seep into the Tamil community at large, but in 1977 this very sentiment was put to a plebiscite of sorts when Tamils chose a slate of MPs in parliamentary elections who promised to work for an independent Tamil nation. "What is the alternative now left to the nation that has lost its rights to its language, rights to its citizenship, rights to its religion and continues day by day to lose its homelands to Sinhala colonization?" read the election manifesto of the winning Tamil party. "What is the alternative left to a nation that has lost its opportunities to receive higher education through standardization and equally its opportunities in the sphere of employment? What is the alternative to a nation that lies helpless as it is assaulted, looted, and killed by hooligans instigated by the ruling race and the security forces of the state? Where else is the alternative to the Tamil nation that gropes in the dark for its freedom?"

Just as Sinhalese nationalism was given propulsion by Dharmapala's national mythology, so, too, did Tamil nationalism gain power by a set of myths that embraced messianic destiny and cultural superiority. Although Tamil scholars had dismissed the substance of the *Mahavamsa* and other Sinhalese chronicles as "nothing but a tangled web of cleverly contrived fiction," they had absorbed the form and answered the glorification of the Sinhala people and their Aryan roots with their own celebration of a noble Dravidian past. And like the Sinhalese middle class who used myth to justify their grab for secular power, middle-class Tamils justified their assertiveness with allusions to an older order they wanted to recapture.

Sri Lankan Tamil nationalism had its roots in the Tamil nationalism on the Indian subcontinent, particularly in the linguistic nationalism of the nineteenth century which, for a time, centered on the writers of Jaffna. At first, for the upper-caste Sri Lankan Tamils at the head of this cultural reawakening, Tamil revivalism in the north was like its Sinhalese cousin in the south—a way of answering the presumed cultural superiority of Western colonialism. It was a companion to Sinhala nationalism, "one eye for two sisters, or two strains of harmony that sang of a happy home," as one Tamil historian described it. In the fifties, however, as relations began to deteriorate, Tamil nationalism became much more exclusive and began to define itself in opposition to the Sinhalese and their supremacist mythology.

According to Tamils, *they* were the chosen people of South Asia, the heirs of an old and ancient civilization that had its roots in the mythical Dravidian civilizations of Mohenjo-Daro and Harappa. Once they had dominated most of the Indian subcontinent, until destroyed by the less developed Aryans who had migrated from West Asia. Jaffna had been a sanctuary for that lost glory, a kind of South Asian Athens where erudition and argument were valued and achievements were many in medicine, astrology, and engineering. One of the three wise men who journeyed to Bethlehem was Tamil, it was alleged, and the mariners who routinely passed from the ports of northern Sri Lanka to the Annamite kingdoms on the coast of Indochina might also have been the first to visit America, centuries before Columbus. In some accounts, Tamils were the original ancient inhabitants of the island, and used it as a launching point to sweep through southern India, establishing a domain west and east across the entire Indo-European landmass.

To Sri Lankan Tamils, their Tamil dialect was the most pure, the closest remaining cousin to the Tamil that was spoken in the ninth century in India, a tongue that had been referred to, in the classical literature of the time, as "a goddess." The Tamil language, they claimed, was the oldest, richest, most copious, refined, and polished language spoken by man—more polished than Greek, more copious than Latin. "Of all the Dravidian tongues, Tamil is the most fitted to be the instrument of exact thought," wrote one linguist. "It is impossible for any European who has acquired a competent knowledge of Tamil to regard it otherwise than with a respect for the intellectual capacity of a people among whom so wonderful an organ of thought has been developed."

Like the language, the religion that predominated among the Tamils, a form of Hinduism called Saivism, was equally magnificent, "the high-water mark of Indian thought and Indian culture." And the culture that the language and religion produced was one of exceeding moral superiority, pervaded, it was said, by "an earnest aspiration after righteousness and a desire for peace," which put the Tamils at a disadvantage when faced with less civilized "bloodthirsty races" like the Aryans and Muslims.

The thrust of Tamil mythmaking was to disparage the boasts of the Sinhalese. It was pure myth that the Sinhalese migrated to the island ahead of the Dravidians, finding only Nagas and Yakkas, who were no more than beasts. In fact, the Sinhalese were actually Tamils by blood who took on a separate contrived racial identity after getting to Lanka and embracing Buddhism. Both ancient names for the island, Eelam in Tamil and Lanka in Sinhalese usage, had Tamil roots, and a wide range of place names assumed to be Sinhalese were in fact of Tamil origin, proving that at one time Tamils held sway over the entire island. And it was the Tamils who introduced the science of irrigation, not the Sinhalese, as most of the related terminology has Tamil roots, too. The imagined Sinhala Golden Age was hardly the peaceful, prosperous time it was held to be. Rather, it was time of incessant struggle between contentious Sinhala princes, attended by patricidal and fraticidal slayings, conspiracies, and internal chaos that would have made the building of a great and glorious civilization impossible.

However much Sinhalese domination may have imbued Tamils with a shared sense of distinctive national identity, their political unity was fragmented by caste and class dynamics, as well as by religious and regional differences. Tamils of the Jaffna peninsula disdained the Indian Tamils of lower-caste origins who had been brought to the island a hundred years earlier to work on tea plantations. During the debate over the Citizenship Act of 1949, for example, which had stripped Indian Tamils on the tea estates of their citizenship, few Jaffna Tamils objected to Sinhalese talk of deporting these stateless Tamils. Neither were Jaffna Tamils above exploiting Indian Tamil labor when violence in the hill country in the seventies sent thousands fleeing north for safety. Solidarity among Tamils was also undercut by differences between Hindu Tamils and those who had converted to Catholicism. Finally, the Tamils were also fragmented regionally. Those in the north were patriarchal and more orthodox in their caste traditions, and those in the east were matriarchal and had more flexible ideas on caste.

The drive for separatism was so slow in coming partly because of the tactics of the Tamil political elite. Although they had embraced the concept of a separatist homeland, nearly all Tamil politicians, initially, were steadfastly opposed to violence as a means of attaining it. Most Tamil leaders were part of an upper-caste Anglicized elite who were committed to a gentlemanly, courtly vision of politics and would pursue separatism only through constitutional means. This reflected the general feeling of the great majority of Tamils, who, despite prejudicial treatment, nevertheless retained traditional loyalty to the central government and the country's democratic traditions.

Many of the leaders used the issue of separatism to win power within the existing power structure. Many also had significant financial and career interests in the south which they did not want to jeopardize. But what most diluted the separatism of the Tamil political establishment was its upper-caste identity. Sinhalese actions against the Tamils as a whole did not affect this class. In fact, within the psychology of caste, the increasing marginalization and degradation of the lower castes actually buttressed the traditional caste order in the Tamil north, particularly the domination of the top caste, known as Vellalas, who had long held a monopoly on landownership and political leadership.

As in its Sinhalese counterpart, caste in Tamil society was an outgrowth of Indian social thought. Each person had a place in society and a function to fulfill, with its own rights and duties. Caste was a matter of social order, of hierarchy, a way of assuring that vital social and ritual functions were performed and that society could operate harmoniously. Just as an inverted pyramid put more than half the Sinhala Buddhists in the top caste position, the cultivator class of Govigamas, more than 50 percent of Sri Lankan Tamils were in the Vellala caste, who occupied a similar niche as landholding cultivators.

The key to the Vellalas' power over other castes lay in part in false claims that they had mystical power over the reproductive sources of farming life and were ritually "pure." It is, broadly speaking, still believed that Vellala men have a supernatural force that brings them, and the community, "increase"—abundant progeny, fortune, and bountiful harvests—and that such mystical power confers upon them the "right" to possess the lion's share of those things. By the same reasoning, the Vellalas had the right to suppress non-

Vellalas because they represented "disorder" and were a threat to the welfare of society.

In pre-British times the Vellalas lived like feudal barons. Non-Vellalas had to give a deep bow when passing their superiors, were not allowed into Vellala temples, and could not participate in the same rituals. According to the traditional ritual code, if a non-Vellala uttered a ritual chant his tongue was to be uprooted, if he heard one his ears were to be filled with molten wax, and if he remembered one his body was to be cut asunder. Vellalas forbade Untouchable women to cover their breasts, wear gold earrings, or live in concrete homes. Untouchable men were forbidden to wear shirts, cut their hair, use umbrellas, or ride bicycles. All Untouchables were forbidden to sit higher than superiors, buy land, cremate their dead, enter Vellala homes, or walk on the pavement if a Vellala was passing. Nor could they insult a Vellala or marry without Vellala permission.

The British tried to break down the caste system in Tamil society, but couldn't. Vellala domination continued after independence, too. Lifelong and indentured servitude persisted. Non-Vellalas were still denied access to wells, temples, and cremation grounds and still couldn't own their own land. Only with the onset of free vernacular education were lower-caste Tamils allowed access to schools, and even then the upper castes had to be forced to let them in. The lower castes sat on the floor.

Gradually, however, failure to check Sinhala domination through constitutional means cost this political class its credibility and its mystique. Even though it was passed in legislation, a bill calling for the "reasonable use of Tamil" to allow use of Tamil as a "national language" in courts and government bureaucracies was never implemented, and proposals for Regional Councils that would have permitted more Tamil autonomy and self-determination were defeated on the floor of Parliament in Colombo. While Tamil leaders were able to take some of the sting out of the standardization of marks with quotas more favorable to minorities, Tamils were still unable to reinstate the concept of ethnic-blind university admissions.

But what finally discredited Tamil moderates was their inability to shield the Tamil population from violence. Very early in the political struggle between the two groups, the Sinhalese established a precedent for vicious repression of Tamils supporting separatism and other unpopular issues. (In 1956, a crowd of Tamils protesting the passage of the Sinhala Only Bill were stoned and assaulted while practicing *satyagraha*—a form of protest by prayer—in front of Parliament.) The result was a spreading militancy and the growth of a martial spirit in a people who had long been known for passiveness. The British had thought the Tamils so unsuitable for the military that they did not recruit them into the colonial army. But a generation of Tamil youth, raised in an almost perpetual state of conflict with the government—boycotts of schools, picketing of government offices, the performance of *satyagraha*, and the hoisting of black flags to protest government actions—had been radicalized.

Then, in the seventies, a small group of radical young Tamils took up arms, vowing to wage a struggle for Eelam through violence, answering government heavy-handedness with their own form of revolutionary brutality. Choosing to go after their own first, in a campaign to purge Tamils of opportunists and sellouts, their first target was the mayor of Jaffna, a well-respected upper-caste lawyer. In 1975, Vellupai Prabakeran, a son of a Tamil civil servant from the lesser-caste fishing area of the Velvetaturai peninsula of northern Jaffna, led a small band into Jaffna town and killed the mayor. In response, the police and army detained and tortured one hundred Tamil students for a year, without ever formally charging any of them, establishing a pattern of collective punishment for acts committed against Sinhalese authority.

Such repression only escalated the level of violence, of course, which widened to include armed clashes between Tamil rebels and government police and army units. Usually, the rebels incited these battles seeking vengeance against particular officers or units who were known for brutality against civilians. In April 1978, a Tamil group slipped a police net and murdered an entire patrol unit. They later claimed credit publicly for the act. Afterward, the militant movement was outlawed and security forces poured into the Tamil areas of the north and east.

Ironically, the spiral of repression came at a time when Tamils had been given a great deal of hope for improved relations with the Sinhalese. Running on a platform that had denounced detainments, arbitrary arrests, police excesses, and judicial partiality, J. R. Jaya-wardene had won the national election for Prime Minister in 1977, buoying Tamil faith in the democratic system. Jayawardene had, after all, said that his policies would usher in the *dharmistra* society, which would extend social justice and economic opportunities to all Sri Lankans. Jayawardene, too, had expressly included Tamils, whose grievances over education and employment he recognized.

But Jayawardene's reassurances were mere electoral platitudes. In July 1979, Jayawardene gave top officers of the Sinhalese Army a mandate to wipe out terrorism within six months. Instead of an All-Party Conference to air their complaints, Tamils were met with Sinhalese troops and commando units and new restrictions on civil liberties enacted to wipe out Tamil terrorism.

Most of these restrictions were allowed under the Prevention of Terrorism Act, or PTA, passed in 1979. The PTA allowed govern-ment forces to deny trial by jury, to make confessions under torture admissible evidence, and to detain suspects without trial or access to counsel for up to eighteen months on suspicion alone. It also banned the expression of sentiments and opinions that could cause religious, racial, or communal disharmony, authorized stop and sei-zure at will, authorized arrest without a warrant, and banned sup-port, espousal, or financial backing for separatist causes. In addition, its powers were retroactive. Basically, the PTA suspended civil gov-ernment and fundamental rights and substituted police and military rule.

At first, the generally conservative Tamils resisted the Tigers, or, at least, their program for violent action in the pursuit of an independent Tamil state. Many Tamils had suspicions about these young men. It was believed, as an old Tamil proverb remarked, that "the cultivation of the young will never reach home." But the degree of humiliation inflicted on civilian Tamils was such that many began to see the militants as the only capable form of resistance. Outside their areas in the north and east, Tamils were at the mercy of the unpredictable Sinhalese, who often went after them in mobs. And what little reprieve they got in their own areas was evaporating as government security forces retaliated there for acts committed by the rebels. Gradually, many Tamils forswore their passivity and began to look more supportively on the small but growing core of rebels. "Increased police and army surveillance of the population has not curtailed violence but seemingly stimulated it," a report written by the International Committee of Jurists declared in 1981. Increasingly, Tamils began to see their struggle against the Sinhalese as more than a contest over constitutional rights and political power. It became a struggle for personal and cultural survival.

Another spate of island-wide violence against Tamils began in 1981, marked by army and police rampages in Jaffna. Roundups had become common, usually conducted by armed men wearing no military insignia and nonregulation uniforms. The prisoners were taken away without official acknowledgment of any kind. The lucky ones were beaten or tortured; the unlucky ones disappeared altogether. That spring, two policemen were killed in response, leading to an orgy of arson, destruction, looting, and killing by members of the security forces, who, it was said, were no longer under the control of their superior officers. The government made only a pro forma investigation of the events.

At the end of May 1981, the police went on another rampage in response to rebel provocation. This time they sacked the house of the Jaffna Member of Parliament, the offices of a pro-separatist Tamil political party, a Tamil newspaper, and dozens of shops in the bazaar. They then destroyed the Jaffna library, burning its 95,000-volume collection of irreplaceable Tamil classics.

The police failed to respond to the attack on the library, though it was taking place not a stone's throw from a major police station. An investigation later revealed that many police had been involved in the carnage. Several days later, a squad of about a hundred Sinhala political goons arrived on trains from the south and, under the pretext of monitoring voting for the district development councils, stole the election. The district development councils, or DDCs as they were called, were a bone that the government had thrown to the Tamils, one that would grant them a very limited amount of

local autonomy in their areas. Tamil rebels had called for a boycott
of the elections, which made the government insistent that they take
place, even though the climate in Jaffna was hardly conducive to
fair balloting. Government officials were also insistent on winning
the vote, and allowed the goons to tamper with the ballot boxes and
to rig the vote count. To make sure there were no surprises, on the
morning of the election two prominent Tamil political leaders were
arrested. The debates in Parliament over the burning of the library
and the rigging of the election were marked by typical Sinhalese
denials. Nowhere was there any remorse for the tremendous cultural
affront that the library fire represented, nor for the continuing reign
of terror that was the Sinhalese occupation of Jaffna.

Acts like the burning of the library and the subsequent rampage
in Jaffna were fuel for Tiger militants, who began to widen the scope
of their operations. Aside from occasional ambushes on Sinhalese
policemen and soldiers, the Tigers, to that point, had concentrated
on a campaign of intimidation and terror against prominent Tamil
politicians and government servants in order to create a leadership
vacuum in their community which the militants would then fill.
Most of these killings had been well-planned hit-and-run attacks or
"lamppostings" in which the victims were tied to a post in a public
area and shot, usually with a list of antisocial crimes posted above
the corpse. But after the bloody spring of 1981, militants in Jaffna
began to strike against military targets, government installations,
banks, and police stations.

By 1983, the strongest and most effective Tamil rebel group,
the Liberation Tigers of Tamil Eelam, had launched sixty assaults,
earning a reputation for revolutionary finesse. Unlike other Tamil
militant groups, the Tigers were not a ragtag band of idealistic
nationalists, but a very well-trained, well-armed, and well-organized
guerrilla band totally committed to revolutionary violence and to the
vision of Eelam, a homeland safe from the Sinhala Buddhist state.
The precision and daring of their well-chosen hits on Tamil "collab-
orators," as well as on the Sinhala military, had made them seem
larger and stronger than they really were. Their mystique was certainly enhanced by such acts as the bombing of the Jaffna Municipal

Building during a meeting between Sri Lankan police and army officials to discuss the deteriorating security situation. By the early eighties, nearly all mainstream Tamil politicians lived under death threats. When the Tigers called for a boycott of municipal elections in 1983, claiming they were a sham, they got nearly 95 percent compliance.

Increasing violence in the north, particularly attacks against the Sinhala military, was met by rage and clamors for vengeful retaliation among the Sinhalese. Many of them saw Tamil violence as something that had been lurking in the Tamil community since independence.

The attacks by Sinhalese mobs on the Tamils of Colombo in 1983 were the final step in the process of polarization that had begun nearly three decades earlier. The riots of 1983 marked the point of no return. After them, Tamils could not trust the Sinhalese. Even the Tamils of Colombo, who had been relatively nonsectarian, began to talk about the inevitability of separatism. As refugees streamed north, the country began to take on the demographic complexion it had before the British arrived: Tamils in the north and Sinhalese in the south. De facto separation.

As Colombo lay in ruins, Sinhalese MPs passed the Sixth Amendment to the constitution, which outlawed separatism and any utterances in support of it. Rather than take what amounted to a loyalty oath, the moderate Tamils in the Tamil United Liberation Front (TULF) quit Parliament and exiled themselves to Madras. Within the Tamil national liberation struggle, the field was now open for the militants.

10 · War

AFTER THE RIOTS OF 1983, the various Tamil rebel groups launched intensive recruitment drives in the refugee camps of southern India and in Tamil areas under occupation in the north and east. Issues such as national self-determination, university admissions, and equity in land settlement paled before the basic desire for vengeance and the quest for safety inside an independent Tamil state. Thousands joined the movement.

The Tamils, however, were still not politically unanimous. At one time there were over twenty-three different rebel factions, splintered along lines of caste, ideology, and personality. While some groups favored Marxist ideology, others had no grander thoughts than seizing power. Some advised patience and eschewed guerrilla conflict, while others said that the best strategy was a head-on conventional war. There was also division over the question of whether the militants should settle for an autonomous state within a federal setup or press for total independence. In 1984, the five leading rebel groups joined together in a short-lived united front called the Eelam National Liberation Front, but the Liberation Tigers withdrew a year later, and this caused the front to collapse. Factional battles between various rebel groups cost the Tamil movement almost as much blood as direct confrontations with Sinhalese security forces. Both the city of Jaffna and the south Indian city of Madras became battlegrounds, and nearly 1,700 rebels of various groups were killed. The feuding also fed Sinhalese propaganda that the rebels were more interested in power and its perquisites than "national liberation."

Eventually, the Liberation Tigers of Tamil Eelam came to dominate the rebel movement. The main source of LTTE power was their leader Vellupai Prabakeran. Born in 1954 on the eve of the Sinhalese Buddhist resurgence, Prabakeran was the son of a minor government civil servant, a strict but gentle man—the personification of an old Tamil proverb: "When he walks, he does not even hurt the grass under his feet." The younger Prabakeran led what is said to have been a shy and lonely childhood. Increasingly caught up in the ferment of the Tamil youth rebellion, he dropped out of secondary school and went underground, to become part of a shadowy revolutionary organization called the Tamil New Tigers. When interviewed later about his formative experiences, Prabakeran told of witnessing a Sinhalese mob burning a Tamil Hindu priest alive in 1958. "This left a deep impression on my mind. If such innocent lives could be destroyed, why could we not fight back?"

Prabakeran received the bulk of his training in India from intelligence operatives of RAW, the Research and Analysis Wing (the Indian equivalent of the American CIA), and from retired servicemen in Tamil Nadu sympathetic to the cause of Eelam. Returning to Jaffna in 1975, Prabakeran established his control over the LTTE by the daring assassination of the mayor of Jaffna, which was carried out in broad daylight.

Prabakeran's nom de guerre, "Thamby," an honorific term of affection meaning "Little Brother," was in stark opposition to his capacity for rage and calculation. It was said that he could hit a cigarette in a cadre's mouth at a hundred paces and could break down and reassemble an automatic weapon blindfolded. It was also said that he personally cut down nine Sinhala soldiers with a machine gun in the ambush that triggered the riots of 1983. Clint Eastwood movies were his favorite form of entertainment, next to *Soldier of Fortune* magazine, and he kept a leopard cub as a pet. After his return from India, he spent the bulk of his time underground, going from safe house to safe house, well served by his capacity for disguises—he once escaped capture by posing as a peanut vendor and once as a Catholic priest—and by an uncanny ability to anticipate ambushes and the arrival of government troops.

Functioning as both chairman of the Central Committee of the LTTE and commander in chief of its military wing, Prabakeran insisted on tight discipline, killing anyone in his organization, and often his family, who threatened him. Neither a smoker nor a drinker, he demanded asceticism from his men as well, banning the consumption of alcohol and tobacco, as well as sex, though he married himself, taking for his wife a former student whom he had carted away from a Tamil hunger strike at Jaffna University.

He also favored the cyanide capsules that the Tigers carried on their persons. "It is cyanide that has helped us develop our movement very rapidly," Prabakeran said in another interview. "Carrying cyanide on one's person is a symbolic expression of one's commitment, our determination, our courage. You won't find many people from our movement in jail, at any rate. No more than you can count on your fingers—perhaps two or three people. But never those involved in our inner circle."

During the initial phase of the insurgency, little was known about the Tigers. Although an early estimate by *Jane's Defense Weekly* said Tiger cadres numbered around 1,500, by the time of the peace accord of 1987 it was thought that there were almost 4,500 young men in the movement, split evenly between the Political Office and the Military Office. Political officers were responsible for the administration of areas that had come under the control of the rebels—staffing courts, collecting taxes, and controlling media and propaganda. Most of the fighters were divided up into small combat units, without a conventional hierarchical chain of command. There were various ranks, and officer status was given to those who showed bravery in combat, but there were no obvious distinctions or insignia. To preserve secrecy, ordinary cadres often did not know the true rank of their superiors. The role that any one officer played at any one time was extremely flexible. "If you have any conventional military training, you would find our military structure very confusing," one Tiger cadre told an interviewer.

Most of the weapons used by the Tigers were those that typified low-intensity warfare—large-caliber machine guns, AK-47 assault rifles, mortars, grenades, and rocket-propelled grenades, which they had well before the Sri Lankan Army. The Tigers had ample international as well as Indian sources for their weaponry. They were also adept at building weapons of their own, displaying great ingenuity and resourcefulness in putting together homemade grenades, mortars, and large-caliber mortar shells that had a range of more than a mile. According to several reports, the Tigers were in the middle of testing a rocket when the peace accord came about. It was the diabolical brainchild of a cadre who had been denied entrance to engineering school. When they discovered the rocket, the Indian military and intelligence officers were absolutely dumbfounded. The Tigers were also allegedly ready to move into biological warfare. Such reports were probably propaganda, however, which the Tigers used to intimidate and outrage the Sinhalese, preying upon their many insecurities and vulnerabilities.

The key to the Tigers' military success was the use of powerful land mines in conjunction with guerrilla warfare, an innovative strategy said to have been devised by Prabakeran. The most powerful mines, 55-gallon barrels filled with anywhere between 50 and 150 kilograms of explosives, were usually placed in culverts under roads and ignited by wires from houses nearby. The mines were capable of throwing packed buses twenty feet into the air or ripping holes in tanks and armored personnel carriers. Few bodies were recovered in these attacks.

The Tigers' primary strategic aim was to consolidate the north and the east by driving off Sri Lankan government forces and government-subsidized colonists who had been settled there. The first part of this goal was achieved through hit-and-run attacks on police stations and army strongpoints, and by making the roads in Tamil areas so hazardous that government forces were wary of leaving of their bases. The colonists—part of the central government's military strategy to thwart Tamil expansionism—were driven off by fierce attacks.

The second aim of the Tigers' strategy was to install a govern-

ment in Jaffna that would serve as the political base of Eelam. The
Tiger militants ran Jaffna as a liberated zone, with its own civil
administration, courts, traffic police, lotteries, and nursery schools.
Judges who presided over Tiger courts were not lawyers, but they
were established professional men, and cases were handled according to Sri Lankan law, though with revolutionary haste. Repeat
offenders were often lampposted. To lay a financial base for an
independent country, militants collected taxes on all transactions,
and even had their own taxes on liquor and cigarettes. They raised
other funds by marketing soft drinks, sweetmeats, and soap.

So as not to lose face in Jaffna and to avoid alienating Tamils
who might still be loyal to them, the Sinhalese government kept up
the flow of pension money to retirees and paychecks to civil servants,
700 of whom showed up for work every day in government offices
in the Jaffna area. Such concerns for face also forced the government
to keep the electricity from the national power grid flowing, too,
enabling the rebels to use government current for their ammunition
and weapons factories. Until a blockade was enforced in January
1987, foodstuffs and fuel were also sent from the south. After the
blockade, softhearted Sinhalese officers and calculating black mar-
keteers kept those supplies flowing, although to a limited extent.

Though they had little regard for national politicians, Tiger
leaders in Jaffna got on fairly well with local Sinhalese army commanders, communicating with them over radios, making arrangements to ferry journalists into Jaffna and bringing them back for
return flights at prearranged times. Militants and local commanders
were able to set up prisoner exchanges from time to time, and shook
hands in formalized, though fraternal, rituals that often left observers in Jaffna baffled. "It's like Alice in Wonderland," one Sri Lankan
officer said upon returning from a tour of duty in Jaffna. "Just when
you think you have understood what everyone is up to, you notice
something that makes it appear to be something else again."

Tiger efforts to consolidate the north and the east were greatly
aided by assistance from the government of India and sympathizers
in Tamil Nadu. Although Indian intelligence operatives had proba-

bly been in contact with Prabakeran as early as the late seventies, after the riots in 1983 the Indian government openly provided the Tigers with arms, training, and sanctuary, issuing the most transparent official denials. Such assistance was a function of two forces: political pressure from the 55 million Tamils living in India and India's increasing desire to destabilize the Sri Lankan government in Colombo.

After sending rescue boats for refugees fleeing the riots of 1983, India began to focus attention on the rebels, assigning top-level liaisons from the intelligence and defense establishments to oversee their operations and, occasionally, to help to execute them. (According to some reports, Indian operatives planned a massacre at the holy Buddhist city of Anuradhapura and stayed in radio contact with the rebels while they carried it out.) Officially, India denied its role but its support was an open secret. Journalists actually visited LTTE training camps on the Indian mainland. Many of the rebels carried Indian passports, enabling them to travel abroad to buy arms.

All of the rebel groups benefited from Indian aid, but Tigers received the most, both from Delhi and from the chief minister of Tamil Nadu, M. G. Ramachandran, a former Indian film star, with whom the Tigers had a special relationship that allowed them to import guns and stockpile weapons freely. Prabakeran was also able to set up headquarters in Madras in a hotel usually reserved for state legislators. When Delhi grew cool to the Tigers, after realizing that it did not have as much control over them as it had assumed, the Tigers still could rely on Ramachandran.

But contrary to Sinhalese opinion, Indian adventurism played only a limited role in the Tigers' military success. A more important source of strength was popular support. Regardless of Sinhalese propaganda, Tamil civilians spoke of the Tigers as "the boys," the only force capable of advancing their cause after nearly a decade of state repression.

The Sri Lankan security forces, meanwhile, were poorly led, poorly equipped, and even more poorly trained, especially for a full-blown counterinsurgency, and their response to the Tamil rebels was slow and inept, hampered by organizational confusion and a lack of transport capability. Few Sinhalese soldiers spoke Tamil or knew the terrain of the north, severe liabilities in a guerrilla war. Government intelligence was bad, which made it impossible for the army to anticipate rebel moves. "The initiative is with the Tigers," said one high-ranking counterinsurgency specialist in the Sri Lankan military at the time. "They choose the time and the place. We can only react." Several cease-fires declared in the interests of peacemaking only put the government forces further at a disadvantage, allowing the rebels to lay carpets of land mines around their forts and barracks. As a result, by 1985 the rebels had driven most of the police and soldiers stationed in the north and the east back into their quarters. For all intents and purposes, Jaffna was a liberated city.

The poor performance of the Sinhalese troops in the field was also related to corruption behind the scenes. Unscrupulous ministers were often able to turn huge profits through sweetheart deals that saddled the government with unnecessary and often substandard weaponry.

As a result, the forces in the field became hard to discipline. Massacres of whole Tamil settlements, or at least the male youth in them, were common, largely in response to devastating land-mine casualties. The officer corps maintained professional standards, but the rank and file ran amok, and officers sometimes had to confine men to their barracks. The authorities even disbanded some units. Few individuals were court-martialed, however, out of concern for morale.

Human rights groups said that between 1983 and 1987 over 6,000 people were killed in the fighting in the north and the east, few of them combatants. Many now think the figure may have been as high as 16,000. At the time the peace accord was announced, more than 5,500 young Tamil men were detained in Sri Lankan army detention centers, mostly in the south. In 1985, Amnesty International reported that torture was carried out in these and other detention centers on a "widespread and persistent" scale. Detainees were stripped and beaten, struck on the knees, face, neck, and feet with iron rods, bound in chairs and lowered into wells, suspended from the ceiling and beaten, tormented with hot chili powder rubbed into the eyes and genitals, burned with hot rods and cigarettes, and often subjected to electroshock and mock executions.

At one refugee camp I visited in 1987, men who had been held in the notorious Boosa detention camp showed me scars from cigarette burns all over their bodies. Hospitals in the north and east routinely admitted boys who had emerged from detention with broken heels and other injuries inflicted by pipes filled with sand. Many detainees were required to admit their own complicity and that of others to avoid further torture. "I lost consciousness and was splashed with water," one victim later told *The Times* of London. "I insisted that I was not a terrorist and did not know any terrorists. So they brought in a man who had earlier identified me and asked him why he had pointed me out. He said it was to avoid another beating himself. So they beat him again and later I heard that he had died."

Amnesty International also documented nearly 700 cases of "disappearances" in the period between 1983 and 1987, though other estimates run to 1,000. In some cases, those "disappeared" included many who had been shot and burned in mass reprisals; others were killed while in detention, often after being seen by detainees who reported their whereabouts to their families. Some were killed after family members failed to make ransom payments to Sinhalese guards.

Amnesty International also documented significant obstruction on the part of the Sri Lankan government during this period. The government imposed costly and time-consuming requirements on families seeking information about the missing. Requests for government cooperation and entry permits from Amnesty and other international human rights groups were repeatedly denied throughout this period.

Human rights abuses were in part the fruit of the Prevention of Terrorism Act. In 1983, the government applied an even more draconian amendment to the PTA, Emergency Regulation 15a—an old provision dating from colonial times intended to prevent the spread of disease—which allowed officers in the security forces to dispose of corpses without the need for a postmortem inquest. This enabled security forces to kill civilians or guerrilla suspects and burn their bodies right on the spot.

The government's human rights record provided the rebels with fantastic propaganda for recruitment drives. It also threatened the government's relationship with international aid donors, whose funds it desperately needed. Without international aid, the government would have no choice but to suspend either the war against the Tamils or the effort to develop the country economically, both of which were central to its legitimacy. Consequently, the government went to great lengths to deny Tamil accusations of rights abuses, claiming that civilians had been killed in cross fire and that "disappeared" Tamil men had really joined the rebels on the sly or had given false names while in detention to spare their families shame.

Pressure from international aid donors to settle the conflict forced Colombo to enter into negotiations with the rebels. Little resulted from these lengthy talks, which provided an opportunity for both sides to build up strength.

Negotiations were complicated because of the referee role India insisted on playing, even as it was continuing to supply the rebels with arms and sanctuary. India had got on the bad side of the Tigers as well by backpedaling on its support for Eelam. The Tigers were also dubious about India's proposal that they scale down their military campaign while talks were in progress. "In serious politics," Prabakeran once lectured Rajiv Gandhi, then Prime Minister of India, "it won't do to concentrate on talking. You must act and then talk."

At first, the government wouldn't negotiate with the Tigers, preferring to carry on talks with the members of the Tamil United Liberation Front, a moderate group composed of older, upper-caste Tamils who at least understood the complicated proposals for constitutional reform that were beyond the Tigers' comprehension. The Tigers did not recognize the legitimacy of these talks. When the government did agree to sit down with the Tigers, it insisted that they lay down their arms, which the Tigers would not do. The talks were also hampered by espionage, which worsened the atmosphere of bad faith. All through the negotiations, Colombo was able to anticipate the Indian proposals thanks to a high-ranking Indian intelligence official who had provided information to the American CIA after being trapped in a potentially embarrassing sexual affair. Nor were negotiations helped by the repeated breaches of cease-fire agreements committed by both sides.

In a very short time, the peace process was completely deadlocked. For their part, the Tamils were absolutely unwilling to accept anything short of a separate state. On the other side, the Sinhalese could not muster the consensus required to offer even the most limited form of autonomy.

Much of the Sinhalese resistance to the peace process was the product of hysteria fanned by Buddhist monks. Asserting themselves as the traditional guardians of the national flame, the monks played the role of spoiler, shooting down any proposal for concessions as soon as it was made and cheering opposition politicians who pledged to rescind any settlement as soon as they came to power. Some of the more reactionary monks even formed a secret ultranationalist cell called the Circle of Sinhalese Force, whose members greeted each other with Hitler-like salutes and spewed apocalyptic bombast from the *Mahavamsa* about the end of "the land, the race and the faith," which narrowed the latitude that the government had in reaching a settlement.

Although he realized that the ultimate solution to ethnic violence lay in a negotiated political settlement, President Jayawardene also knew that he might lose his Sinhala constituency and thus control of his country if the necessary concessions went too far. In the atmosphere of 1986 and 1987, the specter of Sinhala Buddhist extremism cast its shadow over the country's political life. Even those who were nominally behind Jayawardene were beginning to bite their tongues in public, leaving their positions ambiguous. As a result, the deadlock continued well into 1987. "Neither side is strong enough to win, so there has to be a political solution," declared a British military attaché at the time. "But if J.R. gives away enough to satisfy the Tamils, he is giving away too much to stay in power. The only political solution that will work with the Tamils will be one that gives away too much for the Sinhalese to accept."

Jayawardene's response was to play a double game, giving the appearance that he was the tortured conscience striving for ethnic peace even as he readied his forces for an all-out offensive against the rebels. To the international press, he posed as trying to hold his country together against the forces of extremism on both sides. To his Sinhalese constituents, he made pledges to bring the terrorist scourge to an end. Soon, however, Jayawardene gave up the quest for a political solution and embraced the military option. "Today, the whole future of the Sinhala nation, the custodian of Buddhism, is in danger," wrote one academic at the time, expressing the thinking of the hard-liners. "The only solution to the problem is a military one. The government should mobilize the armed forces and defeat the armed Tamil youth in battle. If necessary, military help should be obtained from whatever international sources are available. No further concessions should be granted to the Tamils . . . and the Sri Lankan state should continue as a unitary state with a preeminent position for Buddhists."

The increasing support for a military solution was a reflection of the improving field performance of the Sri Lankan military, a function of the training, matériel, and money it was receiving from foreign allies. After putting out calls for help, Colombo began receiving arms and equipment from Pakistan, China, and South Africa. A new security unit, the Special Task Force, was also created, receiving its training from British mercenaries in the Keeni Meeni Services, the group that also provided men for U.S. Lieutenant Colonel Oliver North's operations in Central America. Although Keeni Meeni was supposed to provide helicopter training and advice on fighting a guerrilla war, it was widely believed that some of the Keeni Meenis personnel also flew combat missions and participated in the "interrogation" of prisoners. What help the United States rendered is unknown, but it was widely suspected that the Israelis gave assistance, as American proxies, supplying experts in counterinsurgency.

Between 1983 and 1986 the Sri Lankan military budget swelled nearly sixfold. As a result, what had been a largely ceremonial army grew to a force of nearly 75,000 men. Intelligence services were also improved. The security forces now claimed to be able to pinpoint

Tiger positions and limit the loss of civilian life in Jaffna, where the final assault would start. Sri Lankan intelligence had also concluded that the number of Tiger cadres were fewer than originally thought, and that the level of popular support was dipping, which would make the drive against the rebels less costly than previously calculated.

In the spring of 1987, the series of gruesome bombing attacks launched by the Tigers on the capital made military intervention unavoidable. In the wake of the bombings, talk of a coup in Colombo intensified, and the JVP, the ultranationalist Sinhalese extremist group, began raiding small military and police installations for weapons, a harbinger of what was to come.

Just as the Sinhalese seemed to be readying their military solution, I met with an officer at the U.S. embassy. "The Sinhalese seem quite ready to accept the disintegration of their country rather than dispense with their pride," she said. "It's a terribly self-destructive form of masochistic nationalism. But at least they are consistent. Every choice they have made that might have been able to unite the country since independence has been the wrong one. It's spooky, almost as if they have a collective death wish."

At first it looked like that collective death wish might find its expression in Operation Liberation, launched in May 1987 as the first stage in the military solution that hard-liners had clamored for. Although it was successful in driving the Tigers from areas on the Jaffna peninsula where they had been thought invincible, Operation Liberation inflicted sizable civilian casualties, which India could not ignore. At the time, it appeared that India would invade outright, leading to war between the two countries and inevitable partition, if not Sri Lanka's demise as a sovereign nation. In June, the ancient dagoba built by Duttugemunu in the sacred city of Anuradhapura cracked open and collapsed into slabs, which was taken by many as a portent of the country's looming dissolution. President Jayawardene, in the sacred city at the time, was reportedly so shaken that he turned ashen, hurried back to Colombo, and forbade the press to report on it, fearful of what it symbolized about his mandate.

Instead of invading Sri Lanka, India proposed the peace accord. Technically speaking, it was invited into the country, forestalling a military showdown. Nevertheless, the Accord was only a holding action. Should deeply ingrained masochistic nationalism on the part of the Sinhalese get the better of more moderate impulses, the country could easily slide into the fractured state of Duttugemunu's shrine to royal Buddhism, which was now as much a symbol of the country's ancient grandeur as of its ongoing self-destruction.

THREE

11 · The Sinhalese South

TRAVELING BY train along the coast to Matara, the farthest point south on the island, we passed tiny fishing villages and empty beach resorts. The heat and sun were stupefying. Across the aisle from me, two sleeping young girls were tangled in a single seat. Outside, fishing boats bobbed in the evening tides, their crews sprawled listlessly on deck.

As we left Colombo behind, the number of middle-class homes fell off; most of the dwellings were now either woven cadjun shacks or one-room structures made from a wattle of sticks and bright red clay. Occasionally, an old colonial-era bungalow would be visible in the jungle. These were usually designed in the old Dutch style, with walls of heavy masonry and windows laid in carved wooden casings. They now stood in phenomenal decay, porches rotting, roofs sagging. Some of the bungalows seemed abandoned, while others housed several families together.

The shores of the southern lagoons were lined with acres of rotting coconut husks, which, corralled in bamboo pens, would ferment in the brackish water until the fiber, called coir, could be extracted for spinning into rope, one of the area's few sources of income. The process exuded a sharp, pungent sourness that mingled with the smells of small coral-processing plants strung along the coast.

According to Sinhalese tradition, it was the south that came to the rescue of the rest of the nation whenever Sinhalese Buddhism was in jeopardy. Long serving as a sanctuary for Sinhalese patriots, the kingdom of Ruhuna, an area roughly covering the southernmost fifth of the island, had produced the hero-king Duttugemunu who vanquished the invading armies of the Tamil Elaru. It was in the south, too, that the millennial expectations of 1956 were highest and where the JVP was most popular.

Since my last brief visit two months before, what had been a low-level insurgency had widened into a full-scale revolt against the government. By then, early December 1987, the JVP had killed several hundred officials of the ruling United National Party (UNP). Those MPs who had not abandoned their districts for Colombo were reluctant to stay in their own homes and moved about like fugitives. The JVP had also assassinated several high-ranking government officials, including the police chief in charge of countersubversion. The coordination of these operations suggested an organizational capacity unsuspected before.

Some reports from the south spoke of it as a liberated zone, not unlike Jaffna in the north. Whether the JVP was capable of maintaining something on such a scale was unclear, but they were able to deprive the government of its ability to control this area. Death threats against government functionaries had triggered massive resignations from the UNP and from party-appointed posts, which brought civil administration and development work to a halt. In some cases, the JVP had forced UNPers to make their resignations in public, furthering the sense of lost government power.

Even in towns where the government still nominally ruled, the JVP was able to exert its influence, banning the sale of government-controlled newspapers and lottery tickets, forcing doctors to charge lower fees to the poor, running protection schemes for businessmen, abolishing taxes and water bills, and punishing "enemies of the people." During the day, police and security forces moved around untroubled, but by night they did so cautiously. Some policemen were afraid to sleep inside their own installations.

Threatened with the loss of power, the government organized

death squads to root out JVP suspects and sympathizers. Dieter Ludwig had been the first to get information on this nasty turn of events. In Matara, a suspected JVP sympathizer had been seized in his home in the middle of the night by men dressed in civilian clothes. Taking him to a bakery, the men locked the suspect in an oven and turned up the heat, extracting the names of other sympathizers, who were later found shot in the jungle. "I tell you," said Dieter, shaking his head by the pool at the Hotel Meridien, "this means there will be trouble down there for some time. When it gets to the stage where the death squads come in, everything escalates."

Although the presence of Indian troops in the north had freed Sri Lankan forces for redeployment in the south, these forces had been unsuccessful in stamping out or even minimizing the presence of the JVP. As a result, grass-roots elements in the UNP were up in arms. "A few more deaths and my party will break up," Jayawardene had told *The Times* of London, shortly after the chief of countersubversion had been murdered in broad daylight. "I can't deal with it in a democratic way."

Jayawardene, though, was careful to depict the death squads as private security groups, created for the sole purpose of protecting the MPs of each district. He also denied that many of these "home guards" were recruited from jails. At a luncheon for the Foreign Correspondents Association in Colombo, I made the mistake of asking him about the backgrounds of some of these new militiamen. Jayawardene reared back and bared his fangs. "Nonsense," he sneered. "Their backgrounds have been checked very thoroughly."

In preparation for a major confrontation, the government had just shipped 2,000 guns to the Hambantota district at the southern tip of the island. My plan was to head there and then into the interior, to look into the magnitude of the JVP insurrection. Uncertain of the situation, I didn't want to travel alone, so I went with a British photographer named Stephen Champion, who had been coming to Sri Lanka over the past three years to do portraits of the war for a show he was putting together. We put in, the first night, at the

Paradies Guesthouse in a little seaside town called Marissa, where Stephen had stayed the year before.

The Paradies was a collection of small cabins set on a wide arc of beach. Though it was beautiful, the owner, a Sinhalese named Ananda, made it unpleasant. After assuring us a half dozen times that we would have mosquito nets, it became clear that nets were unlikely. When we pressed him, he did come back with one—an old moth-eaten net that was half green from mold. Without a guarantee that there would be more travelers behind us, he didn't want to purchase new nets. "Maybe better you go, then," he said testily after we gave him an ultimatum about mosquito protection. "But don't think I would tell you I had one and not give you one."

As a result, we headed farther south to visit a friend Stephen had made the year before, a Sinhalese fisherman named Bonasuriya, who lived in the town of Welligama. Bonasuriya was a walking compendium of Sinhala woes. Until the UNP came to power, he had been a superintendent on an up-country tea estate. Although fishing was one of the lower-caste occupations, Bonasuriya had no other options. As a partisan of the discredited Sri Lanka Freedom Party (SLFP), Bonasuriya was also on the outs with the local power elite, making life difficult for himself as well as his children, two girls and an adopted son, who wanted to go to university one day.

People flocked to greet Stephen, who had become a celebrity from his work photographing the village the year before. They were also desperate for lodgers. We were being offered rooms for practically nothing. "Please, sirs, please," the villagers cried, following us along the road.

We stayed in the Welligama rest house instead. While we were settling in we learned that someone—the JVP or another group pretending to be the JVP—had warned several Westerners living in the town to leave. On the porch of the rest house, a loud, drunken German woman was sputtering apoplectically about having to leave her property behind. It might even have been her servants who had rigged the threat. The writer Paul Bowles had run into similar trouble. Robbing him blind, his servants had forced him to give up his beautiful Dutch mansion on an island off the Welligama coast.

Meanwhile, Stephen was trying to get a sense of what the situation was like farther on. The managers of the rest house assured him there was "no problem" and that our holiday would continue undisturbed. "You know," Stephen said as we walked over to Bonasuriya's house in the middle of a sun-shower, "it's crazy the way they'll deny it so brazenly. It's a little bit like saying it's not raining out right now."

The most formidable powers of denial couldn't have comforted Bonasuriya and his family. Their home had once been a small adjunct to a larger Dutch-style bungalow. It was now little more than a shell. Whole sections of roof were missing in two rooms, but the rain fell through elsewhere, too, forming puddles all over the floor. The furniture was limited to two or three frayed wicker chairs. Four or five cats prowled and poked through the mess, knocking over pots meant to collect rainwater. Tattered curtains hung between the rooms. The plaster on the walls, where there was still plaster, was pocked and crumbling and coated with moss and fungus.

In one corner of the main room, however, was a model of Bonasuriya's dream house, a low one-story structure made of pieces of bamboo that looked like a cross between a Frank Lloyd Wright and a houseboat. Bonasuriya hoped someday to renovate the ruin we were standing in so that it would resemble this model.

The previous year Stephen had lent Bonasuriya some money to make mortgage payments on the house. At first, Bonasuriya's family had refused the money. After accepting it, Bonasuriya had given some of it to Raja, the adopted son, so he could get married. Thus the family's current precarious state.

Bonasuriya had recently been slashed with a machete by a neighbor. The neighbor had paid off the police and local officials in order to complete some illegal construction work. In the process, Bonasuriya's house was damaged, and the neighbor refused to pay compensation, prompting a fight, which police refused to break up.

The machete had left only superficial wounds, so Bonasuriya was hospitalized only for observation. We visited him there. The hospital ward, like most in Sri Lanka, was open to the air. Dogs prowled between the beds, licking that night's meal from the dishes of those who weren't quick enough to shoo them away. Many of the patients had wounds whose dressings needed changing. They would get attention only when their families ponied up bribes for the staff.

Bonasuriya's large hands were as cracked and dry as old leather from his work as a fisherman, of which he was deeply ashamed. He was thin and emaciated after his week in the hospital. Many of the other patients were also victims of violence. The man next to Bonasuriya had been set on fire by his own son, and was also lacking an ear from a similar fracas years before. Bonasuriya's attacker had also been in the hospital, at the other end of the ward, but had been moved when some of Bonasuriya's fishing buddies came by one night and threatened to set his bed on fire.

Bonasuriya heaped tales of woe on Stephen before we left. Although the government owed him back pay and pension from his job on the tea estate, he was not able to press his claim. "They know we are not of their party," he told Stephen forlornly. "And they will not give us anything because of that. We will starve, it is quite possible, unless there is an intercession."

Back at Bonasuriya's house, we ate *wadis*—a spicy Sri Lankan pastry—and little sweet bananas, served by Lillian, Bonasuriya's wife, and the two girls. Raja, his adopted son, explained that survival over the next year was threatened more by the political situation than by starvation or foreclosure. Although Welligama was not as much a JVP hotbed as other areas, they had a presence there and would send cadres into the area from other villages to intimidate the population. The government was in control, but its grip was slipping. The JVP had been able to prohibit local news vendors from selling the government papers. "I do not sell the *Daily News*," one vendor wrote on the side of his stand, as per instructions. "And that is why he is alive," rejoined the JVP cadres who had issued the orders. Another news vendor had a grenade thrown through his window, with the pin still in it, to persuade him. "First time they send a letter," Raja explained. "Then they kill."

People were not afraid of the JVP as much as they were of the government, added Raja bitterly. This was especially so now that the Green Tigers—the name for the UNP death squads—were beginning to operate in the area. The Green Tigers were everywhere, Raja said. Anyone who voiced criticism of the government might be taken away. The Green Tigers abducted people and never turned them over to the police. A few days later, a body might be found, trussed up and shot or charred beyond recognition. And now that the Green Tigers were operating this way, the JVP was doing the same, rounding up UNP supporters and activists, often wiping out whole families.

Our discussion was cut short by a scream from the kitchen. Lillian had been bitten by a snake or a scorpion and was writhing on the floor. Although the government hospitals were supposed to have adequate stores of antivenin, doctors were known to hoard these supplies. Lillian would die if we didn't get her to an Ayurvedic doctor whose herbal cures and *mojo* were often a reliable alternative. We searched the kitchen for whatever had bitten her. Soon neighbors were roused from across the street.

According to lore, the Sinhalese learned what herbs to apply to snakebites by watching what the mongoose ate in the jungle after a fight with a snake. A neighbor came in and, after a look at the bite on Lillian's ankle, declared it was inflicted by a centipede. Its bite wasn't as dangerous as that of a snake like a krait, but it could trigger a stroke or a heart attack in an older person. There was no antivenin in the hospital where Bonasuriya had been admitted, and a drive to a bigger town such as Matara or Galle would risk drawing fire if we crossed an army roadblock or ran into the JVP along the way. In any case, there might not be any antivenin in these towns either; in the last month, fourteen people had died inside one of those hospitals from snakebites because supplies had been pilfered for sale on the black market. In the meantime, as Raja and the girls decided what to do, Lillian continued to howl, having now taken up a position on the floor just beneath Bonasuriya's dream house.

The neighbor who had diagnosed Lillian's bite put a tourniquet on her leg and then set about making a poultice of leaves, bark, and lime. Apparently unconcerned about infection, he mixed the ingredients right on the floor. He then spread the greenish paste on the wound. In theory the mixture would draw the poison back to the original point of entry. Lillian was already rubbing her leg above the kneecap, however, indicating that the toxin was moving quickly.

We sped through the deserted streets of the village toward the house of a medicine woman in a nearby town. Lillian moaned, "*Aiyo, Aiyo*," a traditional Sinhalese lament.

No one stopped us along the way, but when we reached the medicine woman's house, she wouldn't let us in at first. The week before, I had heard about a doctor who, for fear of the JVP, had refused to come out of her house to help with a difficult home birth. The mother died. It was also not unknown for these doctors to let a patient or two die now and then in order to underscore their power over life and death. Finally, amidst a chorus of crying children and barking dogs, the medicine woman agreed to treat Lillian. We put her in a shed next door that doubled as a storage room for a grocery.

In the weak light of kerosene lamps and flashlights, the "doctor" bent over Lillian's pallet and held her foot over a clay pot of incense while she chanted a spell. By this time, Lillian was calmer. Next to her, one of her daughters brushed back her hair, whispering encouragement. As the doctor heated some green leaves and oil in a smudgy-looking black pot, she scolded Lillian. Bedside manner was obviously not in the traditional course of Ayurvedic study. The next step was to place Lillian's foot over the top of a huge, black double boiler that had been brought in by an assistant. Shrouding the top in a gauzy white cloth, the doctor held the foot over it for a few minutes, causing Lillian some pain. "It's like a Devil Dance," noted the neighbor who had first helped Lillian. He was referring to the practice of drawing demons out of a body during a Sinhalese exorcism.

As Lillian writhed and squirmed on her pallet, the doctor scolded her some more. If it was a really bad bite, the swelling would be much worse, she told her; what are you crying about? There was only a little more poison left inside anyway. She, the doctor, had been treating bites all night—the night of the new moon, or "Black Poya," as the Sinhalese call it, when snakes, scorpions, and centipedes were said to run amok. "Don't tell any other people I'm open for business," she warned the girls as she rubbed Lillian's foot over the caked, blackened pots. "I want to get some sleep one of these nights."

Stephen, quiet throughout the ordeal, was upset at the way the doctor was treating Lillian. "Not only do they have to deal with their own bad fortune," he complained, "but they have to endure what others heap on them as well. You'd think that when they were down, others would treat them nicely. But it doesn't work that way here. Instead, they pounce. Good Buddhists, very good Buddhists."

Wrapping Lillian's foot in a cloth bandage, the doctor told her the pain would wear off sometime in the night. In an hour or two, Lillian would be able to sleep, she added, as she pocketed the money that the girls had brought along to pay her. Back at Bonasuriya's house, one of the daughters shook her head wanly as Lillian resumed her fetal position beneath her husband's dream house. "We've had too many unfortunate incidents for one family, no? So many problems. So very many problems."

The revolution of 1956 had promised the Sinhalese masses a panacea, but it had left behind a bitter taste of messianic disappointment instead. Culturally, 1956 had encouraged a greater Sinhala self-consciousness, but the psychological imprint of colonialism proved harder to erase than expected. Despite the glorification of Sinhala Buddhist cultural superiority permeating media and government rhetoric, a certain degree of Westernization was still a prerequisite for those aspiring to topmost social status and English was still *kaduwa*—the sword—which had cut off earlier generations of Sinhalese from opportunity under colonialism. Socially, the promises of egalitarianism had been betrayed by the persistence of caste—as ubiquitous in Sinhalese life as water was to fish—which continued to encourage a deeply hierarchical vision of society, crimp educational opportunity, and inflict stigma on those at the lower end of the scale. Politically, candidates genuflected to a broad-based Sinhala triumphalism that resonated in the middle and lower classes, but in an electoral system heavily gerrymandered by caste, upper castes were assured domination. Meanwhile, economic nationalism took precedence over rational economic planning. Policies such as the Sinhalization of industries and other racially preferential measures, expensive social welfare schemes in imitation of Sinhalese kings, and the priority given to the agrarian smallholder at the expense of industrial development may have been consistent with the ideology and symbolism of the Golden Age as outlined in the *Mahavamsa*, but the country had become an economic basket case.

Though the forces of nationalism itself were to blame for their plight, the Sinhalese preferred to blame other factors. This was a boon to the JVP, which had emerged in the wake of the peace accord as the true avenger of the sons of the soil. In fact, many in the JVP had fathers or grandfathers who had been vernacular schoolteachers, a key group in sweeping Bandaranaike into power.

But unlike 1956, when the sons of the soil thought they could win power through the political reforms promised by S. W. R. D. Bandaranaike, this generation of aggrieved Sinhalese were desperate. This made them vulnerable to the JVP's vision of total revolution. "There is a dangerous absolutism in their [the JVP] vision of politics," noted a news analyst in Colombo. "Their idea is to raze everything to the ground and start anew. It is a product of the despair that they feel. They have a sense that there is nothing in it for them anymore, so why not kill everyone. You've got it, I don't, and I will never be able to get it anyway either, so I don't care about you, your house, your car, or your political system. Politics is dead for this generation. They are absolutely disgusted with it. They think that it's merely another dance, a game, and that it should all be blown away. The political class has forgotten the most fundamental lesson of all: never give a man nothing to lose."

Tapping into this deep well of historical frustration and bitterness, Rohanna Wijeweera, the founder of the JVP, wooed an increasing number of recruits to his cause. This was not the first offensive in Wijeweera's revolt. In 1971, he had launched a similar rebellion with a similar social base: the vernacular-educated Sinhalese youth of the far south.

Wijeweera had founded the JVP in 1967 in opposition to the traditional left in Ceylon, which he and his comrades believed had been co-opted by its participation in parliamentary politics. Wijeweera, the son of a Communist Party activist who had been physically beaten during the 1947 elections, attended Sinhala medium schools and won a scholarship to a university in Moscow. He was the youngest student in the university and gave up his medical studies early on to become a revolutionary. In 1963, after he sided with the Chinese faction of the Ceylon Communist Party in a doctrinal dispute with its Moscow wing, he was refused a visa to return to the Soviet Union. Soon thereafter, he set about laying the base for the JVP. Crimped by the economic downturn that took place in the sixties, and impatient with the traditional parties of Ceylon, a generation of Sinhalese youth was electrified by Wijeweera's fiery oratory.

The ideological core of the JVP was contained in what Wijeweera called his "Five Classes," a course of study that examined Ceylon's revolutionary potential. Some of these classes were conducted openly by Wijeweera, who would often give two or three a day, in union halls and among clerks in government service. Other classes were held clandestinely, sometimes led by men wearing masks or speaking from behind screens.

Wijeweera's vision of society was forged in a sense of absolute national self-sufficiency, which reflected the same romantic longings that fed Sinhala national myths of agrarian prosperity. The JVP advocated autarky, a complete disengagement of the economy from the "imperialist" international order. In the future, Wijeweera imagined, tea plantations would be planted in crops that predated the colonial order, such as rice and manioc, and all buildings over two stories were to be razed—a program for change that even Communist Party members, agreeing with leading Ceylonese intellectuals, denounced as "a passport back to the bullock-cart age."

Wijeweera said that revolution in Ceylon was inevitable but called for a strategy of "scattered and sudden struggle" culminating in an assault on state power that was called the "One-Day Revolution." This carefully planned revolution never came to pass. Although Wijeweera maintained an obsessive level of secrecy, government security officials got wind of his plans and arrested him, and over 4,000 suspected JVP cadres, in the latter half of March

1971. In response, on April 5, the remaining JVP launched an abortive rebellion throughout the island, attacking police stations with homemade hand grenades and shotguns.

In three weeks' time the JVP was brutally crushed, with the help of the Pakistanis and the Indians. The police and the army, given unlimited emergency powers, jailed up to 18,000 suspected JVP members and sympathizers and killed about 10,000 others, even though the number of actual JVP cadres never exceeded 2,000. According to a retired Sinhalese policeman I knew, torture was routine. Bodies were cremated without inquests or due process. "Thousands of young men and women were arrested, tortured, mutilated, shot, and even burned alive," wrote the Sinhalese Buddhist monk Walpola Ruhula. "Dead bodies, some decapitated, floated down rivers. Girls were stripped naked, raped, tortured, and killed. Hundreds of bhikkhus were arrested and humiliated, tortured, or killed—atrocities and cruelties not heard of since the time of the Portuguese in the sixteenth century."

Though devastated by the government's victory, Wijeweera refused to concede defeat. At his trial he claimed that "the capitalist class was only temporarily victorious" and that the failed uprising was only a "big retreat, not a defeat. No revolutionary movement has raced nonstop to victory in a straight line. Forward marches followed by retreats are quite common."

When the UNP came to power in 1977 it paroled Wijeweera and the other JVP cadres who were still in prison, whereupon the JVP reconstituted itself as a legitimate political party, gaining a considerable popular base. In 1982, Wijeweera even ran for President, garnering more than 200,000 votes, many more than anyone would have predicted. But after the riots of 1983, the JVP was proscribed from politics, though it had little to do with the chaos. Its most extreme, uncompromising members seemed thereby to rise in the leadership. In secrecy, unnoticed by the government, the JVP recruited new cadres, built up weapons stockpiles, and made a hard right turn on its policy toward the Tamils, all of which put it in an excellent position to capitalize on widespread Sinhalese rage triggered by the Indo-Sri Lankan peace accord.

After the ordeal with Bonasuriya's wife, I woke with a feeling of dread. What would it be like if I was stuck, like Bonasuriya and his family, in that part of the south forever? Where would I fit in, and how soon would I become subjected to the system of denigration and intimidation, forever prey to hateful envy and blackguarding by my neighbors? What caste would I be assigned to, low or high?

Stephen and I hitched a ride to the next town, Matara, in the back of an empty coconut truck. From there, we took a bus the rest of the way to Kataragama, on the island's southeastern flank. Kataragama was a pilgrimage site, holy to both Sinhalese Buddhists and Hindu Tamils who lived in the nearby eastern province. In the summertime, there was a huge festival commemorating Skanda, the god who resided there, bringing pilgrims from all over the island. Along with the more conventional ritual observances during the festival, there were yogic rites performed by Hindu holy men who pierced their bodies with pins and hung themselves up on hooks.

The ride offered pleasant scenery: greens in every imaginable shade and variation, punctuated by brief stops in market towns stunned by a brilliant white sun, with monks in electric saffron cutting a swath through the hawkers and the cows. But the poverty of the people living in the area was stark. Many of them looked severely undernourished—odd considering the vegetable abundance around them: squashes, breadfruit, coconuts, pumpkins and other gourds. On the bus, a young girl slumped over and passed out. From the Sinhalese I could decipher, I learned from the girl's mother that the child had not eaten in several days because they were too poor to afford food. As we stopped to leave the two of them in front of a small roadside clinic, a convoy of security forces roared by, heavily armed.

In a downpour, we headed north, right through the heart of what had historically been considered the kingdom of Ruhuna, stronghold of Sinhala patriotism. Along the road, there were cow skulls set on pikes, presumably to scare away crows from the rice paddies. They lent the day an eerie energy.

We passed the entrance to a game sanctuary called Bundalla

and, later, the famous dagoba at Tissarahama, a "temple moun-tain," in the shape of a bell jar. According to myth, Tissa was where the princess of Kotte landed after being set adrift in a boat for the crime of injuring a monk. Marrying a local prince, she produced two sons, one of whom was Duttugemunu.

The Kataragama pilgrimage site, initially Hindu, had become more Sinhalese over three decades of Buddhist rule. With its newly laid roads festooned with an abundance of Buddhist flags and its bazaars crammed with baubles and trinkets, Kataragama had a feel-ing of almost complete inauthenticity. The place was desolate except for a few beggars. It had the kind of moodiness I associated with Coney Island in the off-season.

But we weren't there to explore the area's religious significance. Kataragama had been a JVP stronghold in 1971 and was rumored to be so again. It was a good place to size up how powerful they really were, and perhaps to make contact. In the back of my mind I fantasized about stumbling upon Wijeweera in an obscure jungle redoubt.

According to some accounts, the area around Kataragama con-tained nearly five hundred well-armed JVP cadres. This explained why plainclothes Sinhalese soldiers with assault rifles were circulat-ing through the grounds. Their commander, whom we met later at our rest house, dismissed the JVP as a relatively minor nuisance. He was especially insouciant about the reports that the JVP had infiltrated the army, explaining that though it might be easy to get through the perfunctory background check, as soon as they got their first paychecks the soldiers were loyal once more.

"Some patriots these JVPers are anyway," he snarled. "They talk about saving the Motherland and all that crap, thinking the people will see them as their salvation. But where the bloody hell were they when we were fighting in the north and my men were losing their lives? Bloody cowards. They are only using this concern for the Motherland as a cover for grabbing power and installing Communism. That's what they are really up to."

The head of the government tourist office at the shrine, how-ever, didn't take the JVP so lightly. He had fled to Colombo—"for a meeting," we were told by his subordinates. "That's the way it should be, right?" Stephen asked one of the subordinates, trying to sense what they thought about such intimidation. "Yes," the man said, laughing, conveying his JVP sympathies. "That is correct. That is the way it should be."

The next day we headed into the backcountry, hoping to make contact with the JVP. I was interested in exploring the Bundalla Game and Bird Sanctuary—a long narrow stretch of scrub jungle that ran between the coast road and the sea, which at that time of year was treacherous with heavy surf and undertows. There was more to the area than game, however. After the 1971 uprising, the remnants of the badly battered JVP had holed up in the park, eluding capture for years. It struck me that we might hit pay dirt inside Bundalla. We rented a jeep for the afternoon.

Our guides were two Sinhalese boys in their late teens or early twenties. They made jokes about the good times they had had with women tourists before the south got too dangerous. Both dismissed any suggestion that the JVP was using the game preserve as a sanctuary, but they did give us a great tour.

For several hours, we followed sandy tracks through the low scrub and open pastures inside the preserve. Flocks of painted storks fed in the marshlands and shallow ponds. Cattle, water buffalos, and jackals slunk around in the brush nearby, and an occasional crocodile wriggled through the mud flats. I was riding in the back of the jeep, where I was exposed to the ravages of overhanging trees and cacti. Occasionally we would stop and listen for elephants, but all we heard was the faraway crash of the sea.

The year before, I had been helped out by a local fisherman, a deaf-mute who lived in a small shack on the edge of the preserve. The Fisherman, as he was called, lived by himself, communicating with people only with his bright eyes and the occasional grunt. For his living he tended water buffalos, fished, and acted as a guide. It was believed that his muteness gave him special powers to summon elephants out of the deepest bush.

He luxuriated in our attention. He led us to the crest of a dune so we could see the pristine beach that was his backyard. The heavy seas had churned up a Shiva's Eye, a shell with the yin-yang symbol naturally occurring on its flat side, which he scooped up and brought back to us with relish. Then we bundled him into our jeep and headed into another part of the preserve, where he said, through grunts and hand signals, there had been a herd of elephants earlier in the day.

We tracked far and wide through the preserve, but found no elephants. I was getting a little worried. The sun was going down, and if we were caught out after dark, there would be trouble with the police at the roadblocks or with the JVP, who could mistake us for a government security patrol. The Fisherman insisted, however, that we try one more spot, which was outside the preserve in another section of scrub jungle.

We drove into an area thick with impenetrable brush. It seemed unlikely that we were going to see any elephants in that kind of growth, much less a herd. But as we rose over the top of one hill, we came upon several other jeeps, parked in a grassy savanna. Inside a grove of tall bushes was the herd, which we could hear thumping and snuffling amid the din of the jungle.

The Fisherman grabbed me by the hand and led me up to the edge of the clearing. When my eyes adjusted to the shadows, I found myself staring into the dull, ageless eyes of an elephant, a female, it seemed, whose lover was mounted behind her. They were aware of our presence but heedless. The two of them groaned and shuddered and trumpeted. Then they emerged from the bush, followed by nearly a hundred other elephants. Majestically, they marched across the grassland, an ancient processional, and were swallowed up by the dusk.

As it turned out, our elephant hunt had not been frivolous. The next day our guides let it be known that their safari business was only a sideline. "Please don't make me admit that I am a member of a proscribed political party," said one of them, smiling. They apologized for holding out on us, but they had wanted to make sure we weren't spies or weren't being followed by government informers. They also apologized for refusing to take us to a nearby JVP camp.

If they took us and something happened to the camp later, they would be suspected of disloyalties and would be shot. "This is the way that informers are dealt with," the driver said. "They are shot and killed." It was safer to sit and talk in the shade of a tree, though they both grew anxious when several small convoys of police commandos and nonuniformed thugs with AK-47s passed by.

The boys confirmed that there were between 400 and 500 JVP cadre in the Hambantota-Tissa area, most of them recruited locally in the last few years. The fact that the JVP grew in size and power after the signing of the Accord might have seemed anti-Tamil, said the driver, but that charge of racism was spurious; there were, in fact, Tamils in their own group. Most cadres joined for other reasons—the lack of opportunities available to them in the society, the rampant corruption of the ruling party, and the heavy-handedness of the police in dealing with their protests. "We have studied very hard," one of the boys explained. "We are intelligent, but there are no jobs for us. And since we are young, the police have been brutal to us."

The JVP had infiltrators everywhere, they told us, among students, the police, and the army. The driver also verified what I had been told in Colombo—that the JVP issued cards to its members. Most hid them well, producing them only for meetings. The JVP, we learned, had networks in Europe and the Middle East, mostly to raise money for the cause.

The two JVPers wouldn't let Stephen take photographs unless he allowed them to wear a mask. They were no more fearful of the authorities getting hold of the pictures than they were of their superiors in the movement, who might find it arrogant that they had accepted such attention from a foreign journalist. "They might get mad at me even for having my picture taken," the driver's assistant explained, smiling broadly. "They might get mad and shoot me."

The point of their activities, they said, was not to gain power, not yet anyway. Now was the time for "criminal rehabilitation," the punishment of corrupt government officials and other enemies of the people.

"We don't want to take over the government," the driver insisted. "But we do want to identify the people who've made mistakes against poor people. This government will not punish them, so we will." Ninety percent of JVP targets had been criminals, he maintained, killed by special punishment squads of four or five cadres who traveled between different districts to do their work. For now, their campaign had met its objectives.

"The officials are no longer stealing," the assistant said with a smile. "Our punishments have worked well." "We would like to replace the politicians in power and run the government ourselves," the driver continued, "but we can't do that now. Maybe in ten or fifteen years. Now we haven't the power or the guns. We have some guns," he said, "but not enough."

The JVP that emerged from the shadows after the signing of the peace accord was essentially the same as its earlier incarnation. One fundamental change, however, was the near-dictatorial control that Rohanna Wijeweera had come to hold over it. The most recent JVP was far more authoritarian than before, allowing Wijeweera to obliterate all internal dissent on even the most minor matters.

One of the ways that Wijeweera consolidated his reign was to purge the ranks of the old guard, who were a reminder of the failure of the "One-Day Revolution" of 1971. Many of the old guard left out of disgust with Wijeweera, though they were loath to voice those sentiments publicly. Those who had spoken out against him were maligned as traitors, spies, and police agents, and often wound up dead.

Wijeweera had become the core of the party's organizational structure, breaking down the JVP's far-flung units into tightly compartmentalized cells where comrades were known to each other only by their code names. This left local cadres with limited discretion for low-level assassinations and little more.

Wijeweera's solidification of total control over the JVP was helped by the persona he projected. Quite self-consciously, he had cultivated the impression that he was the great prophet and messiah come to save the Sinhala people. Even his first name, Rohanna, had a messianic resonance, invoking the name of the Sinhalese kingdom of Ruhuna, the land of mythic Sinhalese heroes like Duttugemunu.

By the time he launched the second JVP uprising, Wijeweera's stature as an ideologue had risen to that of Marx and Lenin in the minds of his Sinhalese followers. The peace accord validated his prophecies, from the sixties and seventies, of Indian expansionism and the resilience of the neocolonial element in Sri Lankan political life. He had also demonstrated considerable prowess as a guerrilla leader. Like Prabakeran, the Tiger leader in the north, Wijeweera had achieved folkloric stature, evading manhunts with the help of disguises and a sixth sense for the movements of security forces. His ruthlessness with traitors quieted many potential informers. "You may win a medal for capturing me," he allegedly told a police inspector who once cornered him at a funeral, "but your entire family will be dead."

Strategically, the JVP shunned the tactics of 1971. This time around, they were satisfied with denying the government, from a concealed position, the ability to function effectively. "Like Duttu-gemunu, we do not eat hot rice haphazardly," Wijeweera told one of his few interviewers. "We methodically cool hot rice and then eat it," as an old woman in the mythic story had shown him.

Besides building up a weapons stockpile, presumably for larger frontal attacks in the future, and inducing paralysis in government operations at the grass-roots level, Wijeweera's other strategic aim was to make the JVP seem ghostlike and unstoppable, able to move with impunity no matter how hard the government seemed to crack down. The key to the pattern was the JVP's ability to produce a climate of fear in the region through selective high-visibility assassinations as well as intimidation of ordinary citizens, which made it appear bigger and more omnipotent than it actually was.

While the JVP had chosen a much different road this time around, its ultimate destination was still unclear. Had Wijeweera matured as an ideologue or was he still peddling vague romanticism and destructive nihilism that did little but serve as an outlet for violence?

In refashioning its image, the JVP had shed its primary identity as a Marxist-Leninist party and had embraced a new, virulent form of Buddhist nationalism. This new form of nationalism was called

Jatika Chintanaya, which was loosely translated as "National Ideology," "National Ethos," or "Indigenous Thought."

National Ideology was highly racist, xenophobic, and romantic. It called for a return to cultural values, systems of thought, and economic approaches to the country's development that predated the impurities of Western colonialism and its neocolonial heirs. "We have arrived at the darkest hour without a ray of light anywhere around us," wrote Gunadasa Amerasekera, a Sinhalese dentist and ideologue, in a pamphlet entitled "A National Ideology for Liberation." "I do not think that our society reached this depth of depravity and degeneration even during the times of the Portuguese or the Dutch. . . . To sum up, one could justifiably say that forty years of independence has only taken us back to where we were, back into the clutches of our colonial masters."

At the core of the National Ideology movement was the belief that the Sinhalese could achieve independence both from geopolitical realities and their own racial complexities. Those adhering to National Ideology envisioned a society based on self-sufficiency, in which the consumerist, acquisitive culture of the West would be held at bay by the inherently superior nonmaterialist values of traditional Sinhalese Buddhism. Reflecting a Luddite disdain for technology, National Ideology imagined a society that put cultural integrity ahead of economic productivity, a society structured, like that of the Golden Age of yore, around the Sinhalese trinity of tank, temple, and rice paddy.

According to the proponents of National Ideology, the crisis facing the country was rooted less in a political struggle with separatists than in the continuing crisis represented by neocolonialism. "The present crisis has brought the national liberation struggle to its final stage of crisis," wrote Amerasekera, "soon to decide whether we will go on as an independent or an enslaved nation. . . . The solution as I see it, to put it rather bluntly, lies not in solving the ethnic problem or in destroying the Tigers, but in destroying the real enemy—the neocolonial imperialist forces. . . . If the present crisis does not provide this insight, we may as well resign ourselves to our fate and face annihilation." Or as Wijeweera put it in a communiqué: "We have now recognized our enemy and at a suitable time we will destroy this enemy. . . . We know who these traitors are and there is no mistake about this. . . . All these bastards should be driven from power. That is the only solution to save our fatherland and the people from this grave." Elsewhere, Wijeweera again: "We shall climb over mountains of corpses, we shall swim across lakes of blood. We shall sacrifice our lives; we shall fight for the independence of our motherland. This we swear to you."

As the shape of the present incarnation of the JVP became clearer, many observers saw disturbing parallels between it and the Khmer Rouge of Cambodia. Besides ideological similarities, foremost of which was a romantic vision of a Golden Age lost to foreign aggression, both movements put tremendous emphasis on purgation. "Yes. That will happen here, too," said a Sinhalese intellectual, referring to the brutal restructuring of society after the Khmer Rouge seized power. "Kill all the rich people. Make the country pure again—and poor again, too."

Backtracking along the southern coast, we stayed overnight at the Hambantota rest house. The shoreline there was fringed with palm trees, and the town was a jumble of white plaster and red clay tiles. Unlike the Sinhalese in some of the towns we had visited, the predominantly Muslim people in Hambantota were not as preoccupied with themselves or with Western visitors.

The commanders of the police and the air force who had been assigned the job of keeping Hambantota from falling into JVP hands tried to downplay the extent of the unrest in the area. "Lies, lies," said the senior superintendent of police. "The press is making up all these lies just to sell more papers. There are no hard-core people here, just a few uneducated people using the fear for criminal purposes. There is no problem at all. No problem now at all."

Just down the street, however, a detachment of commandos had set up camp, filling sandbags and installing machine-gun emplacements. Yet even their commander was dismissive of reports of JVP strength and influence. "There is more fear than actual threat," he said. "This fear has sensationalized the situation. Frankly there are

not that many JVP around here, and the people are not in support
of them. All right, there was an outburst of feeling when the Accord
was signed. The JVP was very quick to capitalize on that, but now
the people realize what fools they have been played for and the
situation is quite normal. Public sympathy for authorities has increased substantially, in fact. Now we are even playing volleyball
and cricket together."

Such glib dismissals were not forthcoming from the local Government Agent, the ranking civilian official in the district. I had
gone to see the GA in the bungalow he lived in on the promontory
above town.

It was the same bungalow Leonard Woolf occupied when he
was the Government Agent in 1910 and 1911—a colossal structure
with thick walls and a sweeping view of the sea. When Woolf was
the GA, he wrote in his memoirs, he had been able to control the
entire district with just a few constables. The present GA, however,
had a lot more on his hands.

A servant in a white sarong and shirt opened the door warily.
A few moments passed, and a short, balding man emerged from
around the corner of the foyer. He resembled the typical lifelong
civil servant, paunchy and a little standoffish. But oddly, he was
more than willing to talk. First he insisted on a tour of the bungalow.

"You'll have to excuse the music," he said—a radio screeched
classical music as we swept through the empty rooms. "But I'm
alone here now. I have sent my wife and children away to where
they will be safer and I like to keep the place feeling full at least.
And such loud music keeps others thinking the house is full, if you
know what I mean."

The GA had been in his post since 1983, but was now thinking
of retiring. Like many government officials in the outstations, the
Situation had led him to consider other opportunities for work. "J.R.
says it is better to die with a bullet in your heart than withering away
like a vegetable in a hospital," I said. "I guess it is easy for him to
say that with his bodyguards in Colombo around him all the time."

"Oh, in that regard I think he is entirely right," the GA replied.
"You can't spend your entire life living in fear. There are, however,

measures you can take, and precautions to prolong your life when it is in danger."

The GA agreed with the assessments that there were over 500 JVP cadres in the jungle nearby. They were not about to launch any kind of frontal assault, but they were intent on paralyzing all government operations. The GA had received three death threats, one coming in the mail just the day before. Either pay us a hundred thousand rupees, get a transfer, or leave immediately, the note had said. It was hard to say, however, what the source of the threat was. In fact, the GA thought it might have come from some of his own subordinates.

He did take precautions. When he traveled within the district he did the driving and the driver sat in the passenger seat. When he traveled to Colombo, he took circuitous, unpredictable routes. Every day his secretary posted a false schedule. But there were only a limited number of things he could do. "Have a biscuit," he said as the servant brought in tea and cookies, turning the side of the plate facing him around so that I would get any cookies that might have been poisoned.

The JVP phenomenon was understandable, he said, as the UNP's ten-year rule without elections had produced great disaffection. Only UNP supporters were getting the jobs, land titles, and privileges that the local MPs had at their disposal. And even supporters were getting angry. "The MP can only satisfy a few people this way and it winds up alienating the rest. Opportunity has been denied these people for ten years now. If it was five years, people could hold their breath and wait for the government to change. But this government has an indefinite writ. It's too long for the people to be denied basic expectations."

The GA saw a worsening situation ahead, with the possibility of a full-blown civil war. For now, the GA said, he was trying to minimize the appearance of a government under siege. One tactic was to maintain the illusion that there was little to worry about by refusing to post a guard around the house. But there were risks to such tricks. "Then again," he said gravely, "I have absolutely no protection here now. Absolutely no protection. No protection at all."

* * *

The next morning we set off for the interior, where JVP activity was most intense and where the government's counterinsurgency campaign had generated reports of fearsome repression and atrocities. As we neared Embilapitya, the scene of much recent conflict, we encountered several South African-made Buffel armored personnel carriers. Inside were commandos belonging to the elite Special Task Force, which had raised havoc in the north with the Tamils and had now been sent to quell the burgeoning unrest in the south.

As if to underscore the furtive air, a magician was performing in the street as we entered town. From what we could make out, he was trying to sell some kind of snake oil and was using the magic tricks to get attention.

Seeing us approach, his eyes lit up and he went into one of his better tricks, cadging a cigarette, tearing it in half, putting one piece in his mouth and the other in his pocket, presumably for after the show. Lighting the piece in his mouth, he took a couple of puffs, then put the whole thing into his mouth. Making an exaggerated effort to gulp for air, he opened his mouth wide, but there was not a trace of a cigarette. Then, as he exhaled smoke from both of his ears, he worked the cigarette back between his lips and puffed on it nonchalantly as if it had never left his mouth.

Originally, some of the senior police and army commanders had counseled that the forces should adopt a hearts-and-minds strategy, asserting that if they captured one terrorist by killing twenty others, then they were creating more problems than they were solving. But the hearts-and-minds approach lost out to those with a heavier hand; in fact, those field officers who resisted force were demoted or transferred. After the assassination of his chief of counterinsurgency and countless of his party subordinates, Jayawardene saw force as a matter of survival.

"They think and act like brutes," the President said in a speech to UNP officials that month, scoffing at advice to go "soft" on the "misguided youth." "We cannot treat them as humans. We have to be tough if we are to free the country from the calamity they represent. We will start the fight tomorrow. Of course, this will be by the bullet, not the ballot."

Most of the victims of the security forces were Sinhalese youths between the ages of fifteen and thirty who were either indiscriminately detained, summarily executed, or shot after they had been nominally released from custody. Most were of the lower castes; in fact, lower-caste identity itself was often incriminating enough for upper-caste police and army officers conducting the campaign. But the prosecution of the JVP often got bound up with the common feuds and envy of Sinhalese rural life. Seeing an opportunity for revenge or to vent jealousies, villagers were accusing their enemies of JVP sympathies, which was enough to bring down the wrath of government forces. Likewise, minor UNP political bosses often used their influence with the military to rid their areas of legitimate political rivals in the opposition party. Additionally, some of the more enterprising in the security forces were operating as contract killers or kidnappers.

The horror of the human rights picture in the south had bitter irony, too. Back when the government was only fighting the Tamils, the Sinhalese of the south had either ignored or cheered the atrocities and other abuses committed under the Prevention of Terrorism Act. They had also been hostile to the Colombo-based groups that had worked with international human rights organizations and had cheered the JVP when it called many of those groups traitors to the Motherland for supporting the peace accord.

However stark reports were of human rights abuses in the area, Embilapitya did not immediately seem affected. We put up at a recently built tourist hotel on the shores of a beautiful tank, an ancient one with the trunks of gnarly trees standing in its shallows. In the early morning, when the dawn was still spectral and gray, herds of water buffalos would sink up to their necks in the muddy water. The hotel manager was happy to see us; he had had few guests other than a local Peace Corps volunteer waiting out the Situation. "Oh, no," the manager laughed when we asked him about the climate around town. "There is no problem now. No problem at all. You can see with your own eyes when you are out, no? No. No problem at all."

The Peace Corps volunteer, a woman from the American Midwest, had a different take on things. She couldn't even tour her district without a military escort. She showed us a map of the areas she was allowed to travel in by herself and those areas where she was not to go. Out of thirty-six rectangular-shaped zones marked on the map, she was permitted to travel into four of them, all within the confines of the town.

She had been the target of an oblique threat delivered in a letter to the District Agent. She represented, it was said, the government's plans to give away land to foreign investors and corporations. The District Agent, a retired colonel, privately told her that the number of incidents of attacks and assassinations was increasing and wouldn't stop for years. Nevertheless, not wanting to signal a lack of confidence in the government, the Peace Corps insisted that she stay in the area, even though she could do nothing other than mark time in the district offices.

We tried to get her boss, the retired colonel, to talk to us, but he wouldn't comment on the political situation. For that, he referred us to the commanding officer of the district, a man named Colonel Lalgama, a young Sinhalese officer who had been handpicked by the brass in Colombo to mop up the local JVP.

Colonel Lalgama was of a type indigenous to the Sinhalese upper classes who dominated the UNP and the Sri Lankan military. Well spoken, natty, handsome, and youngish, he was the epitome of the Sandhurst tradition. Although we were sitting in the garden of the district offices he was using as a headquarters, I could picture him in the Blue Elephant disco at the Hilton, Lacoste shirt and a drink in hand. He was a terrible liar.

The colonel had been newly assigned, receiving his orders just after several top-level UNP officials were murdered by the JVP in Colombo. Embilapitya had had ten political killings by the time he got there, but lately there had been none. No local officials had resigned; no government bureaucrats had asked for transfers. There was fear in the minds of the people, incapacitating fear, but it was largely unnecessary.

The struggle against the JVP was like a block war, Lalgama told me, confined to a couple of villages. "They are not a swarm of flies as they've been depicted, but are only a few flies landing in a few places. The rumor is that the south is not a safe area, but you should know that rumors spring up fast in our country and are not always true. Do you feel fear here, see a lack of public life? No. There is normal life here—transport, public fairs and markets. Everything you could want."

In the colonel's view the best way to fight the JVP was to keep them on the run. The trick was not to let them settle. The other trick was to address the people's fear and dispel it. "Treat the fear and you treat the whole problem. If you take the fear out of the people, they will take care of the problem themselves. The people are against these JVPers. This is a very Buddhist area, and they do not condone the violence and the killing."

Part of taking the fear out of the people involved arming them. This was what I must have mistakenly been referring to, he noted, when I brought up this insidious claim that the government was sanctioning paramilitary squads. Yes, he did acknowledge that some of the citizens in the area had formed private "vigilance" units, but these were only in existence to treat this problem of fear. "I try to get the ones who would be likely targets to arm themselves and be ready."

The real thrust of his strategy was to get close to the people so that the forces could anticipate the JVP's moves. "You get close to the people and it makes your task easier," he explained. "It's more than a matter of hearts and minds, but hearts and minds are the critical factor. It is through hearts and minds that you gain their confidence and eradicate their fear. You don't go for the flies, you go for the breeding ground. That is how we try to eradicate malaria, correct?"

"Mainly, I have two tasks," he concluded. "Public relations and maintaining discipline in the army. But both are essential to one aim: being with the people. We have learned our lessons from the north: the best strategy is to be with the people. Now, granted, I have to take in a hundred suspects to root out the five JVPers among them. It is inevitable that innocents are taken in. So every time I take in a hundred suspects, I risk making ninety-five enemies. The trick is to make those ninety-five go away with a good feeling, and to come back another day as informants."

"This is the problem," said a guide at the temple I visited on my way back to Colombo. We were discussing the spiral of violence, near "The World's Most Colossal Image of the Lord Buddha," a statue that was more than nine stories tall. I had to chuckle at its sheer size, recalling a favorite Peace Corps quip: "The bigger, the better, the Buddha." We were on the top deck of the temple attached to the statue, about even with his nose, looking over the jungle canopy below. "This Buddha will last five thousand years. In 1956, at the Jayanthi, he reached his midpoint, twenty-five hundred years. He will live another twenty-five hundred years until another one is born, but now his power is running down. For the first twenty-five hundred years this power was going up, but now it is going down. This is the problem. For the next twenty-five hundred years, his power will be running out. Now there will be more problems in Sri Lanka—all these problems—politics, economics, this ethnic tension, the activities of the priests that are not for the good." He took out a pen and drew a rough graph on his arm. "Twenty-five hundred years up, and twenty-five hundred years down. Another Buddha is on the way, but it will be a very long time and much suffering before he comes.

"You are an American, no?" he asked beseechingly. "Can you please leave something for the priests? There are so few tourists these days."

12 · Christmas in Batti

I GOT BACK from the south a week before Christmas. Colombo was gripped by holiday fever. A giant Santa traversed the rooftop of the Intercontinental Hotel downtown; on television there was a "White Christmas" special: the star, a Katharine Hepburn look-alike, sang in a candlelit yuletide room. You couldn't sit in a coffee shop or read a newspaper without being bombarded by complaints about holiday obligations. While it was good to see the city rise above its state of siege, there was an edge of desperation that made it all seem false and brittle.

Christmas was a time for the Christianized elite in Colombo to assert itself, a time when even the most chauvinistic Sinhalese Buddhist shrugged and indulged. "I hate to use a ragged phrase," explained columnist Reggie Michael when I asked him to fix the phenomenon in context. "But Christmas comes but once a year. Any year, we wait for it anxiously, but this year even more. It is heightened because we have a need to escape. We are all desperate to break away from our sorrow. All the merrymaking, all the partying is increasing in pitch in proportion to the violence around us."

I didn't relish the idea of spending Christmas in Colombo. In addition to fending off the assiduous holiday beggars, I had had my heart broken, in a way, by a young Sinhalese lady. She was a waitress in the coffee shop at the Hilton Hotel. When I returned to Colombo,

I found out that someone had stolen her away. She had fallen for the appeals of a young Frenchman, a gem trader, I learned, who had proposed marriage. He had whisked her away to the Maldives, after which they were to go to Thailand. Without Amitha, the Hilton wasn't the same. Since I'd shown a preference for her, her partner, who remained behind, was less than friendly. I then committed the ultimate cultural faux pas and asked whether she and Amitha's replacement were sisters. The two were dead ringers for each other, except that this new girl, a Tamil, was slightly darker in complexion. "Sisters!" she screamed. "But she is black and I am white!"

My friend Dieter had the pre-holiday Scrooges himself. He had been waiting around Colombo hoping for something big to break, without much success. His one effort at a photo story had been absolutely frustrating. Another source of irritation that week was our landlady at the Ottery, Mary. She had become irate when she learned that one of the guests, a Peace Corps volunteer, had taken a Sinhalese girl—one of his pupils at the school where he taught in the provinces—upstairs into a room to have some privacy. The volunteer, who suffered from cerebral palsy, had developed an intense romantic attachment to the girl over the last semester, and she to him. Because of sexual strictures, however, the romance had never gotten off the ground. At the end of the term, the two wrote letters back and forth, though, and they made a date to meet in Colombo. The girl told her parents she was going to the city for a job interview.

It would have been bad enough had they been discovered in public together—recently a young couple necking in the up-country had been stoned by villagers. But being found alone in the same room was truly scandalous, though they were only kissing over tea. Mary, joined by her boyfriend, Nimal, screamed at the girl in Sinhala, calling her a slut, and cursed at the volunteer for soiling the reputation of the Ottery. "People will think we have no morals," Mary ranted. "People will think all kinds of bad things about me." (An Australian girl who'd had a succession of Sinhalese boyfriends caused no problem, however.)

Meanwhile, the volunteer, who had never had a girlfriend before, was worried that Mary might "blackguard" the girl by sending back a report to the village, which could make her unmarriageable and prompt her to kill herself. Such an act was common in Sri Lanka, which had one of the world's highest suicide rates, especially in amorous situations. (Ultimately no blackguarding occurred, but the incident caused an interruption of several months in their relationship, which resumed, furtively, before ending when the volunteer returned to America.)

What put the cap on my Christmas blues, however, was the party that my friend Tilak threw one night down on the beach at Mount Lavinia, the tourist town just outside of the city. It was a party for the Black Sheep Society, an organization that Tilak and friends had formed in the last few weeks to lend some structure to their otherwise aimless social life. I should have known better. I had also attended the planning session a few days before, which ended on an ugly note.

There had been a lot of drinking. They were all friends from childhood, and their parents had all been friends, too, as part of the upper class of Tamils and Sinhalese who were free from ethnic divisiveness. Their children, however, were not immune from these forces. That night, when they were settling the bill, the group started teasing their friend Herzan about his "Tamil cheapness." The discussion then turned to the practical jokes they played on him every year around New Year's Eve—blowing up his mailbox, setting his curtains on fire—pranks that hardly seemed friendly.

"Go ahead, you fuckers, try something like that and see where it gets you," Herzan shot back scornfully. "Come on, I'm inviting you to try it."

"Ooh, it's a challenge, then," said one of the Sinhalese archly. "A challenge he has thrown down."

"Yes, come on. I've got friends in the Special Forces. Deep boys, they are. Choice boys. Come on. Come over to visit some night, I'll have the booby traps ready for you. You should know. Those fellows are deep fellows. They've shown me what to do. Come on. Come over. Just try it. I'll have all the bombs set up and when you come in, you'll have had it. And then I'll tell them you were JVP or the Tigers and they'll lock you up, if you are lucky and they don't shoot you right on the spot. Come near my house and I'll make the call and have those fellows over in flash."

"We'll cut your wires," one of his friends said. "You won't be able to reach them."

"Yeah, just try it," Herzan shouted. "Just try it. Last year they firebombed me in my room as I was sleeping. Nice sense of humor, huh? This is a nice way to treat their friend. Come on, just try it this year. I'll be ready."

I shouldn't have been surprised, then, when the party turned out to be less than cordial. Tilak was presiding over the affair in his sarong, standard local beachwear. He had made a potent fruit punch, which his friends had started to hit on pretty hard. Grateful Dead music was coming from the tape player, and hash pipes were making the rounds.

On one of the chaises, Christo, already drunk, was having a nap. Stephen Champion was there, along with Dieter, on his last night in town before heading back home to Delhi, as was Nigel, a huge friend of Tilak's who started out full of good cheer but after a few drinks began to make stupid jokes about Westerners.

Beneath the superficial hospitality, there was subtle resentment. I wondered why I had even been invited, and why the group pretended to get along. In the course of things, Tilak got into a tangle with the man who managed the beach club where we were holding the party. It seemed that the group was trying to stint on paying up in full.

Since I knew the manager from the year before, I was caught in the middle. Meanwhile, Stephen had begun to tangle with Nigel, who was harassing him about being English and about making money as a photographer out of Sri Lankan sorrows. I decided to leave. Halfway back to the hotel, my taxi driver tried to raise the fare on me, which I refused to pay, a stupid decision given how easily revenge could be had in the current breakdown of law and order.

With such a sour atmosphere in Colombo, it was easy to accept an invitation from the Bishop of Batticaloa, Kingsley Swampillai, S.J., to spend Christmas with him and other Jesuit priests in that former Dutch trading town in the eastern province. There had been a mission in Batticaloa since the first French Jesuits arrived there in the late nineteenth century. Most of the current group, six of them Americans, had been there since the late 1940s. Although they were all over sixty, they were still spry and hardy, and I couldn't think of a better group with whom to spend Christmas. And besides, Batti was now located in the middle of the area in which the Indian Army was at work hunting down the Tigers.

Just as the Tiger ideologue Anton Balasingham had predicted during the siege of Jaffna, the battlefield in the war between the LTTE and the Indian peacekeepers had shifted into the scrub jungles of the eastern province. The Indian Peacekeeping Force had poured thousands of troops into the area, and Prabakeran, in response, had ordered his cadres to attack Indian troops directly, a change in strategy that promised to escalate the violence.

The Indians were trying to encourage the impression that they had the LTTE on the run and that they were taking extra care to avoid alienating Tamil civilians in the process. Despite passionate Indian denials, however, reports filtering back to Colombo already told of the heavy hand with which the Indians were conducting searches and interrogations. There were also a growing number of reports concerning atrocities against Tamil civilians. The Tigers were equally brutal, dealing harshly with any Tamil suspected of consorting with Indian officials and planning land-mine ambushes on Indian patrols, which were guaranteed to incite reprisals against nearby Tamil civilians.

Just how we reporters would be received by the Tigers was the subject of some concern. A Tamil lawyer named Sam Tambimuttu, who, as the chief contact for international human rights organizations in Batticaloa, had worked as an intermediary between authorities and the rebels, had warned us that they were growing increasingly desperate. In the past, he had been on fairly good terms with "the boys," but the situation had recently grown much more desperate. He had been forced to flee to Colombo after the Tigers tried to assassinate him.

"They are killing people for merely talking to the IPKF," Sam said, citing an instance in which a school principal had been lamp-posted for merely asking if his students could play a game of soccer on a field the IPKF had said was off-limits.

Given the current mood, Sam warned us not to be too hard-edged in interviewing them: they were very sensitive to criticism. He also warned against going out into the bush to meet them. "They might kidnap you," he insisted. "Let them come to you in town if you arrange any meetings with them. Remember, they have their backs to the wall."

Getting into the eastern province was a complicated matter. As I expected, the Indians denied me permission, which would make it hard to get past their roadblocks and checkpoints. That problem was solved in conversation with the Bishop, who suggested an untraveled route that would bypass most of the Indian checkpoints. The longer route would take two days instead of one, but we'd be able to meet up with some priests who were traveling the road for a funeral and join them, posing as former students back for a visit. The Bishop assured us of hospitality in a college run by an order of Catholic brothers in a town called Kalmunai, three hours south of Batti. If we could get there, we could spend the night, and arrive in Batticaloa the next day, on Christmas Eve.

Our bus took us through some of the most spectacular areas of the up-country. Unlike the soporific calm of the coast, there was an exhilarating edge to the area, its air sharp and clean. As we climbed higher and higher, the hill country spread out in sun-drenched panorama, cut by deep grooves of late-afternoon shadow.

Passing over the highest part of the road, we descended into the beginning of the dry zone. We were now in some pretty dangerous country, an area of the central province where both the JVP and the Tigers were said to maintain camps. The road was almost completely empty. From time to time, we would slow to a halt and the driver would ask for information about the road up ahead.

It must have been the tension of the ride, but I sensed a real nastiness developing among the passengers. Although there was room enough for the man—a Burgher, I thought—clinging to the side of the bus to put his bag inside, the driver wouldn't allow it, making him hold it under his arm as we sped along. "Good Buddhists they are," Stephen hissed as he lit what must have been his hundredth cigarette of the trip. "Lovely people."

Kalmunai had a remote feel to it, but it wasn't so far away that bad news from the capital didn't travel there quickly. That evening, there was a report that one of the highest-ranking leaders of the UNP had been assassinated, a confidant of the President who was said to have coordinated the private death squads. He had been hit in his car, at a busy intersection, with two bodyguards in the front.

The next day we made our way toward Batticaloa. We got past the Indian Army checkpoints with a note from the Catholic brothers. The brothers were concerned about traveling with us, so we went on our own. Several of their colleagues in the north and east had had to pay with their lives for acts that had been interpreted by the Sinhalese military as antigovernment. A Jesuit in Jaffna, for example, an older man, hard of hearing, had been tied with his hands behind his head and shot by the Sri Lankan forces for not revealing Tiger hideouts. And the last time there was a clerical gathering in Batti, the Sri Lankan forces fired randomly at the church, hitting the Bishop's car. In trying to put down the Tamil rebels, the government had found itself repeatedly catching the Catholic Church in the cross fire. "Everyone is worried when they travel in and out of town," said one of the brothers, a Tamil in his late forties. "We can never be sure of arriving or getting back alive."

Although it was Anglicanism that was the official church of the colonial power, the Catholic Church had borne the brunt of Sinhalese Buddhist antipathy. Sinhalese nationalists had targeted it from the earliest phase of the Buddhist revival through the revolution of 1956, decrying the conspiratorial influence of Catholic Action. Relations were hardly bettered by the military coup in 1962 mounted by Catholic officers. Nor were they helped when Tamil Catholic priests, inspired by Liberation Theology after Vatican II, condemned government repression and defended Tamil militants, a stance that estranged them from Sinhalese Catholics, too. The Sinhalese backlash against the Accord revived anti-Catholic paranoia; according to many Buddhist monks, the concept of a "multiethnic" Sri Lanka was really just a code word for Catholic Action, a thinly veiled plot to destroy their religion.

With the animosity toward Catholics, there was probably little remorse among the Sinhalese over the death of a well-known Jesuit priest in Batti that week. We arrived in the middle of the services. Signs of tension were not obvious in town, although there were Indian Army troops patrolling the streets. But when we checked into the Subaraj, the only hotel open, we began to hear tales of Batti's darker side. The outside wall of the hotel, in fact, was chipped and pocked from Indian fire.

After the funeral, we spoke to some priests and parishioners inside the walled courtyard of St. Michael's Cathedral, a large Gothic-style church painted baby blue. The Bishop, a youthful and slender man, told us they were working to keep a lid on the situation so that they could arrange a cease-fire for Christmas. The Indians might then permit midnight mass, if the Tigers could be persuaded from using it to launch an attack. One of the American priests told us that denials of rape and abuse circulating in Colombo were pure propaganda. He swore that he himself had seen the victims. "The forces want peace. The government wants peace," a Tamil priest added. "The people want peace. The Tigers want peace. The Indians want peace. All these people say they want peace. But somehow we don't have any peace. Something must be wrong."

"I respectfully beg to differ," interjected an elderly Tamil man who happened by. "The Indians do not want peace. They have come to put us in pieces, that is what they want."

Just yesterday, the man explained, "these buggers, the Indians," took him into the jungle and roughed him up. "If I hadn't offered resistance they might have shot me. As it was, they belted me on the head a few times and let me go. They are bad people, barbarians. They take our money at the checkpoints, and have a weakness for wristwatches. They rape. They see a woman—mother, sister, daughter, it doesn't matter—all they think of is sex. And their officers cover up for them. They say, we'll make an inquiry and call you back. But they never do. No wonder these Tiger boys are mad at these activities. They are very concerned at what is happening to us."

A woman and her daughter stopped us as we were trying to leave the courtyard to go over and interview the Bishop. Both the woman's sons had been detained by the Indians. One of them had been taken that morning, pulled right from his bed. "Please," the woman cried. "Please ask them to leave us alone and let them go. I beg you. Tomorrow is Christmas, and they wouldn't even let us see them today."

The year before, on my first visit behind "the cadjan curtain," as Tamil territory was known, I had heard very similar stories in Batti. Four years of fighting had devastated the countryside, putting the area on the doorstep of famine, and had resulted in the disappearances of more than 700 young Tamil men and the detention of almost every other young male in the area.

At that time, the Sri Lankan military had just launched a major offensive, an operation that was a rehearsal for the final offensive on the Jaffna peninsula. The operation had involved 3,000 soldiers and commandos as well as a complement of helicopter gunships and took place in the neighborhood of 20,000 civilian residences.

During the offensive, Tiger rebels had detonated a land mine outside the Serendip Prawn Farm, owned by the Colombo-based Serendip Seafood Corporation, in a small hamlet on the peninsula, killing a dozen commandos from the elite Special Task Force. In retaliation, the STF rounded up the employees of the farm and tortured them, in some cases reportedly scooping out their eyes. Then they shot them, along with other Tamil civilians, the toll reaching more than a hundred. Afterward, according to eyewitnesses cited by the local Citizens' Committee, the bodies were burned, inside an army camp, on a pile of automobile tires, in accordance with the Prevention of Terrorism Act; this tactic left no evidence for later investigation and prosecution.

I had also learned, the year before, about Tiger brutality. Tamil priests in the town told us that it was common for militants to set off land mines near civilian settlements, knowing full well that the security forces would mount reprisals. This was part of their strategy, the priests explained. "Better that they were killed, Father," a militant had told one of them. "More propaganda for us."

The trip that year offered the grisly spectacle of a Tiger lampposting, too. On what was to be my last morning in Batti, I woke to the sound of a single gunshot, and was told by the hotel proprietor that the victim was still tied to a post at a nearby bus station. I got there before the security forces. He was a Tamil man in his early thirties. The scene was overwhelmingly still. When troops arrived, they approached the body in formation, walking slowly backward toward it, as if they expected an ambush.

On our way out that afternoon, we were stopped by a young Sinhalese army captain. He fingered our passes with great suspicion. "A very beautiful country, no?" he asked in a mocking tone. "You have seen the body this morning, the lampposting? Yes. Maybe it is best you leave." He withdrew his pistol and buffed it with a small cloth. "Yes. Better that you leave."

"If they gave me an injection to die, I would take it," a retired Tamil railroad clerk later told us. The train we were on finally lurched forward after soldiers discovered no bombs aboard. "It is no longer good to live here. Hitler was a good man. At least he killed the Jews all at once. Here they are doing it slowly."

Relations between the military in Batti and the priests, whose humanitarian work earned them the name "the white Tigers," had been strained from the onset of militancy. Just a few days before, a joint patrol of Indians and Sri Lankans had fired into the dining room at St. Michael's College during dinner. Father Weber, one of the priests there, recounted the incident. "They were firing machine guns—machine guns, I tell you. AK-whatevers. They peppered us. And I mean peppered us, kid. You know, before, when the Accord was signed, it was like V-J Day around here. We were all so happy. Then these guys started it up again. It was so sad and stupid.

"You can still see the bullet holes," he said, emphatically gesturing around the room as he spoke, his skin flapping on his aging arms. "They were serious. They stood down there for five minutes just pouring fire into the room. Later we found over seventy-five shell casings downstairs. Seventy-five! They are small but lethal. Look at those holes! For a while, we thought it was going to be a real miracle, and that our picture of the Last Supper on the wall wouldn't be hit. But they got that, too. And look at the size of the hole it left in the wall!

"Their excuse was they thought there were some Tigers inside the building, but the real reason is that they were mad at us. They were mad because every day we go and try to get releases for boys who have been detained wrongly, who have nothing at all to do with the movement. Boys who go to school. And they hate us for that. Think we are working on behalf of the Tigers. We took the bullet jackets down to the commander and he admitted that they belonged to both the Sri Lankan Army and the Indian Army. But he did nothing about it. He told us it wouldn't happen again. Can you imagine that? That it wouldn't happen again."

Next door, while waiting to speak to the Bishop, I sat with a Tamil man whose nineteen-year-old son had been killed a few days before. The son had been on his way back to Batti from Colombo, where he had interviewed for a pilot-training course in the air force. On the way back, the van he was riding in had been stopped by the IPKF, who took the boy and several other passengers into custody. "They took them into the compound and shot them on the spot," he said. "Two of the others escaped. They were shot in the process, but survived and told us what happened.

"There was no need for them to suspect him of any associations with terrorism; he had his heart set on becoming an air force pilot, my God! But they have taken him away from me. What am I to do? I was totally dependent on him. I have no one to help me now. I have to live totally on my savings. And there are many others in my position."

The Bishop confirmed the man's story, and agreed that there were many others whose relatives had been killed or injured by the Indians on the merest suspicion of association with the Tigers. "In the period before the Accord, at least we knew each other. At least the Sinhalese respected the clergy and the women. But many of these Indian soldiers have never seen a priest, and they've certainly never seen a bishop."

When the Bishop and his priests tried to get higher-ups in the Indian Commission to exercise some control over officers in the field, there was little satisfaction. "They refuse to believe us when we make our complaints. They simply say, 'Oh, our army wouldn't do that. Give us an eyewitness and some evidence.' Then when we persist, they get angry. Can you imagine it?" the Bishop said. "They are angry at us!"

Such indifference put the Bishop in a tough position. Although he had the stature to publicize their abuses internationally, he didn't want to blow his relationship with the Indians, which on a case-by-case basis did save some lives and ease suffering. "I try to keep a good rapport with the IPKF for the sake of the people who come to me with their grievances. I report the matter to the Indians and sometimes I can be effective. But I try to keep aloof as much as possible. I do not want them to think that we are involved in passing information beyond Batticaloa to Amnesty International, the UN, and all that. They are very sensitive. They are very concerned about what gets outside."

The core of the problem, the Bishop explained, was that the Indians were frustrated. "In my opinion they do not understand terrorism properly. You can never put them down. When you are able to crush some, there are many others in the wings ready to jump in. Before, the Tigers trained their cadres in camps. Now they are training them in homes, in the villages. You don't need to go to the jungle for training—to lay land mines or throw grenades. Any one can do it. Seven- and eight-year-old boys can do it. Yes, they are that young now. And girls, too. It is catching on in every home. It is not a question anymore of recruiting formal cadres. That period is over. Everyone is part of the effort now. At home the man is normal. Then he goes out and throws a grenade, but he goes home again and is normal once more. True, there are those in the towns with ambition who want the war to end so they can get on with their lives. But those in the villages whose lives are dull, they can easily be led into this. And the Tigers are their own flesh and blood. Do not ever forget that. That is the key factor—the emotional identification."

As I was wrapping up my talk with the Bishop, he was called outside into an outer office. He came back in and told me that the man I had spoken to just before the interview had been worried about speaking to me and wanted to remind me not to use his name. "So you see, these are the fears we have to live with day to day here. He is worried that if you used his name, the Indians might come after him."

I walked down the hill from St. Michael's to the Subaraj at dusk as curfew fell. In the middle of town, in front of a row of ragged-looking stores, was an incongruous statue of Mahatma Gandhi.

We had a tremendous dinner that night, a Christmas Eve celebration accompanied by fine wine and liquors supplied by the French medical team staying at the hotel. Over pâté de foie gras, a bottle of St.-Emilion, seerfish steaks, and curries of shrimp, lentils, and egg, we toasted each other and Mr. Joseph, our intrepid, sad-eyed host.

Joseph was full of nostalgia for "those days," when instead of gunfire they could stay up late listening to the "Singing Fish" in the Batticaloa lagoon, or go out to the beach whenever they wanted to get crabs. "We would club those little fellows, cook them and eat them and come home without a worry in the world. Now, though, we don't dare to go. The camps are too close by, and we don't know from minute to minute what will happen. We know we will have to live with this problem for some time now. It will be like Beirut. We can't run away."

"Those days" were full of curious tourists who flocked to the east coast when the hotels were first built in the seventies and early eighties. Joseph recalled how it was often difficult to find a room anywhere in the area.

The Indians and the Bishop had arranged to lift the curfew that night to allow midnight mass to take place, but Joseph was hesitant about our plans to go. He was unusually emphatic about it, retaining his smile but nervously pounding his hands on the sides of his legs as he explained that he didn't trust the Indian commanders to relay the message to their troops. A few quick calls to the Bishop and to the police reassured us, though, and Joseph finally let us go, reminding us to return promptly. He would leave the gates open until one-thirty, but after that the guards in the tower next door would shoot anything that moved.

Batti was motionless and dark as a tomb. We heard voices from the guards posted at the end of the bridge into town, and I turned on my flashlight to ensure that they saw us coming. I was worried that the LTTE might be near and would shoot at us, thinking we were Indians, and that the Indians, thinking we were LTTE, might do the same thing. As we passed the guards, we told them we would be returning at one-thirty. "Right," the guards said heartily. "Cheerio, then."

"It's amazing," said Stephen, scanning the rooftops. "We can walk through this town unharmed when people who live here are terrified of poking their noses out their own doors."

Lit by a single light, St. Michael's looked more like a hulking sepulcher than a church. We thought we would be late, but the pews were almost empty when we arrived. Soon, however, a few older women appeared in brightly colored saris and long lace mantillas. Bells marking the beginning of mass coincided with an amplified, indoor rendition of "Jingle Bells." The church began to fill. I was struck by the incongruity of it all: Tamil Catholics and Hindus listening to tacky Christmas music while outside Indian troops manned sniper posts.

Not a man between the ages of fourteen and forty was visible in the church.

The choir of young children began the preludes, a medley of Christmas carols in English, including a robust "Go Tell It on the Mountain." The second choir, made up of older children—girls in bright yellow frocks, boys in white shirts and slacks—was even more energetic, singing Tamil tunes accompanied by what sounded like a carousel organ. By now the church was packed. The aisles were full, and there were even a number of young men, though they clung to the outside doors of the church and visibly braced when they heard the growl of an Indian jeep.

Though it was a grand celebration, St. Michael's emptied right after the liturgy was finished. The soldiers we met on the way back were the same ones we had passed earlier. One Indian hung over a rooftop, his gun muzzle off to one side. "Sir," he called cheerily. "Merry Christmas, sir."

The next day we were invited to have lunch with the American Jesuits up at St. Michael's. Before the meal, Father Cook, the oldest of the Jesuits, buttonholed me on the porch for a discussion about the Marian cult. Mary had predicted that the end of the world would come when the big nations overwhelmed the small. That was India in Sri Lanka, wasn't it? he asked. Soon, according to prophecy, Mary would ride the horn of the moon and rise from the dead to cure the sick, in apparitions that would take place in Spain. "I will lead a tour there," he explained. "By then I will be totally blind, but I would like to get my sight back. Three days after that will be the beginning of the end. I've calculated that with a fifty percent reduction in missiles, it won't be all that bad."

The other priests greeted us and led us into their library for a few drinks before our meal. Father Weber told us a little about the mission, how some of the priests were chaplains during World War II and had come to Ceylon to take over from the French Jesuits after the war. Although the rise of Buddhist nationalism in the fifties had prompted government officials to deport some missionaries—like the convent of French nuns who cared for lepers on an island just off the Batti coast—the Americans were allowed to stay. Yet their close affiliation with the Tamil cause did feed a popular resentment.

"Of course we are not neutral," one of the other priests explained. "You see, these are our people. We have raised them, schooled them. We have seen them suffering, seen them getting shot and killed. How can we remain neutral? We are not in favor of them killing, but when we see them being killed and tortured, we have to take a side. When you've been here as long as we have and see that every ten years there is a pogrom against them, you can't help it."

We sat around for a while sipping arrack while the priests passed Christmas presents among themselves. Most of the gifts were gags—a deflated basketball to Father Hebert for his "coaching prowess" (St. Mike's had a losing season), an award to Father Miller for incessant talking, and one to Father Weber for contrariness. The cook was warmly feted for his ability to feed them, even in the face of three-day curfews, and his assistant for talking his way out of detention by the Special Task Force. While this was going on, Father Del Mar did magic tricks with his handkerchief, and Father Cook snoozed, snapping awake from time to time to continue his disquisition about Mary and the end of the world.

We ate a hearty meal in the bullet-scarred refectory. From a table in the middle of the room piled high with roast duck, turkey, stuffing, and pumpkin pudding, Father Weber served us ample helpings. In the background, a cassette played "Silent Night." "In case we are being bugged," Father Miller joked, "the music will filter out our seditious comments." Father Miller also made light of the recent attack on the dining room. "If they really wanted to kill us they would have had any number of other opportunities to do so. If they really wanted to kill us, they wouldn't have wasted so much ammunition."

The priests were the only ones in Batti, Father Weber said, who had any potential for making life at all tolerable for the civilian population. "We have to consider the reality here: these are people being treated unjustly, people who have had their rights taken away from them systematically over many decades. We are defending them in the best way we know how: to make sure that the innocent are not abused. If they say we are behind what the Tigers are doing, behind the violence, they are wrong."

But, I asked, didn't they wind up sometimes going to bat for boys who were in fact Tigers? "Yes, we worry about that and wonder whether someone we are trying to free might really be in the movement and the parents are just telling us he's not to get him out. But that's the risk we have to take. And anyway, even if he is guilty, they should let the law take its course and give him a fair trial instead of beating him to death as they were doing."

"You have to understand," interjected Father Miller. "The Indians are assuming the same attitude toward the notion of guilt that the Sri Lankans did. Guiltiness for them is anyone who knows the slightest bit about the Tigers, which is almost everybody in the district. Association is guilt in their book and we have to work to stop the abuse and brutality that this notion of guiltiness leads to."

Many times, the priests intervened in cases where government soldiers were detaining Tamil boys to extort money from their wealthy parents, the priests maintained. In one typical case, a boy was taken in, but when the parents went to find out where he was being held, they were told he wasn't in custody. They were then told by lower-ranking officers that he *was* in custody, but that he had confessed to hiding two guns for the movement. If they paid up, however, they might be able to get him out. But if they went to a higher officer, their son's legs would be broken right away, and the officers would see to it that he was killed, after which they would burn the body immediately. Finally, the priests were able to get this boy released, but in other cases they weren't as lucky.

I spent the next two days trying to nail down exactly what was taking place in Batti. I tended to believe the Bishop and the Jesuits, but in such a highly charged political climate I did not discount the possibility that they, too, had an agenda. In order to give their allegations credence, I needed documentation.

It wasn't hard to see that there were many civilian casualties in the hospital.

In the men's ward, there were a number of civilians recovering from war-related wounds. Some of them were from an incident in a town called Ottomadavilli, where an LTTE ambush had elicited an hour-long reprisal against the townspeople, twenty-seven of whom were killed and scores more injured. One of the wounded was a sixteen-year-old boy whose father had been killed outright.

Down the ward from him was a forty-one-year-old Tamil man, a clerk in the municipal offices, who had been tortured under interrogation, his arms and feet broken. Across the aisle from him was a twenty-five-year-old Muslim who had been hit by a mortar shell, one of three fired by the Indians into a predominantly Muslim area which the Indians claimed was sheltering Tigers. Were the people in the area LTTE supporters? I asked the man. "We are Muslims," he answered, chuckling.

Next morning, there was a line of haggard Tamil civilians waiting outside the Batticaloa Trade Union Federation. The group's
representatives were functioning as an ad hoc human rights monitor
in the absence of anybody else. Spearheading the work were two
retired Tamils in their sixties, Kingsley Rajanagan, a former government servant, and his assistant, a retired accountant named S. R.
Rajah. "People were scared when the Sinhalese forces were in control here," said Rajanagan. "But now they are even more scared. At
least the Sri Lankan forces worked under the law of the country,
nominally speaking anyway. But now people do not know under
what law we are working. Civil? Military? Indian? Sri Lankan?"

Rajah shook his head. They were trying to capture Tigers, but
the real Tigers were trained to get away in any situation. "The result
is that only the innocent are apprehended or killed."

The first case they processed that morning was that of a forty-
three-year-old Tamil mechanic and his wife, who had been taken
into custody on suspicion of being LTTE supporters nearly two
months ago. While Rajanagan asked questions, Rajah bashed away
at an old manual typewriter. (The file would later be forwarded to
contacts in Colombo.) While in custody, the man had been tortured
some, but his wife had been tortured badly. Guards had tried to
rape her. Although he was released, his wife was transferred to a
maximum-security prison more than a hundred miles away.

The second complaint was brought by a woman in her late
forties whose two sons had been in detention during the earlier
phase of the war and had been detained anew, without explanation,
by the Indians. The family was now without income, a typical predicament for Tamils in that area. The third case involved a fifty-year-
old fisherman whose sons had been "disappeared" by Sri Lankan
forces earlier in the war and who had himself been taken by the
Indians just the week before, though he was obviously too old to be
a militant.

The half dozen other cases I heard that morning continued in
a similar vein. Besides the basic violations of human rights they
represented, the cases demonstrated that the Indians were abusing
their authority in other ways as well. One such abuse was the use of

informers, like the young Tamil who was sitting on the bridge in town that morning. He was being paid to finger LTTE suspects, but in reality he was using his newfound power to vent a lifetime of grudges. Even his own mother, I was told, had disowned him. The Indians were also detaining Tamils who had shown support for the LTTE during the brief time it was legal to do so, right after the Accord, using videotapes of post-Accord parties and rallies to identify them.

Such heavy-handedness was totally counterproductive, according to the Trade Union Federation. "If the Indians are treating the unarmed Tamils this way," said Rajanagan, "how do you think the ones still with arms are going to think they will be treated if they surrender? Legally speaking, anyone who was in the LTTE before the Accord was given amnesty, and should have been left alone. But if the ones who have quit the LTTE are being roughed up and jailed, what about the ones who are still active? In fact, some of the ones who had quit the LTTE have gone back to it after the treatment they have received at the hands of the Indians."

Yes, agreed Rajah, peering over the typewriter. "Most of those taken into detention are not LTTE at all. Most are innocent civilians who have no involvement, except for maybe giving food to the boys when they were asked. But if you are going to arrest all the people who have given food to the militants, you'd have to take the entire town."

I spent a little time following up on the rumors of the prawn farm massacre. Sam Tambimuttu, the very man who had briefed us the year before on the details of the massacre, had, according to reports, played a role in that incident.

According to the American who was managing the farm at the time, the farm's directors, of whom Sam was one, had been divided about continuing operations amid the prevailing political chaos. The Tigers had also set up camp right next door, which made it appear as though the farm had close ties to the rebels. Sam, it was said, saw an opportunity to profit from the predicament. If the farm ceased operations, he could buy it from the current owners at a very cheap price and could let it lie fallow for a few years until the conflict was over, at which point he would be the sole owner of a very profitable enterprise. To induce the owners to quit, he had allegedly informed the Special Task Force that the farm was a nest of Tigers, thinking they would close it down. Instead, they had wiped out the entire staff in a frenzy of retribution for the soldiers killed in the nearby land-mine blast.

Sam had dismissed the whole story as Tiger propaganda. According to Rajah, with whom I had a tea later that day, Sam had all along used his position to enrich himself. "How did he get the money to build his two houses?" Rajah wanted to know. "These haven't exactly been boom times for lawyers, you know." And wasn't it suspicious that the man who had replaced Sam doing human rights work in Batti had been imprisoned by the Indians?

Father Hebert, who ran the technical institute from which several of the massacred workers had graduated, made the most convincing case. Hebert believed Sam was still angling to assume ownership of the potentially lucrative prawn farm. "He gave information to the Special Task Force to better his position, but it wound up boomeranging on him. It backfired much bigger than anyone could have imagined, and made him a hunted man."

I didn't know what to believe. Most of the rumors I dismissed as disinformation. But if Sam had "collaborated" with the forces in the prawn farm incident, he wouldn't be the first to put self-interest ahead of Tamil solidarity. Many of the informants were members of other militant groups who were offering their services to the Indians in return for protection and advantage at a later date. Others were lone operators, like the one I met on the bridge into town.

By and large, the soldiers on the bridge had been suspicious of me at first, but eventually they believed that I had once been an exchange student in Batti—which was easier and more effective for me to tell them than presenting my credentials. The informer, however, was intent on flexing his power, and one afternoon he called me over.

"What are you doing here?" he sneered. I gave him the story about being a student there years before, but he wanted to know who my teacher had been. "And where are you from? Some days you say America, some days England." He obviously couldn't tell me apart from Stephen, whom he had been badgering that day too. Behind him, the Indian soldiers manning the checkpoint closed in. "We are very concerned about foreigners being here," the informant said. "There are Pakistanis here wanting to hurt the Indians, you know. I am a special intelligence officer of the Indian Army. You'd better tell me what you are doing here." As things were getting tense, a van full of Tamil men drove up for a routine check, diverting the attention of the Indian sentries. "Let him go," one of them ordered. The snitch glowered as I walked away.

The next day we were supposed to travel up the coast for a meeting with the LTTE that one of the Tamil Jesuits had arranged. In the middle of the night, there was a power outage, stilling the overhead fans in our hotel room. I woke with a start, worried about a Tiger attack on the police station next door. Midway through breakfast the next day, an attack did occur. A short burst of light-automatic-weapons fire sent us scrambling for the safety of the back rooms and courtyard.

Most likely we were caught in cross fire between Tigers and Indian forces, with the Sri Lankan police adding to the exchange. The guard in the tower next door was firing his shotgun at the hotel, as if the Tigers were inside with us, sending chips of plaster and pellets ricocheting into the courtyard. I was alarmed at how many Tamil boys had come inside seeking refuge. If the Indians thought the guerrillas were using the Subaraj for cover, they might storm it.

The boys who were crowded into the room with us were not overly worried, however. Lately, gunfire was passing overhead on a regular basis. As if to underscore his nonchalance, one of them cadged a cigarette and went back outside, where he was in the midst of painting a new addition to the hotel. Just then, there were several dull concussions from somewhere near the police station—grenades or mortars. Large columns of oily black smoke leapt into the sky. A few helicopters began to circle overhead. "Well, I guess there goes our meeting with the Tigers," Stephen said. Meanwhile the French nurse was reading the riot act to her husband: "No more of this. This is the last time. The last time, understand?"

The heavy-machine-gun fire drifted away, beyond the police station.

"They will call this Black Sunday," Joseph said as he entered the hotel from his adjoining cottage. He had already been on the phone with the Bishop, trying to establish what had happened. There had been a number of bodies sighted along the roads, and although the bulk of the gunfire had come from next door, the Bishop reported sentries firing in the direction of St. Michael's as well. "You'll have some work to do," Joseph said gravely to the doctors. "The peace of Christmas is finished. There is never more than three or four days of peace in a row."

We waited a long time in the cramped, windowless room. One of the French doctors resumed reading her novel. Stephen took long pulls from a bottle of scotch. I mistook the ordinary sounds of the day—the closing of a door, the tapping of fingers on a tabletop—for gunfire. From time to time, Joseph would scurry away to the phone, to return later with more news from the Bishop.

Soon we learned that the incident began when two Tigers attacked three Sri Lankan policemen who, in violation of provisions in the peace accord restricting them to their barracks, had been shopping near the police station early that morning. The Tigers had killed one, said to be a notorious torturer, outright, and left the other two wounded. More than twenty civilians in the market had also been killed, presumably in the cross fire. Other eruptions of gunfire were the work of Indian sentries who had begun firing wildly. Much of their fire was directed at St. Michael's, as we had expected, where the Bishop's house was hit by several dozen rounds.

We sat tight for another hour or so. As we waited, more information filtered in by phone, casting doubt on reports that those killed had been victims of a cross fire between Indian peacekeepers and the Tigers. The fighting had involved Sri Lankan troops, although the Indian mandate had expressly forbidden them to carry arms. I made a quick call to John Rettie of the BBC in Colombo to let him know something big had happened, but we were quickly cut off, presumably by someone monitoring the line.

Joseph was worried that several dozen might have been killed. It was the first Sunday after Christmas, and the market stalls were crowded with shoppers, perhaps as many as two or three thousand. When we finally got there several hours later, the market was desolate. About half of the fifty stalls in the market had been destroyed. Some of the stores were still in flames. A sick, pulpy smell hung over the area: the unmistakable aroma of charred human flesh. In some spots, pools of blood and human remains lay drying. On the walls still standing I saw bloody handprints.

I spent a while photographing the scene, ignoring orders from the Indian soldiers who were making their way through the area. As I tried to walk away from a captain, I was ordered to halt and accompany them to their headquarters at the police station.

At first, it seemed a good way to visit with the Indian brigadier general in charge of Batti, who had refused to meet us. But the situation was a lot more serious. I told the captain that he had no authority to take me in and that if his superiors wanted me they could come and see me at the hotel later on. But the captain insisted. One of his aides stuck a rifle snout under my arm.

"Thank you for cooperating," the captain responded as we marched away. "We do not want any international incidents, you see."

When Stephen came around a corner, he, too, was marched over to a command post where Sri Lankan police officers and several Indian officers were conferring. Across the street, about a hundred Tamil men and boys were sitting in the entranceway to the police station. They were civilian shields against further Tiger assaults. "Tiger lovers," the Sinhalese police hissed at us. "Arrest them, arrest them," another chanted from the shadows of a tent.

The officer in charge, a colonel, asked for my camera and film, which I refused to give up until I saw the brigadier. This gave me enough time to reach into the bag and exchange the exposed film for a fresh roll, which they accepted, to my great relief. After fifteen minutes, they let us go.

We were told to return to our hotel, but instead we sprinted up to the hospital and the mortuary. Inside, the families of the dead wailed horrifically in a kind of stylized hysteria. In several rows along the floor—there were only a few autopsy tables—the bodies of the victims were displayed, all of them men.

The families of the dead stooped and kneeled over them. Some of the women pulled at their hair, while others cradled the heads of their relatives. One grief-stricken woman was bent over her dead husband, with her fingers delicately placed in his ear, as if in lovemaking. "Innocent people, sir. Innocent people," an elderly Tamil man said over my shoulder.

I went upstairs to the hospital ward in search of eyewitness accounts. The victims contradicted any assumptions of a cross fire. After the attack on the police, the Tigers had vanished into the crowd. Ten minutes later auxiliary Sinhalese police units rushed in, several dozen strong, and began shooting Tamil merchants on the spot. With grenades and incendiary devices, they destroyed the market in the process.

Another visit to the morgue seemed to confirm the story. Most of the victims had been killed by one or two bullets to the head or the chest. None were women, though many women would have been present. "Ceylon police. Ceylon police did all of this, sir," said one man. "The police called them over and shot them straightaway."

There would be no postmortem to establish the facts, however. The bodies would be released to relatives immediately. Already in the coffin maker's shop across from the hospital, carpenters had begun to work.

"Some were shot right away," the Bishop explained in his recreation room, which had been strafed by Indian gunfire. "Others were dragged out and shot as they went for cover. Others, the wounded, were shot as they were on the ground.

"It was absolute insanity that they started shooting over here," the Bishop said, with considerable restraint. "The action was on the other side of town, the Tigers had fled in an entirely different direction, and they man the bridge. The Tigers could never even have gotten across. Anyone who was in the room at the time would have been killed instantly. As soon as they hear shots, however, they go mad, they go into a mad frenzy. They know this is my residence. It shows how careless they are.

"This incident was absolutely unnecessary. They are supposed to be here keeping the peace, but as you see, just because the Indians are here now the problem is not better. In fact, it is much worse. If they are here, they should be able to control the situation. But they cannot. And so they should go back. I spoke to the brigadier, and he said that he had no idea so many people had been killed. But he assured me he would look into the matter. Can you imagine that?" The Bishop's voice dripped with polite sarcasm. "He'll look into the matter."

"I think I am forced to change these curtains," the Bishop's assistant said, fingering the shredded fabric. Across several roofs, we could see the Indian sentry position that had fired upon the house. "Unless, of course, I want to leave the holes here."

Even though he said it would be good to send the world an SOS, the Bishop was not thrilled about the idea of my talking to the BBC at all, which had been arranged through Rettie in Colombo. At first, he couched his objections in terms of what danger I might be placing myself in. At the very least, I should withhold my name in the report, and make sure I left the very first thing in the morning, he said. I asked him if I could stay the night and do the report from his residence. He demurred, explaining that even that would compromise the effectiveness of his work as a mediator between the Indian Army and Tamil residents.

That evening, as I waited at the Subaraj for the BBC to call back, more facts about the afternoon's incident sifted in. The LTTE had merely wanted to kill one police officer they had targeted and had not planned on reprisals. In all, twenty-four bodies had been brought to the morgue, but there were unconfirmed reports that several other bodies had been found along the roadsides.

Meanwhile in Colombo, the Indians were trying to sanitize the events, in order to absolve themselves of any blame. The ease with which the Tigers had struck in the market substantiated Sinhalese claims that the Indians were ineffective in the east. The Indian inability to restrain the Sinhala police, meanwhile, was proof for the Tamils that they were better off without the IPKF.

Unsurprisingly, then, the Indians circulated a story that the IPKF forces had arrived at the scene only after the fact, and had tried to restrain the Sri Lankan police upon doing so. They also exaggerated the scope of the Tiger action, claiming they had launched a frontal assault on the police station itself. And the Bishop's windows? An earthquake or other form of vibration—a version that the Bishop eventually confirmed, in order to let them save face and earn himself a few points for the next inevitable go-round. The Sinhalese were even more florid in their account, claiming that the brunt of the casualties came from LTTE gunfire and from an electrical wire, shot down in the exchange, that electrocuted several people.

I left Batti the next morning, hitching a ride with one of the Tamil Jesuits who was heading down the coast. Father Weber told me that I would be a "dead duck" if I stayed around any longer and even offered me a cassock as disguise. My broadcast might make the Indians so angry they'd come after me, I was told.

The market reprisal was only the first incident in an orgy of violence that broke out in the Batticaloa area. Less than a week later, the Tigers attacked the Muslim town of Kathankudy, about five miles down the coast. This brought me back to the Batti area after a quick pit stop in Colombo and a short trip to Kandy on New Year's eve for a ceremony at the Temple of the Tooth.

The attack on Kathankudy took place after the town put up resistance to a Tiger plan to control the civil administration of the town, a plan which included "taxes" on local merchants. Two Muslim members of the LTTE, residents of the town, had tried to extend the Tiger writ and were attacked by militant Muslim youth loyal to the UNP member of Parliament. One of the Muslim Tigers was killed and the other wounded critically. In reprisal, the Tigers swooped down for a thirty-six-hour spree of burning, killing, looting, taking nearly two dozen Muslims hostage and killing thirteen of them the next day. In response, a Muslim youth group named Jihad called for a holy war—until the IPKF arrived. The Tigers scattered, leaving behind Muslim extremists in search of revenge.

Through the earlier phase of the war, the militant Tamils had assumed that Tamil-speaking Muslims in the eastern province found solidarity in the separatist cause, despite ethnic differences. Muslims saw things differently, however, fearing that they would become a minority within a minority, fears that were exacerbated as peace proposals included them in land conceded to Tamils. Such fears made them ripe for Sinhalese manipulation. In time, the government in Colombo began arming the Muslim home guards.

The Accord had left them in no better position. The Tigers, fearing the Muslims would vote against a referendum on the merger of the north and east, were growing increasingly heavy-handed toward them. In response, young Muslims began to embrace Islamic fundamentalism, rejecting the moderation of the traditional national leadership.

At present, most Muslims rejected a separate Muslim state, but they were growing increasingly worried, however, as young Muslim militants bought arms from other Tamil militant groups. The experience of the Tamils taught a bitter lesson: those who took to arms in the name of protecting the people often won the right to articulate that group's political vision. "Even if it takes a thousand years, there must be God's rule," one Muslim militant told a Muslim journalist friend, envisioning the day when all of the country would live according to the Koran.

After the Accord, the Tigers had begun to use Muslim areas to stage assaults on the IPKF, which caught the Muslims in cross fires and subjected them to atrocities. Such cynical tactics shot sparks back into India itself, where Hindu-Muslim relations were already tense.

Although the town of Kathankudy was large by eastern province standards, it was isolated. Bounded on two sides by Tamil villages and on the other two by water, its 40,000 Muslims—the largest concentration of Muslims on the entire island—were cut off from any other Muslim enclave. The town itself was a labyrinth of narrow streets, impossible to negotiate without assistance. Bruce Palling and I were met by a young Muslim boy who took us to the town's principal mosque. A group of Muslim elders were gathered there to assess the situation. After they finished, we were ushered inside. The cool Islamic green of the decor was a tonic.

We met with A. Mohammed Lebbe, the president of the Federation of Mosques and Muslim Institutions of Kathankudy. Despite the mob of people around him, Lebbe gave off a sense of personal isolation as stark as the collective isolation of the Muslims in that part of the eastern province.

"This is the worst incident since independence," he told us. Afternoon prayers drifted into the conference room. "There were always incidents between the communities, but now the militants on both sides are involved, making it much more dangerous." Many people had been wiped out, he added, their homes and businesses wrecked. People couldn't sleep, children were frightened, and although area leaders had been able to arrange a cease fire, there was still no transportation in or out, no trucks for bringing in food.

It was clear that the Tigers were trying to drag the Muslims into the fighting. "They use the area as a base to confront the Indians and then we are caught in the middle. They think that we should be under control, but we do not want that. We do not want to be slaves to any community. We want to be neutral, but we have been put in a very bad position."

Because extremist youth were a direct challenge to the authority of the elders in the mosque, Lebbe downplayed their size and power. He admitted that there was an armed group, but dismissed reports that they had formed a group called Jihad. These extremists had, however, been very successful in rallying the local youth to fight against the Tigers. At one point, one of them had climbed up into a prayer tower and called upon the men of the town to fight "with their bare hands and the help of the Almighty." The extremists had also let it be known that they would consider it treason if any of the elders negotiated with the Tigers.

The elders, in the meantime, wanted the Indians to stay in the area, but they did not want them to set up a camp near the town, as the Indians planned to do. "Asking them to stay here is to invite too much danger. It is asking for our town to be destroyed."

As darkness was falling, we made a quick tour of a refugee camp to try to corroborate what Lebbe had told us. We also spoke to some Muslims who had been taken hostage and later escaped, one of whom told us how he had watched through a thin blindfold as others were shot point-blank by the Tigers.

It had been an exhausting day, and it wasn't over. As we were threading our way through the back roads of town, all hell broke loose. A group of young Muslims, carrying shotguns and long curved swords, rounded the corner in front of us. Harry, our driver, slowed down, but instead of attacking us, all the Muslims wanted to do was say hello to the Western visitors. One even stuck his hand inside the car for us to shake.

Then, as we turned onto the main road, we saw what the commotion was all about.

Ahead, a crowd of Muslims had gathered at a roadblock fashioned from tree trunks and 55-gallon drums. They were armed with shotguns, bricks, razor blades, and swords. Across a no-man's-land of about two hundred yards, a restive crowd of about a hundred Tamil civilians from a nearby village were gathered. The scene reminded me of old newsreels of India during partition, Muslims and Hindus facing off in murderous rage. Fortunately, Harry's instincts carried the day. Pedal to the floor, we sped away from the Muslims, some of whom seemed to be trying to use us as a shield to attack the infidels up ahead. On the other side of the no-man's-land, however, we were met by a Tamil brandishing a brick. Inexplicably, instead of smashing our windshield, he, too, was cordial and broke into a wide smile.

Batti was filled with all sorts of rumors about what had happened in Kathankudy. A Tamil Jesuit with good contacts among the Tigers claimed that the Indians had made a gentleman's agreement with the LTTE to wipe out the Jihad. Another Tamil priest said that the Jihad group claiming to be the town's defenders were actually extortionists in the pocket of a corrupt local UNP political boss.

The Indian brigadier in Batti still refused to see any journalists, but we were able to meet the Tigers and interview their area commander, a twenty-one-year-old whose nom de guerre was Sitha. He could be met, we were told, less than a quarter mile from a major Indian Army encampment.

Sitha and his band of rebels were playing cricket on a nearby field when we arrived, with their AK-47s in bat bags on the sidelines. "They are very fond of cricket," an older man told us. "But they will be finished soon." Evidently, despite the supersaturation of Indian troops in the area, the Tigers were not too worried.

We were brought to a house on a nearby beach. The occupants sat in a corner while Sitha answered our questions about the attack in the market and the recent trouble in Kathankudy. Harry, a trilingual Tamil, translated. To make sure he was getting it right the Tigers were recording the interview.

Sitha had been in the movement since he was sixteen, rising through the ranks to area commander. He wore a black string around his neck, which bore his cyanide cap, and a pistol and several grenades tucked under his shirt.

Sitha explained that the policeman who had been targeted in the market that day was killed because of his unreasonable arrests of Tamils, his brutality, and his thievery. After the hit, the Tigers involved had warned the civilians to get out of the market immediately, and had tried to divert the police by shooting into the air as they fled. The attack on the Muslims, meanwhile, had come only after many warnings. We had been misled, Sitha said. The people of the town supported the attack on the Jihad. The Tigers respected the wishes of the Muslim elders, who wanted to avoid violence against the IPKF in their communities.

But, Sitha added, the Muslims had to see that the Tigers were the principal power in the area. The Muslims were gaining political power without having to fight or pay for it themselves. It was only right that the Muslim merchants give the Tigers money to keep the struggle going.

If the Indians were prepared to keep the peace, the Tigers were, too, but if they were intent on conflict, the Tigers would attack in return. New members were joining every day, Sitha said. "And we are used to guerrilla warfare here in the east. It is what we were fighting right from the beginning. They will not be as successful as they were in Jaffna."

13 · Kandy

IN BETWEEN MY two trips to Batti, I headed up-country from
Colombo to Kandy on New Year's Eve. The government had just
finished building a Golden Canopy over the sacred Temple of the
Tooth and was celebrating with a daylong series of dedication ceremonies and processions. Said to be a bicuspid of the Lord Buddha
himself, the tooth relic was perhaps the most enduring sign of the
continuing role that religion had in legitimizing secular power. According to legend, the relic was spirited out of India by a beautiful
princess who had hidden it in her hair when forces hostile to Buddhism tried to crush the religion in the fourth century A.D.

The tooth was considered a symbol of the Buddha's righteousness, and in ancient times the mere possession of it was enough to
confer legitimacy on the king. Conversely, without the tooth no king
could command a mandate. As a result, it was fought over constantly.

In the Great Rebellion of 1818 against British rule, British capture of the tooth relic was a great victory, signalling that the British
were fated to rule Ceylon. While the disestablishment of Buddhism
caused the relic to lose its official aura, as Sinhalese Buddhist nationalism mounted, the tooth relic regained its lost force. It was now
symbolic of an idea of national sovereignty that was exclusively
Sinhalese. "As long as our great shrines such as that of the sacred
tooth relic exist on the soil of this island," a leading archconservative

monk wrote in a newspaper column, "it will remain a Sinhala Buddhist country. The presence of non-Sinhala and non-Buddhist minorities will in no way make it a multinational, multireligious country."

Since the great Sinhalese political and cultural resurgence of 1956, the veneration of the sacred tooth relic had become a virtual state cult, with the Temple of the Tooth in Kandy taking on a significance akin to Rome's St. Peter's Basilica or Jerusalem's Dome of the Rock. The government spent great amounts of money on the temple itself and also on the annual ritual called the Kandy Perahera. Once a year, during the full moon of July, a cask containing the tooth relic was paraded around the sacred Kandy Lake in a procession of thousands of dancers and grandly caparisoned elephants.

Rituals connected with the tooth were a way for the government to fulfill its mandate to preserve and protect Buddhism. But the procession this New Year's Eve was also an opportunity for rebel groups, particularly the JVP, to contest that mandate.

Despite the certainty that the JVP would try to attack or disrupt Kandy during the ceremonies, people from all over the country were flocking there to witness the unveiling of the temple's new roof. As a result, train service was miserable. The train I got made all local stops.

The trip was also unpleasant for the unmistakable impression I was getting from the other passengers that I was an unwelcome outlander, "thuppai" to the max. It was interesting after spending time with Tamils in Batti to compare them with the Sinhalese, who seemed more suspicious, insular, and racially prejudiced than ever. The Tamils, however long they had been living in the chaos and uncertainty of war zones, had a lot more warmth and generosity.

Although I had arrived later than I wanted to, the ceremony had yet to start. I amused myself looking at the elephants that were being led through town. They were strolling, chewing a few clumps of grass and branches from trees as they lumbered past. Later that night, there was to be a Perahera, which would transform the elephants into creatures from another world, bedecked with lights and the finest silk brocade. While this mini-Perahera would not be as awesome as the annual ten-day extravaganza in July, it would still be impressive.

Security seemed curiously light in town. It would have been simple for the JVP to have planted a bomb in the temple amidst the last-minute rush there to complete the Golden Canopy. In the distance, beyond the massive throngs, the new canopy was visible, wrapped in crimson-colored ceremonial bunting, which would be removed after the afternoon's ceremonies. Adding to the sense of pageantry were lines of monks marching into the area from their monasteries around the lake, columns of saffron emerging out of cool green shadow. Depending on their caste, some monks carried umbrellas to ward off the sun, while others bore wide ola-leaf fans.

At just about noon, the crowd surged to welcome the Prime Minister, Ranasinghe Premadasa, the master of ceremonies, who bowed low from the waist and gave the Buddhist high sign. The Golden Canopy was his project, conceived of as part of his Million Houses Building Project, one of the government's most ambitious social welfare programs. It was considered of the greatest merit that a "house" for the Buddha's tooth relic was constructed as part of the program, which put the Prime Minister in a position to gain a great amount of popular Sinhalese support.

Into the empty, cerulean sky, the Prime Minister raised the Buddhist flag on the temple's flagpole outside. At no point was the Sri Lankan national flag, with symbols of the Tamil and Muslim minorities, run up beside it. As the flag went up, people in the crowd were wearing the most rapt expressions, transported by the rite. They broke into a solemn chorus—"Sadhu! Sadhu!"—over and over.

The Prime Minister led a procession of dignitaries along the walkway approaching the temple. Lining the route were men dressed as ceremonial guards. They bore long wooden pikes tipped with polished brass tridents. Among them were musicians, who blew on long curved horns or ceremonial conch shells. Others beat drums. Also in the procession were traditional Kandyan dervish dancers, their white sarongs pleated in a feminine fashion, with breastplates and hats made of jingling shells and pieces of polished silver that shivered when they twirled and jumped.

The temple resembled a fortress. It was hard to muscle into the more interior precincts of the temple, which were stifling from all the people who were packed inside to see the rituals dedicating the canopy.

A crowd of dignitaries stood in front of the tooth relic room in the middle of the temple. The crowded galleries around them continued the mantric chant of "Sadhu! Sadhu!" Although many scholars have scoffed at the notion that the relic in question was indeed the tooth of the Buddha—Leonard Woolf, who claimed to have seen it, said it looked more like a dog's tooth than a human's—whatever was in there possessed an extraordinary holy force for those who believed.

The relic room was a wooden structure, like a little chapel, with huge ivory tusks flanking its doorway. On an earlier trip several months before, I had been able to get close enough to look inside, where I saw a cluster of monks sitting around what I took to be the cask containing the tooth. Due to the crowded conditions, I was unable to get close this time. Instead, I stood on a small flight of steps in the back of the chamber, just able to see the dignitaries pass a line of monks in front of the relic room.

There was a lot of confusion in the chamber, no clear sense of what was going on or who was doing what. The ritual, it seemed, was taking place on its own, through the people performing and witnessing it, as if it were a living entity. The first part, called a *puja*, involved veneration of the tooth and was performed to demonstrate a commitment to protect it. The second part of the rite, called a *dana*, involved a ceremonial feeding of the monks to show official support for the members of the sangha and deference to the role they played in society.

Later that afternoon there was an impressive moment when the bunting covering the Golden Canopy was removed. As the cover blew off into the wind, the Golden Canopy itself was left gleaming in the afternoon sunlight. At that, a loud, profoundly resonant cheer went up again, before the crowd filed out of the temple to an open-air hallway next door. There, a long afternoon session began, with one of the country's most senior monks giving a convocation address, flanked by men dressed as warriors who blew martial-style horns.

In traditional Sinhalese society, royal patronage for rituals like the ones at the Temple of the Tooth that day was only part of the king's claim to legitimacy. According to the Sinhalese version of classical Theravada Buddhism, the individual quest for spiritual perfection was only possible in a state actively devoted to Buddhist ideals. Therefore the king was also expected to exemplify personally Buddhist morality and values as if he himself was a bodhisattva, or Buddha-in-progress. Another obligation was to provide for the general social welfare of his subjects through large-scale public works, like the ancient irrigation system of the Golden Age, so that their spiritual development would not be hindered by a lack of prosperity. Most importantly, the king was expected to show respect and deference for the members of the sangha and to heed their advice, an obligation that made it difficult to wield royal power arbitrarily.

Although many Colombo analysts balked at suggestions that provisions in the 1978 constitution to "protect and foster the Buddha *sasana*" made Buddhism the state religion of Sri Lanka, many of the classical expectations of Buddhist kingship had been tacitly absorbed into the country's supposedly secular political culture. As a result, the President's political legitimacy rested upon fulfilling many of the same responsibilities as those of ancient Sinhalese kings, intertwining the country's modern democratic expectations with religious precepts of the past.

The government in power under J.R. had demonstrated its commitment to Buddhism in the form of lavish patronage to Buddhist temples and shrines. Nevertheless, there was a deepening popular impression that it had failed to live up to its constitutional obligations to preserve the Buddha *sasana*. The signing of the Accord strengthened this impression. Maintaining the *sasana* entailed a lot more than building shrines, explained one highly respected Buddhist layman, who was also a critic of the ruling UNP. "This government has done everything it can to destroy the Buddha *sasana* in this country," he insisted. "And the people know it. It is rotten to the core."

The case against the government contained a number of charges. First was its failure to maintain basic security for the Sinhalese, especially those in the north and east. The government's dereliction of duty on this count also extended to its failure to protect Buddhist shrines, which were in many cases desecrated by Tamil rebels. There was also considerable dissatisfaction tied to the spreading lawlessness in the south. Though the JVP was largely responsible for the chaos, the government was unable to stop it.

Another violation of the *sasana* involved the socioeconomic conditions government policies encouraged. Instead of providing for general prosperity and social justice, the UNP regime had promoted gross economic disparity, institutional corruption, and "false" materialistic values akin to those of the old Anglicized elite that were at odds with Buddhist expectations. Signs of these false values were everywhere—in the kind of sex- and violence-ridden movies that were shown in Colombo, in the egregious greed and corruption of "baby farms" run by illegal international adoption rackets that were winked at by government officials, and in the policies that encouraged gambling and the consumption of alcohol while turning a blind eye toward petty exploitation in the form of food adulteration and usury.

Most of the responsibility for these perceived violations of the *sasana* was laid at the feet of J. R. Jayawardene. Although he had tried to portray himself as a pious Buddhist, his critics said he was concerned with the building of shrines at the expense of the substance. He reveled in his Westernized orientation, his reading of *The Times* of London, his status as an alumnus of the Royal College. "What good is culture?" he had once asked an audience at a literary awards ceremony. "Can you eat it? Can it get you a telephone or a car?"

Furthermore, Jayawardene made intemperate remarks about the JVP, using terms usually reserved for animals. "They are not animals," chided one monk. "They are human beings. We should teach them to be better." That J.R. had also issued death threats against the JVP was considered particularly offensive. "Where has a political leader in the world ever publicly given people a license to kill as he did in that speech?" asked a prominent Sinhalese attorney. "The speech was shocking." Added another lawyer: "Would you expect a respectable head of state to summon his security forces and his own private forces and say, 'They are animals, brutes—go kill them and if you're in trouble I will pass legislation in Parliament absolving you for what you've done'? It is unheard of—here or anywhere else."

Jayawardene's worst lapse in terms of his obligations toward the *sasana*, however, involved his running feud with the monks. Even before the war flared in the mid-eighties, the sangha was complaining that it had grown isolated from the mainstream of the country's political life once again. Once war broke out they grew even testier, deeply resentful that Jayawardene appeared deaf to their counsel on dealing with the Tamils.

Antipathy between Jayawardene and the monks came to a head after the signing of the peace accord. In a bid to discipline the monks for rioting after the Accord, the government withdrew the subsidies used to pay salaries for monks teaching in Buddhist schools and passed legislation requiring them to possess identity cards. It also began arresting and detaining many of them, which violated deep-seated taboos against using violence against the clergy.

As doubts about its legitimacy began to harden, the government initiated a very subtle effort to retrieve its mandate from the public. The rhetoric of government ministers as well as the President began to brim over with self-conscious allusions to Lanka's glorious Buddhist past. The government also announced jobs and housing programs, scholarship funds for poor rural students, and school lunch programs, all of which were designed to fulfill expectations of long-standing traditions of state welfarism and royal largesse.

But the most self-conscious bid to create the impression of government fidelity came in the form of government patronage to the sangha—lavish gifts to influential monks and generous outlays for building and refurbishing shrines. Whether the politics of placation would work was another question. Symbolic displays of support for Buddhism like the Golden Canopy and the festivities accompanying it helped the government restore some of its lost luster. But the more substantive complaints against the regime were harder to beat back.

To mark the importance of the dedication of the Golden Canopy, the ritual procession known as the Perahera was scheduled for later that evening. The Perahera was the most vital manifestation of the link between politics and religion. In it, a people divided by caste came together in ritual harmony to enact a pageant that stood at the heart of their shared sense of sacred mission. The Perahera, in essence, was a microcosm of the entire society, and even provided a place for certain castes of Tamils who were acknowledged as a valued constellation within the wider galaxy of the Sinhala Buddhist kingdom.

In the days of the Kandyan kings, the Perahera also played an important political role as well, providing an opportunity for the king to meet his chiefs and appointees from scattered points around the island. Back then, between preparations for the festival and the festival itself, the king would have his chiefs in town for up to a month. During this period, differences over important political issues were bridged and alliances crafted, leading to harmony in the land. If the king's powers of persuasion didn't hammer out consensus among his chiefs, another dividend of the Perahera was that it allowed him to exhibit his warriors and weapons.

As darkness fell, Kandy began to look festive. The town was bedecked by garlands of electric lights and Buddha statues in gaudy shades. The Temple of the Tooth was illuminated by powerful spotlights, in contrast to the inky stillness of the lake and the moody hills surrounding the town. Crowds assembled in anticipation of the procession, and late-arriving elephants, their trunks curled around grass and leaves, were routed through town by their mahouts.

But the anticipatory air had an undercurrent of tension. Last year's Perahera had been truncated by the first wave of violence protesting the peace accord, and there was fear that this night's mini-procession might suffer a similar fate. Although the JVP had made no statement about the event, I had heard stories that they looked disparagingly upon the dedication of the Golden Canopy as a thinly disguised bid to manipulate popular emotions. Attacking the Perahera might be bad karma for the JVP, but it would be effective strategy.

The JVP had ample opportunities to disrupt the procession, since it was hard to make the city of Kandy totally secure. Although Kandy had been spared the violence afflicting the rest of the south, the JVP looked like it was about to bring Kandy into the fray, expanding its operations there.

Many of the Western reporters in Colombo at that time had dismissed the Perahera as a quaint local custom with little importance for the country's political situation. My friend Stephen and I therefore attracted a fair bit of attention, not all of it good. At one point, a policeman motioned me out of the street, and, unsatisfied by my haste, he overreacted and grabbed me by the hand in an extremely painful way.

We also ran into a lot of resentment in the Muslim café where we ate. At the counter, Stephen got into an altercation with a drunk who exhibited nationalist proclivities, after a fairly even-tempered political discussion about the Prime Minister's chances in the next election. "Don't you dare call him Premadasa," the man shouted. "Show some respect. Call him Prime Minister Premadasa."

Throngs packed the procession route. Many more were perched in the windows along the way. The sheer number of people jammed into town would make any rebel activity very messy. "Have no worry," said a constable assigned to crowd control. "The situation is normal. There is nothing to worry about. We are always here to help you. These terrorist fellows are only in the south. Nothing to worry about."

"Yes," Stephen replied facetiously. "They probably all went away on holiday, correct?"

The constable guffawed at the thought, his reaction very much out of proportion. "Correct. Correct. Holiday. That's a good one."

He told us that there were at least 2,000 police commandos in town, which looked about right. Some were on foot, others on bicycles or on horseback. Pushing and surging, the crowd seemed like it would be hard to contain, but when a group of masked men wearing ceremonial garb came up the street, slashing the air with broadswords and cracking whips, the crowd fell perfectly silent and still. The Perahera had begun.

After the swordsmen came the fire jugglers, some with long batons lit at either end, others twirling pinwheel-like contraptions that created freestanding circles of fire. Soon the whole street was lit up by flames. Posted ten feet apart, a line of pickets had materialized on each side of the parade, holding long staves cocked at sixty-degree angles with buckets of burning pitch at the end. They strained to avoid being burned by the flames that leapt back at them as the wind shifted.

The main procession consisted of groups of dancers, each representing a different caste or regional group. One unit of teenaged boys carried small brooms, another carried broadswords gleaming in the firelight. A contingent of older men, a hundred or more, carried the blue, orange, white, red, and yellow Buddhist colors. Other dancing troupes moved through the streets in paroxysms and fugues, gyrations and shivers, as cymbals clashed and drums beat insistently. Jugglers, acrobats, and magicians rounded out the parade.

Between each contingent were grandly decorated elephants in capes of crimson, maroon, orange, and black that were studded with blinking electric lights. Accompanied by a mahout and ridden by men who wore the historical garb of ancient Kandyan chiefs, the first few elephants marched in single file, but as the parade progressed, they marched two, three, and even four abreast. Around their feet were chains.

The Perahera was by far the most intensely authentic and alien thing I saw in my time in Sri Lanka. Often the Sinhalese seemed to suffer from cultural deracination, or from an overcompensating tendency to make culture a fetish object. But here the Sinhalese were more substantial and more natural than I had ever seen them. This piece of sacred traditional culture invigorated them with the strength of identity. It was an utterly transportive experience.

This feeling, however, did not come without a sense of estrangement for me. I could see how the first Englishmen to have seen the Perahera must have thought they were witnessing something from the bowels of a pagan hell. It was a fiery hallucination of voodoo intensity that would give any Westerner pause.

As the last elephant passed, the crowd began to surge and swell a little bit. Physically, the sensation was like wind filling out a sail, but there was something baleful about it. The crowd dynamic had an intensity that I normally associated with India, where people are routinely crushed to death at festivals. Across the street, a whole tier of people standing on the steps lining the route fell off into the road, prompting police attention.

I assumed that there was a robbery or some youthful unruliness. Back at my hotel, however, the clerk told me that a number of bombs had exploded at the tail end of the parade, perhaps the first salvo in a JVP assault, or a lure to draw a police response for an ambush.

I hurried back outside. The smells of gunpowder and burned human flesh hanging in the streets were unmistakable, but it was unclear what kind of bomb had gone off. As I tried to follow a group of police commandos, I was stopped by an officer, his pistol drawn. He told me that I could not go any further—it was a restricted area. Other pedestrians were also stopped and searched. The bomb, it seemed, had blown up not three blocks from the reviewing stand, along a side street that was part of the parade route.

I managed to get past the police. Not fifty feet from where the blast occurred, about a hundred police officers were assembled in riot gear. It wasn't a terribly big bomb by Sri Lankan standards, but it had done a fair bit of damage. There were unconfirmed reports of five or six killed and eleven injured. Luckily, the tail end of the parade had moved faster than usual. Those still marching, the trustees of the temple and the custodian bringing up the rear, had passed the site of the explosion just a few minutes before the bomb went off.

I headed back to the hotel to see if I could get a phone line and make a report, but just as I got out of the cordoned-off area, there was another explosion and then a third. Two more bombs in almost the exact same spot as the first. Luckily, no one was hurt, not even the explosive-sniffing dog that had its snout in a pile of garbage and debris about ten feet away.

Back at the hotel, I found the Minister of Justice, an aristocratic Sinhalese whose family had long connections to the Temple of the Tooth. His father had been a compatriot of Dharmapala; his son was the custodian of the temple and he, although a stalwart of the UNP and a supporter of the peace accord, was quite revered by Buddhist laymen. "I wish I was an astrologer," he replied when I asked who he thought had set off the bombs and why. "Maybe then I could answer your question."

He was heading down to the hospital soon to check into the casualties, and he invited me along so I could get the facts right, since exaggerated reports would make the government look shakier than it already looked.

The hospital was more crowded than the initial casualty reports would have suggested. Patients were sitting on benches in the corridors to make room for the more seriously injured. A deputy police inspector on the scene gave us the official version: four dead and eighteen critically injured. "Happy New Year, sir," another police inspector said sarcastically to the minister as we were leaving the hospital ground. "Yes," said the minister, copying the tone. "Happy New Year to you, too."

The attack was clearly incoherent, the minister said, applying his spin as we drove through the dark streets. It showed there was serious dislocation in their movement. If not, they wouldn't be targeting innocent civilians to make themselves appear strong and unstoppable.

But the minister wasn't very convincing. Kandy had been ringed with security officers and crawling with undercover agents on the lookout for suspicious parcels. Nevertheless, someone had gotten through with not one but three separate bombs. "We were lucky," the minister admitted, letting his relief show through his otherwise casual air. "It would have been too horrific to consider, because if the bombs had gone off with the elephants still around, it might have started a stampede."

14 · Waiting for the Soldier

BACK IN COLOMBO later that month, N., my articulate Tamil friend, called, after a long lapse. I had heard he was worried that I wasn't trustworthy and that his disparaging comments about Sinhalese Buddhists might wind up in the magazine I was now working for. In the current climate of extremism, that could have meant death, from any number of corners. "You have to understand. We are all living under extraordinary pressure now," he explained agitatedly. "The fear. The madness of the situation now. Every day we all hear horror stories about people we know. It's an awful reality we are now living. We're all just trying to hold it together."

So I visited him at his house, where he introduced me to an Englishman dressed in the saffron robes of a Sinhalese monk. He wore his gray hair tied in a bun on top and he called himself "Swami." For almost two decades, he had lived at the odd intersection of the expatriate academic community, the local intelligentsia, and the community of Lankan spiritual seekers.

N. and Swami were arguing over a soon to be published book that examined the importance of S.W.R.D. Bandaranaike and the legacy of 1956, a subject under much discussion as the new wave of Sinhalese nationalism engulfed society.

"There was something to be proud of, something to exalt. I will grant you that, Swami," said N. "But we never saw the great capacity for destruction within the tradition we were enshrining. That was all pushed under the carpet. No one would ever admit how much of an enemy institutional Buddhism has been to intellectual life, how much it has suppressed critical inquiry."

Swami, on the other hand, defended Bandaranaike and what he represented to the Sinhalese. "They were humiliated by the British," he said. "They wanted revenge. Even today, they don't really own their own culture, their own country, their own destiny. They are still foreigners in their own bloody country, with no one to stand up for their rights. If they want a job, they need to speak English, they need to wear pants. And they still have to fear the Tamils, even after all these centuries."

N. countered that Swami was only responding to myths about cultural engulfment. In fact, he said, there were long periods when Tamils ruled the country at the invitation of the Sinhalese, and ruled it well. How could the Sinhalese be victims when they had over 90 percent of the public-sector jobs and 90 percent of the investment resources of the country, as another book he handed Swami contended.

Hearing this, Swami grew peeved. "It's very easy to write shit like this," he sniffed. "All I know is that you and all your liberal-minded intellectual friends in the bloody liberal press are full of bloody rubbish. If it was up to you all, the Sinhalese wouldn't even exist as a people, you'd have them all believing they were really Tamils."

N. told Swami he needed a text to back up his contentions.

"I'll give you a bloody text," Swami shouted. "I've been keeping files on those bloody fucking think tanks and the liberal-minded press. Stick it up your ass. They're all full of shit."

At that point N. seemed to sense danger and was trying now to keep the lid on what looked like a volcanic situation. He had obviously had experience with Swami before. "Swami," he pleaded nervously, "please postpone this discussion until we can cite the proper texts."

"Stick it up your ass," Swami shouted once again, grabbing the book and throwing it to the floor.

At that point N. told Swami that if he continued to use such foul language, he had no other choice but to ask him to leave. In response, Swami told N. to "stick it up his ass" once again, and promptly stormed out the door.

"Get the real facts," he called over his shoulder to me. "There's nothing but lies being told in here."

Unsure of what had happened, I smiled nervously in hopes that it would help N. to keep from losing face. But N. was slumped over in a chair across the room. He looked like he'd been mugged. He got up and made a beeline to the liquor cabinet. "I've known him for thirty years," he said in a monotone as he began to circle the room in a counterclockwise direction. "I shouldn't have shown him that book. He'll go out and tell everyone I'm harboring Tamil propaganda in my house. That man is very dangerous to me. He'll go away saying I am propagating Tamil lies. I know that he will. I know him. His reaction is very widespread. You saw the way it comes out. This chauvinism is everywhere now, like a poison. He's an Englishman, but he's adopted the views of the Sinhalese. He's scared they'll suspect him, so he has to be more Sinhalese, more rabid than even they are.

"Now you see why the JVP is murdering people who disagree with them. If someone like Swami can erupt like that, imagine the Sinhalese youth who has no culture or education, who has been intellectually debased by years of Buddhist propaganda. Forget he's English. See him as a representative of a particular reactionary tendency running through this society. Look at the way he treated this book. And he's wearing the robes of a holy man, purporting to be a gentle Buddhist. He was going to tear that book apart. And attacking my friends for publishing the truth. So you see the enormous precipice over which we are looming. If someone like him, someone with spiritual aspirations and intellectual training, can fall over it into the pit of myth and propaganda, imagine what can happen to others with less awareness and critical detachment. It's like Nazi Germany living here now. We, the thinking people, live as if in a time of witchhunts. We all live under the threat of death for simply underlining the truth, lucky not to be dragged through the streets. Intellectual skepticism has no place anymore. To be in favor of detached inquiry and intellectual freedoms, to be in favor of fundamental political rights regardless of ethnic background, or to support the accurate writing of history as opposed to this pro-Sinhala view has become an unpatriotic act.

"My friends all tell me to avoid confrontations like that, that I'll suffer for them. But I am the kind of person who wants to discuss ideas, who can't stop doing so. How can you not discuss ideas if you are an intellectual? But that is the attitude of ninety percent of the intellectuals in this country now: Don't talk. Don't talk. You want to know now why I was treating you so standoffishly the first time we met? I wanted to figure out what side you were on, and how trustworthy you were. I was checking you out. We have to be careful."

We headed out for lunch. At the door, though, N. drew up short. Sticking in the door was a replica of a spear-shaped Hindu trident—a gesture on Swami's part, I presumed, to remind N. of the unpredictable times they were living in.

"Let me have a glass of water first," N. insisted, retreating inside. "Let me find my other pair of slippers," he called over his shoulder, heading again for the liquor cabinet. "Oh, what a day it's already been. And I was just coming out of yesterday."

Although I was a bit bewildered by the exchange between Swami and N., time spent among the Colombo intelligentsia made clear that this disagreement represented the polarization that had overtaken the Sri Lankan intellectual community. At one time, Sri Lanka boasted a vibrant and assertive intellectual elite whose scholarship far exceeded that of any other Third World nation. But in the rising tide of Sinhalese Buddhist nationalism and the leaden orthodoxy it imposed on academia and the press, the remnants of that once flourishing intelligentsia were driven to the margins.

Prior to Sinhalese Buddhist hegemony in 1956, the intellectual elite, like their counterparts in the political ruling class, prided themselves on their attachment to the Western political tradition and to the cultural ideals of secularism and cosmopolitanism. For them cultural true north was an arrow that pointed indisputably to England, to Oxford and Cambridge, to advanced degrees and places at the bar.

The intellectual balance of power shifted abruptly in 1956, however, when Sinhalese Buddhist nationalism captured the popular imagination and state power along with it. Just as the bright saffron of monks and the traditional Sinhala trumpets at the opening of Parliament after that watershed election heralded a new era of Sinhalese political power and cultural pride, so too did they foreshadow a new intellectual order. Although the Westernized intelligentsia would still have a great deal of influence in society, an intelligentsia that embraced Buddhist revivalism and its ideological cant came to rival and overshadow it, resulting in a rapid decline of old intellectual traditions.

In addition to policies that yoked academic scholarship to the exigencies of Sinhala nationalism, intellectual life suffered under the pressure of the new affirmative action policies, which admitted many unqualified students to universities. It was further damaged by university curriculum reform which accented heavily politicized courses in Sinhalese arts and literature at the expense of the old classical course of study and did away with the mandatory study of English. Nor was intellectual life advanced by government failure to sponsor the translation of Western works into Sinhala, which limited exposure to ideas outside the rather narrow indigenous tradition.

In the face of this far-reaching cultural transformation, Westernized intellectuals were largely impotent. In fact, at the beginning of it, many liberal-minded Ceylonese were in favor of the Sinhalese Buddhist nationalist agenda, particularly university reforms, seeing them as progressive measures that would offset the cultural oppression of the colonial era. "People were lyrical, in rapture," remembered one Burgher. While some worried that changes would lower academic standards, their reservations were ignored or dismissed. Standards were really nothing more than a code for the former elite's waning power and privilege.

Many intellectuals, especially those in the universities, also used ethnicity to enhance job mobility. As the climate inside academia grew more politicized, embracing or rejecting the Sinhalese Buddhist orthodoxy became a factor in the competition for positions.

In time, though, many intellectuals who originally supported the changes lived to regret them. "I've seen a whole generation go through the system since we've changed," explained the Burgher, the daughter of a prominent historian. "I am not in the least procolonial, but I would say that the wider knowledge has been lost. Their awareness of things has shrunk. In hindsight you cannot blame them. We were living in the wave of euphoria after independence. But what happened in the process was that we threw the baby out with the bath water. Standards have declined, and as a result, we have moved only backwards."

"The voices of caution were ignored at the time," lamented another Colombo intellectual, a columnist drummed out of print for her unpopular views. "I feel sorry and sad for our country now because we have withdrawn from the rest of the world. We have to survive in the modern world and we won't be able to do that by shrinking back into this Sinhala Buddhist attitude. It won't take us anywhere. We have now severed the lines of communication with the outside world and in another generation we will be completely isolated, our second-rate educations making us prey to all manner of romantic ideas and the manipulations of demagogues."

Another front in the country's intellectual bankruptcy was the press. Like their counterparts in academia, the country's journalists were also impaled on the spear of Sinhalese Buddhist nationalism. Assertively Anglophilic before 1956, the press, particularly the influential Lake House publishing group, was decidedly hostile to Sinhalese nationalism. While it often applauded the democratic impulses that were intertwined with Buddhist political and religious elements, it dismissed Buddhist pieties with an imperious condescension that was offensive to the Sinhalese. Sinhala politicians were disparaged as "betel chewers." "The people who used to climb trees are now trying to get into Parliament," they said. The anti-Buddhist tone of the press made it one of the targets of the infamous "Betrayal of Buddhism" report of 1956. In it, Lake House was termed "an instrument of a subtle and carefully calculated anti-Buddhist campaign." Not long after 1956, though, things started to change. Responding to government pressure, the press gradually lost its critical independence and made self-conscious efforts to identify with the new order.

Lacking an intelligentsia capable of challenging it, the more racist aspects of Buddhist nationalism rose to the surface of Sri Lankan culture in the seventies and early eighties. The onset of war only made relations between secular intellectuals and their vernacular counterparts more poisonous. During the war, secular intellectuals who dared quote facts or accurate historical interpretations to disparage the nationalistic legends became the target of ugly, McCarthyite smears and accusations. As a result, the reams of reports, studies, monographs, and books that were produced by secular-minded think tanks did little to curb irrational Sinhalese war-lust.

The slide into war through the seventies and early eighties saw the press become an instrument of Sinhalese jingoism, too. As relations between the two major ethnic groups grew more rancorous, secular-minded journalists as well as Tamils, who had once formed a big part of the profession, found it harder to get and keep jobs in the country's major news organizations. Those taking their places were much more susceptible to a tribal mentality.

The increasing Sinhalization of the country's major journalistic outlets made it difficult to introduce any criticism of the quest for Sinhalese hegemony and to describe the extent to which Tamils had been alienated by that process. The Prevention of Terrorism Act made it even more difficult. With the prospect of a prison term hanging over their heads for even interviewing militants, reporters who might have explored the subtleties of the insurgency shied away. As a result, through most of the war, the press functioned as a kind of adjunct to the government propaganda machine, puffing up the Sinhalese cause and accenting the racial overtones. In cases where Sinhalese civilians were injured or massacred, there were pages upon pages of stories bewailing "the murderous blight that stalked the land," but when it came to Tamil civilians, there was hardly a mention.

The inability of the Sinhalese-dominated press to resist the pull of jingoism ill served the Sinhalese themselves. By publishing such highly politicized and biased reportage, the press encouraged the public to believe that government forces were doing better in the field than they actually were. It became difficult, therefore, to accept the need for the kind of compromise embodied by the Accord. Furthermore, ignoring the international outcry over human rights abuses failed to relay an accurate picture of how internationally isolated the Sri Lankan government was becoming. The press also ignored the sizable body of Sinhalese monks who wanted peace, instead focusing on the alarmist rhetoric of the more conservative clergy.

Another way that the performance of the press ultimately harmed the Sinhalese was by failing to point out how the political elite was able to invoke the specter of the Tamil threat in order to choke off legitimate criticism of its spreading authoritarianism and rampant official corruption. In essence the press failed to show how the cause of "defending the Motherland" provided an opportunity for the ruling party to loot the national treasury and erode civil liberties so that it could solidify its hold on power.

Although the Westernized intelligentsia was not overjoyed at the Indian military intervention, it did see the peace accord as a chance for the country to collect itself after four years of violent polarization. Accordingly, most of the Westernized intellectuals threw their hearty endorsements behind the Accord, in the form of newspaper pieces, petitions, and resolutions. But since the Accord only redoubled the forces of nationalism, the Westernized intelligentsia became the target of death threats and intimidation.

Even a normally intrepid person like Krishnaswamy, a Tamil who supplied hard-to-find books to the journalistic, diplomatic, and think-tank crowds and who had weathered the riots of 1983 living right in the middle of a Sinhalese neighborhood on Slave Island—a locale known for its rough criminal elements—was scared. "Please, sir," he asked me one afternoon while I was over at his shop, a small ramshackle place with but a few narrow pathways through rooms piled floor to rafters with dusty old tomes. "Please do not get caught

with these books. They are banned, sir." Although terrified, Krishnaswamy giggled nervously. "Those days they didn't bother me, but
maybe now if they trace them back to me, I do not know. Please be
careful."

While most of the JVP death threats leveled against intellectuals
supporting the Accord were real, some of the "threats," true to
the Sri Lankan capacity for envy and opportunism, were issued by
intellectuals to intimidate rivals. Some intellectuals told me that the
letters were so commonplace that if you didn't get one, you didn't
feel important. Some people had even fabricated their own, they
maintained, to enhance their own status. But threats against the
liberal intelligentsia deprived the country of a very vital part of what
peace constituency remained in Sri Lanka at that point.

Journalists had to worry about JVP terror, too, but they were
also being squeezed by the government, which wanted no discussion
of the social and political conditions it was responsible for that had
given birth to the JVP. As a result, the press was caught in between,
afraid to assert a vision for peace that would offend the JVP and
fearful of raising even the most tepid criticism of the government
that might incite government repression. "We all know," said one
reporter in reference to the subject of official corruption, "that if
someone did a story like that we would pay with our jobs. And even
if we had all the evidence, no one would print it."

Reportorial courage in writing about the dark side of the UNP
or the JVP was also not encouraged by the backstabbing and opportunism of the journalists themselves. Reporters knew that if they did
publish something, even under a pseudonym, they had to worry
about collegial betrayal.

In the especially sensitive political climate, even normal diplomatic reporting could get one in trouble, too, as my friend Q., a
Muslim journalist, found out. One night after New Year's I met him
at the Arts Centre Club. He was gulping his beer and smoking
incessantly. "Relax? How can I relax?" he scolded me. He had taken
a bullet covering the Jaffna offensive—half his face and his left
shoulder were paralyzed. "Relax? It is a very nervous time in my
country right now. There is no way to relax."

Q. was young, a little more than five years out of university, but one of the country's ablest journalists. And one of its boldest. Because he was a Muslim, he could operate within the camps of the two opposing groups without generating friction. He was also passionate about what he was doing. He was a stringer for a foreign publication, and had the protection of this to keep government officials at bay. Still, there was fear. He had a father who was dependent on government permits for his business, a brother still in university, and his family's house was very close to the street, making them an easy target.

"When I first came into journalism, I thought I could end this thing all by myself. I had a tremendous cockiness about the power that a writer had in this situation—how I could change the way people think and all that nonsense. I'm much more realistic now, though I still think we could all do more. These guys are simply gutless. They could test the limits a little more but they don't. I'm trying all the time, and to a certain extent I have gotten away with it. They should try a little more, too, throw off the shackles in their own minds and then maybe we'd all be able to say the things in print we say to ourselves in private. I don't know"—a wry grin spread across his face—"maybe we should hope this thing gets really bad, all the Western organizations have to hire stringers, and then the government will not be able to come after us the way they can now."

Now Q. was in hot water, and the foreign magazine had not come to his aid. He had written about a meeting between the President and Rajiv Gandhi that had taken place in Delhi the week before, and had quoted the National Security Minister, Lalith Athulathmudali, without attribution. The minister had been cynical, and had told Q. that "the birds and the trees in Delhi had been nice," which had enraged the President. Lalith had told Q. he'd better watch out, that J.R. was incensed and there was no telling what would happen. Better he leave the city for the week and let the heat blow over.

"Crazy things are happening," Q. told me later, upon his return. "I don't know what is happening. All I know is that I was told in no uncertain terms that it would be best for me to leave town. So there I am, hiding out in the south somewhere, worrying for my life and what might happen to my family. I tell you. For the first time I know what it must be like to live in bloody Czechoslovakia."

While the JVP's death threats and the specter of government retaliation made members of the country's intelligentsia nervous individually, as a class the greatest threat was represented by the rise of Jatika Chintanaya, or National Ideology. Just as a broad-based cultural despair had led the Germans to embrace romantic myths of cultural superiority, so, too, did the sense of broad cultural and political despair induced by the peace accord lead the Sinhalese to embrace an ideology offering similar cultural redemption. To its proponents, National Ideology was a prescription for cultural deliverance, but to its critics it put the country on the same road as Cambodia under the Khmer Rouge.

Secular intellectuals found National Ideology disturbing on a number of levels. First, they bristled at the way it rejected the very idea of a secular culture that transcended race, religion, and ethnicity, and they were appalled at its rabid insularity. "What strikes me as most tragic," explained Reggie Siriwardena, an analyst with the secular-minded International Institute for Ethnic Studies in Colombo, "is how the stress on cultural purity runs against the grain of increasing cosmopolitanism in intellectual pursuits worldwide. All great cultures are based on borrowing from others, but here, among the Sinhala intelligentsia, there is a notion of preserving cultural purity that makes them believe that if something is borrowed from another culture it should be condemned."

"The idea of reviving the 'national mind' and 'national soul' is fine," noted a Sinhalese university professor, "but there is great danger in doing so here because to a large extent the national mind is deeply anti-intellectual and deeply xenophobic."

Another troubling aspect of National Ideology was its unbridled messianism. "It is a combination of millenarianism with a kind of primitivism," noted Reggie Siriwardena, "a harking back to an earlier time of primal simplicity and a dismantling of the modern economy and the modern pluralistic state in order to revert to a purer, more autarkic form of society."

But the most threatening aspect of National Ideology was its justification of Sinhalese racism. "It all boils down to this," explained a Sinhalese editorial writer who first introduced me to the Jatika Chintanaya movement. "This is a Sinhalese Buddhist country. Minorities here are okay, but there is to be no other consciousness recognized except Sinhalese Buddhist consciousness. Others can have their identity, of course, but they must defer to the Sinhalese, who have cultural primacy over the entire island."

To bolster their case against National Ideology, secular intellectuals pointed to the climate of profound intellectual intolerance and intimidation on the country's university campuses, where National Ideology was popular. By 1988 any instructor or lecturer who dared to challenge the Sinhala Buddhist consensus could be sure of at least a hectoring, if not a physical assault, a profound phenomenon in a culture where almost all teachers were usually accorded Confucian-like deference. As a result, most of the Westernized intellectuals, already driven out of the mainstream of academia, hardly set foot on campuses, fearing a hostile, if not a violent reception for their politically incorrect opinions.

As students fell prey to National Ideology and the JVP, student politics took on a bloody edge as well. The spring before, a student leader opposed to a competing organization controlled by the JVP was abducted, tortured, and stabbed to death.

"The campuses are like the ones in Iran, except it is a secular fundamentalism that has taken them over," said P., a Sinhalese law student who had been a JVP member but had quit in disgust at their tactics. The student who had been murdered was one of his best friends, and he was devoting his time to writing in denunciation of the people and the intellectual forces that had killed him. It had earned him no popularity at all, and he was living in a hostel downtown with a guard in the lobby to protect him from any unwanted visitors in the night. The afternoon we spoke we had wandered carefully through rush-hour Colombo streets and settled in a sleepy Chinese restaurant for a chat, P. facing the door and looking up nervously when anyone came in.

He was especially upset by the demagoguery of the Sinhalese ideologues on campus, whom he considered little better than thugs.

"They are actively encouraging students not to think. Is it any wonder, then, that no one is confronting these myths of Sinhala greatness, these myths of the glorious past, these so-called facts that have been gleaned from fairy tales? They have idealized a condition that never existed, although it is popular to say it did exist and to back it up with texts that are much in vogue, calling them 'authentic records' when in fact all they really are are fundamentalist fantasies—part of the fundamentalism that limits intellectual freedoms, a fundamentalism that is dangerous and filthy.

"These ideologues supposedly teaching them have put an intellectual gloss over what is essentially a bankrupt ideology. They are second-rate intellectuals leading a herd of unthinking minds in deep cerebral paralysis. Whatever the teacher says is considered the truth—beyond challenge by facts or reason. You don't dare dissent or contradict. A few years ago we might have been able to debate whether the Sinhalese really had Aryan origins and whether the Tamils were primordial enemies or not. Not now. The penalties for doing so, for violating in any way the Sinhala Buddhist worldview, now include political and social ostracism, demonization, and an intolerance that is extreme and absolute: murder."

What P. feared was amply demonstrated to me a few days later. At the university to interview a professor who had been critical of the National Ideology crowd in an essay, I was startled at how quickly the professor took a hundred-eighty-degree turn in his opinion after one of the campus's more notorious Sinhalese ideologues walked into the faculty canteen. "You have to be very careful," he apologized as soon as the bête noire of the campus was out of earshot. "You never know what he might hear and take out of context. He can call out the student brownshirts in a flash."

"There is in the air now a moral justification for eliminating those who interfere with the march of Sinhala triumphalism," the editorial writer Ajith Somaranaike explained, "which of course means anyone who wants a political solution with the Tamils based on giving them their rights. It is a Nazi-like attitude of 'either with us or against us.' "

For members of the older generation, those who originally

warned of the dangers of politicizing university curricula, the dynamics on university campuses were a grim vindication. Absurdities were in fact leading to atrocities, in the form of JVP intimidation, murder, and the total rejection of the liberal tradition. "Students simply do not have the intellectual equipment to criticize the JVP's paucity of ideas," said Reggie Siriwardena. I met him one afternoon before a seminar at his think tank on the topic of "The Crisis of the Intellectual in Sri Lanka Today." "The vast majority are Sinhala-educated with no access to large areas of modern knowledge because of the lack of books translated into Sinhala. Very often they live in a world of slogans and formulas which have, to my mind, no kind of depth. That's why they fall for that utterly stupid JVP ideology."

There was faint comfort in being proved right, however. Like many others, Reggie was filled with a deep pessimism, however much his Buddhist equanimity might mask it. It was not surprising, then, to read a poem he had written called "Waiting for the Soldier," which evoked the world-weariness and despair of intellectuals in the face of totalitarianism.

> *After the Roman army took Syracuse*
> *A soldier in the midst of the looting and the raping*
> *Stopped when he saw a Greek bent over*
> *Figures inscribed in the sand.*
>
> *The Roman watched his strange absorption*
> *In that magic of lines and circles. He,*
> *Not looking at the soldier, said, "Move*
> *With your shadow there, it is hard to see."*
>
> *The soldier hit him on the head and so*
> *Archimedes died. If then today I turn more and more*
> *To this ordered world*
> *Of sixty squares, the mimic play*
>
> *Of forces in a field where nobody bleeds,*
> *Where in the intervals of the game my silent friend*

Won't annoy me by spouting racist drivel
Or Marxist simplicities; if the chief end

Of life at present seems to be to find
An infallible answer to the French Defense
(My opponent's favorite opening), don't say
I am escaping. In a world without sense

One must look for meaning wherever one
Can find it—if only perhaps for a day
Or two. I know—in one shape
Or another—the Roman soldier is on the way.

The seminar that day was more lively than usual. The think tank's seminars were often deathly boring, full of the Westernized intelligentsia's stiff academic formalities. The topic that day, however, had drawn a large, feisty crowd. Although they were united in their sense of crisis, they were bitterly divided on where the real crisis lay—the authoritarianism of the government or the incipient Fascism of the JVP. Almost forgotten was the problem of Tamil separatism. The speaker, Ajith Somaranaike, said that the present condition of the intelligentsia was unprecedented in the country's post-independence intellectual life. "Decency has departed from public life almost altogether," he warned. "And the barbarians are at the gates."

"And why have we been so silent about all this? Why haven't we taken to the streets?" cried D.B.S. Jeyraj, one of the few Tamil journalists still writing for the mainstream English-language press. "We have no one to blame but ourselves. We were without guts and without courage. We preferred to sweep it all under the carpet. But the carpet has become a mountain."

The urgency, however, seemed lost on most of the attendees. Later, at the Arts Centre Club, a Tamil academic who had recently returned from Cambridge said I shouldn't be fooled. "You have to listen to them and realize that what is not being said is the most important thing. We Asians think differently, communicate differently, much more subtly than you Europeans. They will all say this and that and put a good gloss on things and go about the room making themselves feel good. But it is no secret to anyone. At bottom they have been betrayed. They have believed in the idea of a liberal secular state when in fact it never really existed. That's why they have refused to believe. The real crisis of the intelligentsia in this country is that the intelligentsia would rather not see that it is irrelevant now. That is the real crisis."

15 · Prawn Farm

IF YOU WERE to draw a map of the homeland that Tamil separatists want to establish in the northern third of Sri Lanka, its southern border would run not too far from the prawn farm that an American biologist named Dale Sarver had been hired to build and manage about sixty miles up the coast from Colombo. Sarver's prawn farm was one of Asia's most ambitious aquaculture projects. It stretched between two traditional Sri Lankan fishing villages, one Tamil, the other Sinhalese, in an uneasy no-man's-land of salt scrub, marshes, and lagoons.

On a soft sand beach near the farm, villagers had whittled the trunk of a palm tree into an ominous point and had painted it white to mark the boundary line between the two settlements. Mostly, the two villages ignored each other, focused as they were on their larger adversary, the sea, but occasionally the two would have a go at each other, knives in hand, around that shiny white totem.

When I met Sarver, my first year in Sri Lanka, I thought it would be instructive to see how a development project like his coped in the midst of a civil war. Yet, while Tamil militants sometimes used one of the villages for smuggling weapons and the Sinhalese villages in the area were hotbeds of JVP extremism, the farm was largely on the peripheries of any fighting. It was, however, in the center of another kind of conflict. This was the war against chronic underdevelopment and poverty, a contest that played a large role in feeding ethnic tensions. "Do you think we'd have this war if we had the general economic prosperity that you have in America?" the heir to a brewery fortune asked me one night at a Colombo party. His blue-blazered friend added: "So few jobs, so much unemployment. Everybody wants to satisfy their own community first. It is natural, no?"

Arriving in Sri Lanka for the first time, I shared the conventional wisdom about Third World development favored by bureaucrats, economists, and bankers who saw the problem as one of insufficient investment capital, technology, and professional expertise. Put in money and ideas, send in technicians and experts, and it would only be a matter of time before development took root and flourished.

But gradually I began to doubt that pat formulation. Sri Lanka, for example, was awash in development dollars, receiving more foreign aid money per capita than any other country in Asia, half its annual national budget. And Sri Lanka had many engineers and scholars scattered about the world, so the country's problems with development were certainly not a matter of intellectual inferiority or a lack of indigenous expertise. The problem also did not seem to be a function of the punishingly hot climate, inherent native indolence, the distraction of the island's beauty, or any of the other racist saws that an earlier, less enlightened era used to explain away impoverishment. This was, after all, a culture that had built an awesome hydraulic civilization during its Golden Age that had turned ancient Lanka into the granary of Asia. What, then, could explain why its current level of development was so mystifyingly low?

Located on 1,000 sun-blasted, salty acres, the prawn farm was the kind of relatively low-tech, labor-intensive project that should have had very pleasing prospects in Sri Lanka. The flat akaline marshland of the site and the presence of a nearby lagoon fit the required specifications to a tee. The company building the farm, a Sri Lankan-owned consortium, was well capitalized and equipped to take on the project, and had experience as well, having cut its teeth on large-scale contracts it had as part of the Mahaweli Development

Scheme. Although past approaches to development in the country had always focused on large public-sector projects, the Western-leaning Jayawardene government was eager to support a private-sector initiative like the prawn farm in hopes that it would generate jobs and foreign currency. Accordingly, the prawn farm received a special presidential endorsement and preferential status at customs to cut through red tape.

Each pond at the farm was about ten acres square, arranged like ice-cube trays on either side of a narrow dirt road. A network of feeder canals circulated fresh water from the lagoon into the ponds through a series of locks and concrete gates.

Inside Sarver's air-conditioned office, in the trailerlike building that functioned as the project's headquarters, there was an aerial map of the farm, courtesy of the Ministry of National Security, which had stopped giving aerial maps out—shortly after Sarver got his—as a precaution against insurgents. On this map the portions of the farm already completed made the area look like a quilt of giant rice paddies, the most compelling icon in Sinhalese culture and one of the earliest forms of agriculture known to man. One could easily imagine how a relatively unsophisticated technology like shrimp farming could be grafted on top of the cultural fabric and how it would then thrive.

"That's what I thought, too," Sarver said to me in a characteristic growl. "You learn pretty quick around here that nothing is as simple as it should be."

A biologist in his late thirties, Sarver had come to Sri Lanka four years before at the invitation of the farm's owners to manage its construction and to guide it through its initial operating stages. His predecessor, who had originally conceived of the project, was an eccentric British anthropologist who had fled the country, half crazed by the inertia and frustration he experienced trying to get the thing off the ground. Other Westerners involved with the project had also not lasted long. Two New Zealand investors had pulled out after an attack on their house in Colombo during the 1983 riots.

Sarver was the personification of American can-do, his up-front manner of doing things a vivid contrast to the prevailing culture of indirection and obliquity. This was an approach that proved counter-productive at first. But even the most culturally sensitive demeanor wouldn't improve the project's performance or dissolve the resistance and inertia he had encountered.

On the surface, the government could seem persuasive in its commitment to development efforts like Sarver's. But frequently that persuasive rhetoric rang hollow. That morning of my second visit, for example, Sarver had just been notified that three years after making a commitment to lease two pieces of land critical to the project's completion, the government was now reneging, after caving into complaints from factions in the neighboring villages.

Most of these objections were in fact merely efforts on the part of certain groups within the villages to shake down the farm for more money, even though each village as a whole would stand to lose significant income if these protests drove the farm away. Sinhalese farmers on one side of the farm were saying that they still had leases on the land, despite the fact that no one had cultivated it in over eighty years. On the other side, in the Tamil settlement, villagers were alleging that the farm had dried up its wells, destroyed a cemetery, and spewed poisonous toxins into the air, and that "magic dust" had caused a drought—all charges rooted in the pervasive suspicions toward business organizations in the minds of uneducated, easily manipulated villagers. Although the land in question was too salty for growing anything and too flood-prone for habitation, the village now said it wanted it for grazing, for future expansion, and for the women of the village so they could use it as a toilet on their way into the jungle to gather wood.

It was unsurprising that the local politicians were quick to pander to these doubts and suspicions. Worried about the JVP or the Tigers—a local UNP leader was killed and castrated just the night before I arrived—the local government agent had issued a stop-work order on the farm. The issue would now be referred to a ministry in Colombo for further hearings and deliberation, where it would be either strangled in red tape or resolved along the path of least resistance—in the villagers' favor.

Sarver suspected that the villagers' newfound resistance reflected the increasing influence of a faction of amnestied Tamil militants returning to the village after release from government internment camps. No matter how useless the land was to them, the militants were claiming that the farm was an attempt on the part of the government to nibble away at the "Tamil homeland."

But whatever the specifics of the case, it was an example of a casual attitude toward contracts. "They always leave themselves a back door so they can get out," Sarver explained. "You spend years filling out the forms—so many forms they could choke a horse—and then the government gets a complaint and they say, 'What to do? What to do?' I told them what they could do. They could shove it, that's what they could do. 'Homeland' my ass. That land is a goddamn swamp."

Sarver's bosses, however, were more worried than he about the possibility of personal retribution. We drove out on a high point of land and watched the women from the village bathe in the pools of collected rainwater that had formed where holes had been dug for the aborted ponds. "According to our original projections," he told me, "that land should already be in production. Instead, it's the country's biggest bathtub and toilet."

Another objection to the farm seemed to lie in the fact that high-caste groups in the villages would be deprived by the farm of a cheap, easily exploited pool of labor and a needy market for moneylending. With steady work and upward mobility, the lower castes would no longer be beholden to the old feudal hierarchy.

The fact that most jobs at the farm required manual labor upset the sensitivities of the upper-caste villagers, too. "All these guys want to do is grow their fingernails long," Sarver explained, referring to the habit that symbolized exemption from low-status manual toil. "Then they want to sit behind a desk all day and grow shrimp in little teacups. I had one guy whom I made get down in the mud just as everybody else does when they first start out and he started getting hysterical. 'What if people see me working?' he cried." Sarver also explained that the nephew of the village headman expected a supervisor's job right off the bat and a motorcycle on which to get around the farm. But when he wound up with a job several notches lower down, and a pedal bike as well, the taunts of his village cronies made him lose a great amount of face and he quit—issuing a blanket death threat to anyone who had anything to do with the farm.

Caste conditioning was obvious in the Tamil village next to the farm, which I visited later that day. Though it was a vivid, timeless place, the village was badly in need of some kind of economic infusion. Passed over for any development but a government clinic, it reeked of squalor and abjection. Many of the villagers wouldn't talk to me, because, as one of them explained, "I was not from there." But those who did talk voiced a battery of complaints about the farm: that it was exploitative and multinational (though, in fact, it was wholly Sri Lankan-owned); that they had been sold out by Sinhalese politicians (the agreements were actually with their own village elders); and that the farm was taking the best land in the whole area (by all measures it was a swamp with little value for anything else). Soon, however, I got to the core of the problem. "Our men don't want these laborer jobs," one Tamil named Nal told me. He admitted that the term "our men" meant those in his caste group. "They have studied. Some of them even have their A- and O-level certificates. They deserve better. Now they only have work in their fields for us at that farm. We cannot do that. And neither can our women. Our women cannot do that kind of work either." And what about the overall benefit to the community as a whole? Wasn't that something to think about in assessing its value? Nal stared at me blankly.

At the farm, high-caste workers were unable to accept orders from lower-caste superiors. Caste also made it hard for Sarver's workers to absorb the idea of being rewarded on the basis of merit and abilities, something most Westerners take for granted. "They look at a job and see absolutely different things than we do," Sarver explained. "Work here is a matter of fulfilling a role, having a title and a position detached from what you produce or how you perform. A job here is about fulfilling obligations on the surface with little sense of the substance underneath it.

"The main point of my job is to get them to change their values, to recognize that their rewards on this job should be based on what they produce and the decisions they make, and not on their titles and backgrounds. But that is asking a lot—it goes completely against the grain. You just can't be part of this culture psychologically and do the kind of jobs we have here. It takes a flexibility of mind we would take totally for granted but one they simply don't have."

Sarver and I had planned a trip for the next morning along the coast road toward the local *kachcheri*, or district offices. Despite the backing and blessings of the central government, Sarver had to get approvals at the local level and from every one of the many ministries regulating the project in Colombo—more than a dozen. Not only were these agencies frequently conflicting, but each was paralyzed by bureaucratic inertia.

That day, Sarver was going to try to get the *kachcheri* to hurry up on a plan he had submitted nearly eight months earlier. Since his assistant who had been handling the matter wasn't of a high enough caste, apparently, to deal with the situation, Sarver was going to go himself. He was already irritable. He had gotten up early for a 5 a.m. meeting with an important government minister, only to find that his assistant had made a mistake and the meeting was supposed to be at 5 p.m.

Part of the reason the skeins of red tape were so impenetrable was that the government civil service had become swollen with Sinhalese clerks who would go jobless otherwise; many of these clerks had sympathies with socialistic policies of the past and were resentful of private-sector initiatives like the prawn farm, especially since the private sector paid better. Like the rest of the country's political institutions, the civil service was less concerned with administration and governing than with asserting its own status. Often deeply in debt because of the spiraling cost of living, the burden of feeding an extended family, and providing for funerals, bureaucrats at every level used their positions unblushingly for personal enrichment. At almost every point in the system, some kind of bribe or back scratching was required, although Sarver resisted, because once he began doing so, there would be no end to it.

An emergency that afternoon held us back, but as we drove around the farm on the daily rounds, Sarver regaled me with some of his personal frustrations with the bureaucracy. The week before, he had gone up to the *kachcheri* and had sat for hours watching clerks snooze at their desks while villagers with petitions sat forlornly waiting for an audience. That day Sarver sat for most of the day waiting for the man he was to meet. Every half hour the secretary assured him that "he will come now" or "he will come soon." "They'll just say that over and over again," Sarver said in a trauma-tized monotone. "Over and over, instead of telling you plain out that he isn't coming back that day. I once sat in an office in Colombo all day listening to that. Turned out the guy I was looking for was in Africa on a trip. You never get a straight answer."

Even when the right person was there, however, there was little satisfaction. "Most people who petition the *kachcheri* for anything just wind up throwing in the towel," he said, scowling. "You can get the runaround for years. No one explains what the procedures are and they are never consistent two different times anyway. No one takes any initiative or approaches anything with any foresight or takes responsibility for seeing something through. There are always a dozen people to see before you get to anyone who can make the final decision, but there's never really any final decision because no one ever has full and final authority—or exercises it, anyway—be-cause they always want a back door out of the decision to avoid accountability. They will say yes just to shoo you away, but there is a genetic propensity against making decisions here and the matter just stays on some guy's desk, never acted upon. You know there's a good chance he won't act upon it, but you don't want to force anything, because that will really stop him from doing anything, and he knows that and can blow you off with a 'yes, yes' and there's still nothing you can do when nothing happens. He'll blame the mails, or the guy in the other office. If what you are asking him requires a decision on his part, he'll avoid it. Really, I've seen them run right out the door when I've come in needing a signature. Usually a guy will dodge it until you go over his head and his boss orders him to do it and then its okay because it's not his ass on the line anymore, and if anyone down the line gets upset at the decision, they won't come after him."

Once Sarver had to go all the way to Colombo to get a minister's authorization for a *kachcheri* surveyor to come to the farm. When they got back to the *kachcheri*, however, the chief of surveyors balked, claiming that he didn't have a vehicle or a spare crew to do the job. The real reason he balked, Sarver later found out, was that the authorization letter from the ministry bore the previous day's date and he didn't want to act too quickly and give the impression that he had been bribed. "Obviously," Sarver explained, "it is so rare here that anything gets done in a timely manner that when it does, it means the guy has been paid off." Sarver says he had to wait a week before the chief wrote the authorization for a surveyor to come out. The surveyor then waited a week himself before he arrived to do the job. "I was dumbfounded," said Sarver. "But stuff like that happens all the time."

In Sarver's office there was a sign hanging beside his charts and schedules: "Doing Something Wrong Is Better Than Doing Nothing at All."

"I keep trying to tell them that," Sarver explained as we took a tour of the hatchery where the growing of prawn larvae would take place once the facility was completed. "But they are so deathly afraid of doing something wrong that they will often just stand there and do nothing. Their eyes glaze over, their faces lock up, and they just go completely blank."

However simple the mechanics of prawn farming actually were, disaster could strike with lightning speed, which required workers with fast reflexes. Most of the jobs, even those performed by supervisors, could be handled by high school dropouts in America, Sarver said. But getting his workers, who often lacked confidence and initiative, to make those relatively simple on-the-spot decisions was a major challenge.

Part of the problem was that the Sri Lankan family structure led individuals to defer to authority in almost every decision. Another factor was the deep concern for losing face, which made workers overly cautious about even the simplest responsibilities to the point of paralysis. In addition there were the basic conceptual orientations of Sri Lanka: an Eastern notion of time, in which the concept of five minutes meant something entirely different to Sarver and to his workers, and a hazy sense of accuracy, which made precise measurements difficult. Beyond these there was also cultural resistance to the Western notion of cause and effect.

"The point of the task happens on a level they just don't grasp," Sarver said. "They approach everything with incredible tunnel vision, thinking only about discharging their obligation to you, not the substance of the task. Rote tasks are fine, but if the job requires the least amount of creative interpretation or foresight, you are cooked. They do everything by program, and if the program doesn't fit exactly, they just stand around and say, 'What to do? What to do?' We go over the procedures again and again. But the connections are just not made."

Another problem hindering operations at the farm, especially those like running the hatchery that required a certain amount of coordination, was the fragmentation of the workplace. Besides the obvious fault lines of ethnicity and caste, there was the Sri Lankan capacity for envy, which discouraged cooperation and often prompted workers to undermine each other's labors so they'd look bad, since one worker's gain was seen necessarily as another's loss.

To compensate for all these traits, Sarver said he had been forced to break down tasks, even the most elementary ones, "into the tiniest components—to a very specific and simple chain of command that doesn't require discretion, or even common sense." The hatchery, for example, would have to be manned by twice as many workers as were necessary in other parts of the world.

Nevertheless, mishaps were impossible to prevent. Just the day before, workers had emptied a pond prematurely, a mistake that killed most of the shrimp. Another day, a senior supervisor was asked to post a sign requesting that a generator not be turned off, and thought a tiny index card would suffice, resulting in a ruined generator. An old man was hired to release water through a feeder canal when the depth reached three feet. Since, however, he put his measuring rod into the water at a forty-five-degree angle, he released the water at two feet. Even the professional staff made obtuse and expensive errors, like the engineers who failed to account for topographical adjustments in their blueprints.

Besides the constant aggravation of having to cope with mistakes, there was the added frustration of not being able to hold anyone accountable. "If someone screws up, it's never their fault. They are never confronted or fired. It's like the rain. Things just happen. No one ever makes this or that happen. They just happen."

With subordinates unable to make decisions independently, even the most minor matters were pushed upstairs for his review. "It's all pissant stuff. But no one else will make the call. It may seem comical, but taken together, it's torture."

Just then, a man came to Sarver's door and looked inside apprehensively. He stepped away, but returned a few moments later looking even more anxious. Finally, he approached and whispered something to Sarver, who scowled and began pulling on his gum boots. One of the ponds was going through an oxygen crash, threatening more than a ton of shrimp.

When we got to the pond it was half drained. Thousands of shrimp wriggled in the mud. The man had started to harvest the pond later in the day than he should have, and the hot sun had caused an irreversible depletion of the oxygen in the pond, suffocating the shrimp. As workers picked their way nervously around him, Sarver stood on the bank of the pond, arms akimbo, trying to restrain his volcanic temper. He would have loved to throw a fit, but in that control-conscious society doing so would have caused him to lose face in the eyes of his workers. I had seen the foreman pacing around outside his office for several minutes before coming in, trying to think of a way to avoid being the bearer of bad news. "It's the old lockup syndrome," Sarver replied, shaking his head back and forth in frustration. "Once he takes his thumb out of his ass and works up the nerve to tell me something's wrong, it is too late."

Although Sarver put extra time and effort into training his workers, many of them were reluctant to ask their trainers to clarify their instructions. To do so in South Asian culture was an affront to the teacher's abilities and a challenge to his authority. Asking a simple question was also an admission on the part of the questioner that he hadn't understood what was just conveyed. To a Western trainee, this would be a minor matter at most, but to Sri Lankans it was fraught with much heavier implications, involving concepts of face and shame.

As the shrimp hopped pathetically on the bottom of the pond straining for oxygen and dying from overexposure to the sun, workers flailed their arms wildly to shoo away a flock of birds that had swooped down for a feed. Surveying the wreckage, Sarver shook his head disappointedly. "An hour is all it takes around here for the whole house of cards to come tumbling down."

Having gotten a pretty good sense of ground-level development problems as Sarver had experienced them, I was eager to talk to international development officials in Colombo to get their idea of the role that social and cultural factors played in frustrating their expensive efforts. But the people I spoke to were either unable or unwilling to talk about such problems. Few development officials ever got out into the field to get an appreciation of how profoundly different Sri Lankan society was, and with their focus on gargantuan budgets for economic stimulation, the practical issues of front-line development simply didn't engage them.

Behind this official avoidance, though, lurked a theoretical inability to deal with the cultural basis of chronic underdevelopment as well as a fear of being labeled "ethnocentric"—or worse. Ironically, the single development official in Colombo who was candid about culturally rooted development problems was the one who enjoyed the greatest popularity among Sri Lankans, John Guyer, who had run the Asia Foundation in Colombo for more than five years. Guyer's friendships, however, did not make him shy away from making honest, and in many cases unflattering, appraisals of the society, although, with his keen cultural sensitivity, he was usually discreet when expressing them.

"There's very little interest in exploring the facts of life that make most things tick here," Guyer told me one morning in the interior courtyard of his home. "There are professional no-nos in the official community here and an insularity. They have a kind of professional immunity from having to confront these things. They are allowed—no, encouraged—to ignore these things. It is a strange vacuum that they allow themselves to live in—an air-conditioned, sealed-off world of the bungalow, the office compound, and the club. And the walls get higher every day because every one is afraid to leave Colombo. People inside simply ignore the realities on the ground. There's not much curiosity to begin with, and they know they are going to spend a few years here and then move on to a new assignment. The constraints of time and the constraints of the contacts they are allowed to make give them a superficial feel for the real rhythm of life here. And even if they did focus on what was really at work here—or not, as the case may be—there's no way for them to channel it. The real bases of things here, psychologically and culturally, the things that the charts and graphs and budgets are all anchored in, are studiously avoided—or denied."

Even if the development community at large could admit social and cultural barriers, however, it would be unlikely that their insights would be appreciated, given the resistance imposed by the prickly climate of Sinhalese Buddhist nationalism. To challenge Sinhalese culture and customs was "an unpatriotic act—an affront to national self-esteem and dignity," as one former columnist asserted. "Their attitude is: 'This is the way we are. Don't ask us to change.' It is our nationalism and the feelings of specialness and superiority that make us feel this way. We Sinhalese see ourselves as the sons of the soil, entitled to the fruits of development without ever really having to work for it ourselves. Politicians inculcate people with these attitudes, never mentioning the duties and responsibilities we should have, but always harping on our rights and due rewards. They emphasize the duties that the employer has to workers, but never the reverse, what the workers should give in return. The same goes for foreign aid. We think we, the superior Sinhalese, are entitled to this money, and never think that we should make adjustments in ourselves to make things work. In the popular mind, the money is completely disassociated from the results it should have. And in the process we have not seen that we have become a beggar country, always with our hands out. We are so busy harking back to our past glorious heritage that we don't see we are losing our self-respect in the here and now."

Rather than acknowledge the liabilities of tradition, nationalists blamed the country's development dilemmas on the intrusion of the West; were it not for Western colonialism, they said, Sri Lanka would have become one of the more sophisticated countries on earth, through its superior Buddhist values and heritage. Development had failed because, so far, development efforts had been insufficiently nationalistic. What was really needed was a model for economic development that tapped into the power of traditional values and culture, one contained in Jatika Chintanaya—National Ideology—as espoused by the JVP.

To think otherwise was to be a Western supremacist, I was told by one of the more ardent nationalists teaching at the University of Colombo, a Sinhala Buddhist ideologue named Naline De Silva. His ideas had a great deal of influence with the JVP and its student supporters. We were sitting in De Silva's tiny, sweltering office, though the campus had been closed for weeks because of JVP-inspired unrest. I was a little leery of being so close to De Silva: in addition to having set student brownshirts on colleagues who had crossed or challenged him, he had "cuffed" at least one other academic who had made the mistake of debating him in public.

If his bearing was unnerving, his ideas were even more so. Policies shaped by Sinhalese Buddhist nationalism after 1956 were basically on the right track, he said. The problem was that they just hadn't had enough time to take root and flourish. It was the same in Pol Pot's Cambodia, Khomeini's Iran, and Mao's China, he maintained. They were all guided by basically sound ideas that had somehow been twisted: "logical responses to colonial domination and Western influence that were perverted because people did not think things through enough."

The point of my questions was basically straightforward: however much one could argue or bemoan it, development, in both the East and the West, had only come to countries that had a culture of productivity, which was very much at odds with the prevailing cultural ethos in Sri Lanka. How, then, could a vision for economic development that self-consciously celebrated traditional "cultural purity" spur needed change and economic growth?

Although I phrased my questions as gingerly as I could, De Silva took almost immediate offense, accusing me of using terms such as "efficiency," "productivity," and "supply and demand" that were "value-laden" and implied objectivity when in fact they were not. "That's the problem with all you Westerners," De Silva yelled at me. "You think there is only one way—your way!"

De Silva's values were similar on the subject of teaching English in the universities. Arguments in favor of English, he replied, only showed how brainwashed people had become by the myth of Western cultural superiority. But, I asked, wasn't it clear that increasing the number of English speakers would help the country compete internationally and thereby increase general levels of prosperity? Wasn't that the nature of the world these days, and wasn't that hard to change without allowing the country to turn in upon itself in a ruinous economic insularity?

De Silva glowered. "But we Sinhalese want to *change* the world," he responded. "We want to and we will. At least the Sri Lankan world."

But what about countries like Singapore and Hong Kong? They didn't get to their level of economic prosperity by fetishizing their traditional culture and refusing to learn English.

De Silva paused for a second and then exploded. "That's the whole point. We don't want to be like them. Who ever told you we wanted to be like them? They are only an imitation of New York and Paris. We do not want that. They have had to sell their souls for that."

Then which country provided a model for the kind of development they foresaw?

"What kind of country is a model for us?" he pondered. "That's just the problem. There is no country that provides us with a model because the whole world has been ruined by Western domination. Africa, Latin America—areas that could have developed great cultures on their own were ruined."

Then, as if a light went on over his head, De Silva's face brightened. "What do you know about Burma?" he asked me, his eyes narrowing as if he had a secret.

I told him what I knew. Ruinous economic policies and isolationism. Worthless currency. Staggering official corruption. There probably wasn't a country on earth that had made as many mistakes except maybe Cambodia.

"Well, yes," he mused, still attached to his fancy. "I guess what we would want is Burma, but Burma without the mistakes."

The Burmese experiment was cited positively by another Sinhalese proponent of Jatika Chintanaya, a left-leaning MP. "The elite in this country still looks to the West for its values and modes of living and for solutions to the country's problems," he said, "but their way has not worked for the bulk of the country. We are in a mess today because we have tried to follow a Western approach and it hasn't worked. For forty years we've followed a path of nonindigenous development and where has it taken us? We should have development here. We are a rich tropical country. We have the highest literacy rate in the Third World. We have the sea. We could make power from the sea.

"All we are asking is to revive indigenous assets and resources in our culture that have been destroyed and suppressed by the dominating social classes for the last four centuries. What we need is a development program more in tune with our national culture and its primary values—harmony with nature, egalitarian fairness, equality. There could be a lot of romanticism in that, yes. But one has to have a certain amount of romanticism to keep idealism going. Forty years of these Western-style policies have brought complete failure and an incredible level of debt to foreign lending organizations. We have to search our souls and think what else we can do."

My friend N., on the other hand, found much of the nationalist nostalgia contradictory and unsupportable. Yes, colonialism might have damaged the culture's creative capacities, but it did not follow that reviving traditional Buddhist culture would undo that damage or meet contemporary needs. "Like it or not, we are no longer living in the tenth century and have to depend on the outside world," he insisted. "Their vision is absurd. Who will bring the letters, run the telephone service? What role does the bus system play, the motorcar, the modern hospital? Nostalgia won't get us anywhere. Maybe you can do it if your population is stable and all your wealth is self-generated. But never here. If the harbor is closed for three weeks, we'll starve. There will be no food and no fuel. It'll be a disaster."

A colleague of N.'s known for sympathies with the nationalist sensibility, at least on an emotional level, saw cause for alarm as well. "It doesn't make sense except in the most insular political and economic terms," he warned. "This ideology, with its concepts of cultural supremacy and its Luddite approach to modern economics and industrial production, can't work in today's world. But as we know, a lot of things that cannot work have an awful lot of appeal."

Sarver almost choked, a few weeks later, when I told him about my conversations with some of the proponents of National Ideology. "Burma without the mistakes! Burma without the mistakes! There is no Burma without the mistakes!"

Throughout its life, nationalism in one form or another had posed persistent problems for the prawn farm. Originally, the government had made an attractive promise to help the owners capitalize the project, but loans to small Sinhalese farmers, the literal "sons of the soil," took precedence. A tract of nearby land that the farm could have used as an alternate site couldn't be leased for prawn farming because it had at one time been planted in rice, after which it was virtually impossible to use for anything else, under legislation passed in the fifties when smallholder rice farming and the pastoral tradition it represented were apotheosized. Furthermore, there was the trouble posed by the very nature of shrimp farming itself. Although the Sinhalese ate seafood as a regular part of the diet, the more fundamentalistic Buddhists objected when the government put its institutional support behind "inland fisheries" like the prawn farm, claiming it violated Buddhist prohibitions against unnecessary slaughter.

Work that week, as it was one week every month, had been greatly slowed by an observance of the full moon called Poya. Workers would take not only Poya day off but the day before and the day after, to travel—via a heavily subsidized transportation network—to visit relatives. When all the traditional holidays were added up, along with the dozen Poya days thrown in, the law mandated nearly 180 days off for workers.

But on my final visit to the farm, Sarver had more on his mind than the problems posed by the politics of national identity. The JVP had recently tried to assassinate a bank manager in Colombo who was known to be a strict disciplinarian with workers. Sarver was beginning to worry that a disgruntled employee might cook up a story to get the JVP to put a hit on him. The JVP in the area was assuming a much more visible profile, prompting security forces to make more frequent stops at the farm to interrogate workers. The JVP had also recently declared that nongovernmental organizations doing development work, like Save the Children and various European groups, were actually "agents of neocolonialism" and were therefore unwelcome. People in the area often mistakenly thought that the farm was one such project. "Their attitude is totally paranoid," a former JVPer had told me in Colombo, describing the reasoning behind the JVP declaration on nongovernmental organizations. "They think they are all out to undermine our culture and must be stopped."

And then the prawn farm had run into its most life-threatening snag to date. The trouble involved a lawsuit between one faction of the board of directors and the other. One group, predominantly Sinhalese, was accusing the other, predominantly Tamil, of management improprieties and playing with the books. The real issue, however, was that the Sinhalese faction did not want company revenues to be reinvested, but instead wanted them issued as dividends to stockholders, many of whom were assembling funds in order to leave the country. If the faction wanting the dividends won out in court, there was a chance that they might pull the plug on the farm, flushing four years of Sarver's life down the drain. Fortunately, the court was nowhere near to a resolution, as the judge had still not decided whether he should allow testimony to be given in English, the first language of the two Tamil partners, or in Sinhala, that of the other board members.

In the meantime, however, the court action made it impossible for Sarver or anyone else at the farm to make authorizations for major purchases and currency transfers. As a result, equipment vital to the hatchery operation was stuck in customs at the port. The port was a renowned sinkhole of corruption, red tape, and bureaucratic intrigue, and Sarver looked with dread upon an expedition there.

The last night there, I stayed with Sarver and his wife, Anne, at their bungalow. That evening a blizzard of butterflies swarmed around the house. It was an arresting sight, yet Sarver, suffering from burnout, didn't seem to notice. He spoke now more like a jaded Peace Corps volunteer than a frustrated professional. He had originally envisioned the prawn farm as a way to put poor villagers to work in an area that really needed it. He had also hoped that Anne would use the farm as a nucleus for health and nutrition improvement programs, her specialty. But while the farm had brought benefits in the form of new houses, marriages, and confidence for those working there, it had also generated an incredible amount of resentment and resistance.

"You could build someone a house here and they'd send it back and order you to put another room on it," he complained in a rare moment of self-pity. "Sometimes I get the feeling that they just don't want all this stuff. It's put on them by Western organizations, and they go along with it because here they go along with everything, at least on the surface. And if they see something in it for themselves, so much the better. That's why the politicians are gung ho for it, because of the money they can rake in. But personally I don't see any real striving to improve things from their end, any solid commitment to development at any level. They want it both ways, I guess. They want the consumer goods and the trappings of modernization that come with development, but they do not want to lose their identity or look at their values and blame themselves for the way things are going here. The trouble is, they can't have it both ways."

16 · Jaffna II

DESPITE INDIAN ARMY claims that the Tigers were a spent force and that the area they had once dominated had been brought back to "normalcy," I had been told that the militants were still to be reckoned with. Five months after it had routed the Tigers from Jaffna, there were rumors in Colombo that the Indian Army was hopelessly mired in the north. It would be easy to speak with the Tigers, I was told, provided I contacted them in advance from Colombo.

But when I arrived in Vavuniya, a dusty town on the northern fringe of what was considered Sinhalese Sri Lanka, I found out that my telegram to arrange a meeting had not been cabled to the Tiger office in London. Worse, there were two Sri Lankan police inspectors sitting in the hotel manager's office when I got there. Apparently, I thought, someone in the National Security Ministry didn't want me roaming around up north on my own.

The manager, a Tamil man in his forties whom I knew from my last trip to Jaffna, gave me the high sign when I walked into his office, so I pretended we had never met before. As it happened, our charade wasn't necessary. The police were only paying the manager a courtesy call. Soon they were speaking freely: the Tigers were now able to roam in the jungles outside town, while the town itself was controlled by factions of Tamil militants allied with the Indians. The police also gave me a roster of people to see while I was there. Many of these officials probably would not receive me, they added. The Tigers had issued orders that no civil servant should go to work. This seemed to make the police feel happy, since it meant that the Indians had had no more success in stopping the militants than they did.

After they left, the manager went on to brief me in more detail on what was happening. The Tigers had paralyzed the entire civil administration of the district. For the last three or four days, the Indians had been on an offensive against them, and had brought in about three dozen tanks and a whole convoy of troops from Trincomalee to bolster their ranks. In the meantime, the Indians had attacked a number of nearby hamlets by air, the result of which was to swell the town of Vavuniya itself with refugees, most of them elderly. The Tigers, meanwhile, simply melted into the jungle.

The manager showed me a map of the area and pointed out the places where he thought the Tigers could be met. Getting there would require some stealth, he said. The roads in the area were patrolled regularly by Indian helicopters.

The manager came by his information about the Tigers from his brother, who designed mortars for the LTTE. They had come from a fairly well-to-do Tamil merchant family whose holdings in the south were lost in the ethnic violence of the late seventies and early eighties. He apologized for the condition of the rest house—his last remaining establishment—which was decrepit, dusty, and without water. But it was better to leave the place like this, he explained. In the current climate of opportunism, making it more attractive would only make it a more appealing target for someone else.

Stephen, whom I had lost track of since the Kandy Perahera at New Year's, had made arrangements while in Colombo to meet with the Tigers. This came in handy because the manager at the hotel was not as helpful as he had promised. As we rode in our taxi through town on our way out to attempt contact with the Tigers, the heavy Indian presence was unmistakable, but as soon as we passed an Indian Army checkpoint on the far side of town, there was hardly a sign of military activity.

The driver had originally balked at taking us out to meet the Tigers. Earlier in the war, he had been caught in a land-mine explosion while driving a van on the very same roads. To boost his price, he took off his shirt and showed us the scars and ruts that crisscrossed his chest and back.

After an empty stretch of road, we stopped at a small store, where our driver palavered with an old man. "We are free and happy citizens of Tamil Eelam, sir," the man explained, as if a prerecorded tape had been triggered at the sight of Western journalists. "Free and happy citizens of our own free and happy country."

As if on cue, just then a group of Tigers rode up on bicycles. As it was now getting dark, their leader wouldn't be able to meet us today, they said, but he had set aside some time tomorrow at nine in the morning. In the meantime, could we lend them our taxi, just for a few minutes?

There wasn't much of a choice, so we let the Tigers have the vehicle. Our driver was none too pleased, having feared just such a hijacking. We were also facing a five-mile walk back to town. Luckily, though, the car reappeared.

The next morning, although the manager had instructed the driver where we wanted to go, he seemed confused, and stopped often along the way, asking directions from the boys who drove cattle along the road. As we bounced along, the driver honked his horn at regular intervals, presumably so we wouldn't take any of the militants by surprise. About a mile from where we met the Tigers the day before, we came upon a couple of them standing in the bush with their weapons aimed right at us. "Contact," said Stephen excitedly as a group of Tigers prowled from the bush.

With their AK-47s hidden between their legs the eight sarong-clad Tamil teenagers surrounding us hardly looked like seasoned guerrillas. Their leader would be along in a little while, one of them explained, urging us to sit in the shade by the side of the road. While we waited, they showed us large pieces of the rockets that Indian helicopters had fired into a nearby hamlet.

From what we could glean from one of the cadres who could speak a little English, a man named Jude, there were over 2,000

Tigers in the Vavuniya area, camped throughout the jungle. The Indians were much better fighters than the Sri Lankan forces, he said, but the reports that 800 Tigers had been killed by them since the offensive were exaggerated; at most there had been only 75 Tigers killed, while Indian casualties were edging toward 1,000. The Indians were also lying about Tiger land-mine attacks and the indiscriminate killings of civilians they themselves caused.

Although the loss of Jaffna had been a setback, the cadre explained, the Tigers had reorganized themselves. Training had been disrupted but was now continuing all over the north in secret locations. "These are our training camps," Jude said, pointing to a small clearing in the jungle. "Daily we are training new cadres." Many of those new cadres were boys as young as twelve.

Jude received radio instructions to have us meet the Tigers' Vavuniya area commander, Jeyam, several miles down the road. While we waited for another half hour, more Tigers drifted into the compound. Many of these were wild-eyed. They looked like they had been living in the jungle for years. Many of them wore Christian crosses or rosaries around their necks. One of them had a "Rambo" decal on his gun and wore a bright black-and-red shirt with emblems of racing flags on it, and called himself "Disco," another colorful LTTE nom de guerre.

Instead of an assault rifle, Jeyam carried a sidearm in a leather purse and had a long fingernail on his pinkie as a sign of status. He had a graduate-student air about him and hardly seemed the killer he undoubtedly was. But despite his soft-spokeness, Jeyam too was full of LTTE bluster.

Jeyam disagreed with many of the impressions circulating in Colombo about the Tigers. Popular support for the Tigers was not dipping. Only rich people in Colombo felt that way. A split in the leadership? Bah! There was only a problem with communications, given the now decentralized chain of command. Everyone still took orders from the central leadership. And even if that leadership was caught, they would all continue to fight, contradicting another popular supposition that arresting or killing Prabakeran would suck the wind from the movement altogether. Up to now, the Tigers were focusing on rebuilding, but next month, watch out, he said, for they would soon launch a major offensive against the Indians and show them they were still a force to be reckoned with.

As Jeyam was finishing, we heard a vehicle roar up the road and brake sharply in front of the compound. It was a battered Japanese van, its windows removed in the style the Tigers preferred for combat operations, carrying a load of Tiger guerrillas and a lone Indian soldier, his head bloodied and his hands bound. He had been captured when the Tigers ambushed an Indian jeep. Two Indians were killed outright and one escaped, but this one, dazed and terrified, had been apprehended and brought in at the end of a rope for interrogation.

As the Tiger commander asked the captive a few questions, the other Tigers crowded around speaking excitedly of the ambush and the Indians they had killed. After the attack, they had set fire to the jeep, immolating the corpses, and had made off with a number of weapons, which they proudly showed their leader. The face of the prisoner, meanwhile, grew more ashen, as if he was realizing that he was soon to die.

The Tigers said that the Indians would soon be sending up helicopter gunships to look for the captured soldier, which prompted Jeyam to order everyone to move out. This was no longer a safe area, he explained in an oddly apologetic manner.

Worries about the helicopters proved unwarranted. It was nearly two hours before the Indians put up a chopper. By that time, the Tigers were probably miles away in a safe hideout.

Later, at a roadblock the Indians had set up on the outskirts of town, I watched a detachment of bedraggled, footsore troops walk back into town after being confounded by a Tiger hit-and-run operation. At the head of the column, wearing a helmet that was too small for his head, was a pompous-looking lieutenant colonel, who seemed to be having a hard time refolding a map.

Although it might have been an exaggeration to say that the Tigers had tied the Indians up in knots to the same extent that they had trussed up the Indian prisoner that morning, it was clear that the Tigers had put the more than 50,000 troops in the Indian Peacekeeping Force in a classic military and political quagmire. Back in October 1987, Rajiv Gandhi had told an interviewer that he didn't envision the Indian peacekeeping effort getting "stuck or bogged down" in Sri Lanka, even with the problems they were already having in disarming the Tigers. But Sri Lanka soon became independent India's longest conflict to date, a protracted guerrilla war in which the world's fourth-largest army was neutralized by a group of teenagers in sarongs and rubber slippers.

Earlier, when it had sided with the Tamils and served as an intermediary in peace negotiations, India had warned that a military solution to the problem of Tamil separatism was impossible. In failing to heed its own counsel, however, India was being forced to learn a bitter lesson about the pitfalls of intervention. "It is easy for an army to march proudly into a foreign land," a British correspondent had written after the siege of Jaffna. "It is sometimes much harder to march out again."

Although men in the field had been trained to answer reporters' questions about the situation by describing it as a "picnic," they were starting to see that they might be in Sri Lanka much longer than they imagined, and that terms such as "mop-up," "residual terrorism," and other euphemisms employed by their commanders were unrealistic. Reliable estimates of Indian casualties ran into the thousands. Even the conservative estimates, however, meant that the Indians had lost more men in nine months than the Sri Lankans had lost in all the years they had fought the Tamils before them. How much the Indians were spending on the effort was also subject to widely disparate claims, but some observers estimated the cost at $3 million per day, a huge drain on the national treasury.

But despite the money and the manpower, the Tigers continued to elude capture and to wreak havoc in the north and east. Having assassinated five Government Agents in the last six months, they were able to paralyze the civil administration and to call out crippling strikes against all commercial activity in the north and east as well as to intimidate moderate Tamils and rival militant groups cooperating with the Indians. So confident were the Tigers of holding off the

Indians that they wouldn't even agree to negotiations until India rolled back its positions to where they were before the Jaffna offensive. The situation was completely deadlocked.

The costs in men and matériel, however, paled beside the political costs of the misadventure. Internationally, the quagmire had made a mockery of India's pretensions to the status of a regional superpower. Domestically, instead of distracting attention from Rajiv Gandhi's leadership it had provided new grist for critics.

But the greatest costs were in Sri Lanka itself, where India had forfeited its role as a peace broker. In the eyes of the Tamils whom its army had brutalized, it had turned from savior to enemy; in the eyes of suspicious Sinhalese, India's inability to crush the Tigers was only further proof of its ulterior motives and its sympathy for the Tiger cause. A pull-out, though, was unthinkable, since it would represent a huge loss of face and credibility, precipitate the collapse of the UNP government, and leave the Tamils to an uncertain fate at the hands of Sinhalese nationalists. Nevertheless, liquidating the Tigers wasn't an option either, even if it was possible, which was dubious given India's clumsy and ineffectual performance in the field so far. Without the Tigers there would be little leverage on the Sinhalese to follow through on their promises to grant the Tamils some autonomy. Consequently, India was attempting to declaw the Tigers without destroying them, a policy having little impact besides alienating Tamil civilians through the brutality of the troops and the extortion that Indian forces allowed other Tamil rebel groups to practice in return for their support.

Although what I had seen in Vavuniya was telling, the ultimate fate of the Indian intervention would be determined in Jaffna. But ever since the Indians launched their offensive there, a security curtain had come down on the rebel bastion.

Despite the news blackout, some information filtered through. A Tamil doctor on holiday from London at the time of the siege wrote a harrowing eyewitness account of what she had seen before she was able to flee. "Those who were lucky enough were bundled up in sacks and dumped in the hospital morgue," she wrote of the many dead bodies she remembered. "For others, there were long delays before being cleaned up. Crows were sighted on trees eating human flesh."

Such accounts by Tamils were easily dismissed as LTTE propaganda, but a report written by a Sinhalese doctor now living in Australia echoed the basic charge of immense brutality and suffering. Over 3,000 civilians died, according to his statements, though the toll could have been higher, as many bodies were eaten by rabid animals or disposed of by families and never counted. "What was important to keep in perspective," the doctor wrote, was that "this was a major military offensive by a peacekeeping force on a town packed full of civilians."

Information about what was happening in Jaffna since the offensive was a little more reliable. Although the Indians claimed to have reduced Tiger resistance to "residual terrorism" and to have established authority in a miraculously short time, Jaffna was still far from under control. According to some accounts, the LTTE still had a presence on the peninsula and could operate in town quite easily. For their part, the Indians had tempered their conduct toward civilians but were still being accused of wrongful detention, rape, and collective punishment. "This is the situation now," said one of the editors of the *Saturday Review*, an English-language weekly that had published all through the war but was driven out of Jaffna by the Indians. "Just a short while ago I would have been arrested in an instant if I stepped foot in Colombo, but now it is safer here for me than in Jaffna."

Reports of Indian brutality were confirmed through intelligence gathered by the U.S. embassy's human rights monitors. Although the Indians were not being accused of the same brutality as the Sri Lankan forces before them, they were still violating many of the international standards on human rights. The Indians had also turned down a request from the International Red Cross to send a delegation, claiming that the Indian Red Cross, known to be a cover for the Indian intelligence service, would suffice. In addition, the Indians had detained human rights workers and destroyed affidavits.

For the international journalists who had relied on the flow of information from Jaffna during the earlier phase of the conflict, the news blackout and harassment of reliable human rights monitors made it hard to refute Indian propaganda. "What you do know is that nothing is what people are telling you," complained John Rettie of the BBC. "It's not what the Tamils say and it's not what the Indians say. All you know is that it is something in between."

Occasionally, the Indians did allow journalists into Jaffna on brief, closely supervised junkets, with little opportunity to pierce the façade they wanted to maintain. For me, in disfavor with the Indians because of some of my reporting, even the dog and pony shows were off-limits, leaving me no other option but to go overland and hope that I could get through the Indian checkpoints along the way. Lacking the required passes to do so, I decided to go by bus instead of car, which might confuse the Indian soldiers enough to let me slide by.

Before I left Colombo, a Tamil friend, a journalist, had offered some sage advice for the road. "Don't complain about a slow driver or waiter," she said. "They might just save you from a land mine," the inconvenience a chance to let someone else's vehicle set off the explosion. Thus forewarned, I could see some utility to the roadblock outside of Vavuniya, although standing in the sun all morning took its toll. The soldiers manning the roadblock were only letting vehicles pass in sets of ten, to thwart robberies by militants farther on up the road, although the hijackers were just as often rebels belonging to groups siding with the Indians as they were Tigers. Soldiers were also levying their own tolls by helping themselves to produce carried in the trucks waiting to pass.

Once past the first checkpoint we were hardly home free. The Indians had nearly fifteen checkpoints strung along the road due north to Jaffna. At the second checkpoint, our bus was stopped and all the young men were forced to line up for interrogation. After checking the boys for weapons and cyanide caps beneath their sarongs and for the calluses on elbows, knees, and backs that were the marks of guerrilla training, the soldiers separated eight of the boys from the rest and marched them off into the jungle, presumably for further "interrogation."

Having seen other boys marched off in a similar way never to return, relatives of the young men pleaded with the major in charge to let them go, to no avail. I tried to take a picture, but was stopped at gunpoint by one of the officers, who yelled at me and warned me that I should be more careful while I was in "his" country.

Demonstrating an impressive flair for underhandedness, the commanding officer let me continue on up the road, though he radioed ahead for me to be stopped and turned around about an hour farther north, which meant it would take two hours to get back to Vavuniya instead of one. I was offered a ride back in an Indian Army jeep, but I didn't want to risk being ambushed.

It was the unhappy task of a young Indian captain to wait with me for the public bus. As we sat on a log at the side of the dusty, untraveled road, the captain proved he was a philosophical sort, with the Hindu knack for cosmic irony and a sense of the grand sweep of time. "It is like the way you Americans went into Vietnam after the French had already lost. History tells it is a lost cause, yet history is a concept the human mind will not accept. What are we in this bloody country for anyway? Nice game it is, eh? These Tigers are trained killers, and we will never win. The Buddhists are to blame. They have turned these Tamils into killers, and we are their dupes for coming to the rescue. In fact, it is highly ironic I am here, for I am a Tiger supporter. I sympathize with their cause and I want them to win. But first I must do my duty, for they are trying to kill me and my men. We are actually here to fight for them, but they do not realize that."

True to their reputation for inconsistency, the Indian sentries let me through without a problem the next day, though the rest of the passengers on the bus I was riding in faced the usual harassment.

As we proceeded along the peninsula toward Jaffna, we passed the coconut groves where we had been attacked by mortars the previous October during the fighting. I could still see some of the trenches and other fortifications the LTTE had dug to hold back the Indian armored columns, but the groves looked peaceful now, full of animals and dark-eyed Tamil women. Outside Jaffna a large Rotary Club-style sign told us: "The IPKF Welcomes You to Jaffna."

There were also signs telling residents to feel free to make sugges-tions or register complaints, as well as blackboards scattered around town devoted to "IPKF News"—information about curfews, restric-tions on fishing hours, and other quotidian matters.

Every once in a while, though, I could still see traces of old LTTE posters—the cartoonish, larger-than-life depictions of Pra-bakeran or the pantheon of Revolutionary Martyrs that once were ubiquitous. In fact, right below an advertisement for the Hotel Ashok—"We take care of you"—was the faded likeness of Praba himself, which had somehow been overlooked.

Indian military commanders had claimed that they had re-frained from using heavy weapons and air power in fighting the Tigers and hadn't done any damage to buildings in Jaffna "because of our consideration for human lives," but the condition of the city even after five months of Indian control clearly showed that this was a lie. Over 75,000 houses and buildings had been either destroyed or damaged, largely by indiscriminate Indian shelling. Churches and temples were pocked with heavy-machine-gun fire, the fronts of many stores still looked like Swiss cheese, and many houses were pulverized.

In certain sections of town, in front of buildings still pocked and shell-shattered, retired Tamil civil servants had set up outdoor businesses as "sworn translators." Using their trilingual skills, the sworn translators functioned as scribes for other Tamils to submit petitions to the government in Colombo for war relief, which was slow in coming, just one of many signs that government officials had other feelings beneath professions of amity toward Tamils. All over town, squadrons of black crows with incredibly swollen bellies picked through debris and offal, barely able to fly for their bulk. The crows made me queasy, reminding me of the Tamil doctor's macabre report.

From the rubble of the houses and buildings that were destroyed in the fighting, the Indian Peacekeeping Force had built a city of pillboxes and fortified bunkers within Jaffna itself. They were still dug in deeply in the town, with troops on virtually every street corner. The army also patrolled the streets in jeeps and trucks.

Despite the military presence, the city was still bustling with activity, the bazaar packed with customers—many of them off-duty Indian soldiers hunting for electronic goods unavailable in protectionist India—and the streets were thronged with scooters, trishaws, and commuters. At a movie theater we passed, a gaggle of Indian troops waited to see a film called *Lady Select Your Lovers.*

In the open-air bus station, I listened to the screechy Tamil epic that was playing over the loudspeaker, a rousing, athletic tribute to one of the Tamil gods. The atmosphere in Jaffna was tense. Many of the people I tried to speak to simply went about their business, pretending not to understand me. One older man, a retired civil servant, gave a polite, but furtive explanation, looking over his shoulder as he did so. "There are still incidents every day. People are nervous. Even now, you can't say it is peaceful here. But people are living, that is all I can say."

All through the fighting with the Sri Lankan forces, Gnaniam's Hotel was the place where journalists made their contacts with the LTTE, courtesy of the clerks and room boys. But close IPKF surveillance—there was a machine-gun emplacement on the roof next door—had put Gnaniam's out of the "facilitation" business. The head clerk sadly informed me that I, like all visitors now, had to see the brigadier in charge of operations in the town. Given the fishbowl nature of Jaffna, it would be impossible to ignore Indian orders. "Better for you, sir, if you go and see the brigadier," said the clerk. "Better for us, too."

The brigadier in charge of Indian peacekeeping efforts in the town was a Sikh named Kahlon, who kept a tidy office on the top floor of an old Raj-era building. His beard was neatly combed and the prow of his turban swept forward dramatically, giving him a pudgy, though distinctive appearance. He was obviously burdened by my arrival, as I was the first correspondent to reach Jaffna independently. It had been a mistake, he said, for the Indians down the line to have let me through. I was there, however, and there was little he could do about it at that point. He had more than an unauthorized reporter to worry about. "We never foresaw the delay we have had," he said. "Remember the original schedule?" He recited the timetable Rajiv Gandhi had set when the Accord with signed: seventy-two hours to disarm the LTTE, Provincial Council elections shortly thereafter, followed by an Indian withdrawal in less than two months. Lasting peace after that. "It's anybody's guess when we will be out of here now."

At the moment, he was most absorbed by Jaffna's mounting crime problem. For years, the LTTE provided law and order to the town, if in a crude form. But now, the incidence of robbery and other forms of crime was skyrocketing, complicating what was an already challenging administrative burden. "I have bigger guns and could break some more heads, but I have the reputation of a nation to consider," the brigadier complained. "You know how bad we are looking already."

The real problem facing the IPKF, however, was the resiliency of the Tigers. Lately several mid-level rebel commanders were reported to be on the prowl on the peninsula, having infiltrated from the jungles of the north and east by blending in with civilians. Something big might be in the works, the brigadier surmised. But even if the LTTE kept its low profile, it was still capable of intimidation of civilian officials and civil servants in Jaffna. The latest LTTE threat—a single letter—had closed down the entire civil administration. A follow-up threat looked likely to stop all commercial activity in the next few days. "People are absolutely terrified of the Tigers," the brigadier explained. "They may not believe in God, but they do believe in the wrath of the LTTE. Today, the IPKF is here, but tomorrow we may go back and the Tigers will still be here. That is why they listen to them, do what they say, and keep quiet."

Questions about Indian Army brutality and allegations of human rights abuses brought the brigadier's rage to the surface. "They'd be sitting in darkness if we hadn't come here and brought electricity back to them after October," he insisted. "They'd be starving if we hadn't brought food. They don't realize that those buggers in Colombo talking about sovereignty of the country don't care a fig about them at all. Bloody ingrates. I feel sorry for them. They haven't seen what we have done for them. Our munificence. When we first came here in October, this was nothing but a city of corpses and rotting flesh."

Another official who wasn't too happy with the deadlock between the Indians and the LTTE was the Bishop of Jaffna, who, like his counterpart in Batticaloa, was a Jesuit. The Bishop was a tall, burly man with the build of a fullback and a way of laying out an argument that was just as delicate. It was inevitable, in the face of Sinhalese political demagoguery since independence, he maintained, that the Tamils wanted to have their own state, but India would never allow it to happen. The only hope was autonomy within a federal setup, though that was something the Tigers would never settle for.

The situation had grown so extreme that not even the feelings of the people mattered to the Tigers anymore. Anyone who voiced any position that diverged from the Tiger line of complete and unending struggle for Eelam was silenced. "People won't say anything about the LTTE. It is a very delicate matter. As a result, we are living between two fires. If you say anything about India, they will take action against you. And if you say anything against the LTTE, they will take their revenge. So we all follow the best course and say nothing. How will this be solved?" he asked despondently, as church bells next door rang to signal the start of curfew. "I do not know."

As I pedaled back to the hotel, already in violation of curfew, I passed three funeral homes. Inside the Bright Funeral Home two coffin makers were busily at work. "Business is good, sir," one of the men said.

One of my missions while in Jaffna was to investigate several reports about the fighting several months earlier. There was still considerable ignorance about what had taken place. The Indians, for example, had reportedly overrun Jaffna Hospital—the rumor I had first heard in Jaffna at the time of the fighting and been unable to pin down.

At first, the Indians claimed they did nothing to the hospital, that the first time they entered it, during the fighting, they had walked through ambushes and booby traps to deliver medicine to the poor. Later Indian accounts acknowledged that there had been some fighting, but only to rout the Tigers who had taken up positions inside. Of course, some civilians had been caught in the cross fire.

Other versions, including a report from the humanitarian organization Doctors Without Frontiers, seemed to corroborate the Tiger
side of things, describing a harrowing atrocity in which Indian troops
shot patients in their beds, as well as doctors and nurses attending
the sick.

By now I had been joined by another journalist, Catherine
Manegold of *The Philadelphia Inquirer*, who had shown up at Gnaniam's with a car and a pair of drivers, making it easier to get around.
The directing physician of the hospital had tried to brush us off the
day before, claiming he wasn't allowed to give interviews. But he
had mentioned he was going to be home the next evening, a clear
signal that he wanted to talk. When we arrived at his house, located
in an upper-middle-class suburb that had been shelled heavily during the offensive, the doctor welcomed us, though he was now joined
by another man, who I supposed was an LTTE supporter, perhaps
assigned to monitor what the doctor was about to tell us.

That the Indians attacked the hospital was a bad enough violation of the Geneva Accord, the doctor said. All through the earlier
phase of the war it had been off-limits to all warring factions—the
Tigers and other militant groups as well as the Sri Lankan
Army—the single point of humanitarian refuge in the entire city.
But two weeks into the Indian drive on Jaffna that immunity ended.
Every other day, the doctor said, he had waited at home for an
ambulance to fetch him so that he could attend to the increasing
numbers of wounded civilians, most of them hurt by indiscriminate
Indian shelling. On the day of the hospital attack, however, the
ambulance never arrived. But although he had not been at the hospital, he had been able to piece an account together from the stories
of eyewitnesses.

As the Indians crept forward, a few Tigers had taken up positions behind the hospital compound's walls to fire on them. Although
the staff inside had pleaded with the Tigers to leave, they refused to
do so. When they did go, it was through the back door, leaving the
Indians with the impression that they were still somewhere inside.
As a result, the Indians decided to storm the hospital, under the
direct supervision of one of their brigadiers. He was eventually com-
mended for the action.

The doctor drew a diagram of the hospital, and told us what he had learned. An entire hour elapsed between the time the Tigers fled and when the Indians stormed the walls, laying down a heavy barrage of machine-gun fire as they did so and throwing grenades through the front doors. After that, Indian troops roamed the hospital wards, firing indiscriminately. As a result, fifty people died in the attack itself, twenty of them hospital staff. Many others were badly wounded, some so terrified that they pretended to be dead and lay among the corpses or hid in closets all night as the Indian troops ransacked the hospital. Even the next day, a doctor who came to the hospital from his home, unaware of what had happened, was shot dead at point-blank range by an Indian soldier with a machine gun, even though he had a stethoscope around his neck and the nurses accompanying him were in uniform. When doctors with the IPKF finally arrived later the second day, the wards were still full of bodies, the floors still flooded with blood.

"I feel the Indians could have saved the hospital if they had made an announcement before they attacked, ordering those with guns inside to come out and letting the patients move to another part of the building," the doctor said sorrowfully. "But I suppose in warfare this could not happen."

Another report from the October offensive concerned the Nallur Kandaswamy Temple, Jaffna's most revered Hindu shrine, where many thought the Tigers would make a suicidal last stand among the thousands of refugees who had fled there. On the bus trip into Jaffna I had met a Tamil man, a retired bank manager named Sellakandu, who had been in Nallur through most of the siege; he invited me to drop by if I was in the neighborhood so he could tell me more about it.

Having just dismantled their bomb shelters in the wake of the peace accord, Sellakandu and his neighbors had been caught completely by surprise when hostilities were renewed. "They were welcome here, the Indians," he explained. "We had high hopes for this peace. Reconciliation. Reconstruction. Then all of a sudden, things took a turn for the worse."

Luckily for them, Indian reprisals against civilians who were mistaken for Tiger supporters were inflicted only on other neighborhoods. Still, Sellakandu's family barely got behind the thick six-teenth-century walls of the Nallur Temple. Outside, shells were raining down on the area. There had been no preparations for the hordes seeking sanctuary in the temple. Conditions inside were al-most as deadly as outside in the fighting. More than 10,000 had sought refuge there. With heavy rain and no sanitation, dysentery broke out, killing some people and threatening mass infection. "If we were there one more week," Sellakandu said, shuddering. "It would have been the end of us."

Although Sellakandu and his family slept every night at the temple, he himself would go back to the house from time to time to check on the goats he kept in the backyard, a mission that often had him picking his way through the shifting lines of fire. Indian commanders told him he'd probably be shot if their men came across him at the wrong time, but he kept going back, out of an attachment to the goats. The Tigers he met along the way were no more reassur-ing, he said. "We are dying. Why aren't you ready to die?" the Tigers asked him when he complained about their foolish resistance in the face of such superior Indian forces, a logic that eluded him. "If we are supposed to die, then who are these fellows fighting for?" he asked me rhetorically. "People don't accept death all that easily, even though one day we all will die."

When Sellakandu returned to his home to feed the goats the first time, he hardly recognized the scene. He had to step over dead bodies to get through his own gate. The roof of the house had also been blown apart. Four goats were missing right off the bat, having probably been taken by the Indians and eaten. Then, as shells began to fall again, he was trapped inside the cattle shed, where he was later caught by the Indians. They accused him of firing at them, and beat him hard all over his body, shooting rifles just over his head as they did so. Then they bound and blindfolded him and ordered him into a truck. He was given the impression that he was to be driven somewhere and shot. Instead they took him to their commanding officer, who, after hearing his story, allowed him to go.

In another week, he returned once again to the house. All the goats had escaped and were grazing around the neighborhood.

Somehow he found them, each in terrible condition. An old woman who had remained at home throughout the ordeal told him the Indians had come over each day to slaughter a goat for food. The goat bones were not the only ones that were left behind, however, Sellakandu explained, showing me the skull of a corpse he had found in his backyard on one of his visits.

"Was it an Indian, a Tamil civilian, or a Tiger?" I asked. As he answered, Sellakandu held the skull up at eye level. "I am deadly sure, one hundred percent sure, this skull belongs to a Tamil," he told me. "In fact, I think it is one of my relatives." Then he lowered the skull and tried to hand it to me. "Go ahead and touch it," he said matter-of-factly as I declined. "It is indeed what we all are, isn't it?"

After satisfying my curiosity about what had happened several months before, I spent the next few days trying to get a sharper picture of the present. What, in fact, constituted "normalcy," as the Indians liked to characterize the current situation? Were the Tigers on the rebound, as some of their supporters said? And what did people caught in between the two fighting forces think about all this? To answer these questions, Manegold and I took a long winding tour by car one day through the small towns on the peninsula where the LTTE was said to be regrouping.

The atmosphere outside of Jaffna was both somnolent and surreal. It was hard to fight off déjà vu, as people peering from their doorways and over their ratty fences had the same look as they did months before when shells were flying. Houses, many of them with huge holes in their walls and roofs, stood like derelict hulks in a thick fog. In a small town called Nillady, about ten miles outside of Jaffna, we were stopped by Indian troops who demanded to know who had authorized our presence there. Contrary to the brigadier's wishes, who had asked that we notify him daily about our itinerary so that there wouldn't be "any international incidents," we had not telephoned him that morning. Now we had strayed into a major Indian operation. One of the soldiers grabbed Catherine's camera, and another glowered menacingly at me when I objected.

The Indian troops were overwrought. A major, summoned to deal with us, was abrupt and smarmy, scoffing at the permit the brigadier had issued me to travel on the peninsula. "This says you have permission to travel through Jaffna," the major snapped. "However, it does not say you have the right to conduct journalistic research or take photographs." After a radio call to headquarters, we were allowed to proceed, although along a different road, and the major changed his tune. "Thank you very much for the inconvenience," he said politely. "Have a safe journey under the circumstances."

Indian control in the area was minimal. "People are afraid day and night," said a shopkeeper we met on the road who declined to ride with us and act as a guide. "Night particularly." There had been no fighting here during the offensive, he explained, but now the Indians believed a major concentration of Tigers was being organized nearby. In response, the Indians were blockading the area, closely monitoring what vehicles went in and out and the flow of essential supplies like oil, gas, and diesel fuel.

We drove to the northernmost tip of the peninsula, where Prabakeran had been born, passing the house where, in October, I had waited to interview him and other Tiger leaders during the height of the fighting. Signs of the LTTE were almost nil, except for a black hand painted on a door to mark where an anti-LTTE informer had once lived.

Later on in the day we stopped off at the Uthyan Press, which at that point was publishing Jaffna's only newspaper, a weekly. Before the Indian offensive there were six papers, including several dailies and an English-language weekly put out by a Sinhalese with a staff of Tamil editors and reporters. Most of the papers stopped publishing because the Indians put them out of business. The Indians took the added step of expropriating typewriters around town to prevent the publication of unauthorized broadsheets. Not that the Tigers were paragons of free speech either: just the week before, they had blown up the presses of a paper that was deemed partisan to the Indians.

The lack of competition did not sit well with the editor of the

Uthyan Press, however, who greeted us just as a contingent of Indian troops was entering the building for overnight guard duty. "We didn't ask for protection but they gave it anyway," sighed the editor, a squat, middle-aged man in his early forties. "Actually it will be a problem for us. The Tigers will think we are now siding with the Indians and come after us all the more. We are being pressured from both sides. Running a newspaper these days is like walking on the edge of a blade. It is like wartime, no matter what the Indians say."

Such forthrightness did not make its way into the columns of the newspaper, though. What he tried to do, the editor said, was to take a very neutral stance, which meant that commentary and opinions were not the things he was interested in publishing. He also said that the prevailing conditions made it hard to publish the more sensationalistic stories, by which he meant reports of Indian atrocities and human rights abuses, especially reports of rape.

"All those incidents took place before we resumed publishing," the editor stammered sheepishly. "So therefore they are not news, no? And anyway, our culture doesn't like these stories, so we leave them alone."

The next day I met somewhat clandestinely with a member of the Jaffna Citizens' Committee, an organization that had formerly devoted itself to monitoring the human rights situation in Jaffna but had lately become a propaganda outlet for the LTTE. Although they had gotten out of the "facilitation" business, the staff at Gnaniam's had arranged a meeting for me, and served us lunch in my room so that the Indian Red Cross workers set up in the hotel wouldn't see us together. The reason the Citizens' Committee man had to be so furtive, he explained as he peered through a crack in the drawn curtain, was that the Indians were emphatic about blocking information on human rights abuses. Those known to be activists had had their travel passes revoked, and the Indians had set up an informers' network to monitor their movements. A barbarous situation had been allowed to develop, said the man. "We have seen rape, molestation, the killing of entire families," he exclaimed, intent on being convincing. "The killing of grandmothers and grandfathers, of invalids and the blind, of brides and bridegrooms together, of mothers, fathers, and lovers as they slept. All these things have happened since these Indians have come."

Although I sensed that the Citizens' Committee man was a full-blown LTTE operative, it was hard to dismiss his charges outright, especially in light of allegations I later heard at a demonstration organized by the Jaffna Mothers' Front, a group of women that had been formed to protest the conditions of the Indian occupation. The mothers of Jaffna were not a force to be shrugged off. Even the most swaggering Indian commander knew the influence they could exert, as motherhood was a profoundly powerful concept in Hindu culture. Over in Batticaloa, for example, the Mothers' Front had staged a death fast, which could have triggered violence all over the north and east if carried to its gruesome end.

The Hindu temple outside of which the protest was taking place still bore the gouges of grenades and heavy-machine-gun fire. The mothers had called the protest to complain specifically about arbitrary Indian detention policies, which in some cases had led to disappearances of people with no political involvements whatsoever and of family members of LTTE cadres.

Most of the cases that the Mothers' Front presented were documented as best as they could be under the circumstances, although there were no lawyer's affidavits as was customary. Any lawyer who notarized any such affidavit would have been arrested by the Indians for fomenting discord. One of the cases that seemed particularly poignant involved a man in his late thirties whose wife and three children were taken away by a detachment of IPKF soldiers in the second week of November. "I have lost all sources of energy and strength in the search for my family and have become a mental wreck," said a letter the man had written to Indian authorities, making unintentionally comic use of the English language. "As my family life is now disrupted, my home broken up, I have taken refuge at my mother's residence and am subject to the treatment of the inmates."

I heard another poignant story later that night. In the hotel coffee shop, a young Tamil woman who worked in a camera store attached to the hotel came over and asked if she could speak to me in private. She had asked the same thing the day I had arrived, obviously agitated about something. I made a motion that she should sit at the table so we could talk, but she said it wouldn't be proper to be seen alone with me. Instead we stood in the doorway, out of earshot of the clerks sitting at a nearby table, but within the code of modesty that restricted Tamil women.

She had been working, she told me, as an au pair for an American woman in France, but had returned home when the peace accord was signed, thinking things would be all right in her homeland once more. "But then these problems didn't go away, sir, they got worse," she explained, looking over at a table of Indian Army officers having a drink in the bar. Had someone been bothering her? I asked, phrasing it vaguely. Yes, she answered, clearly understanding what I meant.

An Indian soldier had been coming into the store and had recently told her that she should start learning Hindi because he was going to take her back to India with him. "He said even if I don't want to go, he will force me, and that he would hurt my family if I refused," she said, breaking out in a panic. "He said I had three days, and that he would come back at the end of the week for me. I told him to stop talking nonsense and to get out of the shop, but I am now very worried, sir. That is why I want to go to America, sir, to leave this place. It has been three days now and he is going to come back very soon."

Though the lack of regard for the Indians in the north and east was manifest, it was unclear to what extent the Tamil population supported the LTTE. In Colombo, there were two schools of thought. One held that any visible support for the Tigers was actually coerced and that the average Tamil rejected the LTTE's claim to leadership because the Tigers were too young and low-caste, too politically inexperienced and overly authoritarian. If there ever was genuine support, it had evaporated, since the LTTE had overplayed its hand in defying the Indians and had inflicted enormous suffering on the people of the north and east in the process. The other school of thought discounted these contentions and claimed that popular support was still high.

As the Bishop had warned when I first arrived, the people of Jaffna were very careful when speaking of the Tigers. Among the forthright was a man I met the day we were touring the northern tip of the peninsula. The man was yet another Tamil pensioner. Well preserved for his age, he wore white athletic clothes, a terry-cloth hat, and a pair of dark sunglasses. India would never allow Eelam, he insisted, so why did the Tigers continue with their fight? "War must end. Peace must be restored," he whispered as if committing sedition. "Men must begin living like men. Right now we are living like less than men. The Tigers have successfully drawn attention to our grievances. Yet at the same time, the remedy they are prescribing is worse than the disease itself. They might be ready to fight and die for their cause, but they shouldn't expect civilians like us to die with them."

Such an equivocal stance toward the Tigers was, I concluded, typical of the average middle-class Tamil's feelings. But this under-lying ambivalence did not threaten the LTTE's power or its base of popular support. However much the Tamils objected to the extremist demand for a totally independent Eelam, however much they fa-vored a more moderate negotiated settlement that would create a separate Tamil state inside a federalized Sri Lanka, the bulk of the Tamils were never going to renounce the Tigers entirely, for reasons that were subtle and simple.

The continued popular support for the Tigers was mainly a function of a fundamental fact of Tamil political life: while the Sinhalese government in the south might promise concessions, it would only follow through with them if there was pressure on it to do so. The militant tone of the clergy and the rising specter of the JVP had Tamils worried. "We know J.R.; he will be forced to change his conciliatory stance toward us," explained the leader of a Tamil militant group called the Eelam Revolutionary Organization of Stu-dents, or EROS, which was closely allied with the LTTE. "That is why he must be forced to honor his pledges and why we need a structure, an armed structure, to protect our rights and our future."

But popular backing for the Tigers ran deeper than collective self-interest. Many Tamils felt grateful for and proud of the militants, whatever their excesses. Tamils might never accept all the tenets of the LTTE, or justify their cruelty, but they would never turn against them. "For years, the people in Jaffna were brutalized by the Sri Lankan Army, which was running riot with cordons and searches, detentions and executions," the Bishop had explained that first night I spoke with him. "We had no redress. We were desperate. All of the Sinhalese politicians in Colombo had turned their backs on us. It was only these Tiger fellows who were able to fight against the soldiers and the police, who were able to hold them back in their barracks so people could walk freely outside their homes. This is what has given them the irreducible support of the people, their admiration."

To be sure, a sizable portion of the population abhorred the Tigers and their reflexive, unthinking brutality. But even those who were disgusted and fearful saw the efficacy of the Tigers. Like Buddhists in the south who abhorred the slaughter of animals but heartily partook of what the butcher was selling, many Tamils surely disdained the intimidation and violence of the LTTE but would accept whatever benefits that violence brought them. And when all was said and done, the Tigers were family. "We are mothers brought up in the old school," explained the head of the Jaffna Mothers' Front. "And as mothers we do not often approve. But they are our children. If a son does something wrong, we will forgive him, even if we have to do so a hundred times."

If popular support was important for the Tigers to win the legitimacy needed to lead whatever political entity emerged after the struggle, it was not all that important in terms of the more immediate task of beating back the Indians. According to the municipal commissioner of Jaffna, who was close to the Tiger leadership, morale among the Tigers was good, and talk of fragmentation between commanders and rank and file as well as within the leadership itself was bunk. "Their people are always ready to die," the commissioner explained matter-of-factly. "And because of that, they are neither worried nor depressed."

* * *

One night, Catherine Manegold and I were invited over to the Jaffna fort to have dinner with the two ranking Indian Army brigadiers. I wasn't thrilled about the invitation. The day had been a hard one, taking us to all corners of the peninsula, and I was exhausted. I was also less than happy about being out after curfew in the company of the two senior Indian officers—prime targets for an LTTE assassination.

When we arrived back at Gnaniam's from that day's rounds, there was a jeep and an armed escort of two soldiers waiting for us. There was no begging off the banquet. "You need not be worried about anything," one of the generals assured me over the phone. "We can promise you that there will be no problem. Our troops are well trained and disciplined and will make sure there will be no incidents."

Meanwhile, the two soldiers in the jeep were trying to convince Catherine of the same thing.

"Yes. Protection, madam, protection," one of them insisted. "Yes, yes. We will protect you," his partner added.

"Come on, don't be such an old lady," the brigadier chided me, sounding like a golfer looking to get in a quick nine before a thunderstorm. "You have already wasted a half hour on this silly business. The shrimp has already been cooked!"

Finally we caved in. We were allowed to drive over in the car Catherine had rented, although the driver and his sidekick, both Tamils, were not thrilled with the idea of driving after curfew, especially since the headlights didn't work. Both of the brigadiers greeted us warmly when we arrived, dressed sharply for the evening in tight Levi's and crisply pressed sport shirts.

It was actually our second social engagement of the week with the brigadiers. The night before, they had paid a visit to us at Gnaniam's, as much to find out what we had discovered about the Tigers and Jaffna as for the social stimulation. The two of them were real characters. Brigadier Magid Singh, the general in charge of the fort, showed up that first night in a white shirt and tie, while his colleague, Brigadier Kahlon, who had the more difficult task of coordinating civil administration in town, was wearing an off-white leisure suit. Our casual chatter that night in the hotel was punctuated by some pretty good information.

Initially, the brigadiers reminded me of two college frat boys. Brigadier Kahlon complained about his weight, and said that since he only played golf, there was no way for him to get any exercise, as Jaffna lacked a course. Brigadier Singh, for his part, kept in "trim nick" by playing badminton, politely omitting details of the exercise he had gotten leading the charge on the Jaffna Hospital. They joshed each other amiably. "Missy, more scotch?" Brigadier Singh called over to Brigadier Kahlon. "Sir," Kahlon answered rousingly.

The scotch loosened their tongues. In the estimation of Brigadier Kahlon, the Tigers had outlived their usefulness as a military organization. It was time to get down to the hard job of political negotiations. Violence, he said, can only set the stage, can only focus the issues at hand.

Still, Kahlon continued, there was an enormous task ahead in building a bridge of trust between the Tamils and the Sinhalese. He had been shocked when he realized just how deep the breach had grown between the two communities. The prior autumn, he had seen the aftermath when Sinhalese helicopter pilots fired on Tamil civilians trying to flee the Jaffna peninsula. "They are filled with hate toward them, pure hate," Kahlon said in disgust. "How could they fly out to that ferry, hover twenty feet over the heads of the people below, while the people held up their babies so they could see they were not militants, and fire directly on them? The sea turned completely red, bloody pure red. I saw it with my own eyes." In the general's estimation, the Sinhalese used the Tamils as scapegoats for their own inadequacy, like the Nazis did the Jews. "Those bloody buggers in Colombo don't care a fig about the people up here," he hissed. "The moment we leave, they'll be lunging for them two minutes later."

For Kahlon, such hate was especially absurd given the proximity of the two traditions, Buddhism and Hinduism. Buddha was, after all, a Hindu, he explained intently, wiggling his head from side to side in South Asian style.

"Curfew time," Kahlon reminded Singh as it neared eight o'clock. "Yes, we have to go," replied Singh as Kahlon poured him another round.

It was no sweat, they told us, if they were out a little late. They were, after all, in charge of the city. Were they worried about being targeted by the Tigers? Of course, they said, but there was little they could do. If the Tigers wanted to get them, they were going to get them, no matter what. And anyway, there was more to soldiering than constantly worrying about your own skin, said Kahlon, apparently to impress Catherine.

To get into the fort on our second date with the brigadiers, we had to cross the infamous no-man's-land which had, before the Accord, separated the Sri Lankan troops from the Tigers, who controlled the town outside. Often, in those days, mortar shells whistled overhead, as each side tried to unnerve the other. Once the gates closed behind us, it seemed like we were in a different part of the country. "You see, the brigadier here is in the safest part of the city," Kahlon said, razzing his colleague. "As we told you, Jaffna is as quiet as a church, for God's sake."

"Sir!" Singh bellowed, welcoming us to his quarters. Were we spending the night? our driver wanted to know. "We shall see," the brigadier answered for us, his eyes narrowing a bit over a carefully waxed mustache. "We shall see."

We began the cocktail hour with a few quarts of beer, "mother's milk," according to Singh. After that it was shrimp from the Jaffna lagoon and spicy cashews. Even though there was a tacit agreement that the evening was for relaxation, conversation inevitably swung around to the Situation. These two were more candid than I had expected. The Tigers were a unique fighting force, Brigadier Kahlon maintained. Not since the kamikazes had there been a group of fighting men so ready to accept death voluntarily. "They bite into this cyanide like it's a bloody chocolate," he said disgustedly. Even if they were disorganized after Jaffna, they were committed. If he was a Tamil, Kahlon maintained, he'd be fighting as a Tiger, too. "They have definitely been discriminated against, no doubt about it."

In the general's estimation, the Research and Analysis Wing had screwed up in backing the other rebel groups and trying to cut the Tigers out of the equation for power sharing. The Tigers were a factor, Kahlon said, citing the general strike they had called for the next day throughout the peninsula. Gandhi was a child to think he could hold elections in Jaffna without the Tigers' support.

"And for that we are here," exclaimed Brigadier Singh, raising his glass for a toast. "Missy, pass the scotch! And what do you care anyway?" he called to his chum across the cocktail table. "Twenty-four hours and you'll be back in Delhi on leave, isn't that right?"

In order to scribble some notes, I trotted off to the toilet several times, explaining that I had a weak bladder when they remarked how often I was going. It didn't seem to matter too much. They were quite happy to be alone with Catherine, who was pumping them for information, too. Through the wall, I could hear her asking about reports of Indian soldiers raping the women of Jaffna. "Four rapes, forty, four hundred. How can we ever tell how many? It is so very hard to say," said Singh. "Anyway, you don't have to worry about us. We are Sikhs and we like our women fair."

Brigadier Kahlon wanted to know if we would rather stay over that night instead of going home in the dark after so much drink. "It would be easy for you to stay here," he told Catherine. "We could fix up a bed without any bother at all."

The two were very disappointed when we insisted on going home after dinner. Sulking over the rebuff, Kahlon, who was supposed to make sure we got home safely, allowed us to get lost on the way home almost as soon as we got out of the fort.

It was a typical instance of cross-cultural miscommunication, but the consequences were far worse than in any other situation I had been in before. As we were leaving the fort in our night-blind Peugeot, we stopped outside the walls to regroup with the two jeeps that were to escort us back to the hotel, one holding Brigadier Kahlon, the other with several bodyguards. One jeep would be in front of us, the other in the rear, to provide security in case of a rebel attack as well as illumination along the pitch-dark roads.

When we got outside the fort, Brigadier Kahlon waved good night, his turban kicking back on his head as the open-air jeep reared into the dark. But instead of letting us get right behind him, the other jeep cut us off, taking the usual position of bodyguards as close to the commander as possible. We tried to keep up, but the rutted road was slow going for us. We were left in the dust in no time, well after curfew, without any headlights, in a town crawling with guerrillas and nervous Indian sentries.

We didn't want to drive back across the no-man's-land, not knowing what kind of reception we would get from the sentries inside. Very carefully, then, we picked our way through town, getting hopelessly lost as we proceeded. I waved a small flashlight out the window on one side, and Catherine flicked her lighter on and off in hopes that we might be mistaken for people on the way to the hospital.

There was a brief moment of comic relief when the driver and his sidekick tried to switch places in the front seat and got tangled in their sarongs, but most of the drive through town was terrifying. In the sepulchral quiet, the only sounds were the buzzing of street-lamps and the light sprinkling of gunfire. We stopped at one point for directions at a sawmill that was operating an overnight shift. When I got out to ask directions, the two workers jumped a good foot in the air, as if I was already a ghost.

We finally made it back to the hotel, though, however much the odds had been against it. And just after we drove into the courtyard Brigadier Kahlon appeared, wearing a dopey smile. His expression changed completely, however, as soon as he saw how angry we were. "It was something that just happened, don't you understand?" he said as I started to lay into him. "It was not my fault. It just simply happened."

Whatever Asian equanimity I might have gathered was completely inaccessible to me at that point, and I strode over to the general and let fly a stream of profanity, capping my blistering tirade by notifying the general that when I got back to Colombo, I would make a point of telling the Indian High Commissioner what had taken place that night, how the two most senior Indian officers in the town had jeopardized our lives. "And I hope," I screamed at the general, "that when the High Commissioner hears about all this, he nails your silly ass to the wall."

The offense was even worse because I had launched it in front of his men. In response, the general grew equally angry with me, his eyes narrowing as we stood toe to toe. Luckily, Catherine was able to come between us diplomatically, saving me from a fistfight, and perhaps a firing squad.

The general was still insisting that it wasn't his fault. "It just happened. Can't you see? It just happened!"

Deep down, I think he knew he had screwed up, but it would have been completely out of the question for him to acknowledge it. And now that I had polarized the situation with my foolish temper and insulting remarks, there was no way he could back down. East glared at West, West glared at East, the clash of cultures as stark as it could get.

"Americans," he said disgustedly, lighting a cigarette and spitting into the dirt. Brigadier Kahlon then launched into his rap about the mystical nature of warriorhood. "You care so much about your own life? You shouldn't be here, then, my friend," he informed me curtly. "You should come to a place like this for something more abstract, something you obviously don't comprehend. Your life is nothing compared to the essence of what is happening around you. Don't you see that? I am twice your age. I don't have to listen to these things from some little punk like you. Nail my ass. Bah! It's dangerous here, my friend. You have to be built to take it. You cracked, man, you cracked. You don't belong here, don't you see? You shouldn't be up here to begin with."

It was doing no good trying to force the issue. "It must be cultural, then," I said in concession, walking away, as the general once more declared that the incident was not his fault.

"Cultural!" the general erupted. It was the wrong word.

"Don't you try to tell me about culture, my friend. Culture! I come from a culture that is five thousand years old, not two hundred like your bloody country. Culture? Don't talk to me about culture, all right? Tomorrow morning you will regret ever having said the things you've said. Tomorrow morning you'll wake up and want to apologize to *me*!" At that, I simply turned and left. But as I stepped across the patio, I could hear the general resume his courtly manner. He tried, once again, some of his better lines on Catherine. "Ah, but it has not been so bad, has it, now?" he said romantically. "The lady has at least been able to see the Jaffna evening."

FOUR

17 · Mr. Crab

AFTER THE EPISODE with the brigadiers in Jaffna, I refrained from going into forward areas. I had contracted a case of short-timer's dread and was convinced that my number would be up before I left the island. The fear I had repressed on earlier excursions into the war zones was now uncontainable, bringing with it memories of burned bodies, land-mine victims, and morgue scenes. What little relief I found came at the beachside restaurant and cabana bar I had formerly frequented in Mount Lavinia, just outside Colombo.

My students and I had found the place the year before and had called it Mohammed's because of a cabdriver named Mohammed who told us he had a piece of it. This was a fabrication, it turned out, but the name stuck, for that year at least, even after the owners put a big sign outside announcing its real name, the Catamaran. Mohammed's was a modest-sized shack with a woven cadjan roof that had been tricked up with tacky wall decorations for a neo-disco effect. The food was horrendous, but the beer was pretty cold and those looking for a place to drink arrack found it appealing. The breeze was cool and the staff was friendly enough to make you feel like you were escaping. Its owner was a thirty-year-old Sinhalese named Gamani, who, despite a dwindling supply of tourists, was always fixing the place up, using capital of unknown origin.

Though Gamani owned it, the place was dominated by Sena,

the manager, a Sinhalese in his mid-thirties, who was as robust as he was pitiable. Sena was an excellent chef, the result of a few years as a cook in the Iraqi Army, he said, in which he served as a kind of soldier of fortune. He did not get a salary at Mohammed's but worked for tips and commissions he got by bringing in Western tourists. To work for a salary would imply that he was Gamani's employee, and the upper-caste status Sena claimed would not allow that.

Buddhistic piety was neither Sena's nor Mohammed's stock-in-trade. Although Sena always swore about the clientele who frequented the cabana section, he gladly accepted the business, even if he did scowl at some of the touts and massage boys when they came in to place an order for their "friends." Sena also functioned as a liaison with the local police, handling bribes and short-circuiting any situation that threatened the restaurant's status with the authorities.

What was most appealing about Mohammed's was the diversity of its habitués, as well as their color and zest. In terms of nationality and class, Mohammed's always had a great cross section: preppies from the nearby St. Thomas College, expats who preferred a more earthy style than the club scene in town, touts trying to sell any knickknack or trinket they could carry, beggars of every infirmity, merchant seamen, Sri Lankan gigolos, and tourists ready to be their marks. A day spent there never wanted for laughs.

Mohammed's was one of the few places where I was able to overcome a nagging sense of cultural estrangement. Like Robert Knox, the shipwrecked English sailor whose memoirs of imprisonment during the reign of the king of Kandy formed the basis for Daniel Defoe's Robinson Crusoe, the deep cultural barriers around me often made me terribly solitary. Another visitor to the island, Pablo Neruda, who served as Cuba's consul to Ceylon in the 1920s, wrote of that estrangement, too. "You could smash your head against the wall and nobody came. No matter how you screamed or wept. . . . I realized there were hundreds, thousands of human beings who worked and sang by the waterside, who lit fires and molded pitchers, and passionate women also, sleeping naked on thin mats, under the light of immense stars. But how was I to get close to that throbbing world, without being looked upon as the enemy?"

A day at Mohammed's would serve up any number of Gauguin-like scenes: Sinhalese girls carrying clay vessels, their hips cocked to one side as they went to draw water from the nearby well; lovers necking furtively beneath an umbrella along the track; women bathing with their wet sarongs plastered against their skin. But the compelling sensuality of the place only made the fundamental estrangement even more aching.

I was so desperate for some kind of communion that one day I took up a beach tout on his offer to take me to a declining guesthouse up the beach, which in the absence of tourists had become a house of pleasure. Although I was a bit morally uncomfortable with the idea, and was worried about being set up by the police, my stay inside was not uninteresting.

For most of the time I simply sat around with the girls—village girls for the most part, both Tamil and Sinhalese—who marveled at my watch, my eyes, and the newsmagazines I had brought along with me. At one point, we all laughed hysterically when a small poodle came out from one of the bedrooms and dropped a sequined high-heeled shoe at my feet. Ethnic friction, however, was not far beneath the surface. All hell broke loose when, after choosing a Sinhalese woman, I changed my mind and selected a more alluring-looking Tamil girl instead. Soon the women began to fight, as I made my way to the door, mission unaccomplished. The Sinhalese woman I passed over hissed at me: "Tamil lover."

Time at Mohammed's, though, helped me see deeper into the culture and the minds of the Sri Lankans than anywhere else. Gradually a sense of life as the people lived it opened up to me. These epiphanies could be sublime, but just as often there was a profound sadness and melancholy lurking inside them.

I like to think that Mohammed's also made me see the Third World a lot more clearly than I had before. One lesson I remember well was taught by Moses, a Tamil beggar born with no arms, who roamed the beaches forlornly, often joining the Mohammed's crowd on the weekends. Moses was a thalidomide baby, and what passed for his arms were little flippers that extended from his shoulders. With these he ate, smoked cigarettes, and opened up the neck of his T-shirt so donors could deposit coins inside it.

Once, trying to be friendly, I asked him how much he made that day. Forty rupees, he told me, about $1.30. "Forty rupees!" I gushed. "In one day! That's great!"

Moses just stared at me.

"Well, yes, I guess it is better to have two arms, huh?" I said, reading his mind.

"Yes, sir," he answered me politely. "Much better to have two arms."

It was inevitable, given his mystical leanings and nose for a good time, that the Arab would find Mohammed's, and set up residence there for almost two months around the Christmas holidays. Although he was an incongruous addition to the usual crowd, it was fitting to have an Arab in the club. His forebears, traders from East Africa, had given the island one of its first names, Serendip, and had also invented arrack, the national intoxicant. Furthermore, the night he arrived, a bright star sat in the scoop of a new moon low over the horizon, as if the sky had configured itself as a Saudi flag, no small coincidence in a culture so obsessed with astrology.

The Arab was a forty-something bedouin tribesman from Jidda with a very lucrative international construction business. He had three wives, in keeping with Islamic tradition, the most recent of whom was a Sinhalese woman who had been married before and had seven children of her own, adding to the eight the Arab had sired with the others. The Arab and wife Number Three seemed madly in love, billing and cooing at each other and trading Italian pet names which he had learned in Rome.

The Arab and his wife had returned to Sri Lanka to gain custody of one of her children. She spent most of her time with her children and her relatives scattered all over Colombo. He spent most of his time on the beach at Mohammed's and was drunk almost constantly. He was making up for lost time, he told us, having just gotten out of jail in Saudi Arabia after serving out two separate convictions. One was for failing to pay his men on time, a cash-flow problem, he said, which violated the letter of the Koran—a man must be paid before the sweat dried on his back. The other offense was getting

caught with a case of Johnnie Walker in his truck during a celebra-
tory drive just after his first release.

Claiming that one of his wife's relatives had tried to poison him
at their hotel, the Arab adopted Mohammed's as his own, and took
Sena under his wing as a kind of bodyguard. An ardent America-
phile, the Arab took an instant liking to me, and quickly made me
part of his entourage, prohibiting me from paying for anything I
consumed and sending his car to pick me up every morning so I
could sit with him during the day.

The Arab was convinced that our friendship was a function of
destiny and providence. He was deeply superstitious and even paid
one of Sri Lanka's foremost astrologers to do my chart. And like all
mystics, the Arab was an experience junkie. He told me he had spent
a vacation living in Harlem, reveling in the soul and the edginess.
His prison term was one of the most morally and spiritually formative
things he had ever gone through, and, he said, he had once made
love to Sophia Loren, introduced to him by a Mafia chieftain he had
befriended in Rome.

Most of the day he would sit on a beach chair with his knees
drawn close to his chest, gazing westward into the sea while a tape
of Omar Khayyám's *Rubáiyát* played, in Arabic, on a cassette player
at his feet. Morning, noon, and night he played it, over and over,
even prohibiting the boys at Mohammed's from listening to their
disco tapes on the sound system.

At Mohammed's, he didn't easily fit in. When it rained, and
everyone else piled into the restaurant to stay dry, he would take his
shirt off and stand outside in the downpour, as they did in the desert.
The Arab had little regard for the Sinhalese, their endless bickering
and lying and their lax standards of efficiency and service. "Why
are they this way?" he'd say over and over. "What is it about them
that makes them the way they are? Why? Why? Why?"

The Arab's impatience did not make him any friends at Mohammed's nor did the ban that Gamani put on hash smoking and
disco music at the Arab's request. The others were also jealous of
the way he favored Sena and of the job that the Arab promised him
in Saudi Arabia. For a while the Arab was tolerated: between the

couple of cases of Carlsberg beer he'd drink and/or give away every day and the meals he had prepared for him, his family, and any number of beach beggars, his tab amounted to several hundred dollars a day—a king's ransom by Lankan standards. Nevertheless, it wasn't more than two weeks before the staff started looking at him with knives in their eyes. I could sense that their patience was shredding and that a confrontation of some sort might not be long in coming.

In short order, I found that even the simple act of keeping pace with the Arab as we drank was a life-threatening experience. We often drank late into the night, and passed out right on the sand in our chaises. Soon I began to wonder how long it would be before I was as manic and sodden as he was.

Things began to change one morning about eleven o'clock with the appearance of Mr. Crab, a teenage beggar crippled with polio, whose manner of getting around on his hands had earned him his nickname. I had been reading a magazine and having an early beer, and hadn't really seen the form approaching me on the sand. I knew it was a beggar, but I thought if I simply ignored him, he'd go away. Suddenly, however, the form moved through the air in a blur of rags and crooked limbs, as if capable of vertical lift-off, and landed squarely in the chair next to me. Stretching a long hand my way, Mr. Crab bared a huge smile full of mossy impacted teeth and said, quite naturally, "Hello, friend."

If he had been any other beggar I would have shooed him away, but the Crab's jack-in-the-box arrival had taken me aback, and when I saw how badly his legs had been wasted by polio, I felt sad for him, although he hardly felt sorry for himself, as I was to learn. After shaking hands, the Crab waved a waiter over and ordered two Cokes, assuring me that he would be paying for them. He took out a twenty-rupee note to vouch for himself and we sat there looking at the magazine, the Crab entranced by the ads, especially those with Western women.

Just about fourteen years old, the Crab had a kind of irrepressible, beagle-like good cheer, and like most of the beach crowd, he had an appetite for kitsch and bedecked himself in groovy T-shirts and jewelry from around the world.

Halfway through our Coke, however, two policemen walked down the beach, part of the stepped-up effort to throw the touts off the beaches. Instantly the Crab scampered into a cabana stall so they wouldn't see him. At first I thought it had all been a ruse to get me to pay for the refreshments, but I later found out that the last time he had been picked up in a police sweep he had been handcuffed.

Like most Sinhalese, the Crab had a rather plastic sense of the truth, making it hard to secure his biography. In some versions, he was an orphan; in others, he had run away from his home in the tea country, fleeing from an alcoholic father who beat him, but he still sent money home so a brother could go to school. From what I could make out he had been born with his affliction, with one leg attached to the back of his neck, the other locked at the knee joint in a ninety-degree angle. At birth, he must have looked like a contortionist. He had no use of his legs whatsoever other than for balance when he scuttled forward on his hands.

I found out his given name had been Chandana, which means "Child of the Moon." He was lucky to be alive; the Sinhalese were still deeply superstitious and often left crippled children to die. Although begging on the beach was hardly a license to print money, the Crab had done pretty well. After spending the first few months on Colombo's notorious Slave Island, he had landed on the beach at Mount Lavinia and was soon taken in by the crowd at Mohammed's. At first, he was only allowed to sleep in a boat beached outside, but by the time I got to know him he had moved up in the world and was now sleeping in the restaurant itself, curled up inside an inner tube.

In the theater of Mohammed's, the Crab was a little like Lear's Fool, a born comic wit with a keen eye for human folly. As often as not his target was the Arab, who never seemed to be able to get his hands on the Crab. His repertoire also extended to imitations. One of his favorite was a cobra, the kind carried by snake charmers, which the Crab would mime by waving a cupped hand back and forth, pretending to hypnotize me. Then, as in an old Three Stooges routine, he would try to poke me in the eyes. He also loved to imitate Bruce Lee; he'd put on a headband and strike a kung fu pose while sitting on a tabletop.

He kept to an almost daily routine. After waking and shooting the breeze with whoever was around, he took off his sarong to take his morning bath at the well in back of Mohammed's. Sometimes he'd spend hours washing and soaping himself, in the fetishistic style of the Sinhalese, although the concept of brushing his teeth always seemed to elude him. The Crab also knew the city pretty well, and would often go into town for the afternoon, begging rides with sympathetic cabdrivers, or taking the bus, with the conductors picking him up by the armpits and throwing him wherever there was space, usually in the luggage rack. He knew all the movie houses and their managers, who often let him in without paying, although he was a little in the dark about movies in the main, referring to all films as "Rambos" since that was the first one he had ever seen.

He would usually return later in the day for a swim. He kept pretty close to shore, but was an aggressive frolicker in the surf. After that, he'd fly his kite as the sunset promenaders strolled lazily by. Then, in the dark, he'd do his nightly calisthenics, push-ups and wind sprints performed on his hands.

On Christmas Eve, my first in Sri Lanka, there was a disco party at a small beach hotel in the tiny fishing village down the coast where I had gone to get away from the Arab. I took the Crab along for company. Most of the guests were Westerners, but ringing the dance floor were villagers curious about the *suddha* and his sidekick. The Crab was his usual exuberant self and made a big impression, befriending two comely Chinese sisters and comforting Leo, an Austrian diving instructor, whose wife had just run off with his best friend. At one point he had to fight off the advances of a very drunken German woman who had become smitten by his break dancing.

The Crab was also a hit with the local people of the village. Several of the boys there volunteered to carry him around for me, sparing the muscles in my back and shoulders, which had grown quite sore from his weight.

I often laughed, wondering how a crippled beggar with an obsession for kitsch and cheap distractions could become the one person in Sri Lanka I grew most attached to. Friends were hard to make in that insular culture, where there was such a keen sensitivity to status and slights, and I found the Crab compelling because he was so untypical of the society around him. Where most Sinhalese tended toward a sort of fatalism, the Crab had an indomitable enthusiasm. And where the dominant strain in the Sinhalese character was insecurity, the Crab had confidence.

The most important aspect of my relationship with the Crab, however, was the way his experience brought the otherwise lofty and abstract ethical ideals of Buddhism down to earth, particularly the notions of "loving-kindness" and "compassion"—the way he was treated by others around him, the institutionalized way that people fed him and gave him money as a practice of "making merit" for a better rebirth. In Sri Lanka's spiritual life, the beggar played an important role, one that affirmed the dignity and humanity of all beings.

It was assumed by most of the people at Mohammed's, as well as by most of the people we'd run into on our excursions, that I would adopt the Crab. It seemed that the Crab believed this, too. He began to pester me about going up to the tea country so we could get his birth certificate, which would be needed for a passport. For a time, I did think about taking the Crab to the States for medical treatment, as well as for the thrill of showing him New York. I had also developed a kind of parental protectiveness. One day when the Arab and I took him for a motorboat ride and a swim off the Mount Lavinia reef, I dove deep into the water and looked up at the Crab's legs dangling lifeless and tiny against the immensity of the ocean and almost packed him up for America right on the spot.

But after giving it much thought, I began to wonder whether it was such a good idea to take him away from his culture, no matter what the material benefits in the United States, for the web of support and sanctity that eased the Crab's life in Sri Lanka might make the West seem limited by comparison. Despite its many problems, the traditional Buddhist culture appeared rich and vital, and the Crab seemed one of its beneficiaries. However crippled and destitute he was, the society around him seemed to accord him a measure of respect. So I decided to leave him there on the sand.

We parted, however, without being able to say proper goodbyes. The Crab, it seemed, had taken off for a short holiday with another Western friend and admirer, a Swedish prostitute named Coco. He was forever trying to arrange dates for me with Coco, even offering to pay the five hundred rupees he said she normally charged, hoping, I think, that we might together adopt him as our own.

This all took place during my first trip. Away from Sri Lanka, I was often anxious about the Crab. I worried that he might have been hurt or killed in the political violence or mistaken for a Tamil and beaten to death in a communal riot. Or perhaps he had fallen prey to drugs, or the easy money of beach sex. Then, too, I was worried that maybe Coco had carted him back to Sweden, put a fez on him, and turned him into some freak act in a Stockholm bordello.

I tried to find him as soon as I got back. He was right there at Mohammed's, as before, cleaning off at the well after a sea bath, with his drawers halfway down his backside and his hair slicked down on his head like an otter. "Hello, friend." Then, like it was just yesterday, he pointed at my chest and put his finger up my nose in the old Three Stooges gag, and scampered away.

We caught up on old times and laughed about the Arab, as if he had been a military campaign we had fought through together and now looked back upon fondly. And Coco? Remember Coco? he asked me, cupping his hands in front of his chest. Five hundred rupees and she could have been yours, he scolded.

In the months I had been away he had grown. His torso was longer and he was maturing into a young man, no longer the beach kid. He had also taken on a harder look, and he used slang he didn't know the previous year, calling the other touts and beggars around him *mechan*, a Sinhalese familiar term much like the Italian *paesano*. Mohammed's was looking a little rougher around the edges, too. The tourist season should have started by now, but the beach was desolate.

Sena was enthusiastic about seeing me, but moody about life. He had sent me a letter that summer asking for money, a long, wheedling, indirect plea in which he told me about how the Arab had abandoned him without arranging for him to go to Saudi Arabia. This even after Sena had bribed the police to let the Arab go after they had set up a trap for him at a local whorehouse, shaking him down for a few thousand dollars, which the Arab gladly paid. The first thing Sena did, of course, was take me on a walk along the beach and ask me for a loan, which I talked my way around. He wanted to get married, he said, and had been relying on the Arab to help him out.

Sena must have lost a tremendous amount of face when the Arab abandoned him. He was more sullen than I remembered, more hopeless. He had enemies along the beach now. "He'd better watch it," said Richard, an eely gigolo who had gotten into a tiff with him. "He throws his weight around too much, somebody will want revenge. The price for having someone killed here in Sri Lanka is not too high now. Not too high at all."

Later in the day, as I watched the Crab frolic in the surf, I saw that he had lost little of his friskiness in the time I had been away. He retained his lordly little bearing, snapping his fingers to summon the attention of the waiters at Mohammed's and generously dispensing a rupee to the troupe of destitute minstrel girls who sang on the beach, but he had switched his tastes in fashion, exchanging the tacky T-shirts of the past for more trendy disco gear. He was also wearing expensive sneakers, which seemed strange since he wasn't exactly walking with them. To round out the ensemble, the Crab was now wearing flip-flops on his hands, elevator flip-flops that helped him get around better on asphalt and concrete and fostered better posture.

Though I was happy to see him, I was having some difficulty negotiating the cross-cultural gaps and was finding myself a bit squeamish about the Crab's physical condition—the nits in his hair, the thick black crud beneath his fingernails, the ringworm marks on his skin. I couldn't shake the worry that I might catch something from him.

Most of the second year I spent hanging out with the Crab was devoted to missionary work, to trying to find him something better to do than begging on the beach. If I wasn't going to take him home and get him new legs courtesy of Western medical technology, I could at least find him a job or pay for his learning a trade. However jaunty his current lifestyle, he was no longer a kid and would soon probably become just another haggard, disease-ridden beggar crowding the pilgrimage sites for handouts. My efforts were in vain. Anytime I approached the Crab about the prospect of working, he'd jump back from me as if I were a cobra.

Over the course of that second year, I began to see the Crab's existence in an entirely different light, which made me realize how much I had romanticized his life the year before and how much Buddhism in Sri Lanka was that society's true sick man. Instead of enjoying immunity from the petty envy, viciousness, and other depredations of the Sinhalese culture, the Crab, I began to see, was one of its principal targets. Instead of being a symbol of the endurance of Buddhist virtues, the Crab's life became a lens though which to explore their loss.

Having little capacity to resist, the Crab was often forced to "loan" people money, and the kindness and consideration I showed him was deeply resented by others, who felt that they were more deserving than this lowborn boy with such bad karma. Dining out was no easy matter either, as the better restaurants generally wouldn't let him inside, and when they did, they dragged their feet in serving us to make sure we wouldn't return. Many people I encountered simply couldn't comprehend why I, a Westerner, would take such an interest. "Why are you doing this? What do you expect to get out of this?" asked one particularly mystified Sinhalese gentleman. "What can he do for you?"

The decline of Buddhist virtue, of course, was clearly a manifestation of the toll the war was taking on the nation's social and moral fabric. But the society's poisoned moral climate was also a function of something much more subtle and diffused, a product of the way that Buddhist revivalism had actually encouraged the erosion of Buddhist ethics even as it trumpeted their reinvigoration.

One way that revivalism did injury to the moral fabric was by fostering the notion that Buddhism was a national possession of the Sinhalese, which made it more of a badge of ethnic identity than a vehicle for spiritual development. Revivalism also promoted the idea that Buddhism could improve political, social, and economic life for the Sinhalese in the here and now, which contradicted its essentially transcendental purpose. On a more esoteric level, the kind of "scientific Buddhism" put forward by revivalists had been shorn of its oral folk tales and ritual dramas that had been crucial in transmitting abstract Buddhist ethical principles, leaving a moral vacuum, particularly in the uneducated.

Another way that revivalism had detracted from Buddhist morality was in the impact that government patronage had on the spirituality of monks. Although government funds swelled the numbers of young men entering the sangha, most were there for the status that clerical life provided. Patronage also encouraged monks to involve themselves in politics, to bicker over temple assets, and to indulge in worldly materialism at the expense of meditation, the core of Buddhist practice, which many monks no longer engaged in. Nor did revivalism prompt the laity to overcome the sense that they were spiritually inferior to monks and therefore incapable of achieving nirvana in a single lifetime, which generated a moral cynicism and restricted their spiritual enthusiasm to perfunctory merit-making gestures such as donations to temples, acts akin to buying indulgences in medieval Catholicism. As a result, even temple attendance was in decline. "Buddhism is hollow now in Sri Lanka," a prominent Buddhist layman admitted painfully, and discreetly. "We are only going through the motions. There is no sincerity. And so our attitude toward life and the state of our hearts is desperate."

I lost track of the Crab halfway through my second year in the country. Occasionally, my friends around the island would say they sighted him in various places: at shrines favored by pilgrims or paddling his skateboard—his new form of locomotion—down the Galle Road, right in the thick of Colombo's murderous traffic. But there were long stretches when I didn't hear anything at all, which made me nervous. Bodies were beginning to wash up on beaches throughout the south, and newspapers were a steady diet of brutality and gore. (In one case, the diet was literal. One morning, the news carried the tale of an eatery where crows had dropped pieces of a human body into the pots of an open-air kitchen. Customers realized only belatedly.) And not all of these killings were political, for the breakdown of government order had unleashed a torrent of criminal opportunism.

There was no love lost for the Crab down at Mohammed's, where I went looking for him one day. By that time the violence had scared away almost all of the Western tourists, save for a few insistent older German men. The beach had fallen into a state of dereliction.

A legion of idle touts descended on me as soon as I stepped foot on the sand. Sena, who by now had dropped his pretense of concern for the Crab, having realized it wasn't encouraging me to loan him money, scowled. The Crab had taken to drinking beer, smoking dope, and hanging out with people in the cabanas, he told me. "You spend money on that boy, and when I ask you for money you say you have none," he grumbled accusingly. "He tells many lies. He is always telling lies."

Sena had gotten fatter from beer and from idleness, and was also wearing a crucifix around his neck, which was odd, since he was one of the more chauvinistic Sinhalese Buddhists on the beach. "Are you a Christian now?" I asked him. "Yes, I go to church now," he answered me, his face curling into disgust as he neared the bottom of a pile of lottery tickets he'd bought. "But I am Buddhist, too. Why not. Keep both doors open. I always play to win." Then, as the pile was finished, he swept the tickets off the table. "So many troubles we have here now, Mr. Bill. So many troubles. Troubles. Troubles. I think for the rest of my life we will have these troubles."

As I was walking down the Galle Road one night, having almost forgotten about the Crab, I saw him riding in the back of a bus. The hurtling bus screeched to a halt, after which the passengers passed the Crab over their heads to the door. And *voilà*! There was the Crab, smiling broadly, paddling his skateboard down the road to say hello.

Aiyo! He'd tried to call several times, he explained, knocking the side of his head with his hand. But Mary, my landlady, hadn't given me any message, probably out of fear that I might ask the

Crab to stay with me in the Ottery. Then someone stole his wallet with the number inside. *Aiyo!* "Did they steal your mirror and comb, too?" I asked, chiding him for his messy hair. *Aiyo!* "Very funny," he answered, before touching his head to the tops of my feet, a gesture of profound respect and devotion that he also knew would stop me from needling him.

Aside from a few ugly cuts he had on his legs from what he said was an accident, the Crab's life hadn't been all bad. He had hooked up with a tour group from the American Midwest who had taken him around to some of the pilgrimage sites and, it seemed, bought him yet another "polio chariot," or wheelchair, which he had duly sold as soon as they left the country. He had bought a new set of clothes, the latest in surfer chic—clam-digger shorts, a shirt with oversized pockets, and a pair of immensely cool running shoes—not bad for a kid who only the year before had thought all movies were called "Rambo." He was now wearing a wristwatch, too, although he still couldn't tell time, and he had also bought a camouflage-covered wallet, which he had filled with pictures of the ruling UNP leaders. These, I imagined, were an attempt to cover himself in case he was picked up by some government death squad and accused of being JVP.

The pièce de résistance, though, was the Crab's new board, several pieces of wood affixed to a set of casters with a cushion on top. It was emblazoned with the Honda logo. "My car," he said joyously, popping a wheelie and imitating a drag racer peeling out. "Number One. No gas. No license. Number One."

I was a little leery about bringing the Crab to my new digs in the swank Colombo Guesthouse, to which I'd moved from the Ottery a few weeks before. But as the family running it was Anglican, not Buddhist, they had an easier time understanding the relationship, and the Crab was generally made to feel welcome, sleeping in my guest room at night. There was one unfortunate moment when the desk clerk, a Sinhalese girl, squealed like a mouse when the Crab was making his way down the stairs to breakfast. Later one of the Tamil rebels I interviewed in my quarters shot him a look that I thought would kill him on the spot. Otherwise there was no problem, and he passed the next several days in a lordly style he found quite natural.

Later that week the Crab and I headed south for a short holiday in Unawatuna, the tiny village in the jungle I had come to adopt as my second home. According to the science-fiction writer Arthur C. Clarke, the force of gravity in Unawatuna was stronger than in any other spot on earth, a claim I could believe, having been drawn back there many times in the years I lived in Sri Lanka. The village sat on the shore of a stunningly beautiful horseshoe-shaped bay whose turquoise waters smashed up against a natural seawall of boulders at one end before gently rolling to the sandy beach.

The Crab was excited about hitting the road, and sang his favorite song on the train trip down—"Tarzan Boy," a hit that season in Sri Lanka, especially among the beach crowd. For a while, he sat with his legs out the window in a seat that bore a sign reserving it for clergy. Then we sat in the doorway with our legs dangling out the car. Along the way he imitated the weird glottal croaking of the train conductor calling out the names of the Sinhalese towns we passed through. He also threw a few choice barbs at snotty-looking upper-caste Sinhalese women. His irreverence came to a halt, momentarily at least, when we passed through the town of Kalutura and the Sinhalese passengers on the train got up and bowed to the huge bell-shaped shrine off to the right. The Crab, unable to get up, nevertheless clasped his hands tightly to his chest and bowed from the waist, almost toppling over.

Traveling south at that particular time was dicey. Most of the people I knew in Colombo weren't going outside the city limits, for the government's writ had shrunk drastically. Along that stretch of coastline the JVP and the death squads were marshaled against one another. Although the people were still able to force "the smile" that was the Sinhalese trademark of equanimity, it was easy to see their faces cracking nervously behind it from the strain. At one point, the train stopped for nearly a half hour while villagers thronged to the side of the tracks to watch several dead bodies being removed so the train could proceed.

Being back at Unawatuna was like old home week for the Crab, too. During his "disappearance" he had been there several times, using the money that tourists had given him to hire another beggar to carry him around and to rent a room in an economy guesthouse. He had also treated the locals to ice cream and sweets, which explained why he was so heartily welcomed.

On this trip he made some new friends, too—three young English women, secretaries on holiday from London, who sunbathed topless on the beach and frolicked in the surf with the Crab, who had borrowed some scuba gear and was looking quite like a creature from the deep. Whatever magic was passing between them ended rather abruptly, however. When the women insisted on visiting the Buddhist temple at the end of the beach without putting their tops back on, the Crab, good Buddhist that he was, realized he was not dealing with the right kind of people. He shunned them after that.

As a sign of my honorary status in the village, I was invited to a couple of folk rituals that week. One was the exorcism of a teenaged girl performed by a troupe of "devil dancers" making a swing through the superstitious villages of the far south. The other ritual was more arcane, involving the propitiation of a local god known both for his benevolence and for his wrath. According to legend, he had once turned sand into rice to avert a famine. He could also be summoned for vengeance, which made him an important deity among the villagers. What was most interesting about this particular ritual was that it took place at a Buddhist temple, although the Buddhistic side to it was only a gloss over what was essentially a much deeper and darker pagan rite underneath.

As absorbing as the time in Unawatuna was, however, it did not serve up the tonic I needed. I found myself growing short-tempered from the continual nagging of the touts and the constant lying, subterfuge, and suspicion that was so deeply embedded in village life. Like Leonard Woolf, whose novel *The Village in the Jungle* was written about a hamlet not far from Unawatuna, I had originally been infatuated with the Sinhalese of the jungle, but in the end saw a darker side of life. Along with Woolf, I realized that my village was "a strange world, a world of bare and brutal facts, of superstition, or grotesque imagination." Though it had been spared political violence, Unawatuna had not escaped rot and inertia.

I was eager to look up several acquaintances from the year before, but had little luck. One of them was a French woman named Anne Lise, who had once run a restaurant with her Australian husband. He had been framed on drug charges by his Sinhalese business partner and then deported. Anne Lise, however, had stayed on, with her gargantuan German shepherd for protection, living in a house in the jungle where I stayed for several weeks my first year in Sri Lanka.

Although she was much too self-absorbed to be considered a humanitarian, Anne Lise had a soft streak for the people around her, and ran her household like a one-woman development project, contracting out work to be done at greatly inflated rates so that the people she cared for could survive. An entire family lived on the fees she paid for massages alone.

For the most part, though, the villagers despised her. The houseman stole her blind, and while she was gone, the caretaker starved her dog and sold her electrical appliances to buy arrack and drugs. The house now stood empty, almost overgrown by jungle, with dead yellow palm fronds strewn about the front yard like faded streamers from a festival.

I also wanted to stop in on a character I had met briefly the year before, an Englishman who had established a meditation center in Unawatuna three years before and who toured the south as a missionary trying to revive a practice that had lapsed among both monks and laymen. The year before, I caught him in a wry mood as we spoke about the problems confronting those who wanted to follow the dharma in a country where it had been so exploited for political purposes. "It's a nice country, Sri Lanka," he had quipped. "Very tolerant, actually. You can even practice Buddhism here if you want to."

That a Westerner would come to attempt reform in a country that prided itself on preserving and protecting the dharma seemed contradictory. But the Sinhalese were unable to mount any sustained effort at reforming Buddhism's decadent institutions on their own.

This was particularly true of the sangha, which had little regard for self-criticism. To discuss reform in the current climate was vaguely seditious. "We are conditioned to think that Sinhalese Buddhism is the most pure form in the world," one of the Sinhalese laymen working at the meditation center explained. "We are taught to believe that reform is bad. That it will violate the purity of the doctrine. And you must remember that in the East we are trapped by our system of conformity, which deprives the individual of a sense that there are options, other ways of doing things."

The Englishman had taken the name Asvijith, shaved his head, and now wore the saffron robes of a Buddhist monk, although he was only an *anagarika*, or lay cleric. He lived on the bottom floor of the meditation center, beneath the natural-foods restaurant upstairs that catered to the Westerners and wealthy Sri Lankans who stayed at the center for spiritual instruction.

As witty and self-effacing as Asvijith could be, he could also be pompous and aloof. His reputation hadn't been helped when villagers had caught him on the beach in meditation over the corpse of a dog. Although the Buddha had once meditated over the corpse of a man and recommended it as an ideal way of promoting spiritual awareness, the villagers found this too bizarre.

It had not been a banner year for anyone trying to revivify Buddhism, Asvijith admitted. A few months before in the hills around Kandy, the leader of a similar meditation retreat catering to Westerners and Sri Lankans was murdered; the case was never solved. Three years before, when he arrived from India, he had thought Sri Lankans peaceful, but now his opinion was different. "They know nothing about suppressing unhealthy states of mind, anger," he explained, sitting in the quiet of the meditation room one afternoon. "And once you give in to those states, it's back to the jungle. Without spirituality here, you have a jungle mentality."

The primary problem with Buddhism in Sri Lanka was its militancy, Asvijith said. "The spectacle of Buddhist monks exhorting Sinhalese soldiers to go and kill for the dharma was a denial of the whole spirit of Buddhism. Buddhism doesn't need defense by the sword if properly practiced, because Buddhism is an example of kindness toward all humanity, which needs no defense. It's only when people cease to practice brotherhood that it needs defense, and to the extent that they cease to practice brotherhood, they cease to be Buddhists. Tolerance is absolutely fundamental to Buddhism; one sees that men are different and tolerates that; one sees that men have different philosophies and one tolerates that; one sees that even though men may not be good or wise one tolerates them and tries to transform those qualities to a higher state of human development. Not through the bullet, or the sword, but by an example of gentleness and persuasiveness. Buddhism has always wanted to communicate, not coerce."

Although this militancy was intensified as a reaction to colonialism, it had roots much earlier. "If one takes the *Mahavamsa* at all seriously," he explained, "it provides incontrovertible evidence that apparently four hundred years after the Buddha died, Buddhism in Sri Lanka was already degenerating. The moment the bikkhus forgave Duttugemunu for slaying the Tamil king Elaru, that was the end to the claim that Sri Lanka was the protector and preserver of Buddhism."

The moral dissolution of the tradition was also a function of more recent failings as well. "Imagine. There are over thirty thousand monks here and yet look at the mess this country is in. That couldn't happen if they were practicing the dharma. At best, the monks here are social workers. Most often, though, they are political tricksters, political meddlers, political rogues. Monks here do not see themselves as people dedicated to self-transformation and as a source of inspiration for others to seek that as well. Instead most monks have pursued the role of kingmakers, an idea that this society accepts almost uncritically, even though that impulse is an utter disgrace to the spirit of Buddhism."

Asvijith conceded that it might seem odd that a Westerner would be needed to do missionary work in the country which considered itself the repository of Buddhism in its most pristine form, but Sri Lankans lacked enough perspective to see what truly bad shape the religion was in. Underlying that was a basic arrogance and a complacency born of a fundamentalistic frame of mind—"the belief that their form of Buddhism is the only real form," when in fact, as the Buddha himself said, "whatever worked was Buddhism, whatever conduced to dispassion and the end of worldly desires. He never said his teaching could be contained within the covers of a book, so the fundamentalists' attitude here that the last letter can be found in any teaching is fundamentally mistaken."

However formidable the obstacles in his way, the English monk was buoyed of late by modest successes he was having at the grassroots level. He was close to a deal with a wealthy tea planter who would be donating money to his cause, and a group of monks at a temple in the interior were starting to warm to his overtures. "In the very early days I was worried, very worried that the little sapling I was tending would dry up at any moment," he said. "And I am still wondering whether it will ever really take root. But given all the blighting tendencies, there are signs that a small green shoot is starting to grow. If I can risk a generalization, I will say that the Sinhalese, despite all their limitations, have got a transcendental element missing among Westerners—an openness, an ability to overcome their present condition and to look for something else. There is still a greater feeling of spiritual potentiality than in the West which keeps me going, despite all the frustration."

Later that day Asvijith and I took a short sail into the bay on an outrigger owned by a local fisherman. The beach had filled up with a crowd of young people from Colombo, transforming it into a decidedly unholy scene. At one end a herd of young men ogled the Western women lying in the sand, and at the other there was a crowd of what looked to me like army officers or veterans, who were so drunk they could barely stagger. A few passed out right at the water's edge, occasionally waking when a wave washed over them.

Between these groups, swarms of touts tried to foist badly made handicrafts on the few tourists who had come that season. "We'd like to think outsiders see Sri Lanka as a friendly country, smiling and welcoming to strangers," I recalled the Minister of Tourism saying the week before. "A country with a tradition of hospitality, regardless of immediate pecuniary benefit. Tourism is an extension of our hospitality, friendliness brought to another dimension. We want our international friends to come and enjoy our country and our people."

Asvijith and I boarded our outrigger. Soon we were about a half mile offshore, rocking back and forth, the sound of the wind in the palm trees only a barely audible hiss. The action of the waves put him into a dreamy state of mind, and he began telling me an ancient story about a Buddhist saint.

He was an Indian named Nigargena, one of Buddhism's greatest philosophers, Asvijith maintained, who had rescued Buddhism from the threat of dry scholasticism by preaching the importance of meditation. The saint's name meant "one who lived in the depths"; it was common for him to be depicted through the imagery of the ocean. However profound his message, the Sinhalese dismissed him, claiming that because he was an Indian, his insights were unimportant.

The English monk clearly saw himself as the successor to this legacy. Just as I was going to razz him about it, a huge wave rolled across the bay. For a moment, we lurched, trying to regain our balance. Then the boat capsized.

As he clung to the boat, our skipper, who could not swim, cried out, "What to do? What to do?" Luckily, several boatmen happened by in a few short moments. Meanwhile, Asvijith had started floating on his back toward shore, where much of the village had assembled, watching the spectacle with glee. Having lost his umbrella, his glasses, and the top half of his robe in the water, Asvijith emerged from the churning surf in absolute mortification and made his way back to his meditation center, the catcalls of the villagers trailing behind him.

18 · Sri Pada

OF ALL THE MANY shrines and sacred places scattered about the island, one of the most holy, to all four of the major religions of Sri Lanka, was the 7,360-foot mountain known as Sri Pada, or Adam's Peak. To Hindus, the footprint in a rock at the top of the mountain was that of Shiva, the great Hindu god. For Muslims, the footprint belonged to Adam, who waited a thousand years to be reunited with Eve in Sri Lanka, the second earthly paradise. Christians disagreed on whether the footprint was that of Adam or St. Thomas. For Buddhists, the footprint is indisputably that of the Lord Buddha, who left it behind as he ascended into nirvana.

According to legend, Alexander the Great sought the "elixir of life" in a lake inside the mountain; Fa-Hsien, a Chinese traveler in the fifth century A.D., believed invalids could cure themselves by drinking the water that collected in the footprint. To the Crab, who had climbed the mountain several times already when the average Sri Lankan made but one or two pilgrimages in a lifetime, Sri Pada held out the promise of a miracle cure. "Bill," he explained with utmost reverence, pointing to his wasted legs as the triangular majesty of the holy mountain soared above the green abundance of the tea country. "My problem. Sri Pada very good. Very good, Sri Pada, my problem."

We were making the pilgrimage as part of a march for peace

sponsored by an ecumenical array of religious and humanitarian groups. As one of the few symbols of shared national harmony and spiritual devotion, Sri Pada was a powerful backdrop for the march, which was expected to draw more than 100,000. The march's principal sponsor was a grass-roots community development and spiritual movement called Sarvodaya, where the Crab and I headed very early one morning in order to catch a ride with the movement's founder, Dr. A. T. Ariyaratne, who had invited me along as his guest. The Crab was excited. Could he bring his cart? he joked, knowing from experience how hard it was on his hands to crab his way up to the top.

I didn't think it would be a very big deal to bring the Crab along, but I had forgotten that Ariyaratne had a phobia about cripples. If the body is sick, it is just a projection of a sickness in the spirit, I remembered him explaining one time, when a group of crippled women had bent down to touch the tops of his feet with their heads.

Although Ariyaratne had said that I would ride with him to the march, the presence of the Crab seemed to change his mind. He shifted me into a bus that would carry some of the other people in the movement. By the time the bus arrived, morning had broken over Colombo, bathing the markets and the roadside Buddhas in cool green light as we drove into the country. In the interior, the road became jammed with buses and trucks filled with other pilgrims, the vehicles festooned with Buddhist flags, yellow peace ribbons, and bunches of long elephant grass jammed into the front fenders for good luck. Many of the pilgrims wore white, the Buddhist color of peace, and were blowing on horns or blaring screechy music through speakers.

For the past several weeks I had been trying to get the Crab into a training school run by some monks in Colombo, but had had little luck. I was baffled at first until the monk's assistant, who was English, explained that the monks would consider him bad luck and a physical liability who had little to offer them. Some of the monks were on the bus, and I found myself wanting to bait them into an argument. "Why don't you take him on as a novice?" I asked one of them, a middle-aged monk whose shaved eyebrows signified he was part of the highest-caste sect. "The problem is the Buddha said that monks must have all their faculties," the monk explained, smiling nervously. "It says so in the code of rules he gave us. They must be independent people, self-reliant. The sangha is a special organization, reserved for good people. It is not cut out for everyone."

I was then accosted by a young Sinhalese man who, overhearing my conversation with the monk, regaled me with some disconnected trivia about Buddhism—the number of people who had achieved enlightenment, the number of shrines in the country, the number of rules covering monastic life, the number of Buddhas that have been on earth, the possibilities for the Crab's bad karma.

The young man was clearly *tikak pissu*, or "a little crazy," as the Sinhalese say, but it made him a source of shame to his father, a professor of history and Sinhalese archnationalist, who was riding with us too. Feeling a bit sorry for the professor, I began to chat amiably. He had been up Sri Pada many years before with his ailing mother, and reassured me that I would get help with the Crab when, after he was too tired to go up on his hands, he needed to be carried.

Where most of the country was cramped, the scale in the tea country was vast, akin to the Himalayas. "I saw, deep blue and immense, the entire mountain system of Ceylon piled up in mighty walls," Hermann Hesse had written of this vista. "And in its midst the beautiful, ancient and holy pyramid of Adam's Peak."

The Indian Tamils formed the bulk of the labor source in the region. Housed in dank colonial-era "line rooms," many lived little better than their coolie forebears. While Indian Tamils may have differed by caste and origins from Sri Lankan Tamils, they, too, had been systematically discriminated against for decades, deprived of state funds for economic development, of basic services such as schools and medical facilities, and, for a large percentage, of citizenship itself, which made many of them technically stateless.

Ten long, bumpy hours after leaving Colombo we were in Maskeliya, a small town nestled about six miles from Sri Pada, where Ariyaratne gave a dramatic speech about peace and brotherhood before an assembled throng of marchers and dignitaries. These included Hindu priests, Muslim imams, Catholic clergymen, and several dozen Buddhist monks.

The march was to begin when the speeches were over, but after the grueling ordeal of the trip and because of the altitude, I realized I would never be able to climb the mountain with the Crab if I had to first walk six miles to get there. Luckily, several Buddhist monks from Japan who were completing their own pilgrimage in the area arranged a ride in a truck for us.

Along the way, clouds that had been gathering all afternoon burst, drenching the marchers. "Sadhu! Sadhu!" intoned the crowd, as if the chant would bat the clouds out of the sky, which in short order it did.

As we bumped along the road, the Crab was in his glory, shouting out hellos to passersby along the way. There was also a lot of salty palaver with some of the younger boys. We stopped at a temple for a quick devotional *puja*. Crab paid no heed to the stares of the monks and scampered through the crowd at the base of the temple stairs. Then, back in the rear of the truck, he performed tricks for the marchers we passed, doing his favorite break-dance routines with his rubbery arms and slippery joints. "Excuse him, he's a little crazy," I said, getting into the act. "Oh, me crazy?" he asked jokingly, pretending to throw himself out of the truck like a parachutist. "Okay. Thang you veddy much. Okay. Gootbye."

However jazzed up, I could also see that the Crab had not lost his sense of where he fit in on the food chain. Some people he razzed, and some people he bossed out of the way, but there were others to whom he was very deferential, as if his awareness was unconscious. He was also very concerned with not being mistaken for a Tamil, passing a necklace of flowers that had been given to him to me instead, as if the floral necklace were a Hindu custom and might have given people the wrong idea.

The rainstorm had shrouded most of Sri Pada, but as we approached the base, the entire mass of the mountain appeared. It was an awesome sight. Almost a perfectly shaped cone, Sri Pada stood at one end of a broad basin, flanked by a series of smaller hills. Since it was now dark, the mountain was garlanded by electric lights that illuminated the steep switchbacks of the trail, wrapping the steeper upper half like a Christmas tree. The whole scene crackled with a timeless spiritual intensity. "Sadhu! Sadhu!" intoned the crowd. "Sadhu! Sadhu!" came the words to my lips almost unconsciously, although I mispronounced them, which prompted a scolding from the Crab.

At the mountain's base, the atmosphere was not so sacred. Full of gaudy lights and tawdry knickknack booths, the assembly area was the worst kind of tourist trap. Worse still, though, was the way the Crab was treated, stared at in incomprehension and disdain. "What are you expecting to get out of this?" one middle-aged man asked me. "Where are his mother and father?" a crowd of teenaged girls demanded.

With temperatures dropping, I gave the Crab a pair of socks and carried him over to a stall selling statues of the Lord Buddha, where he sat on the end of a table as he donned them. Incensed at the sight of the Crab sitting on his table, the proprietor, a Sinhalese in his early thirties, rushed over and pushed him off the table. The Crab tumbled to the ground onto his crumpled legs and barely stifled his tears. I was livid. I chased the man into the back of his shop cursing loudly. It was all I could do to keep myself from smashing his entire stock of Buddha statues.

Later, I ran into an acquaintance from the year before, a tall, toothy Dutchman in his mid-thirties named Thomas who had been working as a volunteer in the Sarvodaya movement for the last three years. The year before, he'd told me he had stayed in Sri Lanka because it was the one place he could live "with love in his heart," a sentiment I sensed he felt sincerely. But the year had taken its toll on him. A state of what he called "animalism" had taken over, he explained, as we sat having tea in a loud, dingy cafeteria. People had lost all sense of morals and spiritual generosity. He wasn't surprised to hear about what had just happened to the Crab. "Yeah, they treat them just like dogs, don't they?" Thomas laughed sarcastically. "But why do you expect them to act any better climbing a holy mountain than in everyday life?" he asked.

By 9 p.m. reports were filtering down that the trail was already packed. I thought about not going up; it had been sixteen hours since we had left Colombo that morning, and I was already exhausted. Making the climb with the Crab riding on my back at least part of the way would be excruciating. On the other hand, I had looked forward to the climb as the climax of my time in Sri Lanka. I wanted to get to the top and watch the sunrise and look at the shadow of the mountain as it spread over the hills and jungles below, a staggering vision I had heard about for years. The climb would also be a seal, of sorts, on my friendship with the Crab, whom I would be leaving behind. If I couldn't take him with me, I could at least help him reach the top of the mountain, which in his mind was good for "his problem."

Part of me wanted to make the climb as a symbolic gesture for peace, too. For all its maddening pettiness, viciousness, ethnic bloody-mindedness, and cultural inertia, I had grown attached to the country and its people. I knew that once I left I would feel as if a little bit of me was left behind there, among the tea sippers in the Pettah, the fishmongers with their glottal cries, the schoolchildren in their uniform whites in the cool of the morning, the élan of the older men reminiscing about "those days," the piety of the many real Buddhists I encountered along the way, the eccentricities of the characters at Mohammed's, and, of course, the Crab.

We set off at about 10 p.m., crossing a small wooden plank bridge. Below, in a narrow river, pilgrims were washing. According to legend, the pool formed in the footprint of the ascending Buddha was the source of this river, and bathing in it had curative powers. As we walked—or, rather, as I walked and the Crab did his thing beside me—we were overtaken at several points by bands of Sinhalese teenagers singing songs and shouting cheers as if they were at a football game: "Who's gonna help us get to the top? Yeaaaahhhh, Buddha!!!!"

Along the trail, souvenir shops sold cheap religious trinkets and plastic knickknacks; elsewhere, there were shrines and carnival-like booths with monks sitting inside, selling what looked like raffle tickets. There was also a lot of alcohol being consumed along the way. Several times the Crab was almost trampled by drunks. At one point, a Sinhalese man crashed right into him, smacking him hard and cursing him before staggering away.

The Crab was having a ball, though, scampering along, pretending he was a motorcycle, then a car, then a boat, then a taxi, clearing people out of the way with car-horn sounds. The first leg of the ascent was relatively easy, the trail a rocky but gradual climb. When he got tired of struggling forward, the Crab turned around and traveled backward. But when we passed the midway point, the trail steepened dramatically, and we were soon climbing up stairs made out of stones that would have winded a champion alpinist.

The Crab did his best getting up the stairs, using a kind of vaulting maneuver, but it didn't take long for his arms to grow tired and for his hands to bleed. At several points, his elbows buckled as he tried to hurl himself upward, causing him to fall back like a spastic.

For a time I carried him on my back, but every ten yards his grip slipped down around my neck and choked me. I was also badly sunburned. An Indian from the United Nations Mission in Colombo who was climbing alongside us apologized for "not being able to help," by which he meant that he, as a member of a high caste, was prohibited from touching such a lowly creature as the Crab. Two Sinhalese teenagers paused for a few moments to carry him between them, but tired very quickly before hurrying on their way to the top.

With hardly a square foot of open space anywhere on the trail, there were plenty of opportunities to stand and rest. The march up the hill had become gridlocked, and people who had reached the top weren't going to come down until the sun came up. What forward movement there was came excruciatingly slowly, with a great deal of jostling and elbowing. At one point, a Tamil girl fainted from exhaustion, but instead of bringing her directly down, her mother smeared some kind of balm all over her body, trying to revive her.

As we tried to make our way up a particularly steep set of stairs about a mile from the top, the column of marchers came to a virtual standstill. With no way up and no way down, the crowd became impatient, almost crushing the Crab several times. By then, I had become angry myself. People were not only not helping me carry the Crab; they weren't even letting him climb in front of them, so focused were they on getting to the top and accumulating the special "merit" of being there at daybreak to see the mountain's shadow.

One would have thought that the merit involved in helping the Crab would have been appealing as well, but apparently it was the destination rather than the journey that mattered.

We had also become the targets of some cruel jokes by a crowd of young Sinhalese men that had joined us on the small outcropping of grass and rock off the side of the trail. All dressed up in the latest Western fashions, they stood around in affected poses smoking cigarettes like their movie heroes. I could hear them making jokes about us among themselves, ridiculing the Crab's physical condition and the state of my disheveled clothes. Soon the jokes were becoming more direct, and the salty expressions the Crab was whispering into my ear weren't shaming them. Finally, I got up and tried to grab one by the neck, but he slipped down the side of the trail, falling into the trees and rocks that lined it, getting clean away. My heroics did not exactly make the Crab happy. Next time they ran into him, the *suddha* would probably not be there.

We sat shivering by the side of the trail for another hour or so until about 5 a.m., protected only by flimsy blankets. Realizing we were never going to get to the top, we reluctantly started slowly down. But even that proved almost impossible, as marchers continued to climb upward. After some struggle, we were able to get down about fifty yards to a plateau where there was a small tea stall. Getting there was exhausting, like crossing a river of mud. By then, the crowd had gotten even more ugly. Sri Pada was on the edge of a riot.

Worried we might be knocked off the side of the mountain to our deaths, I grabbed the Crab, slung him onto my back, and plowed into the tea stall. "MOVE!" I shouted, scattering as many people with the volume of my voice as with my elbows. Then the Crab went into a panic himself, and began clutching at my neck as he slipped from my shoulders. I tried to pass him over the counter of the tea stall, but the workers inside wouldn't touch him. Finally, completely drained, I pushed my way through to the back, screaming imprecations, before collapsing on the floor while the crowds moiled outside.

That the peace march was not peaceful was fitting, I thought. The prospects of the country's ever achieving peace were about as good as that of a cripple making his way up the side of a mountain seven thousand feet high on his hands. On almost every front—politically, socially, culturally, and psychologically—there were enormous barriers to a lasting settlement and every indication that the tide of violence would rise much higher before it ever receded. In kinder days, the Tamils and Sinhalese used to share a ritual of purgation in which societal problems were symbolically cast adrift in a vessel on a river, to be swallowed by the Makara, a mythical beast that swam in the currents out of sight of man. But even if there was enough amity to get a group of Tamils and Sinhalese together, there was hardly a vessel big enough to hold all the problems facing Sri Lankan society.

One of the most basic problems was the inability to revive negotiations between the government in Colombo and the Liberation Tigers of Tamil Eelam fighting in the north and the east. Besides obvious antagonism between the government and the rebels, India was insisting on brokering the talks and involving the discredited moderates of the Tamil United Liberation Front. But at least there was some prospect, if dim, that these talks would get going. In the south, neither the government nor the JVP was even close to finding a basis for talks, as each was bent on the other's destruction and had no inclination to share power. Peace between Sinhalese and Tamils, as well as peace within the Sinhalese community itself, was also dependent on holding provincial, parliamentary, and presidential elections that were scheduled for the coming year. Without these elections it would continue to be unclear whether the government had a mandate to seek peace with the Tamils on the basis of the peace accord, and without that, the Tamils had little reason to believe the Sinhalese would follow through on their commitments. Elections were also crucial to calming popular discontent toward the ruling party over its antidemocratic character, which was continuing to fuel popular support for the JVP.

Yet even if elections did take place, they would be unlikely to be free of the election abuses and voter intimidation that the UNP had resorted to in the past, since losing would expose its members to the tradition of post-electoral revenge for abuses of power while in office. Nor would these elections produce a mandate for peace with the Tamils, since the presidential candidates of the two major parties had both become stalking horses for Sinhalese nationalism and had hinted they would rescind objectionable elements of the present government's peace plan.

With two theaters of conflict, the process of finding a settlement was raised to an altogether new level of complexity. A perverse dynamic now existed between the two situations, north and south: to quell the Tamil insurgency in the north, the government needed to settle the revolt in the south among the Sinhalese, since that represented a threat to any lasting commitment to peace; to settle the revolt in the south among the Sinhalese, the government needed a solution to the Tamil insurgency in the north that would not inflame Sinhalese fear and provide ultranationalists with fodder.

In the end it seemed that lasting peace would only come when Sinhalese nationalism, the fruit of a persistent cultural identity crisis, subsided and a new, more inclusive national identity took hold that could bring the Tamil and Sinhalese communities together again. But all indications were that the Sinhalese were growing more nationalistic rather than less. Beneath the surface of this ever-surging current of nationalism was the ever-potent mythology contained in the *Mahavamsa*, the ancient chronicle given a new lease on life by the nationalist leader Dharmapala as a stay against cultural dissolution under the British. Whatever energy its more secular-minded intellectuals spent in debunking it, the *Mahavamsa* continued to shape the Sinhalese worldview, encouraging the belief that the Sinhalese were anointed by the Buddha to protect his religion and the land of Lanka from outside depredations and that they would have complete dominion over the island in return for carrying out that sacred mission.

The violence that had overtaken the country only seemed destined to worsen, hastening the country's political and social dissolution. Already the island seemed as if caught in a witch's grasp, as if Mara, the mythic god of evil, had enveloped it in a poison cloud, returning the country to the blighted condition the Buddha had found it in before he consecrated it. In the north, the Tamil Tigers had returned to their old pattern of massacring Sinhalese villages bordering the northern and eastern provinces. In return, Sinhala forces were launching retaliatory attacks on Tamil villages, harking back to the tit-for-tat killings prevalent during the first phase of the fighting.

But it was far worse than back to square one. In the south the struggle between the government and the JVP was coming to what seemed to be a head, as bodies piled up on roadsides, in rice paddies, and in rivers. The decapitated were usually victims of the JVP, the faceless and burned ones those of the government's security forces or paramilitary death squads. Further darkening the picture was the unrest among Muslims in the east and the first stirrings of militancy in the up-country among the "tea Tamils" hitherto on the sidelines.

Speaking of the historical momentum of Sinhalese Buddhist nationalism in the fifties, S. W. R. D. Bandaranaike had once said that "a river never flows backward." Looking out upon the political landscape as I was getting ready to leave the country, it was hard not to come to the same conclusion about the inevitability of violence. Many of my friends had a sense that a purgative bloodbath was unavoidable, making what I had seen over the past year pale by comparison. "It's coming. It's coming. People have this foreboding that something terrible is about to be unleashed," whispered an aging Colombo dowager over tea and biscuits one morning. Violence of epic proportions also looked likely to my friend N., the anthropologist. "In the next three months it will come down to this: either kill or be killed. By the time it is finished, two groups will meet on the road and even though they don't know each other they'll start shooting, not wanting to get shot first. I'm talking about real anarchy—order will break down all over the country."

As I came down the mountain, a sense of the tragic overcame me. The Buddhist revival and the political transformation it sparked had been a necessary reaction to the very real damage of colonialism, but they had ultimately been a cure worse than the disease itself. A great tradition had been perverted in the process, turning the island of the dharma into a hellhole. Bishop Reginald Heber, a missionary who visited Ceylon in the early 1800s, was surely guilty of colonialist arrogance in describing Ceylon as a stricken paradise where "every prospect pleases, and only man is vile." But there really was something deeply squalid and profane about what had happened in Sri Lanka, especially since so much of it had occurred in the name of Buddhist culture and Buddhist cultural identity.

The Crab, however, was in a decidedly different mood, and was having great fun as he slid down the mountain in the dark. For part of the way down, we took a path that ran on the outside of the staircase, stumbling and sliding among the rocks and the weeds. We got separated at several points, but I could hear him crashing around behind me, laughing as he went. Occasionally, the Crab lost his balance and started rolling uncontrollably. Once we got back onto the stairs, though, he really made good time. Throwing his legs in front of him as he jumped by his hands from each landing, the Crab cleared several sets of stairs per minute, leaving a wake of wisecracks behind him. One high-caste woman in a white lace gown almost fainted when he passed; another lifted up her skirts when she saw him, as if he were a mouse. This prompted a gleeful song impugning the virtue of women of a certain caste.

As we neared the halfway point, the sun came up. We could hear the collective gasp at the summit though we were already miles away. First light also filled the air with the long, gnarled shadows of marchers. Stopping just then, the Crab gave me a smile and a knowing wink, after which he turned toward the mountain. Bowing deeply from the waist, he prostrated himself with his hands clasped together over his head. Then, impishly, he raised himself up on his hands and spun around, throwing his limp legs behind him, as an aviator in an open cockpit might throw back a silk scarf. Flying down the trail in a cloud of dust, the Crab resumed his bawdy song about high-caste women, with gusto.

Epilogue

SEVERAL MONTHS after I left Sri Lanka in mid-1988, the situation degenerated into what the more dark-minded had prophesied: armed gangs of indeterminate affiliation roaming deserted streets. Through the summer of 1988, the Indian Peacekeeping Force continued to go at the Tigers in the north. Indefinite curfews, arbitrary detentions, roundups, helicopter strafing, and naval blockades had little effect, however. Although large ground offensives drove the Tigers out of their jungle hideouts and captured sizable caches of weapons, they merely moved to other areas of the north and east, from where they continued to defy Indian power and paralyze civil administration and public life. Indian frustrations began to take a mounting toll; human rights activists decried "horrors of My Lai proportions" and told of electric shock, deaths in detention, and reprisal killings of more than fifty civilians at a time.

The Indians did see to it that the north and the east were merged into a single province, as per the provisions of the Accord. But Provincial Council elections were obstructed by a Tiger vow to kill anyone who participated in them. As a result, Tamil moderates in the Tamil United Liberation Front sat on the sidelines and the candidates supported by the Indians had to be ferried around the northern province in IPKF helicopters. As their quagmire deepened, morale in the entire Indian Army suffered gravely.

Meanwhile in the south, JVP pressure mounted sharply, reducing the government's writ to an ever-shrinking circle around the capital. On the first anniversary of the Accord in the summer of 1988, the JVP launched a wave of arson, sabotage, and intimidation that paralyzed the country. All commercial activity ceased and the entire transportation network ground to a halt. Those tactics were intensified in September as the presidential elections drew closer, firmly establishing the JVP as an even bigger threat to the country's future than the Tiger insurrection in the north. This latest round of JVP activity was marked by a sudden and silent campaign of intimidation and terror unlike anything that the country had seen before: a few letters and posters emptied the streets of Colombo, as civil servants, businessmen, and students stayed home for days in fear.

JVP actions again crippled the country in October, inducing public panic. The JVP ordered all tourist hotels in the south to close, brought the ports, the railroads, and the banks to a standstill through strikes, and engineered a prison breakout that freed over two hundred convicts, many of them JVP cadres. The JVP may not have had the power to topple the government outright or win power in elections, but it could bring about "total chaos."

Shortly thereafter, in November and December—on the doorstep of elections—the two sides went at it furiously. As a result, twenty-five to fifty bodies were found each day all over the south. The government instructed its troops to use "maximum force" to protect campaign activists and voters, equipped its security forces with sweeping extra-democratic powers, and imposed the death penalty for anyone accused of disrupting the elections. "I don't care about human rights," growled a brigadier named Lalgama, the man I had spoken with on an earlier tour of the south when he was a colonel talking a good hearts-and-minds game. "If it is necessary to kill people, then we will kill them."

Although the elections did take place, voter turnout was a weak 55 percent of the normal 80 percent of the electorate, and the losing candidates charged the victorious UNP with fraud and intimidation. In some areas of the south where opposition candidates were expected to do well, the government allegedly never even allowed polling places to open, and at other precincts polling officers were too frightened to show up. The election's failure to deliver a much desired catharsis was clear several days later in the worst single day of violence to date, on December 21, when JVP assassins and government vigilante squads killed nearly 200 people along the southern coast.

Still, the election did offer some hope. The winning presidential candidate, Ranasinghe Premadasa, was an ardent nationalist who was sympathetic to the political feelings of the JVP. Although thousands of his fellow party members had been killed by them, Premadasa had never denounced them and echoed their hard-line stance toward the Indians and the cause of Tamil separatism. He was also from a lower caste, quite a departure from the remote aristocrats who had governed Sri Lanka until then. It was felt that these affinities with the JVP might spur him to alleviate the social and economic conditions that inflamed the movement. The Tamil problem could be solved later on. By that point, Sri Lanka was desperate: tourism was dead, basic food production had fallen to near-starvation levels, and development programs were crippled.

Promising a government of "conciliation, consultation, and consensus," Premadasa extended an olive branch to the JVP, offering an amnesty and an invitation to participate in parliamentary elections in February 1989. He lifted the emergency and its draconian provisions in force since 1983 and released several key JVPers as a sign of good faith. Premadasa also took great pains to reassure Buddhist monks and conservative laymen with calculated affirmations of Sinhalese Buddhist tradition and ostentatious acts of public piety. State television, for example, broadcast instructions showing younger people how to "worship" their parents in the traditional manner and edited out the bathing-suit competition from the Miss Universe contest.

To no avail, however. The JVP spurned Premadasa's gestures and offers of power sharing, demanding that "the whole gallery of rogues must quit." It continued its wave of assassinations and terror in the weeks before parliamentary elections, resulting in 1,000 more deaths. Premadasa had no choice but to brandish an iron fist. "We have to get rid of them one way or another," exclaimed his newly appointed defense attaché in reaction to a JVP massacre in April of a village known for UNP support. "The sooner the better."

With the JVP on the rise, Premadasa tried to remove the primary source of Sinhalese nationalist disaffection: the Indian Peacekeeping Force itself. If the IPKF quit Sri Lanka, Premadasa might also be able to pressure the JVP into talks. He chose a Byzantine route to that end, however, by entering into secret negotiations with the Tigers. In turn, these contacts led to direct talks in May 1989, the first time the Sinhalese government and Tamil militants had sat down together in seventeen years, with the Tigers put up at government expense on the fourteenth floor of the Colombo Hilton. Both sides were there for cynical reasons. The government wanted to embarrass the Indians to the extent that they would leave the country, while the Tigers were trying to gain time to regroup after the Indian offensives in the north. Although peace could have ensued from these talks, it was felt that once the Indians were gone, the two sides would find some excuse to have at it once again. (According to some intelligence reports, the collusion between Colombo and the Tigers was more than political; the government also allegedly funneled arms to the Tigers for use against the Indians. This was eventually confirmed by Premadasa himself more than a year later in a startling admission before Parliament.)

In Premadasa's calculations, the talks with the Tigers would make it look like Sri Lanka could handle its own affairs again without Indian meddling. In June, without briefing his own cabinet or officials in Delhi, he ordered the Indians to quit Sri Lanka within two months, insisting that after July 29, the second anniversary of the peace accord, the IPKF be confined to its barracks and stating that India had "no authority over one inch" of his land.

The move risked a dangerous confrontation with the Indians, who did not relish being ordered out of a country they had spent so much time, lives, and money trying to pacify. (The death toll of Indian troops had at that point reached 1,200.) The other Tamil rebel groups in league with the Indians also cried foul and called it a "devil's pact," realizing that once their patrons in the Indian military departed they would again be easy prey for the LTTE. Unsurprisingly, Rajiv Gandhi categorically rejected the ultimatum. The two countries were on the brink of war yet again, except that this time India had perhaps 70,000 troops on Sri Lankan soil.

Although it was clear that Sri Lanka would lose big in a fight with Indian forces, Premadasa had made the ultimatum such an issue of stubborn national pride that he could not back down. Ultimately, however, the Sri Lankan military explained the facts of life to him and vetoed any confrontation, which sobered Premadasa. Instead of ordering troops to attack the IPKF, Sri Lankan military leaders invited their Indian counterparts to tea.

The showdown did pay some dividends for Premadasa, though. Shortly after, in September 1989, the Indians announced they would cease hostilities against the Tigers and withdraw in full by December. (Delays pushed it to the end of March.) Premadasa's bold maneuvering had also forged a cease-fire with the Tigers that lasted thirteen months, the longest lull in the armed struggle since it began in 1983.

As predicted, however, the Indian withdrawal triggered a bloody struggle for supremacy between the other Tamil groups and the Tigers. As soon as the Indians pulled out of an area, the Tigers gained control. As a result, the Tigers were as close as ever to gaining Eelam.

Meanwhile, in the south, the withdrawal of the Indians put Premadasa in a position where he could take on the JVP without appearing to betray Sinhalese nationalism. The opportunity came just in time. At that point, the Sinhalese south was in a state of "total quadriplegia," as a Colombo lawyer put it.

By then the JVP had killed nearly 4,500 UNP members or sympathizers in the south and had even gone after high-ranking monks who dared to put their support behind government peace efforts. Continued labor strikes orchestrated by the JVP had crippled the banking system, the port, telecommunications, and transport. In July 1989, a ten-day hospital strike produced gruesome scenes in the wards, where the ill were left to die. In August, arriving tourists walked right through customs posts at the Colombo airport because clerks were too scared to show up for work. Schools and universities were still closed and had not held an examination for graduation in over four years. Trains were running on skeleton schedules, two-thirds of the country lacked electricity due to JVP sabotage, and government lawyers, fearing retribution, had refused cases assigned to them involving police officers brought up on charges of indiscipline. In the far south, a JVP attack team had thrown grenades into crowds at the Kataragama festival, killing thirteen. Colombo was a city under siege and a ten o'clock curfew, studded with pillboxes and checkpoints manned by soldiers who often shot first and asked questions after.

The ascendancy of the JVP, now called "the little government" for the obvious power it had gained, had made many lose faith in Premadasa's ability to last. Colombo aristocrats pondered the future gloomily, anxious about property expropriation and a life of forced equality with their gardeners. Anyone who could was trying to get out of Sri Lanka, including many of the country's professionals and expatriate experts. (Dale Sarver had already packed off, passing over a job in Burma for another prawn project in Africa.)

After signing the pact with the Tigers in July, Premadasa reinstated the draconian measures used to crack down on the JVP during the election the year before, again imposing the death penalty for putting up antigovernment posters, attending illegal meetings, or participating in a JVP strike. Premadasa also imposed severe press censorship that limited coverage of the violence in both domestic and foreign reporting and anything else that "threatened the national interest."

This final government push to exterminate the JVP has been called by Asia Watch "a period of lawlessness and bloodshed unparalleled in [Sri Lanka's] forty years as an independent state." Death squads proliferated—Yellow Cats, Black Cats, Green Tigers—killing students, dissident monks, young men, intellectuals, human rights monitors, and the families of JVP suspects and sympathizers. Corpses were found hanging from trees, floating down rivers, and smoldering in what were called "eternal fires," the craters where

JVP land mines had destroyed government vehicles. Often these corpses burned for days because locals were afraid of the same treatment if they tried to bury the remains. Instead of playing cricket, schoolboys in white uniforms stood at the rails of bridges over rivers and tried to spot bodies floating out to sea. During a five-week period in August and September of 1989, an estimated 5,000 people died, more than the casualty rate in Beirut for those weeks. It was the conflict's bloodiest phase.

The government was able to gain control because the JVP had finally overplayed its hand. Threats against the families of policemen and soldiers had backfired, rousing the security forces to overcome their reluctance to kill fellow Sinhalese. Revenge was extracted at a ratio of twelve JVP families for every one military and police family. Those high-level officers whose relatives had been targeted were allowed to exact revenge with little interference from the government.

The government also got a break when its counterinsurgency operatives captured a high-ranking JVP cadre, who told them, presumably under torture, that Rohanna Wijeweera, the leader of the JVP, was living in disguise as a tea planter on an estate outside of Kandy. While this was a neocolonial lifestyle anathema to JVP ideology, it was such an effective cover that even JVP cadres in the area did not know who he really was. Wijeweera was taken into custody sometime in November and died shortly thereafter. According to the government's story, which few believe, he was killed after taking authorities to a JVP safe house in Colombo. A top cadre inside tried to escape and, in the process, shot Wijeweera.

After his arrest and death, the government captured a string of other high-ranking JVPers, all of whom also died while in custody—in shoot-outs or escape attempts. But even after the leaders were dead, death squads continued their activities, as mop-up operations against the JVP provided a cover to liquidate the regime's political opponents and critics. In January 1990 alone, at least 147 headless bodies were found along roadsides in the south and corpses were spotted floating in the sea between Sri Lanka and the Maldive Islands five hundred miles away.

The total number of people killed—young Sinhalese males largely—will probably never be known, since local human rights activists and journalists probing the issue have been discouraged from pursuing it by killings of colleagues. Reliable estimates, however, like that of the London *Financial Times*, range as high as 30,000. It was us or them, Ranjan Wijeratne, Premadasa's top defense aide, said without apology in an interview with the news magazine *Asiaweek* several months later. "I had to get people who were prepared to do the job. They may have been overenthusiastic, a little more perverted than they should have been. We have now eased them out from their charges because they are no longer required for that kind of activity."

Although the decimation of the JVP gave the government more latitude in making concessions to the Tamils, it ultimately did not bring the country any closer to peace. Just as the southern front grew calmer, in the summer of 1990, confrontations between the Tigers and government forces in the north ripped the thirteen-month cease-fire apart, pitching the country back into bilateral conflict.

During the cease-fire, Premadasa had given the Tigers a wide berth in the north, calling off the Sri Lankan Army so that the Tigers could settle scores with those groups who had collaborated with the Indians. But the Tigers also took the opportunity to replenish their arms supplies and fortify their positions around Sri Lankan military camps, which Colombo preferred to ignore.

Negotiations between the government and the Tamils continued, but tensions were rising at the negotiating table over the government's refusal to lift the constitutional amendment banning advocacy of separatism, a sign of the continuing hold that the *Mahavamsa* mentality had over the Sinhalese mind. The situation grew more explosive in June when Tigers manning a checkpoint in the north fired on a patrol of Sinhalese soldiers. Then, a few weeks later, the peace ended abruptly when the Tigers overran twenty police stations in the east and the police inside—800 in all—surrendered on government orders. In keeping with their past pathology, the Tigers murdered many of their captives; in one case, they took over a hundred to a jungle clearing, made them lie facedown, and sprayed them with bullets, leaving only one survivor. Later in the week, there were other attacks and retaliatory assaults in which government forces killed Tamil civilians and Tamils were burned out of areas in the east by vengeful Sinhalese mobs. In that one week alone, over 600 people died.

The Tiger actions were a stinging betrayal and a great source of embarrassment to the President, who had put himself out on a limb for peace. Although the JVP had been crushed, rising Sinhala Buddhist anger over the government's perceived coddling of the Tigers could have raised it from the dead. Consequently, Premadasa had no choice but to throw his forces into another all-out war. "Just as we dealt with the JVP, the scum of the south, we shall deal with this scum of the north," ranted Ranjan Wijeratne, whom Premadasa had unleashed once again. "We got the leadership of the JVP and I have given assurances that we will get the leadership of the LTTE."

There was little to check the government in this, the most brutal round of combat yet. After the massacre of the captured police, the Sri Lankan armed forces were thirsty for revenge. India, savior of the Tamils in the past, found little inclination to return to a situation from which it had just extricated itself. Aid donors, another check on past government excesses, had been impressed by Premadasa's sincerity and did not repeat threats to withhold development dollars. Nor was there any effective pressure from influential parties in the Tamil diaspora, since the standing of the Tigers among expatriate Tamils had never been lower.

Renewed hostilities produced what Asia Watch has called "human suffering on an almost incalculable scale." Strafing helicopters rarely distinguished between civilians and guerrillas, shelling was indiscriminate, and newly acquired heavy aircraft dropped 300-kilogram bombs that left craters twenty feet wide and ten feet deep. Although the government blamed pilot error and wind, the damage done by bombs and shells to temples, schools, and hospitals seemed intentional. A government embargo of the north cut telephone lines to the outside world, closed banks, stopped food and medicine from entering, and restricted access by international humanitarian organizations. As a result, nearly a million Tamil civilians were displaced by the fighting—the largest refugee displacement to date in the war—with more than 100,000 fleeing to south India. Such massive refugee movement also seemed intentional, too, as the government formulated plans to forcibly remove the entire population of the Jaffna peninsula so they could attack the Tigers unencumbered.

During this most recent phase of fighting, human rights organizations documented wrenching stories of torture and mutilation, as well as the destruction of homes, businesses, and in some cases whole villages. Rights organizations claim that government forces used civilians as shields and that the government had organized death squads made up of ex-convicts to abduct young Tamil men and to amputate one of their hands to make them undesirable Tiger recruits. The government also detained young Tamil men fleeing the fighting as they arrived in Colombo, many of whom subsequently "disappeared," and made little effort to locate those Tamil students and faculty at predominantly Sinhalese universities who were abducted and presumably killed.

Not that the Tigers were any less cynical or brutal. Apparently abandoning any concern for Tamil civilian hearts and minds, they laced Tamil areas with land mines, used civilians as human shields, and demanded that each Tamil family give either several hundred dollars in gold or one of its sons. The Tigers also seemed to be encouraging attacks on civilians to push refugees to south India so Delhi might be forced to pressure Colombo once again.

The outbreak of war in 1990 brought the Muslims much deeper into the fray than before, turning the conflict into a three-pronged war. In July 1990, Tiger rebels reportedly massacred several dozen Muslims in separate bus attacks in the east. Then, a month later in a weeklong spree that claimed 300 Muslim lives, they butchered Muslims at prayer in two different mosques, following that attack with an assault on a Muslim village where the inhabitants were slaughtered in their sleep. The Tigers also allegedly desecrated several mosques after driving away villagers, plastering the walls with pictures of Prabakeran, a mortal offense.

The reaction of the Muslims was swift. Mobs armed with shotguns and broadswords stormed neighboring Tamil villages, killing

200. All through August there were attacks and counterattacks; in one incident Muslim home guards, armed by the government, attacked Tamil refugees inside a temple, firing blindly into the crowd. Revenge attacks on Tamil civilians by Muslims then prompted the government to arm groups of Tamil home guards. Although the intent was to arm these groups to prevent communal violence, the result was to inflame it.

That the government was allowing attacks on the Muslims in order to spur them into fighting the Tigers, and that the killings were the work of government forces disguised as Tigers, as the LTTE maintained, was probably untrue. But a great deal of murkiness did surround the Muslim-Tamil clashes. Father Eugene Hebert, the American Jesuit who directed the technical school in Batticaloa, disappeared around this time, after going out one day on a motor scooter to minister to the survivors of a massacred Muslim village. Muslim militants had in fact attacked several Tamil Jesuits in the area, killing two and hospitalizing another, who had been stoned. But it was strongly suspected that the army and the police had a hand in Hebert's death. He had made insistent protests over unjust detentions and other human rights abuses in Batticaloa.

The government talked about a final "fight to the finish," but its real aim was to gain the upper hand and force the Tigers back to the bargaining table. "It's like a tennis ball," said one security official, "The harder you hit it, the faster it comes back to you." But the fighting dragged on for months. Although each side scored impressive battlefield successes against the other, neither could translate them into a decisive overall advantage.

One of those impressive, though ultimately Pyrrhic, battlefield victories centered on the Jaffna fort. For almost three months 200 government troops held on inside it, almost completely cut off from resupply and reinforcement by a constant barrage from Tiger mortars. Tiger attempts to dislodge them were relentless. In one attack, the Tigers charged the fort with fourteen-year-olds wrapped in explosives. In another, they rammed the gates with modified bulldozers. In return, the government forces shelled and bombed neighborhoods around the fort, indifferent to the civilian toll. Government forces fought a long, slow effort to break the siege and rescue their comrades, but they ultimately abandoned the fort since its significance was more symbolic than strategic. After that, the Tigers flew their red-and-gold flag brazenly above its ramparts, a gesture of defiance that made the Sri Lankan forces vow to bomb the fort relentlessly until the flag was lowered.

By May 1991, almost 6,500 had died in the nine months of the latest round, mostly noncombatants. Peace was never further away. The government refused to negotiate with the Tigers unless Prabakeran participated personally. Then, too, there was the problem of renewed instability in the south. "We're still alive," read JVP posters put up in a few towns in the south, heralding a comeback. According to some reports, the JVP was beginning to hold indoctrination classes once again, and had mounted revenge strikes against progovernment vigilantes who had exterminated their comrades.

In response, Premadasa intensified his repression of the country's democratic rights with the Prevention of Subversive Political Activities Regulations, which curtailed virtually all political activity in the workplace and in schools. Such antidemocratic measures only encouraged the kind of opposition and resistance they were designed to contain.

Although the violence in this latest round of fighting was largely restricted to the north, violence did reach into the heart of Colombo again in March 1991, when Ranjan Wijeratne, who had spearheaded the liquidation of the JVP and the renewed effort against the Tigers, was killed on his way to work. As Wijeratne was being driven down elegant Havelock Road, a bomb exploded inside a bus parked nearby, killing him and thirty others, scattering severed hands, heads, and feet about the scene. Neither the Tigers nor the JVP claimed credit, leading to speculation that Wijeratne may have been the victim of a plot from inside the government to head off a coup that he may have been readying with the assistance of disgruntled military officers.

Some hope-starved Sri Lankans chose to view the death serendipitously; with Wijeratne gone, they said, the government would conduct the war less brutally and civilian suffering might ease. That was not to be the case, however, as the government continued to use a heavy hand in the north and the Tigers responded savagely, employing suicidal frontal assaults with cadres barely into their teens.

Suicide attackers were also used in May in the daring assassination of former Prime Minister Rajiv Gandhi as he campaigned for a parliamentary seat in India's general elections, a step toward winning back control of the government. According to intelligence reports, Prabakeran and other top Tiger leaders wanted revenge for Gandhi's treachery; they also feared Gandhi would seek to destroy the LTTE once he had resumed power, and plotted to have him killed. The bomb, a sophisticated device built from the kind of plastic explosives the Tigers had used in the past, was detonated just days before the balloting by a Tamil woman in her thirties outside of Madras as she stooped down to touch Gandhi's feet. Although the Tigers never took public credit, reports in India said that the woman was a member of the suicide cell of the elite Black Tigers, may have been raped by Indian troops, and had two brothers who were killed by the Indians in Sri Lanka.

The picture in Sri Lanka began to brighten over the course of the 1991 summer. Premadasa's economic liberalization programs spurred a surprising recovery in several sectors, arresting the steady downward spiral. The stockmarket took off, foreign investment picked up, and tourists returned, bringing boom times back to Colombo. Another hopeful development occurred in the north when the huge losses the LTTE incurred in a battle over a key government fort at Elephant Pass outside Jaffna seemed to whet its appetite for peace talks. The Tigers were ready, it was said, to drop their demand for a completely independent Eelam for some kind of autonomous state in a federalized Sri Lanka. The Sinhalese were also showing signs of increasing flexibility. Parliament passed a motion to approach the subject of devolution to Tamils in a bipartisan manner, the first move in forty years toward a Sinhalese consensus. "It is through consultation that we find solutions to human problems—not through confrontation," said Premadasa, a far cry from his old Sinhala war whoops.

Yet Sinhalese hawks had gained momentum after beating the

Tigers at Elephant Pass and were ready to fight till the last Tiger was killed. They rightly pointed out that the Tigers had feigned interest in peace talks many times before so they could regroup and fight again, justifying suspicion. Another dark sign was the way the Tigers had fought for Elephant Pass using the set-piece tactics of a conventional force, a departure from their usual guerrilla strategy. This made some observers anxious that if peace efforts crashed once again, the ensuing combat—now between two conventional armies—would be heavier than ever. Grimly, the impasse in the north continued, causing the conditions of daily life in Tamil areas to revert back to those of a pre-industrial era.

Moves toward a settlement were also overshadowed by a Byzantine constitutional crisis in Premadasa's government, when two of his cabinet ministers started a drive to have him impeached. At the very least, such tumult guaranteed that a power struggle, not peace, would preoccupy Sinhalese politicians for the immediate future. Unhappily, for every indication of hope in Sri Lanka there came another reason for pessimism. The war, traveling the same blood-soaked ground, still goes on.

Index